V&R

Novum Testamentum et Orbis Antiquus

Series Archaeologica 6

In collaboration with the foundation "Bibel und Orient" of the University of Fribourg, Switzerland
edited by Martin Ebner (Bonn), Peter Lampe (Heidelberg), Stefan Schreiber (Augsburg)
and Jürgen Zangenberg (Leiden)

Yinon Shivti'el

Cliff Shelters and Hiding Complexes: The Jewish Defense Methods in Galilee During the Roman Period

The Speleological and Archaeological Evidence

Vandenhoeck & Ruprecht

ZEFAT ACADEMIC COLLEGE

The extended English version of this book has been printed
with kind permission of Hakibbutz Hameuchad Publishing House Ltd.

Bibliographic information published by the Deutsche Nationalbibliothek:
The Deutsche Nationalbibliothek lists this publication in the Deutsche Nationalbibliografie;
detailed bibliographic data available online: http://dnb.de.

Typesetting by SchwabScantechnik, Göttingen
Printed and bound by ⊕ Hubert & Co. BuchPartner, Göttingen
Printed in the EU

Vandenhoeck & Ruprecht Verlage | www.vandenhoeck-ruprecht-verlage.com

ISSN 1420-4622
ISBN 978-3-525-54067-1

Table of Contents

Preface

The English edition of this volume is the result of prolonged, systematic exploration in parts of the Galilee that usually lie off the beaten track of both hikers and scholars. The academic research involved clambering up the precipitous cliffs that abound in the region, rising up on both sides of the larger riverbeds. It called for exhausting scrambles across scree slopes and strenuous climbs up rocky outcrops and through dense, thorny thickets. The task of anchoring ropes to boulders and rappelling down 100-meter drops to caves containing signs of rock hewing presents a serious physical challenge. The same is true of the interminable hours spent crawling through underground hiding passages. During such crawls, the entire body struggles to penetrate a thick layer of dirt mixed with animal waste that has accumulated over centuries, engulfed in total darkness while only the glimmer of the flashlight lights up the winding crawlway. The fieldwork and its findings, juxtaposed with the historical sources, provided the necessary academic basis for this volume.

The book is based on the author's doctoral thesis and it documents and classifies two Galilean phenomena that throw light on the history of the local Jewish community in times of adversity during the Hellenistic and Early Roman periods. With an increase in interest in the underground cavities of the Galilee and the publication of the Hebrew edition of this book, other underground sites used principally for hiding have been discovered in the region, thus expanding on research into the question of Galilee's involvement in the Bar Kokhba Revolt.

Two main kinds of underground cavities used by the Galilean Jewish community are found in the region. The first of these are natural caves at the top of cliffs near Jewish settlements known to have existed in the Second Temple period. The caves have been modified and contain clear signs of human activity. Both historically and archaeologically, most of these sites can be identified with the Jewish population that participated in the Great Revolt, although some of the caves were modified at an earlier time. We propose adopting the term 'cliff shelters' for this type of underground cavity.

The second phenomenon discussed here is that of the hiding complexes. The book contains plans of most of the underground cavities with characteristic hiding-complex features. These sites are also compared with the hiding complexes discovered in the Judean Desert. The typology of the Galilean underground cavities necessitated a more flexible definition of the term 'hiding complex', since they do not fully conform to the same criteria as those of the hiding complexes found in Judea. Furthermore, the hiding complexes in the Galilee have their own distinct characteristics. We therefore divided the underground cavities into six categories:

1) Small underground cavities expressly quarried out as hiding complexes. Such cavities are simply hewn, with no attempt to finish them to a high standard, and they are small and similar to the hiding complexes found in Judea at sites such as Horvat 'Etri and to the complexes discovered at Horvat Zit'a. The systems were designed in such a way as to make it as difficult as possible for the enemy to penetrate the underground cavities. The passages do not necessarily turn at exact ninety-degree angles and there is no consistency in the hewing of the different levels of the caves. It would seem that the people who made them were satisfied with the fact that the complexes were dark and narrow and that any progress through them would force a person to crawl blindly into the unknown. Over twenty-five hiding complexes of this type were hewn in Galilean settlements in preparation for worst-case scenarios. Some were apparently made at the end of the Second Temple period. Most

of these hiding places were very probably prepared immediately prior to the Great Revolt.

2) Well-developed hiding complexes. These complexes consist of low, specially hewn winding narrow passages with ninety-degree-angle turns that render any progress along them extremely difficult. The passages lead to smoothly hewn chambers furnished with niches for oil lamps. Many of these systems clearly cut into ancient agricultural installations and earlier tunnels. The complexes are similar to those in the Judean foothills, as at Horvat Midras, Amazya, and Horvat Ga'ada. Since the sophisticated hiding complexes found in the Judean foothills date to the Bar Kokhba Revolt, the approximately thirty well-developed systems of this type surveyed in the Galilee may well also have been hewn during the second century CE. They may also attest to preparations made by the Jews of the Galilee in anticipation of the Bar Kokhba Revolt, even if the Galileans did not participate in the revolt.

3) Hiding complexes that render obsolete previous underground installations such as storage rooms for agricultural produce, water cisterns, olive presses, and ritual baths. Such underground chambers were cool, sheltered, and protected from the rain and could easily be converted into hiding complexes. Similar hiding complexes have also been found in the Judean foothills, as at Horvat Hazan. In the Galilee, hiding complexes have been discovered that rendered previously hewn underground cavities unusable, a few of which were used as olive presses. In some of these, narrow tunnels – some finely finished and some roughly hewn – lead to other man-made cavities. Water cisterns or ritual baths were incorporated in most complexes of this type, for example at Meroth and Zippori, and previous existing installations were damaged beyond repair. The phenomenon is evident at most of the hiding complexes explored in the Judean foothills, as at Horbat Bet Loya. In a few cases, the water cisterns remained viable and could still be used to store limited amounts of water. In such complexes, the entrances to hiding passages were hewn a few meters above the bottom of the cistern and from above only the water was visible. The same phenomenon has been documented at Horvat 'Aqad in the Judean foothills, at Horvat Naqiq, and at the Nahal Yattir site. It is reasonable to assume that the underground installations were sacrificed in favor of hiding complexes during a period of heightened danger. The passages were probably cut into them when the inhabitants of Galilee realized that the hiding complexes could potentially save lives.

4) Underground complexes cut into burial caves. In Judea, this is extremely rare and has only been observed at Horvat Burgin and Horvat Benaya. Three of the six burial caves adapted as hiding places in Galilee are located inside the settlement of 'Iyei Me'arot. The other three burial caves converted for hiding were found bordering on or outside settlements.

5) Escape passages. This type of underground cavity is rare both in Judea and in Galilee. Their scarcity makes it difficult to specify their characteristics and the extent to which they were used. Apart from Josephus' description of the use of tunnels to bring produce and information into Yodefat for the rebels (*War* 3:190–192), no other documentation exists of escape passages in the Second Temple period. An escape passage was discovered at Gush Halav and there are tunnels in Nahal 'Amal and at Tel 'Amal that may also have been used for this purpose. In Judea, there is an example of an escape complex at the Nahal Yattir site (Rasam Yattir).

6) Cavities that cannot be identified as hiding complexes. This category includes underground cavities assumed by some scholars to have been hiding complexes, but which I do not believe should be regarded as such. The underground cavities at Jebel Qat, Eilabun, the passages at Tel 'Amal, and the Tel 'Amal tunnel do not exhibit the characteristics of hiding complexes.

To summarize, the book describes the ways in which the Galilean Jews used underground cavities as places of refuge and as hideouts during periods when they felt under immediate threat from the Roman authorities. It was a constant threat hanging over the Jewish population of Galilee, as in Judea, for much of the Second Temple era.

Acknowledgments

To my parents: My father, R. Isaac Haim Saʿadia (Damati) Shivti'el, may he rest in peace, my leading light and mentor to whom I am indebted for everything. To my mother, Margalit Shivti'el, daughter of R. Eliahu Antabli, of blessed memory, who built her home with wisdom.

"What I have vowed I will make good (…) Salvation comes from the Lord" (Jonah 2:10).

It is impossible to fully express here my gratitude to the following people who contributed toward the completion of the book's English edition, all of whom are the 'gems' that joined forces to create an entire 'necklace'. They include my wife, Hagar, who taught me that her patience, her support, and her love have no limits; my children, Shaham, Yahav, and Nittai, who showed every kindness toward their father as he buried himself in his books; my grandchildren, Amit, Gili, Yonathan, Daniel, Inbar, Ophir, Rona, and Na'omi, who have received far fewer hugs from me than they deserve.

I would also like to thank: The directors of Safed Academic College, for their tireless support and encouragement; the College research committee, who deemed the translation of the book an academic project worth funding; the former college presidents, Prof. Aharon Kellerman and Prof. Baruch Nevo, who helped me gain the support of the academic world; my mentors from earlier times, Prof. Bezalel Bar-Kochba and Prof. Shlomo Giora Shoham, who increased my thirst for knowledge and intellectual curiosity.

I am indebted to the wonderful team of young people from the ICRC (Israel Cave Research Center), who combed the Galilee with me in the quest for caves and underground cavities and participated in the difficult and complex task of mapping. With inexhaustible dedication and skill, they remained undeterred at the prospect of joining me as we crawled through the depths of the earth and rappelled down ropes to caves in sheer cliff faces together with the equipment needed for mapping and measuring: Vladimir Boslov, Shmulik Avidan, Boaz Langford, Nevo Fishbein, Elchanan Kleinberg, Mika Ullman, Shalev Avni, Amit Lev Ari, and the late Ahikam Amichai – of blessed memory – who was murdered by terrorists while hiking in Nahal Telem in Judea. All the new plans in the book were prepared by Reuven Zakai and Yuval Sobolib, who began as amateur cave explorers and became involved in the work of accurate, professional cave mapping. With special thanks to Vladimir Boslov of the ICRC who resides in Galilee and whose contribution to this research has been invaluable. My special thanks also to Professor Amos Frumkin of the ICRC for recruiting the assistance of the younger ICRC members. It was he who developed my love for the subterranean world of Eretz Israel and instilled in me an insatiable curiosity for cave exploration under the auspices of the wonderful ICRC organization, of which I have been a member since its foundation.

To Prof. Israel Amirav, Prof. Haim Goren, Prof. Esther Eshel, Yosef Stepansky, and Edna Tirosh for their wise and invaluable advice. To the Israel Nature and National Parks Protection Authority and the Israel Antiquities Authority for their assistance and for recognizing the importance of studying the Galilean caves. With special thanks to Debi Manor for the English translation of the original Hebrew book and to her daughter, Carmit Massimino, for the translation and graphic editing of the numerous accompanying plans. To Hakibbutz Hameuchad-Sifriat Hillel Ben-Haim Publishing Group for agreeing to the book's translation. To Professor Boaz Zissu for his tireless guidance, comments and clarification in the process of preparing my doctoral thesis for publication in Hebrew and for remaining to be my guide and mentor as I continue to delve into the research of Israel's caves.

Last but not least, to the late Professor Hannan Eshel, of blessed memory, my senior advisor who inspired the publication of this volume in its two versions. It was he who realized the enormity of the task and helped me along the way with strokes of the pen and with his oversight, intellect, wisdom, and kindness. His remarkable ability to differentiate between the relevant and the irrelevant contributed immensely to the doctoral work on which the book is based and the lessons he taught me have been carried over into the present volume.

The English edition of this book would not have been possible without the great encouragement and strong support of Prof. Jurgen Zangenberg, who spent months of his valuable time to prepare an accurate English version.

Dr. Yinon Shivti'el
Zefat Academic College, 2018

Introduction

From the standpoint of archaeological and historical research, the caves in Galilee are less well known than those in the Judean Desert and foothills.[1] Ever since the Dead Sea Scrolls first began to be discovered in the summer of 1947, the Judean Desert has been extensively studied and surveyed. Its caves have been systematically combed and surveyed and the diverse finds discovered in them shed light on many details from the Second Temple period, the Great Revolt, and the Bar Kokhba Revolt.[2] Gradually, a singular pattern of natural karst caves containing networks of crawlways and chambers used as refuges by Jews during the Early Roman period was identified in the Judean Desert. These caves, located in the steep cliffs of large riverbeds descending from the Judean Desert toward the fault scarp near the Dead Sea, were called 'refuge caves'.[3] I recently suggested a new term for natural caves in Galilee, also found near the top of precipitous cliffs containing features that are comparable with those in the Judean foothills. Unlike the Judean 'refuge caves', these natural caves were adapted for human habitation and lie near to Jewish settlements rather than in remote locations. In my research on the Galilean model, I have adopted the term 'cliff shelters' for such sites.[4] Along with the refuge caves and cliff shelters, another type of underground complex was discovered. These 'hiding complexes' were first studied in Judea in the 1970s, where they were discovered and classified by David Alon in 1978. Since that time, they have been extensively researched and documented.[5] Hiding complexes are characterized by two main features: All are underground cavities hewn out by man and all lie beneath the remains of Jewish settlements. They provided places of refuge mainly in the Early Roman period and sometimes afterward, although recent research attests to some having been used in earlier periods.[6]

This book is a compilation of the research into both phenomena in Galilee, including detailed new data gathered in recent years. It contains all the known evidence of the two types of underground cavities that existed in Galilee. This evidence helps us identify Jewish communities in Galilee that were mentioned by Josephus. In particular, the research of cliff shelters and hiding complexes has revealed the defensive methods of the Galilean Jews during times of crisis during the period under discussion.

Two of Josephus' works, *The Jewish War* and *The Life,* describe his operations in Galilee, to where he was dispatched to organize preparations for the Great Revolt. In *The Jewish War,* he writes that he managed to enlist an army of one hundred thousand fighters in Galilee, whom he trained in Roman military tactics, and that he personally fortified seventeen named settlements. These were in addition to Gush Halav, which was fortified by John of Gischala, and Zippori, which organized its own defenses. In his *Life,* the author again lists the settlements he claims to have fortified and prepared in anticipation of the Roman army's mobilization to quell the revolt in Galilee.

On the question of whether he did in fact establish such a large army in the short time available to him from the moment of his arrival in the Galilee

1 Weiss 2005.
2 Yadin 1971; Kloner 1983; Eshel/Amit 1999; Porat/Eshel/Frumkin 2006; Porat/Eshel 2008; Frumkin et al. 2015.
3 Eshel/Amit 1999:8, 11; Porat/Eshel 2008.
4 I am grateful to the late Prof. Hanan Eshel for suggesting this term for the phenomenon I discussed with him while researching it; Shivti'el 2010:41–72; Shivti'el/Frumkin 2014.
5 Kloner, Oppenheimer, Gichon/Yadin 1983; Isaac/Oppenheimer 1985:39–44; Alon 1987:107–114; Kloner/Tepper 1987; Kloner/Zissu 2005; Shivti'el, 2011a.
6 Shivti'el 2016:175–200.

to the beginning of the Roman campaign, there is a general consensus that his description is greatly exaggerated. However, the defenses deployed by the settlements can be archaeologically examined and their finds studied, thus contributing to an understanding of the tactics described by Josephus at those settlements he claimed to have fortified.

The identification and scientific exploration of these settlements has been extensively discussed in the past, but previous discussion has focused mainly on the problem of identification and includes only a general overview of the finds discovered at such sites. The defensive tactics of these settlements have not been sufficiently examined. In the book, I maintain that many of the settlements identified and mentioned by Josephus in both his works are located near two types of underground refuges. Those that I term 'cliff shelters' are different from the Judean 'refuge caves' described above that have no direct association with the communities from which the fugitives fled. During the course of the field work, dozens of settlements described in the book were examined. Six of the villages Josephus claims to have fortified are located near steep cliffs containing karstic caves, the majority of which are only accessible by rope. These caves were adapted for human habitation and yielded plastered water reservoirs, ritual baths, potsherds, coins, a complete jug, an intact jar, and other finds dating them to the Hellenistic and Early Roman periods.[7] The same phenomenon was also identified at other settlements that are not mentioned by Josephus throughout the Upper Galilee. Four ancient villages in Western Galilee lie near steep cliffs containing numerous natural cave complexes in precipitous rock faces that are either difficult or impossible to reach without ropes. Most of the caves were adapted by rock-cutting in ancient times and yielded evidence of their use in two main phases, the Hellenistic and the Early Roman periods. The discovery of this type of cliff shelter in the Western Galilee necessitated an investigation into the existence of Jewish settlements in an area that was known to have had a predominantly non-Jewish population.

Furthermore, the finds discovered in and around the cliff shelters indicate activity in the period preceding the Great Revolt. This proves that the fortifications described by Josephus in both his works were prepared not only under his command and that at least some of them predate the Great Revolt. Even if the use of underground cavities began long before the Great Revolt and continued after it, Josephus' testimony is of great importance to this research since it is the most detailed we have of Jewish life in Galilee at the time. More than any other source, it also attests to the use of caves for refuge during the Jewish revolt in Galilee and Judea. The results of exploring the underground cavities presented in this volume shed light on the defensive tactics of Jewish settlements in Galilee during the Second Temple period and the distribution of the Jewish population in the region at the time. Because the shelters are located in steep cliffs, those sheltering in them must have reached them by clambering up sheer faces of friable, crumbling limestone rock or, as was often the case, by abseiling down from the cliff tops by rope or by some other means. Whichever method was used, it would have involved tremendous daring and considerable hazards. Only a population confronted with extreme danger would have risked reaching such inaccessible locations and preparing them for a prolonged stay. The Galilee cliff shelters are comparable with the 'refuge caves' in the Judean Desert, even if the time of their adaptation and period of use are more difficult to determine than those of the Judean refuge caves, which date to both Jewish revolts. This study summarizes the results of a comprehensive survey conducted in the Galilean caves by the author and colleagues from the Israel Cave Research Center, while discussing the archaeological findings discovered in the cliff shelters and their conclusions.

The second type of underground cavity described here is the 'hiding complex'. Hiding complexes are quarried beneath the sites of Second Temple-period Jewish settlements and bear typological similarities to examples discovered throughout the Judean foothills.[8] The book covers all the currently known hiding complexes in Galilee, including many that were discovered during the current research work, and compares the Galilee examples with the Judean type. It is now obvious that the defensive tactic of hiding complexes was far more extensive in Galilee than has previously been described and extended across Lower Galilee and the whole of Upper Eastern Galilee.

The descriptions of the two groups of caves are accompanied by a discussion of the reasons that prompted the local population in Galilee to prepare these underground cavities, relying on two assumptions: 1. The preparation of shelters near the top of steep cliffs and the hewing out of chambers and narrow underground passages indicates that such opera-

7 Shivti'el, Zissu/Eshel 2009–2010; Regarding the uniqueness of the ritual baths at these sites, see Shivti'el 2012a.

8 Tepper/Shachar 1987b:279–280; Shachar 2001; Shivti'el 2013a.

tions were motivated by a heightened sense of imminent danger. 2. The project would have depended on the local population concentrating its resources and organizing combined manpower. The discovery of the cliff shelters and hiding complexes in Galilee raises the issue of whether some kind of ruling body or military commander was giving directions to the local population. Another intriguing question concerns the relationship between Galilee and Judea, in light of the similar use made of underground cavities in both places. Cliff shelters and hiding complexes appear to have been employed in a similar manner in both regions, prompting us to ask why some settlements opted for cliff shelters and some quarried out hiding complexes. Another question concerns those settlements where both hiding complexes and cliff shelters have been found. Cliff shelters are all typically located near Jewish settlements whose residents can be assumed to have readied them for use. Most hiding complexes bear a striking resemblance to the Judean complexes, which are without doubt related to the Jewish population. During this period, it was mainly the Jewish population who were in most danger. One of the important pieces of evidence for this is given by examples where it is clear that in order to complete the hiding complexes, it was necessary to render existing features obsolete (agricultural installations, storage cellars, ritual baths, water cisterns and burial caves) by cutting through them and joining them together to form a hiding complex. The physical evidence is accompanied by a discussion of the relevant historical sources related to the phenomenon of underground cavities, which can help date the finds. The majority of the hiding complexes published in this book provide evidence of use, or preparedness for use, and continued maintenance into the 2nd and 3rd centuries CE.

The documentation of the underground cavities presented here is based on the accepted speleological practices used by the Israel Cave Research Center in the Hebrew University of Jerusalem's Department of Earth Sciences. In the course of our fieldwork, we documented and partially mapped all the accessible cliffs in the Galilee subject to nature-reserve restrictions (since many are located within such reserves) and accessibility and safety constrictions. In some cases, access to the cliff shelters was so difficult and dangerous as to make it seem incredible that Jews had managed to reach them nearly two thousand years previously, by means that were doubtless far less sophisticated than our own. The book presents plans of all the previously-mapped underground cavities, some of which have been improved, and new plans of all the sites discovered while surveying for my research on the Galilee caves, which were professionally documented and mapped using special computerized graphic processing.

This volume describes 74 underground cavities used as hiding complexes. The terminology is used with extreme caution, since not all the sites have all the characteristics of those hiding complexes surveyed in Judea and Samaria on which the criteria was based to identify the phenomenon, thus enabling them to be compared with the hiding complexes in the Galilee. It is not always easy to use systematic comparison to identify some of the sites surveyed in the Galilee as typical hiding complexes, since some have unique characteristics. I therefore divided the hiding complexes into six categories, adjusted to the categories used for the hiding complexes discovered in Judea.

Locating and accessing the cavities, combined with prolonged crawling along the passages and removing soil and debris or dirt, provided a major physical challenge, as did extensive underground stays in extreme environments. Many caves, for example, are home to ticks that infest every protective garment currently available, and some of the ticks carry tick-borne relapsing fever. The work of mapping and drafting the caves was difficult, as was that of documenting and describing the cliff shelters. All these activities had to be carried out under challenging field conditions. For this reason, there may be small discrepancies between some of the descriptions and the plans. In a few instances the plans are not complete, and where massive tick infestation prohibited work, only schematic plans were made.

Chapter 1:

Identifying the Settlements Fortified by Josephus in Galilee

Two of Josephus' works document the course of events in Galilee during 66–67 CE. The first is *The Jewish War* (written ca. 71–81 CE) and the second *The Life* (written in approximately 94–96 CE). Together, they provide the main historical source for the events of the Great Revolt. Following the defeat of Cestius Gallus near Jerusalem in November 66 CE, Josephus was given command of the Golan and Galilee, which he reached a few months prior to the Roman invasion led by Vespasian and his son Titus (*War* 3:35–43). Various scholars have discussed the credibility of the two sources and the inconsistencies between them.[1]

This book reviews the defensive measures taken by the Jewish inhabitants of Galilee during the Great Revolt, based on surveys and archaeological remains at sites mentioned in Josephus' writings. It is obvious from his testimony that the Jews were reluctant to meet the Roman army in open battle; when circumstances made such a confrontation unavoidable, Josephus' forces would retreat almost immediately as the Romans approached. Since Josephus had no military experience, his only feasible options were to fortify settlements by throwing up defenses and preparing concealed shelters to withstand the might of the Roman onslaught. This volume examines the seventeen settlements Josephus claims to have fortified and commanded in person.[2]

1 *War* 2:568; *Life* 29–30; cf. Broshi 1983: 21–29; Dan 1983: 67–68; Rappaport 1983: 22–65; Schwartz 1994: 291.

2 Josephus notes that he was not personally responsible for the fortification of two of the nineteen settlements he lists.

Josephus begins by describing Galilee's boundaries (*War* 3:35–43):

> Galilee, with its two divisions known as Upper and Lower Galilee, is enveloped by Phoenicia and Syria. Its western frontiers are the outlying territory of Ptolemais and Carmel, a mountain once belonging to Galilee, and now to Tyre; adjacent to Carmel is Gaba (…). On the south the country is bounded by Samaria and the territory of Scythopolis up to the waters of Jordan; on the east by the territory of Hippos, Gadara, and Gaulanitis, the frontier-line of Agrippa's kingdom; on the north Tyre and its dependent district mark its limits. Lower Galilee extends in length from Tiberias to Chabulon, which is not far from Ptolemais on the coast; in breadth, from a village in the Great Plain called Xaloth to Bersabe. At this point begins Upper Galilee, which extends in breadth to the village of Baka, the frontier of Tyrian territory; in length, it reaches from the village of Thella, near the Jordan, to Meroth.

According to his own words, Josephus faced three challenges when assigned command over the two Galilean districts:

(1) selecting and appointing seventy elders to head the districts, together with seven judges for each town;

(2) enlisting and training a Jewish army of 100 000 fighters; and

(3) building and fortifying settlements, some of which were walled, to resist the imminent Roman invasion of Galilee.

Josephus lists the names of seventeen settlements whose fortification he ordered and supervised, adding that Gischala (Gush Halav) and Sepphoris (Zippori) prepared their own fortifications (*War* 2:572–576; *Life*

187 where the nineteen fortified settlements are only listed with no further details).

Josephus' three tasks were supposedly accomplished over the seven-month period between his arrival in Galilee and his capture at Iotapata (Yodefat) on July 20, 67 CE. The account of his appointment of community leaders and judges may be true; however, the establishment of a skilled, hundred thousand-strong army trained in Roman military tactics would almost certainly have required far more than the six months at his disposal. Furthermore, Josephus' Galilee operations were viewed with animosity by key rebel leaders; at least three of the main towns in Galilee rejected his command: Sepphoris, Tiberias, and Gischala, where John of Gischala openly opposed him with support from the local citizens. Josephus' self-professed lack of military experience did little to improve his status (*Life* 1–12). It is hard to imagine that under such circumstances Josephus would have succeeded in recruiting nearly two-thirds of the local population to man his army.

Some of the settlements Josephus lists have been identified beyond question while others have only been located with a high degree of certainty; several have been excavated and have yielded findings consistent with Josephus' descriptions. In some places it is even possible to examine and assess the actual method of fortification and to estimate the minimum time needed to complete it. The seventeen settlements fortified by Josephus are listed with similar words in *The Jewish War* and in *The Life*. In *The Jewish War*, Josephus writes (*War* 2:572–576):

Having established these principles for the internal regulation of the various towns, he proceeded to take measures for their security from external attack. Foreseeing that Galilee would bear the brunt of the Romans' opening assault, he fortified the most suitable places, namely, Iotapata, Bersabe, Selame, Kapharekcho, Iapha, Sigoph, the mount called Itabyrion, Tarichaea and Tiberias; he further provided with walls the caves in Lower Galilee in the neighborhood of the lake of Gennesaret and in Upper Galilee the rock known as Akchabaron, Sepph, Iamnith, and Meroth. In Gaulanitis he fortified Seleukia, Soganae and Gamala. The inhabitants of Sepphoris alone were authorized by him to erect walls on their own account, because he saw that they were in affluent circumstances and even without orders, eager for hostilities. Similarly, John, son of Levi, fortified Gischala at his own expense, on instruction by Josephus. The other fortresses were all built under the personal superintendence of Josephus who both assisted in and directed the operations. He, moreover, levied in Galilee an army of upwards of a hundred thousand young men, all of whom he equipped with old arms collected for the purpose.

In *Life* he states (*Life* 187):

I erected walls at Seleucia and Soganae, villages with very strong natural defenses, and provided similar protection for certain villages in upper Galilee, also in very rugged surroundings, named Iamnia, Ameroth and Acharabe. In Lower Galilee I fortified the cities of Tarichaea, Tiberias and Sepphoris, and the villages of the Cave of Arbela, Beersubae, Selame, Iotapata, Kapharath, Komus, Soganae, Papha and Itabyrion. These places I stocked with ample supplies of corn and arms for their future security.

The existing research into Josephus' fortifications in Galilee has focused on two main issues: Firstly, on attempting to identify the settlements, particularly those whose locations are indeterminate such as Kapharekcho, Meroth, Seleukia and Soganae. The second, related line of research centers on detecting some method in Josephus' references to settlements and the order in which they are listed in the two works, in order to understand Josephus' strategy and the geographical distribution of Jewish settlement in Galilee during the Great Revolt.

Avi-Yonah started the debate by claiming that Josephus planned to form a defensive line along Galilee's borders.[3] He believed that each fortress was assigned a specific role, dictated by its location and the network of roads existing in Galilee at the time. In Avi-Yonah's opinion, the group of fortified settlements in Upper Galilee – ʿAkhbera, (**Fig. 2**) Zefat, Iamnith and Meron – controlled the crossroads between Mount Meron, the Qadesh Naftali ridge, Nahal ʿAmud, and Mount Canaan. Gischala completed this group. A second group of settlements in the Lower Galilee – Tiberias, Tarichaea and the Arbela Caves – guarded the shores of the Sea of Galilee. A third group – Itabyrion and Yifit – was built in the southern Galilee. The fortress of Sepphoris (Zippori) was located at the intersection between the southern and the western lines of defense. Avi-Yonah believed that Iotapata, Bersabe and Selame (together with Kfar ʿAkko and Kfar ʿAta) secured the western border of the Jewish Galilee. Avi-Yonah commented on the fact that the geographical order was not adhered to in the lists and even added Sikhane (Sahnin) to this line.

3 See Avi-Yonah 1951. Avi-Yonah proposed adding Agrippina to the list of southern settlements before it was conclusively located at Tel Faras in the southern Golan Heights. For the identification of Agrippina see Ben-Ephraim 2003:13; Ben-Ephraim/Dar 2007.

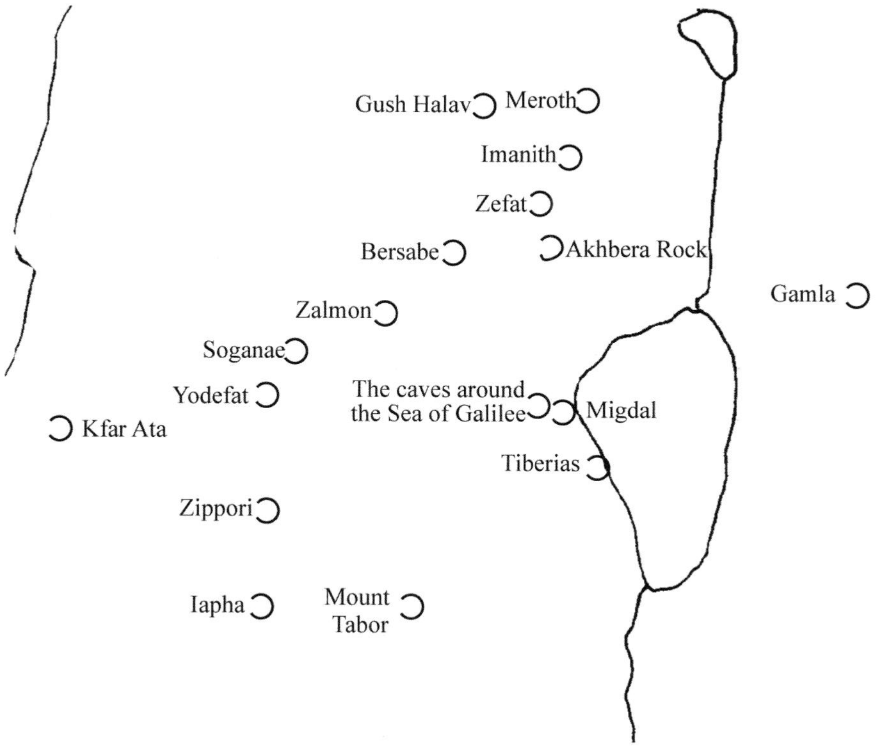

Fig. 1a: Fortification of Josephus Sites according to Aviam, 1983

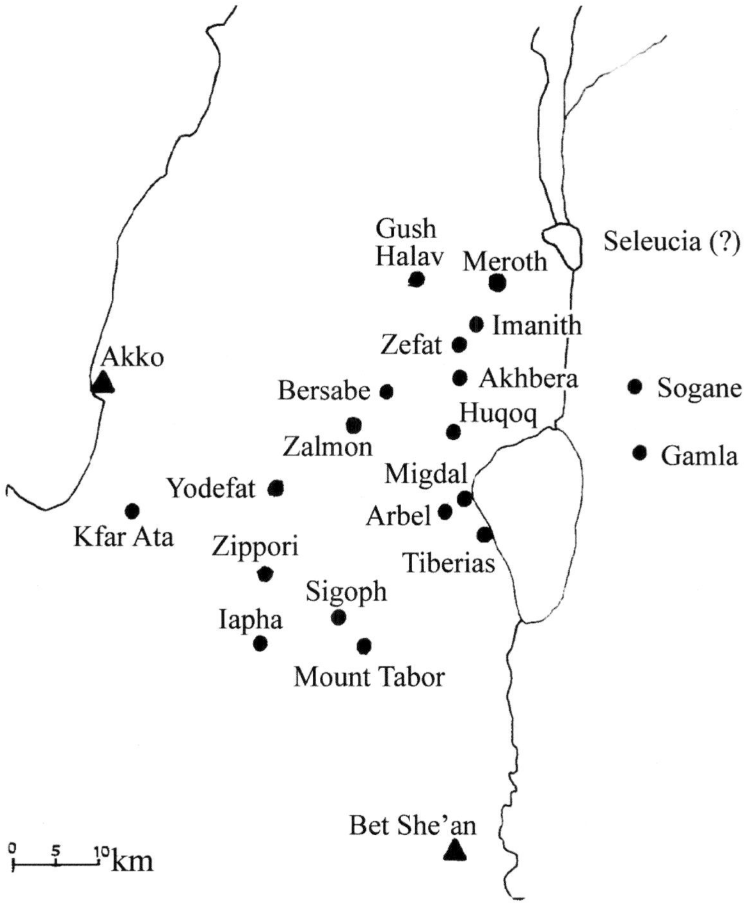

Fig. 1b: Fortification of Josephus Sites according to Damati, 1986

Fig. 2: ʻAkhbera Rock, with the village of ʻAkhbera in the background

Following Avi-Yonah's theory, Menashe Har-El believes that Josephus chose to fortify eighteen sites (although Avi-Yonah claimed that Josephus had only fortified seventeen) from among dozens of other Jewish towns in Galilee according to the following key: Ten in the Lower Galilee, four in the Upper Galilee, one on the border between the Lower and Upper Galilee, and three in the Golan. Har-El's choice of sites was based on the following criteria: (1) a commanding topographic location; (2) easy access and communication routes; (3) signaling visibility between the forts; and (4), provision for stocks of food and water. According to Har-El, six of the main forts were arranged in two triangular formations and were intended to act as the principle defensive centers and lookout positions. He believes that the three main forts are Itabyrion (Mount Tabor), Mount Meron (called "Miro" in *Life,* as interpreted by Har-El and others) and Mount Azmon (near Iotapata). Three additional forts served as lookout posts and defensive positions on the eastern fringes of Galilee around Bet She'an, the Jordan Valley and Transjordan. These were Iamnith, Arbela and Apharatha (Kfar ʻIhka or Kapharta, which Har-El proposed identifying with Agrippina, placed by him at Kokhav Ha-Yarden).[4]

Table 1 compares the two lists given by Josephus in the order in which the settlements are mentioned in *The Jewish War,* then followed by a discussion of each individual site.

4 Har-El 1968; Aviam, 2008.

Location number	Place name in The Jewish War 2:572–576	Place name in The Life 187–188	Place name used in this volume	Modern Hebrew name
1	Ἰωτάπατα	Ἰωτάπατα	Iotapata	Yodefat
2	Βηρσάβη	Βηρσαβεέ	Bersabe	Be'er Sheva Ha-Glilit
3	Σελαμίν	Σελαμίν	Selame	Zalmon
4	Καφαρεκχώ	Καφαρεκχώ	Kapharekcho	Huqoq(?)
5	Ἰαφά	Παφά (corrupt text?)	Iapha	Yafi'a
6	Σιγώφ	Σωγανή	Sigoph (in Galilee) Sogane (in Golan)	Sigoph
7	Ἰταβύριον καλούμενον ὄρος	Ἰταβύριον ὄρος	Mount Tabor	Tabor
8	Ταριχέαι	Ταριχαῖαι	Tarichaea	Migdal
9	Τιβεριάς	Τιβεριάς	Tiberias	Tiberias
10	Τὰ περὶ Γεννεσὰρ τὴν λίμην σπήλαια	Κώμαι Ἄρβηλων σπήλαιον	Arbela Caves	Arbel
11	ἥ τε προσαγορευσομένη Ἀχαβάρων πέτρα	Ἀχαράβη	'Akhbara Rock	–
12	Σέπφ	–	Zefat	Zefat
13	Ἰαμνίθ	Ἰάμνεια	Iamnith	Yavnit
14	Μηρώθ	Ἀμηρώθ	Meroth	Meroth
15	Σελεύκεια	Σελεύκεια	Seleukia	Seleucia
16	Σωγάνη	Σωγάναι	Soganae	Sugni
17	Γάμαλα	–	Gamala	Gamla
18	Σεπφωρῖται	Σέπφωρις	Sepphoris	Zippori

Table 1: Fortified settlements listed by Josephus[5]

5 Greek spelling taken from Thackeray 1926 (LCL 186), 1927a (LCL 203) and Thackeray 1927b (LCL 487).

Fig. 3: Yodefat, looking toward the west wall

We will now individually examine the place names.

(1) Iotapata (Yodefat)

The Battle of Iotapata occupies a prominent position in *The Jewish War,* since Josephus himself commanded its defending forces and eventually surrendered to the Romans in the city, which he describes as follows (*War* 3:158–160):

The town of Iotapata is almost entirely built on precipitous cliffs, being surrounded on three sides by ravines so deep that sight fails in the attempt to fathom the abyss. On the north side alone, where the town has straggled sideways up a descending spur of the mountains, is it accessible. But this quarter, too, Josephus, when he fortified the city, had enclosed within his wall, in order to prevent the enemy from occupying the ridge which commanded it. Concealed by other mountains surrounding it, the town was quite invisible.

The Mishnah mentions "ancient Yodefat" in a list of walled cities from the time of Joshua bin Nun (*Mishna ʿArakhin* 9:6), leading some early scholars to believe that there were in fact two places named Iotapata. Iotapata was first located by Gustav Schultz (1849) on an isolated hilltop 419 m above sea level (asl), northwest of Bet Netofa and at the foot of Mount Azmon. The hill lies above a meander in the Yodefat River and is surrounded by a chain of hills now known as the Yodefat Ridge. Schultz's identification was based on Josephus' description and on the site's name, "Shifat" (Jifat) preserved in local Arab tradition. Both Victor Guérin (1880) and members of the Palestine Exploration Fund recorded the site in the late nineteenth century. Ze'ev Safrai remarked on the unusual position of Iotapata compared with other Lower Galilean settlements, noting that its location at Khirbet Jifat was determined by a compromise between a preference for cretaceous rock sites (into which water cisterns can easily be hewn) near agricultural land, and the need

Fig. 4: Bersabe, Galilee

to exploit the natural fortifications. Mordechai Aviam conducted extensive archaeological excavations on the hill, exposing the city walls, residential neighborhoods, and ample evidence of the fierce battle that had raged there. He also discovered traces of a siege ramp, two hiding complexes, and additional finds consistent with Josephus' descriptions.[6]

(2) Bersabe (Be'er Sheva Ha-Glilit)

Scholars agree on Bersabe's location at Khirbet Abu-Sheva, a hilltop at the eastern end of Bet Ha-Kerem Valley and 472 m asl. Bersabe lies near Kefar Hananya, a site of considerable importance in the Mishnah. Aviam thought that there was probably extensive devastation at Bersabe during the Great Revolt and that for this reason the settlement was abandoned and later rebuilt at a different location, nearby Kefar Hananya.[7] Nevertheless, the finds from Bersabe show that it did in fact continue to be occupied after the Great Revolt, although a marked decline is evident.[8] Josephus mentions Bersabe not just as a town he fortified, but also as a place lying on the border between the Upper and the Lower Galilee (*War* 3:39–40):

> On the north Tyre and its dependent district mark its limits. Lower Galilee extends in length from Tiberias to Chabulon, which is not far from Ptolemais on the coast; in breadth, from a village in the Great Plain called Xaloth to Bersabe. At this point begins Upper Galilee, which extends in breadth to the village of Baka, the frontier of Tyrian territory; in length, it reaches from the village of Thella, near the Jordan, to Meroth.

6 See Aviam 2005:1.

7 See Aviam 1983:38; Aviam/Richardson 2001:182.

8 See Leibner 2009:123.

The location of Kefar Hananya near Bersabe and its attestation in the Mishnah as a town on the border between the Upper and Lower Galilee has reinforced the identification of both sites. In *Mishnah Shevi'it* 9:2 it marked the boundary between the Upper and Lower Galilee, as in the following description: "From Kefar Hananya and upward, where the sycamore fig tree does not grow, is the Upper Galilee and from Kefar Hananya down, where the sycamore fig tree grows, is the Lower Galilee". Ze'ev Safrai noted that the reference to Bersabe and later to Kefar Hananya as marking boundaries inside Galilee attests to the importance of the two towns.[9] Although Bersaba was a major town during the Second Temple period and the Great Revolt (according to Safrai) there is no documentation of it after the revolt, whereas Kefar Hananya is frequently mentioned instead.[10]

Several surveys have been conducted at Bersabe. Guérin observed burial caves hewn into the rock among its ruins. On the same occasion, Guérin continued south from Bersabe to Kfar 'Anan which he believed to be Kfar Hananya where black-ware pottery was produced.[11] Conder and Kitchener also documented the ruins.[12] Yosef Breslavsky surveyed the site in 1934 and observed that Josephus had fortified it not only because of its position on an obvious geographical border, but also because it commanded the most direct route between the 'Akko plain and the heart of the Upper and Lower Galilee. Breslavsky made remarks on the clear line of visibility between Bersabe and 'Akhbera Rock, the Arbela Caves and the heights above Iotapata and Itabyrion – all sites Josephus listed as having fortified. Breslavsky also noted that the mount was surrounded by a large wall built of massive stones. On its summit, he observed the remains of numerous stone-built structures with masonry similar to that of the wall. Breslavsky believed that the entire complex should be attributed to the hasty fortifications Josephus supervised.[13] Eric Meyers, James Strange and Dennis Groh surveyed the site in the late 1970s and identified and recorded the course of the wall.[14] Mordechai Aviam surveyed the site several times in the 1980s and recovered potsherds and other surface finds from various periods, including the Second Temple period, and coins from the 2nd to the 4th centuries CE.[15] On the north side of the hill, Aviam also detected the remains of a wall with traces of three towers.[16]

Oren Tal, Yigal Tepper and Alexander Fantalkin surveyed the site in 1997 and discovered an additional, outer fortification system beyond the previously identified wall. Here, they detected four main stages: (1) outer defenses with a wall approximately 1.65 m thick; (2) a thickened wall about 2.8 m deep constructed on the northeast slope of the hill; (3) the addition of a northwest watchtower whose eastern part was adjacent to the thickened wall and whose western part was next to the earlier wall; and (4), three semicircular towers constructed near the outer face of the thickened wall. Despite the difficulty of dating the first two stages of outer fortifications, the third stage was datable to the Hellenistic or Roman period. The archaeologists believed that the presence of semicircular towers similar to examples found at Mount Nittai and the abundance of Early Roman pottery finds near the base of the towers supported Josephus' testimony regarding the fortification and strengthening of existing defenses at Jewish towns in Galilee prior to the Great Revolt.[17]

(3) Selame (Zalmon)

Fig. 5: Zalmon

The Jewish town Zalmin is also known as Zalmon in Rabbinic literature[18] which cites the name in connection with a war identified by some as the Great Revolt.[19] In *Tosefta,* R. Yehuda describes the town's

9 See Safrai 1981:93.
10 See Klein 1939:165.
11 See Guérin 1880:255.
12 See Conder/Kitchener 1881:235.
13 See Breslavsky 1954:241–245.
14 See Meyers, Strange/Groh 1978:1, 4.
15 At Kefar Hananya near Bersabe, David Adan-Bayewitz excavated a large workshop where cooking vessels and kraters were produced (Adan-Bayewitz 1993:75–77).
16 Aviam 2004:95.
17 See Tal/Tepper/Fantalkin 2000.
18 See *Mishnah Kilayim* 4:9; *Mishnah Yevamot* 16:4.
19 See Klein 1945:165.

spring "flowing down to Zalmon" whose water was forbidden to be used for purification since "it is dry during war."[20] The toponym Dalmanutha in Mk 8:10 might be identified with Zalmon.[21] Priests from the order of Daliah resided at Zalmon. The settlement has been identified on the summit of a hill 304 m above sea level, between Nahal Qamun to the west and Nahal Zalmon to the east. Secondary use of building stones has destroyed most of the site's archaeological remains. Guérin identified another rectangular compound 80 paces long and 50 paces wide, which he believed had a military purpose. In and around the site, he saw ancient remains that he identified as Josephus' defenses.[22] On top of the hill's eastern slope Breslavsky identified a row of roughly-hewn wall stones, which he attributed to the fortification of Selame from the time of the Great Revolt.[23] Ze'ev Safrai noted that Selame's location as a fortified town was the result of a compromise between the population's need for farmland and its defensive requirements. Economic needs dictated its proximity to fertile soil and Nahal Zalmon, which is a perennial water source. In the 1980s Mordechai Aviam recovered a sarcophagus fragment with a Greek inscription on the summit of Tel Zalmon. The inscription was deciphered by Shimon Applebaum, Benjamin Isaac and Yohanan Landau and attributed to a Roman military commander in Vespasian's army called *Lucagus* or *Lucagas*.[24]

Mordechai Aviam also surveyed the ruins on Tel Zalmon and identified the remains of the rectangular compound previously interpreted by Guérin as a citadel dating from the rule of Dahar al-Omar (1750–1775 CE). Among the meager surface finds he recorded a few potsherds from various periods including the Second Temple era, helping identify the site as one fortified by Josephus. Mordechai Aviam also noted the possibility that the place was linked to the site described in the Mishnah in connection with the spring known to have dried up in time of war, possibly implying the Great Revolt.[25] Another survey carried out here by Aviam recovered coins from the Early Roman period as well as traces of an unfinished ditch, which eventually became the town's entrance route.[26] The current survey conducted by the author of this book revealed a number of dwelling caves and a plastered water cistern and one of the caves yielded the fragment of a sarcophagus lid.

(4) Kapharekcho/Kapharath (Kfar 'Ata, Huqoq?)

Fig. 6: Horvat Huqoq

When investigating the area of 'Akko, Shmuel Klein identified Kapharekcho-Kapharath as a village near Kabul, between Signah and Iotapata.[27] Later, he followed Avi-Yonah's explanation of the order in which Josephus lists the towns he fortified and proposed locating Kapharath in the region that he considered to have been left unprotected, namely between Iotapata and Sepphoris, thus placing it at Khirbet at-Taibe, east of Shefar'am.[28] In one of the surviving versions of Josephus' *Life,* the place is called Apharatha (Ἀφαραθα). Avi-Yonah believed that "Kaphartha" had been replaced by "Apharatha" which means "demon" in Arabic. Place names similar to Ofra/Opharta were often changed to "at-Taibe" in Arabic for apotropaic reasons, meaning "The good One."

According to Menashe Har-El, Apharatha is Josephus' Kfar 'Ata and its locatization at Kokhav Ha-Yarden is based on Har-El's concept of a triangular layout. Furthermore, to the west of Kokhav Ha-Yarden lies a village called "at-Taibe", which he believed substantiated his identification.[29] Bezalel Bar-Kochva rejected Avi-Yonah and Har-El's theory and their proposed identifications of Kfar 'Ata.[30] Dan Barag adopted the text variants attested in the eleventh-century 'A' and fourteenth-century 'R'

20 See *Tosefta Parah* 9:2.
21 Sickenberger 1934; Seybold 2000.
22 See Guérin 1880:314.
23 See Breslavsky 1954:249.
24 See Applebaum, Isaac/Landau 1981–1982:99.
25 See Aviam 1983:39.
26 See Aviam/Richardson 2001:96; Aviam 2004:193.

27 See Klein 1945:59, 157.
28 For the Greek versions, see Bar-Kochva 1974; for greater detail see Barag 1981:392.
29 See Har-El 1968:209–212.
30 See Bar-Kochva 1974.

Fig. 7: Nahal ʿAmud Gorge

manuscripts of *Life*.[31] The name Kaphartha appears in both manuscripts. Thus, Bar-Kochva suggested identifying the site with the hill now occupied by the modern residential neighborhood of Qiryat ʿAta. Barag believes that this is a suitable site for a frontline observation post on the western line of defenses that would have made an important contribution to the series of fortresses guarding the western approaches to the Jewish settlements in the Lower Galilee.[32] Ze'ev Safrai sought Kfar ʿAta in the Arab town of El-Macher, some 5 km east of ʿAkko.[33] Paul Romanoff proposed identifying Kfar ʿAta with Horvat ʿAhrosh near ʿAmqa in the Western Galilee,[34] although this is beyond the boundaries of the Jewish Galilee described by Josephus. Kfar ʿAkko (Kapharekcho) – the "missing fort," as Avi-Yonah called it – should probably be identified at Horvat Huqoq, as proposed by Emanuel Damati who based this on the many alterations to the name "Huqoq" in Talmudic literature, which he cited as proof that "Huqoq" is a derivation of ʻIcho or Kapharekcho.[35] Damati's proposal also seems to be substantiated by the cliff shelters discovered in the nearby Nahal ʿAmud gorge.

Already in the 1950s, Bezalel Ravani had conducted a survey at Ramat Huqoq on the eastern slopes of Nahal ʿAmud and discovered eighteen sites from the Roman and Byzantine periods. Ravani recorded the ruins of a fort, which he called a "Roman fortress," on the northeastern spur of Mount Huqoq and near the remains of the village of Huqoq. The fort measures 50 × 55 m and has straight walls 1.1 m thick.[36] The

31 Barag 1981.
32 Ibid.
33 Safrai 1981:65.
34 Romanoff 1937:171–173.

35 See Damati 1986.
36 Ravani's survey has not been published, but is cited by Tepper, Der'in/Tepper 2000:38.

Fig. 8: Nahal 'Amud Gorge

summit provides an excellent view of the entire region and Ravani assumed that the fort was manned by Roman soldiers who controlled the surrounding area and access routes. The fort commanded a view over at least four Jewish settlements existing in the region during the Second Temple period: Horvat Huqoq (Khirbet Yaquq), Sheikh Nashi Hill, Horvat Shuna and a group of caves Ravani called "Caves 25–26."

Horvat Huqoq covers an area of approximately 7.5 acres at Ramat Huqoq. Near Horvat Huqoq, Sheikh Nashi Hill has yielded traces of continued occupation from the Iron Age to the Roman and Byzantine periods[37]. The ancient settlement of Kapharekcho was probably centered on about four acres at Sheikh Nashi. Over the years it spread to seven and a half acres across Ramat Huqoq. Its western side consists of low hills suitable for arable farming. There are several springs in the region, some of which are defunct, but the town's main spring is still an active water source. The site is located on a prominent hill 230 m above sea level, overlooking the Ginnosar Valley and with an unimpaired view of Migdal, Tiberias, 'Akhbara, Zefat and Yamnit. Ramat Huqoq was located on the intersection of several routes: One linked the Ginnosar Valley with the city of Hazor; another led from Huqoq to Zefat via Nahal 'Amud and 'Akhbara; and a third went from Huqoq to Bersabe in Galilee and the valley of Bet Hakerem. North of Horvat Huqoq, Bezalel Ravani excavated four burial caves dating from between the first century BCE and the third century CE.[38] To the south of the village, ritual baths were discovered together with distinctive installations named the "Huqoq installations" by archaeologists, who believed they were used to manufacture mustard-seed oil.[39] In the late 1980s, Yigal Tepper and

37 Grey/Spigel, 2015.

38 See Ravani 1961:128–143; Kahane 1961:121–127.

39 See Tepper, Der'in/Tepper 2000:73, 83–84.

Yuval Shachar surveyed a hiding complex at the site which had been hewn out beneath a domestic house and led to a water cistern.[40] Based on architectural details, a lintel ornamented with a menorah found in the past at the site, and also on a description by Rabbi Ishturi Hafarchi who visited Huqoq in the thirteenth century CE, Zvi Ilan believed that a synagogue had been built in the center of Horvat Huqoq.[41] Since 2011 Jodi Magness has been directing archaeological excavations at Horvat Huqoq, confirming the existence of a Byzantine period synagogue with spectacular results like large areas of a colorful mosaic depicting scenes never previously discovered in a synagogue in ancient Palestine. Above them are scenes from a Samson-cycle showing a Hebrew inscription flanked by a giant and two foxes with burning torches tied to their tails. The north side of the floor depicts a battle scene with an elephant and an animal keeling over with a spear in its stomach. Five symmetrical figures wearing cloaks decorate the lower edge of the mosaic.[42] About 25 m away from the southeast corner of the mosaic floor is an 8 m-deep water cistern. The cistern is linked to a hiding complex that was excavated by the author. The main tunnel of the hiding complex leads directly under the mosaic floor towards a hewn shaft which climbs up to a blocked opening terminating in the middle of the synagogue floor.

Adjacent to the town of Huqoq, on the north bank of Nahal ʿAmud, lay a Jewish village called Horvat Kur. The village was surveyed in the 1980s by Yigal and Yotam Tepper and Gil Der'in.[43] Archaeological excavations began at Horvat Kur in 2008 under the auspices of Kinneret Regional Project with the author's participation, uncovering at least three phases of an

40 See below, Chapter 4.

41 See Ilan 1991a:122; Ishtori Haparchi 1852:46.

42 With thanks to Prof. Jodi Magness for permission to mention details of the mosaic floor before the publication of her report. Now see Britt/Bustan 2017.

43 See Tepper, Der'in/Tepper 2000:67–68.

Fig. 9: Horvat Kur cisterns survey

ancient synagogue (whose existence had already been surmised by Zvi Ilan) dating to the fourth through seventh century CE.[44] The author's survey of the surface remains prior to the excavations showed that the site extends over five acres.[45] Numerous finds were recorded in the field, including many water cisterns, ritual baths, and domestic houses.

In addition to these, a sealed water cistern was discovered next to the synagogue, 6.5 m deep and irregularly built, coated with gray hydraulic plaster and with a second coat of reddish plaster. Test trenches were excavated for two seasons by the author. In 2011, two plain cooking pots dating to the Late Roman period were found at the bottom of the cistern. An excavation of the same locus in 2012 yielded more plain cooking pots and jugs dating to the same period. Samples from the sediment contained in the cooking pots were analyzed and produced helpful insights into local vegetation and micro-climate.[46]

(4) Iapha/Papha? (Yafi'a)

Fig. 10: Yafi'a lintel of the ancient synagogue of Yafa (Vincent 1921)

In addition to the account of its fortification, Josephus mentions Iapha elsewhere in his writings. In *Life,* Iapha is described as the largest and best-fortified village in Galilee (*Life* 230: "the largest village in Galilee, very strongly fortified and containing a dense population"). Iapha is also mentioned in *Life* as a place where he lived for a while (*Life* 270: "I settled at Iapha"). In his *Jewish War,* Iapha is described as having been fortified with a double wall and as the site of a brutal battle. After the attrition of the town by Trajan, commander of the Tenth Legion Fretensis, Titus led the last offensive; the battle lasted six hours and culminated in the massacre of Iapha's Jewish population in a bloodbath in which fifteen thousand people perished (*War* 3:302–306):

> The troops of Titus thereupon scaled the ramparts and were instantly masters of the town. But within the walls, where the inhabitants had rallied to meet them, a desperate struggle ensued: the able-bodied fell upon the Romans in the narrow alleys, while from the houses the women pelted them with whatever missiles came to hand. For six hours the contest was maintained; the more efficient combatants were at length exterminated, and the rest of the population was then massacred in the open or in their houses, young and old alike. For no males were spared, except infants; these, along with the women, the Romans sold as slaves. The slain, whether in the city or in the previous action, amounted in all to fifteen thousand; the captives numbered two thousand one hundred and thirty.

Until now, the accepted identification of Iapha has been based on the preservation of the name at the large Arab village of Yafi'a on the southwestern approach to the town of Nazareth. The village of Yafi'a is built on top of the remains of a large Jewish village where Vincent Louis-Hugues and later on Eliezer Sukenik excavated a synagogue.[47] The few surveys carried out at Yafi'a have yielded potsherds from the 1st c. CE. In 2009 Yardena Alexandre conducted a salvage excavation at the core of the ancient village of Yafi'a. Remains of a settlement from the Hellenistic and Early Roman Periods and a series of subterranean basements that served as a barrier and as a hiding place were discovered in the excavations. Among the finds were stone vessels and coins from the Early Roman Period.[48]

(5) Sigoph (Sogane, Sakhnin)

In describing the location of Sigoph, Josephus states that it is twenty *rees* (about 4 km) from Gavra-Arab (*Life* 265). Sigoph-Sogane is generally believed to lie buried beneath the large Arab village of Sakhnin, southeast of the Bet Hakerem valley. After touring its ruins, Victor Guérin remarked that he found ancient water cisterns and burial places hewn into the rock. In one of the burial places he found a chamber with several niches *(loculi)* surrounded by a square structure built of finely-dressed ashlars. Mordechai Aviam surveyed the ancient settlement and dated the mausoleum

44 See Ilan 1989:19–20; for the synagogue, see Ilan 1991a:132; Zangenberg, Münger, Hakola and McCane 2013:557–576; Zangenberg 2016:166–189.

45 The site (Kur) was surveyed on July 7 and 24–26, 2007 with support from Kinneret Regional Project (http://kinneret-excavations.org/) in preparation for excavations directed by J.K. Zangenberg (University of Leiden, The Netherlands).

46 See Neumann, Zangenberg, Shivti'el/Münger 2013:1–25.

47 Vincent 1921; Sukenik 1951.

48 See Alexandre 2012.

Fig. 11: Sigoph, mark of the grave of Rabbi Yehoshua of Sakhnin (Sigoph)

that Guérin described to the Late Roman period. On the west side of the tell Guérin noticed traces of a building he identified as a synagogue that had been transformed into a church.[49] Guérin's description is one of the most detailed existing of the site. Today, it is difficult to identify the remains he described. Klein believed that Sogane was "Sagnah in the valley" – the valley of Sakhnin referred to in the Mishnah as a place where fine wine was produced. Although Sogane is on a hill, its farmers apparently grew crops in the Sakheni (Sakhnin) Valley.[50] Avi-Yonah maintained that Sakheni was Σωγάνη, one of Josephus' forts between Kfar Sha'ab and Zalmon.[51] Ze'ev Safrai claimed that the similarity in the names and the distance given by Josephus between Sakheni and Gabara confirmed this identification.[52] Bar-Kochva, however, rejected the accepted identification and maintained that Sigoph – as spelt in original manuscripts of the *Jewish War* (which he prefers) – is southwest of Iotapata. Bar-Kochva also believes that Josephus had no strategic justification for building or describing the construction of a fort at Sakhnin, on the site where we now know Sogane existed.[53]

49 For the existence of a synagogue at Sakhnin, see the *yMegillah* 4:1,4b.
50 See Klein 1945:24.
51 See Avi-Yonah 1963:136.
52 See Safrai 1981:85.
53 See Bar-Kochva 1974a:108–110.

Itabyrion (Mount Tabor)

Fig. 12: Mount Tabor

There can be no doubt about the identity of Mount Tabor.[54] As a prominent summit towering almost 600 m above sea level, the mount commands the country's main south–north artery. Mount Tabor lies in the northeast of the Kesulot Valley where the northern arm of the Jezreel Valley ends in a narrow basin between the Nazareth Hills in the north and Givat Ha-Moreh and the Lower Galilee hill spurs in the south. In ancient times this was the main route for the passage of various armies between Egypt in the south and Syria in the north.

With its distinctive summit towering over the valley plain and its steep slopes on all sides, Mount Tabor held a vitally important strategic location. Its top provides an excellent vantage point with views over extensive tracts of land. Mount Tabor is mentioned in the Bible for the first time as the place of the famous battle where the tribes of the Israelites, under the command of the prophets Deborah and Barak son of Abinoam, had defeated the Canaanite army led by Sisera (Jud. 3:12).[55] The earliest Second Temple-period reference to the conquest of Mount Tabor is provided by Polybius (2nd c. BCE), who wrote that in 218 BCE Antiochus III fought Ptolemy Philopator IV and took Philoteria (Bet Yerah), Bet She'an, and Itabyrion: "a place lying on a breast-formed height, having an ascent of more than fifteen stadia."[56] The name, written as Ἰταβύριον, also appears in Josephus' *Jewish War* and *Antiquities of the Jews*.[57] In his *Antiquities of the Jews,* Josephus describes how Alexander, the son of Aristobulus, was defeated in a battle waged on Mount Tabor in 53 BCE after attacking the army of Gabinius, the Roman proconsul and governor of Syria (*Ant.* 14:101–102). In describing the siege of Gamala, Josephus mentions that Vespasian dispatched some of his troops from Gamala to fight the rebels in their stronghold on Itabyrion (*War* 4:54–58). Itabyrion is referred to several times by Eusebius and his descriptions all match its accepted identity.[58]

Ze'ev Safrai noted that its summit once contained not only a military fort but also a civilian settlement with defenses. He maintained that the battle for Itabyrion in the Great Revolt occurred only after the whole of Galilee had been conquered, interpreting this as evidence that those occupying Itabyrion continued their resistance even after Galilee had been subdued.[59] Avi-Yonah determined that Itabyrion was part of the district of Debritah (Daburia) which was a large administrative center.[60] Commenting on this, Elizur pointed out that whenever Josephus mentioned the site he called it "Mount Tabor," inferring that no settlement by the name of Tabor existed at the time.[61] Aviam surveyed the top of the mount and recorded traces of a wall enclosing approximately 100 acres. The author's investigation of a cave at the base of the fort on Mount Tabor (map ref. 187182/292232, elevation 556 m asl) exposed a rock-cut underground dwelling complex divided into five rooms. The system does not have the characteristics of a hiding complex, yet it clearly served as an underground shelter beneath the settlement on Mount Tabor.

Fig. 13: Mount Tabor, rock-hewn underground cavities

54 Safrai 1982.
55 See Malamut, 1951
56 See Shimron 1991:368
57 See for example *Ant.* 13:396–397; *Ant.* 14:102; see also Breslavsky 1951:74.
58 See Melamed 1966:48, 54.
59 See Safrai 1982:21–22.
60 See Avi-Yonah 1963:137.
61 See Elizur 1990:11.

Fig. 14: Migdal, excavations at the ancient synagogue

(7) Tarichaea (Magdala/Migdal)

The accepted location of Tarichaea ("the fish-salting place") is Migdal, also known as Magdala or Migdal Nunaiya. Uzi Leibner believed that rather than being a possible description of the livelihood of its residents, the Greek name for the place (Ταριχέαι) derived from a time when the town was granted certain civic privileges due to its trade links with Greek-speaking populations.[62] Some scholars believed that this Migdal should also be identified with Migdal Zv'aiya.[63]

Josephus mentioned the town several times under its Greek name Tarichaea in the context of the central role it played in the Jewish Rebellion of 53 BCE (*Ant.* 14:120) and above all the Great Revolt. In *Life*, he classified Tarichaea as a city (πόλις) together with Tiberias and Sepphoris (*Life* 188). It was one of four administrative units that were annexed to the kingdom of Agrippa (*War* 2:252) and since Tiberias was founded during the reign of Tiberias, Ze'ev Safrai assumed that Tarichaea had until that time been the main city on the Sea of Galilee, even though it may not have been the capital of a toparchy.[64] The residents of Tarichaea were opposed to Josephus (*War* 2:595–607). Yet later he noted their loyalty to him (*War* 2:608–609; *Life* 59), and Leibner maintained that Josephus based his headquarters at Tarichaea.[65] Josephus recorded that thousands of rebels gathered at Tarichaea, trusting in the city's "strong fortifications" (*War* 3:462–470). In his *Jewish War*, Josephus describes the naval battle between the citizens of Tarichaea and the Roman army (*War* 3:522–526):

Vespasian, when his rafts were ready, put on board as many troops as he considered necessary to cope with the fugitives on the lake and launched his flotilla. The Jews, thus rounded

62 See Leibner 2004:230.

63 Klein 1945:211.

64 See Safrai 1981:111; 1997:15.

65 See Leibner 2004:232.

Fig. 15: Burial troughs hewn in rock next to Migdal

up, could neither escape to land, where all were in arms against them, nor sustain a naval combat on equal terms. For their skiffs, being small and built for piracy, were no match for the rafts, and each was manned by no more than a handful of men who were afraid to close with the dense ranks of their Roman assailants. However, they hovered round the rafts, occasionally even approaching them, now flinging stones from a distance at the Romans, now scraping alongside and attacking them at close range. But in both these manoeuvers they sustained greater injury themselves; their stones produced nothing but a continuous rattle in striking men well protected by armor, while they were themselves exposed to the arrows of the Romans; on the other hand, when they ventured to approach, before they had time to do anything they instantly came to grief and were sent to the bottom with their skiffs.

Magdala also appears in the New Testament as the home town of Mary Magdalene, whom Jesus "cleansed of seven demons" (Luke 8:2; Mark 16:9).

An underwater survey conducted by Edwin Link in 1960 discovered the port of Migdal immersed in the Sea of Galilee. Link's archaeological report describes a paved road and an assemblage of Roman cooking pots. In the 1970s, it transpired that the "paved road" was in fact a wharf made of limestone slabs faced with basalt and containing mooring stones. Recent excavations by Stefano De Luca confirmed this. The wharf was about 90 m long, terminating in a breakwater whose foundations were found to extend eastward into the lake. A second breakwater 70 m long and 4 m wide was built to the north of a small cove, sheltering the anchorage to the north and east. The breakwater was constructed of basalt stones and was paved with flat limestone slabs.[66] Mordechai Aviam noted that no trace has yet been found of the city's fortifications recorded by Josephus.[67] Shelley Wachsmann suggested that the ancient boat found in 1986 near the mouth of Nahal Zalmon – approximately 1.5 km away from Migdal – could be the remains of one of the Jewish craft that participated in the naval

66 See Rabban 1992:77.
67 See Aviam 2004:98.

battle Josephus described. Wachsmann believed that since the remains of other ships were found nearby, the one found near the Migdal anchorage may have participated in the battle on the lake.[68]

Salvage excavations at Migdal in 2009 uncovered the remains of a first-century CE synagogue with a main hall measuring about 120 m^2 and stone benches along its walls. It had a mosaic floor and its walls were decorated with a colorful plaster fresco. A square stone block was found in the middle of the hall, covered with decorative elements on all four sides and on its upper face. The facade of the stone is engraved with a seven-branched menorah with a triangular base, flanked by amphorae (jars).[69] Excavations by Stefano De Luca under the auspices of the Studium Biblicum Franciscanum have brought to light large parts of the harbor area, a *quadriporticus,* a bath house and domestic structures.[70]

(8) Tiberias

Tiberias was founded by Herod Antipas in ca. 20 CE, who intended to make it his capital city and named it after the emperor Tiberias, building it "in the best part of Galilee" (*Ant.* 18:36), not far from the hot springs at Hammata (Hammat Tiberias).[71] According to Josephus, the city was built on graves and Herod Antipas was therefore forced to provide certain concessions to encourage people to live there, since the Jews were reluctant to live in a town founded on graves.[72] Its proximity to fertile land and therapeutic springs added to the town's prosperity. Thanks to its location between the two areas ruled by Herod Antipas – Galilee and Peraea – it became an important administrative and political center. Josephus referred to Tiberias as Galilee's main city. It housed the palace of King Herod Agrippa II who lived here with his sister Berenice. In his description of the Great Revolt, Josephus recorded that the city's council leaders came to Vespasian and pleaded for him to take mercy on the inhabitants and for the safety of the city and not to harm it. In fact they gave up their city without a fight (*War* 3:453–457). According to *The Jewish War,* the people of Tiberias issued an edict ordering Josephus to leave the city, forcing him to capture it by trickery. He then expelled the wealthy citizens and council members who opposed him from Tiberias and confined them to a prison in Tarichaea (*War* 2:638–641):

> Josephus severely threatened and reproached them, first for their folly, after taking up arm s against Rome, in wasting their strength beforehand upon civil strife and so fulfilling their enemies' fondest wishes; next for their eagerness to make away with their guardian and protector, and their shamelessness in closing their city to him, who had built its walls; he declared himself ready, notwithstanding, to receive deputies who would offer an apology and assist him to secure the town. At once ten citizens, the principal men of Tiberias, came down; these he took on board one of the vessels and conveyed some distance from the land. Next he required fifty more, the most eminent members of the council, to come forward, ostensibly to give him their word as well. And so, always inventing some new pretext, he called up one party after another, presumably to ratify the agreement. As the boats were successively filled, he gave orders to the skippers to sail with all speed to Tarichaea and to shut the men up in prison. Thus, in the end, he arrested the whole council of six hundred members and some two thousand other citizens, and shipped them off to Tarichaea.

The remains of ancient Tiberias have been found in the southern part of the modern town, north of the hot springs known as Hammat Tiberias.[73] The level shoreline here, no wider than 400 m, enabled the city to be planned with parallel streets. To the west of the flat coastline on which the city was founded, the land rises up to what is today known as Mount Berenice.[74] Victor Guérin was the first to survey the walls of Tiberias and described sections measuring over two meters in breadth. He also recorded the remains of ruins known by the locals as "the royal palace." Avi-Yonah wrote that Tiberias was a fortified city whose wall abutted Agrippa II's citadel.[75] Numerous excavations have been conducted over the years at Tiberias, exposing the remains of various public buildings, part of the ancient city's cardo, the bath house, the market, and the basilica, which was part of an extensive complex whose first phase dates to the second century CE. In the last decade, renewed excavations have re-exposed the city gates of Tiberias as well as

68 See Wachsmann 1990:129–130.
69 Avshalom-Gorni/Najjar 2013 with thanks to Dina Avshalom-Gorni for the personal communication prior to its publication.
70 See, e. g., De Luca/Lena 2015.
71 See Weiss 1992b.
72 See *Ant.* 18:37–39; Oppenheimer believes that at the time of Herod Antipas, Tiberias was populated by people of dubious moral character (Oppenheimer 1988:24). Later, Tiberias was purged from impurity – see Levine 1978.
73 Savage 2015.
74 See Hirschfeld 1991:15.
75 See Avi-Yonah 1963:139.

Fig. 16: The excavation from the Roman period in Tiberias

Fig. 17: Tiberias, the city's gate towers

the theater from the time of Herod Antipas (**Fig. 17**). At the foot of Mount Berenice, a structure that may have been a public building was excavated. Yizhar Hirschfeld interpreted it as a center for religious study *(beth midrash)*.[76] He also exposed a long wall with traces of red fresco beneath the foundations of a basilica. Hirschfeld interpreted this as part of the remains of the luxurious palace of Herod Antipas, later used by Agrippa II.[77] Furthermore, sections of a floor made of polished marble slabs were exposed in the area where an apse was found and in several places to the west of it. They may well belong to the palace of Antipas. The foundation of Tiberias in 20 CE was commemorated by Herod Antipas in a series of coins with four different values. The coins bear the name of Tiberias on one side and the inscription "Herod the Tetrarch Year 24" on the other.[78]

(9) The Caves near the Lake of Genesareth/ The Arbela (Arbel) Caves

A settlement called Arbela is first recorded in the 9 th-century BCE Book of Hosea, when Hosea prophesied Ephraim devastation on a scale such as that at Arbela: "All your fortresses will be devastated – like Shalman devastated Beth Arbel on the day of battle, when mothers were dashed to the ground with their children" (Hosea 10:14). Despite their similar names, Hosea's Arbel should not be confused with the Arbela listed as one of Josephus' fortified sites and should more correctly be located near Irbid in Transjordan.[79] The use of the term "Mesaloth in Arbela" (1 Maccabees 9:1–2) to describe the site of the battle between the Seleucid commander Bakchides and Judas Maccabaeus seemed to Guérin – and later also to Klein – to point to the Galilean Arbela fortified by Josephus.[80] In the Hasmonean period, Nittai of Arbela – a chief of court and colleague of Joshua ben Perachyah – lived at Arbela, probably in the time of Alexander Jannaeus. His teachings are recorded in *Pirkei Avot* 1:6–7.[81] Before it is listed as a fortified site, the town of Arbela is mentioned in the description of King Herod's rule. Josephus referred to Arbela as the place that harbored the first seeds of Zealot resistance to Herod's rule in Galilee. During the suppression of the Jewish rebellion against Herod (in 37 BCE), the population of Arbela hid in the caves and Herod lowered his fighters

76 See Hirschfeld 1992:561–566.
77 See Hirschfeld/Meir 2006.
78 For Tiberias, see now Cytryn-Silberman 2015.
79 See Ilan/Izdarechet 1988:7.
80 See Guérin 1880:134; Klein 1945:13.
81 See Margaliot 1958:679.

Fig. 18: Arbel Cliff (Photo by A. Greicer)

Fig. 19: Mount Arbel, the method used by Herod the Great and his soldiers to reach the Arbel Cliff Shelters (the caves)

down to the cave openings from the cliff top to drive the Jews out from their shelters. Some preferred suicide over surrender to Herod (*Ant.* 14:413–430; also, with minor amendments, in *War* 1:304–314):

> From here he then sent out a troop of cavalry and three companies of foot-soldiers against some brigands living in caves, for he had made up his mind to put an end to their depredations; these caves were very near a village called Arbela… And he pressed on in pursuit of the enemy as far as the river Jordan (…) and so he got into his hands all the people of Galilee except those who lived in the caves (…). But Herod, who was hastening against the brigands in the caves, sent Silo off to Ventidius, and set out against them by himself. Now their caves were in hills that were altogether rugged, having their entrances half-way up the sheer cliffs and being surrounded by sharp rocks; in such dens did they lurk with all their people. Thereupon the king, whose men were unable either to climb up from below or creep upon them from above because of the steepness of the hill, had cribs built and lowered these upon them with iron chains as they were suspended by a machine from the summit of the hill (…) the men in the baskets fell upon them still more fiercely (…) and threw flaming fire inside, and so the caves, which had much wood in them, were set on fire. Now there was an old man shut up within one of the caves with his seven children and his wife; and when they begged him to let them slip through to the enemy, he stood at the entrance and cut down each of his sons as he came out, and afterwards his wife, and after hurling their dead bodies over the precipice, threw himself down upon them, thus submitting to death rather than to slavery (**Fig. 19**).

In the Mishnaic and Talmudic eras Arbela was famous for its fertile land and the manufacture of linen garments. Klein wrote that priests of the House of Jeshua, who settled at Arbela, zealously guarded their ancestry.[82] Ze'ev Safrai believed that the numerous teachings linking Arbela with redemption derived from the fact that it was the site of the first clash between the Zealots and the Roman rulers.[83] In medieval times, Jewish travelers recorded visiting Arbela and the cave of Nittai of Arbela.[84] These traditions were based on the identification of Galilean Arbela with Horvat Irbid on a spur of the western slope of Mount Arbela above the Wadi Hammam valley. Edward Robinson's placement of Josephus' ancient Arbela at Horvat Irbid in 1852 was confirmed by the discovery of the town's ancient synagogue.[85] Victor Guérin toured the ruins of the synagogue at Arbela and noted that its entrance faced east, unlike the usual orientation of Galilean synagogues.[86] In 1865 Charles Wilson conducted a partial excavation of the synagogue on behalf of the Palestine Exploration Fund. He was followed by Conder and Kitchener who drafted a plan of the building. In 1905 Kohl and Watzinger excavated the center of the synagogue's north and northeast sections and published a report describing its architecture with drawings and photographs.[87] Nahman Avigad wrote that the Arbela synagogue marked a new phase in the development of Galilean synagogues. He interpreted a niche in the southern end of the hall as a permanent location for the Torah scroll, which he believed had not been housed in a fixed place until that time.[88] In 1987–1988, Zvi Ilan and Avraham Izdarechet surveyed Horvat Irbid and further exposed the Arbela synagogue. Together with the Israel Cave Research Center, they also carried out a preliminary survey of the caves on the lower cliff face. Their excavations at Horvat Irbid and the synagogue showed that the site contained numerous industrial and agricultural installations and water reservoirs. They also recovered dozens of coins dating from between the Hellenistic period and the nineteenth century CE.[89] In 2012 the Arbela synagogue was further excavated by Benjamin Arubas, but his results have not yet been published (**Fig. 20**). Mordechai Aviam and later Yigal Tepper and Yuval Shachar surveyed the slopes northwest of the Arbela cliff. Tepper and Shachar also surveyed several caves scattered on the slopes of the cliff known as Mount Nittai on the northwest side of Nahal Arbel. They dated the potsherds recovered from the caves to the Early Roman period. At the foot of Mount Nittai lies a ruin called Hammam where Zvi Ilan identified traces of a synagogue. Uzi Leibner excavated the site between 2007 and 2012 and uncovered a synagogue with fragments of a mosaic floor, apparently also from the Samson cycle, depicting the figure of a gigantic man grasping three people by the locks of their hair, flanked by a horseback rider and a commemorative inscription bearing the name "Safr'a." The floor has been dated to the 3rd or 4th c. CE.[90] Rock shelters are dotted along the cliff of Mount Nittai above the ruins, and similar shelters are located on the facing cliff of Mount Arbel.

82 See Klein 1945:123–124.

83 See Safrai 1981:106.

84 See, for example the visit of R. Petachiah of Regensburg in 1180 CE in Ya'ari 1946:52.

85 See Ilan/Izdarechet 1988:76–123; Robinson 1970 II:398–399.

86 See Guérin 1880:133.

87 See Kohl/Watzinger 1916:59–70.

88 See Avigad 1968:98–100.

89 See Ilan/Izdarechet 1988:30; see also below Chapter 2.

90 Again see the detailed description in Chapter 2.

Fig. 20: Arbel Synagogue

Fig. 21: Mount Nittai facing Mount Arbel, wall and guard tower

Fig. 22: ʿAkhbara Rock

(10) The Rock called Akchabaron/Acharabe (ʿAkhbara Rock)

In his two works, Josephus writes that he fortified the "Rock called Akchabaron/Acharabe." In the *Jewish War,* he specifically uses the term "rock" and in *Life* 187 he lists ʿAkhbara together with three villages that are "very rocky" (πάνυ πετρώδεις οὔσας). These descriptions and the choice of wording are highly significant, yet some scholars have neglected to take them into consideration in attempting to locate the ʿAkhbara fortifications. The search for ʿAkhbara and its placement at Horvat ʿAkhbara, near the route that drops down from Zefat to the Ginnosar Valley and the Sea of Galilee, comes from the fact that ʿAkhbara is listed immediately after the Arbela caves as the first in the series of fortified towns and villages in the Upper Galilee, together with Iamnit, Yavne and Sepph (Zefat?). ʿAkhbara is described several times in Rabbinic literature as the place where Rabbi Yannai lived and taught and where Rabbi Yossi bar Abin provided halachic instruction. Another source comments that its inhabitants raised fine pheasants.[91] Shmuel Klein located the village to the south of Zefat and quoted further references to sages from ʿAkhbara and alternate versions of its name in rabbinic literature.[92] A place marked "Agbara" on the Madaba map shows that it was still occupied in the sixth century CE.[93] A fourteenth-century anonymous student of Maimonides mentioned the town of ʿAkhbara near Zefat, commenting that R. Nehorai, R. Yossi and R. Dustai were buried there: "Among the gardens [orchard] and the water two handbreadths pass between them."[94] In 1521/22, Rabbi Moshe Basola of Ancona described ʿAkhbara and his visit to a collapsed cave inside an

91 See *yEruvin* 8:4,25a; *bAvodah Zara* 70a; *yTerumot* 10:8,7b; *Kohelet Rabbah* 2:8, *Siman* 2.

92 See Klein 1939:117.

93 See Tsafrir 1996:9; Avi-Yonah 1996:60.

94 See Ya'ari 1946:91.

Fig. 23: ʿAkhbara, the ruins of the southern wall of a public building (synagogue) in ʿAkhbara settlement

orchard where he saw the graves of R. Yannai and his two sons, R. Dustai and R. Nehorai, near a bubbling spring. In the village itself, he noticed two walls of a ruined synagogue that were still standing.[95] Ishtori Haparchi stated that ʿAkhbara was about an hour's walk south of Meron and mentioned a "good spring" there.[96] Avillia Tshelebi identified ʿAkhbara Rock as the "Eagle's Mount" about one and a half hours downhill from Zefat. Tshelebi claimed to have viewed 500 caves in ʿAkhbara Rock, where the "Children of Israel" hid to escape a plague in the region, commenting that Allah had sent them a bad spirit and they had perished in the caves. He wrote that their heaped-up skeletons could still be seen there.[97] In 1769, R. Moshe Yerushalmi recorded that R. Nehorai and R. Dustai were buried below the village of ʿAkhbara in a cave inside a beautiful garden.[98] Victor Guérin identified the site of ʿAkhbra and "Wadi ʿAkhbara" in 1870, adding that Josephus had fortified the rock and describing it as a massive, undulating cliff face that had been quarried out. After visiting ʿAkhbara, Guérin recorded the impressive ruins of an ancient settlement that covered a terraced hill. He later saw the remains of a rectangular compound made of fine ashlars. He recorded that the site was called el-Knissa, "The Church," adding: "Yet it is possible that prior to this, the site was a synagogue."[99] Mordechai Aviam agreed with the accepted interpretation of ʿAkhbara Rock as the site Josephus fortified.[100] Emmanuel Damati uncovered ashlar remains at the village of ʿAkhbara that he interpreted as having once been the walls of a large public

95 See Basola 1939, p. 9b.
96 See Haparchi 1852:11, 47
97 See Tshelebi 1980:28.
98 On the travels of R. Moshe Yerushalmi see Ya'ari 1946:442.
99 See Guérin 1880:236.
100 See Aviam 1983:43; Aviam/Richardson 2001:101; Aviam 2004:181.

building.[101] Gideon Foerster, Zvi Ilan and Mordechai Aviam all believed that these ruins were the remains of a synagogue.[102]

(11) Sepph (Zefat)

Fig. 24: Safed, ruins of the town's citadel. The natural location of the fortifications of Josephus

A village named Sepph appears in the list of fortified settlements in the *Jewish War,* but is not mentioned in the list in *The Life.*[103] Its accepted location is on a mountain summit north of the modern city of Zefat, where a Crusader fort was built on ancient fortifications containing remains from the Hellenistic and Early Roman periods.[104] Klein noted that Zefat was a fortified town at the time of the *Jewish War.* His identification is based on the order in Josephus' list of settlements as well as on its name, which indicates that the hilltop town overlooking "much of the land"[105] was founded here. Avi-Yonah placed the site of Sepph fortified by Josephus between ʿAkhbara Rock and Biri (Biri'a).[106] Yosef Stepansky's survey of the site in 1987 produced Galilean Coarse Ware (GCW) and Kfar Hananiya Ware among the ancient potsherds.[107] The hilltop citadel may be the site of the first-century BCE fort captured by Herod during his campaign against the Jewish supporters of Antigonus II Mattathias (the Hasmonean) in Galilee.[108] The following quotation from Josephus may also refer to Zefat: "Marion [*scil.* the governor of Tyre] therefore invaded Galilee, which lay on his borders, and captured three strongholds, in which he placed garrisons. But Herod came against him also and took from him all these places" (*Ant.* 14:297–298). It is therefore likely that when he began to build his defenses in Galilee, Josephus encountered a site that had already been fortified with an existing defensive infrastructure. The recognition that it was one of the chain of settlements fortified by Josephus derived not only from its surviving name, but also from its strategic position commanding excellent views in all directions. The Jerusalem Talmud mentions Zefat as a place where beacons were lit to announce holy days and the appearance of the new moon even after this practice had been discontinued elsewhere.[109] Mordechai Aviam recorded a Roman-period burial cave at the site attesting to the settlement's existence in the Second Temple era.[110] Emmanuel Damati recovered the fragment of a Herodian lamp with a pared nozzle in his salvage excavations at Khan el-Basha (the Jewish Khan) in Zefat's Jewish Quarter, providing the first Second Temple-period archaeological evidence from a stratigraphic context in Zefat. In the same report, Damati published a coin of Alexander Janneus (103–76 BCE) from the area of the citadel.

(12) Iamnith/Iamnia (Yavnit)

Fig. 25: Mount Iamnith (Yavnit). Ornate stone from Mount Iamnith

101 See Damati 1989.

102 See Foerster 1983b:232 n. 32; Ilan 1991:51; Aviam/Richardson 2001:181.

103 Klein believed that the omission was deliberate in order to adapt the number of settlements listed in *Life* to the number in the *Jewish War,* see Klein 1945:42–43.

104 See Foerster 1983a:141; Aviam 2004:101.

105 See Klein 1945:42, 130–131.

106 See Avi-Yonah 1963:142.

107 See Stepansky 2003:51–53.

108 As proposed by Klein 1945:30.

109 See *Talmud Yerushalmi, Rosh Hashana, 2:1 (58a).*

110 See Aviam 1983:43.

Iamnith/Iamnia has been identified with Horvat Yavnit, a site 897 m asl and about 8 km northeast of Zefat. It is recorded as having been the seat of the priestly order of Immer – one of twenty-four orders displaced to Galilee after the fall of Judea.[111] Shmuel Klein identified the settlement from the name Khirbet Banit, preserved in Arabic, and from the geographical order of Josephus' list. Levi Yitzhak Rahmani found two sepulchers at the site that could not be dated with any certainty.[112] Mordechai Aviam detected the remains of structures and pottery from the Roman, Byzantine, and Early Islamic periods.[113] Rafi Frankel and others have reported that the site is located on a summit and surrounded by traces of walls and graves[114]. Since the establishment of the State of Israel, the ancient settlement has been part of a military camp and for this reason there is little information about it. The IDF recently allowed the author access to the site. The visit revealed traces of ancient ruined walls, potsherds, blocked cave entrances, and an ancient ornamental stone outside the administrative offices.

(13) Mero/Ameroth (Meroth)

Until the 1980s, Mero/Ameroth was identified with the ancient settlement of Meron at the foot of Mount Meron[115] or with Maron ar-Ras in Southern Lebanon.[116] Zvi Ilan proposed locating Μηρώθ at Horvat Marus, which lies about 5 km southeast of Alma and about 7 km northeast of Zefat. Ilan's proposal derived from the position of Meroth in Josephus' lists at the northern end of the settlements he fortified in the Eastern Galilee, and from the fact that the site matches Josephus' description of the northern boundary of Jewish settlement in Galilee: "Its length is also from Meroth to Thella, a village near to Jor-

111 See Klein 1945:67; Oppenheimer 1991:53–57.
112 See Rahmani 1994:218.
113 See Aviam 1983:44; Aviam/Richardson 2001:190.
114 See Frankel, Getzov, Aviam/Degani 2001:40.
115 See Safrai 1981:134–135; Robinson, 1970 III:115. Bar-Kochva 1974:73–74.
116 See for example Press 1952:601.

Fig. 26: Meroth, the ancient synagogue

dan" (*War* 3:35–40).[117] The finds recovered from Ilan and Damati's excavations at the site show that Horvat Marus was a large Jewish settlement with a ritual bath, a synagogue, hiding complexes, and defenses that contained a wall, watchtowers, a gate and a moat. Several arrowheads were found near the wall. The area surrounding the settlement also yielded 160 burial caves with hewn *loculi*. Ilan and Damati attributed the assemblage of finds to the period of preparations for armed resistance to the Romans during the Great Revolt.[118] The position of Meroth in Josephus' list, on the northernmost boundary of the settlements he fortified in the Upper Galilee, matches Ilan's proposed identification. Nahal Hazor flows near to the settlement of Meroth; a steep cliff on the southern bank of the river contains over forty rectangular rock-hewn shelters that provide excellent vantage points toward the north bank of the gorge.[119]

(14) Seleukia (Seleukia)

Josephus lists Seleukia as one of the three settlements he fortified in the Golan (with Soganae? and Gamala). In his *Life* he writes that Seleukia is naturally fortified (*Life* 187); however, in his *Jewish War* he describes Seleukeia as being near Lake Semechonitis (*War* 4:2–3). The town was probably named after its founder who was a ruler from the Seleucid dynasty, possibly Seleukos IV Philopator.[120] Seleukia is mentioned in *Antiquities of the Jews* as having been captured by Alexander Janneus (*Ant.* 13:394). According to Josephus, Seleukia did not actively participate in the Great Revolt since the town had been guaranteed its safety by Herod Agrippa II (*War* 4: 4). The Tanhuma Midrash states that "Golan in Bashan is Seleukia."[121] Gottlieb Schumacher surveyed the Golan in 1883–1886 and visited a ruin named Selukiyeh (about 5 km south of Qazrin), which he identified as the town fortified by Josephus. Schumacher detected the foundations of a large square structure and several smaller buildings. He noted that although the site did not entirely match Josephus' description, the marked similarity between the name of the ruins and the name of the fort indicated that it was the Seleukia described by Josephus.[122] Avi-Yonah placed Seleukia in the upper Golan and remarked that after its destruction by Alexander Janneus it was only resettled at the time of Pompeius.[123] Zvi Ilan agreed that locating Seleukia was problematic and proposed seeking it at one of the tells or ruins in the foothills of the Golan Heights toward the Huleh Valley, possibly at Kfar Dabura.[124] Dan Urman noted that because it did not participate in the rebellion, Seleukia was a site of little importance and as such was largely ignored in descriptions of the Golan settlements, which he considered not detailed enough to provide evidence.[125] In his archaeological survey of the site identified by Schumacher (Qusbiyye el-Jdeideh), Haim Ben-David recovered no finds confirming Ilan's identification.[126] Moshe Hartal stated that all the existing proposals were inconclusive and that there was nothing in the finds to provide any corroborating evidence.[127] Seleukia's location therefore remains an unsolved mystery.

(15) Soganaea/Soganae (Sugani)

The settlement's identity remains unclear. In *The Life* it is listed as a naturally fortified settlement. Like Seleukia, Soganaea took no active part in the rebellion. While Victor Guérin was visiting the village of Z'eura in the Golan south-west of Ein Qiniyye (grid ref. 791600–266900) about an hour's ride from Banias, he was taken to a site called Khirbet Sujan. He considered identifying it with Soganaea, but the site had been plowed and sown and only a few structural surface remains were scattered around. Guérin rejected this site as the location of Soganaea, the settlement fortified by Josephus, believing that if it were the site he would have noticed substantially larger ruins.[128] Michael Avi-Yonah identified Soganaea at Kfar Yehudiyah.[129] Zvi Ilan initially supported this view in 1969, but later preferred the site of Khirbet Sujan on the Golan slopes facing the Huleh Valley,

117 *War* 3:35–40. The village of Thella has been identified at the Bnot Ya'akov burial ground near the outlet of the Jordan River from the Huleh Lake south of Armistice Bridge. If this identification is to be accepted, Josephus' determining of the boundary in this way would have resulted in an oddly limited area, see Shaked/Avshalom-Gorni 2004:33.
118 See Ilan 1984; Ilan/Damati 1988:11, 31–36.
119 See Meyers/Meyers 2015.
120 See Ilan 1969:205.
121 Schechter, *Tanhuma,* 1928a:112.
122 See Schumacher 1888:110.
123 See Avi-Yonah 1963:152.
124 See Ilan 1969:205–206.
125 See Urman 1995:481–483.
126 See Ben-David 2006:87.
127 See Hartal 2006:347.
128 See Guérin 1880:185–186.
129 See Avi-Yonah 1963:152.

Fig. 27: Gamla, view from the north

following his survey of this new site.[130] Dan Urman believed that because Soganaea did not participate in the rebellion, Josephus provided few details about its location and merely stated that it was in the upper Golan. Urman maintained that for this reason it was difficult to accept the identification by Avi-Yonah and others.[131] Moshe Hartal rejected the siting of Soganaea at Yehudiya, interpreting the remains of a wall described by Schumacher there, which was cited as evidence for its identification, as nothing more than a field wall. Hartal also rejected Ilan's proposal because of the scant finds at Khirbet Sujan, dating no earlier than the Late Roman period. [132] The town's location therefore remains unidentified.

130 See Ilan 1969:208; Ilan 1964.

131 For the division between the upper and lower Golan, see Hartal 2006:359–360.

132 See Hartal 2006:348–349.

(16) Gamala (Gamla)

Gamala is only listed as a fortified settlement in the *Jewish War*. Together with Sepphoris, Gush Halav and Yodefat, Gamala was described as "a walled city from the time of Joshua bin Nun" (*Mishnah 'Arakhin* 9:6; *Tosefta 'Arakhin* 5:7). Josephus mentions Gamala several times and records its capture by Vespasian in great detail (*War* 4:11–83). In writing about the period of Alexander Janneus, Josephus says that Gamala is "well-fortified." However, the main role played by Gamala in historical events of the time was undoubtedly during the Great Revolt. Josephus' description of Gamla and its capture resulted in several proposed locations: Gustav Dalman, Emil Schürer, Konrad Furrer and Bezalel Bar-Kokhba adopted the identification of Gamla at Tel ed-Dra' (the "humped tell") near Kfar Jamila at the intersection between the borders of Israel, Jordan, and Syria and east of Nahal Rukkad.[133] However, most early Golan scholars – among them Victor Guérin, Gottlieb Schumacher and J.P. van Kasteren – preferred the identification of Gamala with Qal'at al-Husn, a hill on the western slopes of the southern Golan now known as Hippos/Sussita.[134]

Yitzhak Gal, participating in the Golan survey headed by Shmaryahu Gutman, finally identified Gamala in 1968 on a spur resembling a camel's hump and known as Tel es-Salam, between two tributaries of Nahal Daliot and west of the deserted Syrian village of Deir Qaruh. Seventeen seasons of excavations and surveys at the site now leave no doubt as to its identification as Gamala.[135]

(17) Sepphoris (Zippori)

While Josephus claims to have fortified Sepphoris himself in *The Life,* in *The Jewish War* he says its citizens were "authorized by him to erect walls on their own account, because he saw that they were in affluent circumstances and even without orders, eager for hostilities" (*War* 2:574). Josephus calls Sepphoris a well-fortified stronghold of major importance several times, such as in the time of Gabinius (57–54 BCE) when it became the center of Roman government in Galilee, much to the approval of its residents: Gabinius "divided the whole nation into five unions; one of these he attached to Jerusalem, another to Gadara, the third had Amathus as its centre of government, the fourth was allotted to Jericho, the fifth to Sepphoris, a city of Galilee. The Jews welcomed their release from the rule of an individual" (*War* 1:170).

Sepphoris is first recorded during the time of Alexander Janneus in 103 BCE, when Ptolemaios Lathyros attempted to wrest it from Alexander: Ptolemios "also made an attempt on Sepphoris (…) but lost many of his men and went on to fight Alexander" (*Ant.* 13:338–340).[136] The city is next mentioned during King Herod's military campaign, when he captured Sepphoris without opposition during a blizzard in 37 BCE. Herod's troops rested at Sepphoris, which was well stocked with provisions: "He pushed on to Sepphoris through a very heavy snowstorm and took possession of the city without a contest, the garrison having fled before his assault. Here, provisions being abundant, he refreshed his troops, sorely tried by the tempest" (*War* 1:304). After Herod's death, Josephus recorded that Sepphoris was taken by Judas ben Ezechias who based his headquarters there during the rebellion against Varus. Caius, one of Varus' commanders, attacked and took Sepphoris and, according to Josephus, burnt it to the ground and sold its citizens into slavery (*War* 2:68–69):

> At Sepphoris in Galilee and of Judas, son of Ezechias, the brigand-chief who in former days infested the country and was subdued by King Herod, raised a considerable body of followers, broke open the royal arsenals, and, having armed his companions, attacked the other aspirants to power (…). Varus at once sent a detachment of his army into the region of Galilee adjoining Ptolemais under the command of his friend Gaius; the latter routed all who opposed him, captured and burnt the city of Sepphoris and reduced its inhabitants to slavery.

During the reign of Herod Antipas, Sepphoris was rebuilt and renamed "Autokratoris" according to the Greek equivalent of the Latin title *imperator* shared by both Augustus and Tiberius. Josephus called Sepphoris "the bastion of all Galilee" (*Ant.* 18:27; the Greek word πρόσχημα can also mean "ornament").[137] During Caesennius Gallus' campaign in Galilee, intended to quell the rebellion in Judea (in November, 66 CE), the Twelfth Legion was warmly received by the citizens of Sepphoris (*War* 2:510–511):

> To Galilee he sent Caesennius Gallus, commander of the twelfth legion, with such forces as he considered sufficient for the reduction of that province. Sepphoris, the strongest city in Galilee, received Gallus with open arms, and, following the sage advice of this city, the rest remained quiet. All the rebels and brigands in the district fled to the mountain in the heart of Galilee, which faces Sepphoris and is called Asamon; against these Gallus led his troops.

Vespasian's entry into the city is described in the following passage (*War* 3:29–34):

> At this city he was met by the inhabitants of Sepphoris in Galilee, the only people of that province who displayed pacific sentiments. For, with an eye to their own security and a sense of the power of Rome, they had already, before the coming of Vespasian, given pledges to Caesennius Gallus, received his

133 See Furrer 1889:145–151; Schürer, Millar/Vermes 2000:495, note 46; Dalman 1911; Bar Kochva 1976:54–71.

134 See Guérin 1880:6; Merril, 1881:145; Schumacher 1888:205–206; Van Kasteren 1890:213–215 (although Van Kasteren did not reject an identification at Tel Ahdav).

135 On the identification of Gamla see Syon 1996:3–24; Syon 2016.

136 For Alexander Janneus' campaign against Ptolemy Lathyros see Stern 1991:116–118; Bar-Kochva 2000.

137 On these names and titles see Strange 2015a:27.

Fig. 28: Zippori (Photo by A Greicer). Second Temple-period ruins on right

assurance of protection, and admitted a Roman garrison; now they offered a cordial welcome to the commander-in-chief, and promised him their active support against their countrymen. At their request, the general provisionally assigned them for their protection as large a force of cavalry and infantry as he considered sufficient to repel invasions in the event of the Jews causing trouble; indeed, it appeared to him that the loss of Sepphoris would be a hazard gravely affecting the impending campaign, as it was the largest city of Galilee, a fortress in an exceptionally strong position in the enemy's territory, and adapted to keep guard over the entire province.

Josephus records that he also tried to take Sepphoris but did not succeed because of the strong defenses that he himself had been instrumental in building (*War* 3:61):

Josephus did, in fact, attempt an assault on the city in hopes of capturing it, although he had himself, before it abandoned the Galilaean cause, so strongly fortified as to render it practically impregnable even to the Romans; consequently, his hopes were foiled and he found it beyond his power either to compel or to persuade Sepphoris to surrender.

Sepphoris has been conclusively identified on a hill 289 m above sea level in the center of the Lower Galilee, between the valleys of Bet Netofa and Jezreel and northwest of Nazareth. It lies on the intersection between the main routes to Galilee. It had plentiful water sources and was surrounded by fertile land. Sepphoris is mentioned numerous times in Rabbinic literature as Zippori, Zipporin, Zippri, Zipporim, etc. The name Sepphoris appears in the Mishnah as one of the three walled cities in existence since the time of Joshua bin Nun (*Mishna 'Arakhin* 9:6). During the period of the Mishnah and the Talmud, Sepphoris was famous for being a rich and peaceful city where Rabbi Judah Hanasi chose to live in his declining years because of its altitude and sweet air.[138] In the Rabbi's time, Sepphoris was the seat of the president and the Sanhedrin and it was here that the Mishnah was formulated and redacted. Sepphoris was an important center for religious study and retained this importance even after the religious leaders had moved to Tiberias. Until the late fourth century CE, Sepphoris was known as the

138 See for example *bBaba Bathra* 5b; *bKetubot* 3b and 4a.

home of many famous sages including Rabbi Halafta, Rabbi Elazar ben-Azariya, Rabbi Yosef ben-Halafta, Rabbi Yohanan, Rish Lakish and Rabbi Yonah. El'azar Ha-Kalir also probably resided there at a later time. Bronze coins minted at Sepphoris under Trajan (98–117 CE) bear inscriptions recording the city's right to mint coinage. Another series of coins, from the reign of the emperor Antoninus Pius (138–161 CE), shows that the city's name had been changed to Diocaesarea. A third series of coins was minted at Sepphoris by the emperor Caracalla (211–217 CE) and bore inscriptions emphasizing the bond of brotherhood and friendship between the Senate and the Roman people and the "Holy Council" of the city of Sepphoris.[139] During the revolt under Gallus, however, Sepphoris was destroyed (351 CE):

> Gallus suppressed the Jews who had killed soldiers by night and captured weapons for a revolt. Many thousand people were killed, even harmless children; and their cities of Diocaesarea (Sepphoris), Tiberias and Diospolis (Lod), as well as countless villages, he gave over to the flames.[140]

Victor Guérin visited the ruined citadel at Sepphoris and wrote that the *Onomasticon* of Eusebius suggests that Diocaesarea was still standing at the time when it was written.[141] From the 1930s to the present day, archaeological excavations at Sepphoris have uncovered exceptionally rich finds, most of which date from the Roman and Byzantine periods.[142] They include an extensive water system, large reservoirs, and aqueducts dating to the early first century CE that brought water to the city from springs 13.5 km away.[143]

139 See Meshorer 1978:185–200. Also see the multiple author collection of essays on Sepphoris in Fiensey/Strange 2015a:22–87.

140 Hieronymus, *Chronicon, Olympiad* 282.

141 See Guérin 1880:250.

142 See Weiss 1992a:1332–1335; Talgam/Weiss 1989:93–98; Weiss/Netzer 1992.

143 See Tsuk 1995:64–79.

Chapter 2:

"Cliff Shelters" near Settlements Fortified by Flavius Josephus

Having summarized the existing historical and archaeological data on the settlements in Galilee that Josephus claimed to have fortified, this chapter discusses the five sites named by Josephus where the author has explored and documented one of the defensive methods employed to shield the local Jewish population from the Roman army's actions to suppress the Great Revolt in Galilee. In our view, this defensive method ("cliff shelters"), already familiar to the local population, was adopted and perfected by Josephus as a vital tactical defense at the sites described below. The archaeological evidence sheds light on the tactics he used for the defense of this region against the Romans and discusses the phenomenon of "cliff shelters" located near some of the settlements listed by Josephus. Most modern literature distinguishes between "hiding complexes" and "refuge caves", thus differentiating between subterranean chambers hewn beneath Jewish settlements and used as hiding places for the local population and underground resistance forces ("hiding complexes"), and caves occurring naturally in steep cliffs and occupied by Jewish refugees in desperate times, principally in Judea ("refuge caves"). Researchers have found no evidence of a link between the refuge caves and the fugitives' hometowns and villages. The term "cliff shelters" can be applied to hundreds of natural caves in precipitous cliffs in Galilee adapted for use as shelters in times of adversity and that are clearly linked with the settlements fortified by Josephus preceding the Great Revolt (and with a number of other settlements he does not mention).[1]

1 Shivti'el, 2008.

The notorious lifestyle of those living in similar shelters is hinted at by a Greek inscription dating to the time of Agrippa I, found at Kanatha in Trachonitis. The inscription commemorates Agrippa I's war against bandits who had "beastly habits" and preyed on their victims from inside caves.[2] The popular Arabic name for this region of caves is *leja,* which translates as "refuge", and *mleja* means "shelter" in Arabic.[3]

In the course of analysis, our study adopts the following terminology, developed in the course of my work and adopted by the scholars of the Cave Research Center in Israel:

1. According to the types of hiding places:

Refuge Caves: Natural caves occurring in places that are hard to reach and are part of an extensive network of tunnels interspersed with large chambers. Refuge caves were often far from the fugitive's home settlements, which did not have regular links with them.[4]

Cliff Shelters: Caves occurring naturally near the top of steep cliffs in Galilee, close to settlements and with signs of human adaptation for use as shelters and hiding places. Cliff shelters had links with the fugitives' home settlements.

2 On the inscription see Kokkinos 1998:287; Shivti'el 2016:184–185.

3 See Wehr 1974:858.

4 Eshel/Amit 1990:8.

2. According to the components of such hiding places:

Cave: A subterranean cavity greater than 5 m in length whose entrance is smaller than its inner dimensions. It can be part of either a cliff shelter or a refuge cave.

Chamber: An underground cavity not exceeding 5 × 5 m whose entrance is smaller than its inner dimensions.

Cavity: Any kind of subterranean space.

Alcove: An underground cavity not exceeding 1 × 1 m whose entrance is smaller than its inner dimensions.

Complex: A number of adjacent cavities opening onto a specific area.

Rock shelter: An underground cavity whose entrance is greater than its inner dimensions.

Niche: A natural or man-made underground cavity, smaller than an alcove, with one side open to the outside or to a larger underground cavity.

Cell: An underground cavity larger than an alcove and smaller than a chamber, usually rectangular.

Shaft: A natural or man-made vertical shaft between two or more cavities on different levels.

Rock shelf: A shelf hewn in the rock and used as a lookout position outside a cliff shelter.

Cliff Shelters in Galilee

As discussed above in Chapter 1, Josephus claims that he fortified a number of settlements prior to the Great Revolt; archaeological research into five of the settlements in Josephus' lists corroborates the methods of fortification he describes. In the two sources referring to the fortified settlements, Josephus describes the fortification of villages located in "very rocky" terrain, as in the case of Arbela Caves and of 'Akhbara Rock, and he also mentions that he "provided with walls the caves in Lower Galilee in the neighborhood of the lake of Gennesareth" (*War* 2:572–574; *Life* 187–188). Josephus apparently lists the settlements he fortified (Tiberias, Arbela, Kapharekcho-Kapharath [Huqoq], 'Akhbara and Meroth) from

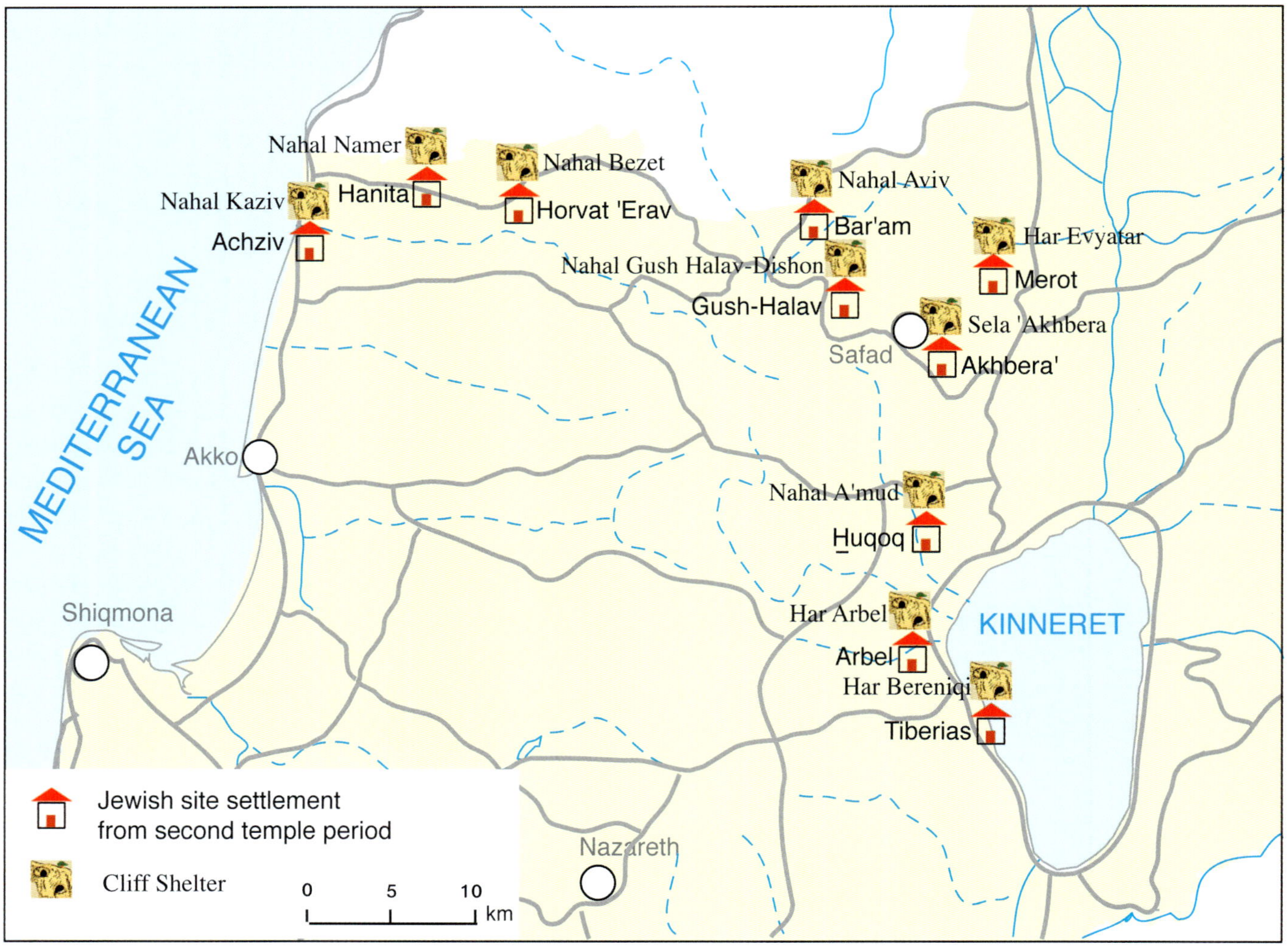

Map 1: Map of the cliff shelters

Fig. 29: Berenice cliff shelters

south to north. During our survey we found that the distance between the settlements and the sheer cliffs where the shelters are located is no more than 2 km. All the cliff shelters described in this book have been surveyed, documented, and photographed and most of the descriptions include map references.

Tiberias: The Cliff Shelters of Mount Berenice

The northeast end of Poriah Ridge, rising 190 m above the Sea of Galilee, is known as Mount Berenice. An uplift of the land mass on the fringes of the Rift Valley exposed rocks from the Upper Cretaceous Cenomanian and Turonian stages. This mass is formed of cliffs with precipitous slopes. The lower part of the eastern cliff consists of thick layers of dolomite and the upper part of limestone layers (the two layers are known as the Sakhnin and Bina Formations). In the lower part of Mount Berenice where the Sakhnin Formation was exposed, numerous karstic caves formed over time. A few caves also developed in the Bina Formation before the uplift of the ridge when they were still below the level of the regional aquifer. At this stage, phreatic caves developed below the water table. After the uplift of Mount Berenice, these caves shifted to the vadose zone, namely above the aquifer. The caves of Mount Berenice are typical of karstic activity below groundwater, a characteristic found mainly in Israel's central hill country.[5]

Herod Antipas founded the city of Tiberias in ca. 20 CE at the foot of Mount Berenice (**Fig. 29**). Josephus records that he surrounded the city with walls (*War* 2:638). Yizhar Hirschfeld believed that Mount Berenice was Tiberias' acropolis and that a citadel was later built there as part of the city walls.[6] In 1983 Yigal Tepper and Yuval Shachar surveyed some of the caves and suggested that they had served as refuges during

5 Frumkin 1990:77–83.
6 See Hirschfeld 1990:19.

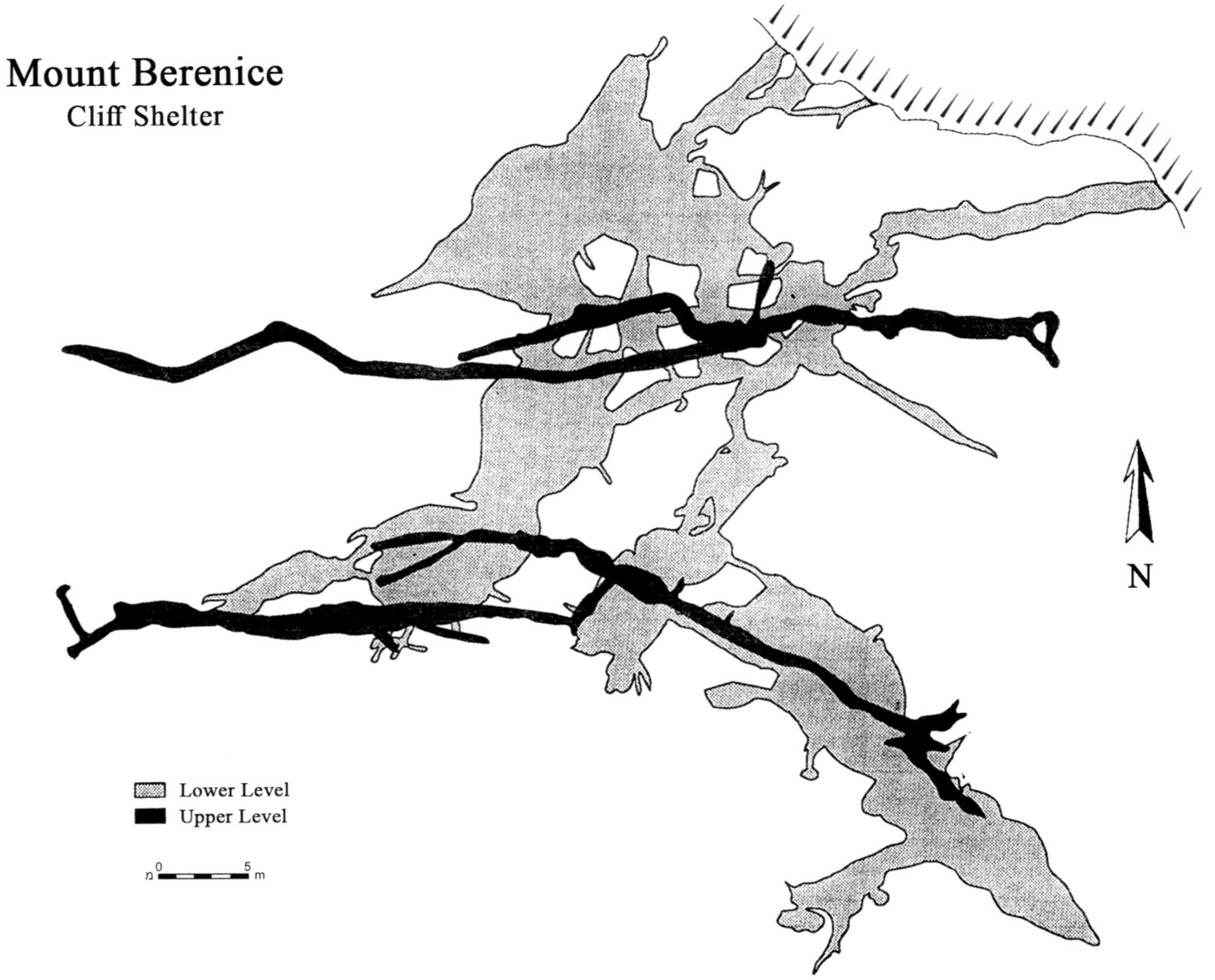

Map 2: Mount Berenice, survey map of cliff-shelter sites

the revolts against the Romans.[7] In 1989 I participated in a detailed survey of the Mount Berenice caves conducted by the Israel Cave Research Center (ICRC).[8] The survey team did not publish a written description of the caves, but 30 of them were recorded and mapped.

According to these explorations, the Mount Berenice caves can be divided into three groups:

1. Natural caves with no sign of human adaptation.

2. Large, natural caves where some cavities have been converted into water reservoirs, some of which retain traces of plaster on their walls. The reservoirs may have been connected to an ancient aqueduct carrying water from the springs of Nahal Yavniel to Tiberias.

3. Seven natural caves forming three levels interconnected by solution domes and passages. Signs of chiseling are visible on the smooth lower walls of these levels. Small niches for oil lamps are present in crawl passages between the different chambers. Rock-hewn staircases are also evident and lead from passages to openings to upper chambers. In other places, footholds were cut into the rock to climb from one level to another. The cave area was leveled and a door-hinge socket and bolt hole were hewn out. The largest and most extensive cave is the Berenice Cave, which has a total area of 482 m^2.[9]

Finds from the survey included potsherds from the Early Roman period. Supporting walls built along

7 See Tepper and Shachar 1984:34–35. The first speleological survey of the Mount Berenice caves was carried out on a limited scale by an ICRC team in 1983. See Frumkin 1990:77, note 1.

8 The Mount Berenice survey was conducted by the ICRC on behalf of the Israel Antiquities Authority. See Schwager/Miron 1991. The survey was problematic because of an abundance of cave ticks.

9 See Frumkin 1990:77.

Fig. 30: Mount Berenice, cliff shelter

a geological stratum beginning at the city below and ascending north via Mount Berenice cliff were also found at different points along the cliff, supporting an ancient path. A gradual and easy ascent followed this route along the stratum and over the remains of the supporting wall. The path apparently served in antiquity to link the city of Tiberias with the heights west of Mount Berenice. The supporting walls were only built in places where the route was too narrow for easy passage. The path probably played a vital role in case of emergency, providing a concealed route in and out of Tiberias without needing to go via the city wall.

A clue to the use of caves in Mount Berenice appears in the *yPesahim* 1:1,27b. Rav Huna, one of the great amora sages in the fourth century CE, wrote that during the "revolt against the Romans" (perhaps meaning the Gallus revolt) he used to hide out with his comrades for days at a time in caves overlooking the great *beth midrash*. This is generally considered to mean the *beth midrash* established by R. Yohanan at Tiberias in the third century CE. In any case, the only caves that can be identified at Tiberias as the ones described here are those in Mount Berenice cliff. The cliffs have, in turn, also been used in attempts to locate the site of the great *beth midrash* in Tiberias.[10] We believe that the two factions in Tiberias mentioned by Josephus as sympathizing with the revolt had originally made these caves as shelters in which to hide from the Roman army.[11] While preparing this book, some of the complexes and their finds were re-examined and the similarity between them and other cliff shelters in Galilee suggests that the caves were indeed prepared as refuges.

10 See Hirschfeld 1990:22.

11 See *Life* 62–68.

The Settlements of Arbel and Wadi Hammam: Cliff Shelters in Mount Arbel and Mount Nittai

The Arbel Heights (**Fig. 31**) in eastern Lower Galilee tower above the north end of the Arbel Valley. They ascend from southwest to northeast where they have a commanding view of the Sea of Galilee at their highest point. The summit is Mount Arbel, 181 m above sea level and approximately 380 m above the Sea of Galilee. The cliff drops down sharply to Nahal Yonim (Wadi Hammam). The crescent-shaped cliff is approximately 1750 m long and 100 m high. The east slope also drops precipitously to the lakeshore. On the northwestern side of the Arbel cliffs, across Nahal Yonim (Arbel), rises the second part of the mountain. This northern side of the fault is now known as Mount Nittai (**Fig. 32**). The summits of Mount Arbel and Mount Nittai consist of hard limestone rock from the Eocene epoch and are strewn with boulders. The cliff has two geological units, one composed of Bar Kokhba Formation limestone rocks characterized by karstic phenomena, and the other made of jagged Timrat Formation limestone. Hundreds of natural karstic caves are scattered along the north-facing side of Arbela and the south-facing side of Mount Nittai that have been modified for use as dwellings, probably for use in time of dire need.

Three partial surveys of Horvat Arbel and the caves on both sides of the Arbel and Nittai cliffs were conducted some time ago. In the early 1980s, Yigal Tepper and Yuval Shachar's exploration team surveyed some of the Arbel and Nittai caves and found over twenty rock-hewn caves in Mount Nittai containing

Fig. 31: Mount Arbel, surveyed cliff-shelters

potsherds and fragments of oil lamps, which they dated to the first century CE.[12] In 1987–1989 Ilan and Izdarechet excavated the Arbel synagogue and surveyed some of the Arbel and Nittai caves that were accessible by foot.[13] Mount Arbel was surveyed for a third time in 1992 by members of the Israel Cave Research Center (ICRC). The ICRC survey examined and mapped 40 caves, but provided no written description of them. Approximately 120 caves were explored during the three surveys. In 2010–2011 a fourth survey was carried out by myself and Vladimir Boslov from the ICRC, documenting all the shelters on both sides of the cliff. The first stage recorded all the easily accessible caves in Mount Nittai, at the same time documenting the Mount Arbel caves (apart from those shelters covered by the ICRC survey) that were only accessible using rock-climbing and abseiling equipment.[14] The survey of the least accessible Mount Nittai caves was conducted simultaneously by Boaz Langford of the ICRC with the participation of the author as part of Uzi Leibner's excavation of the wall on the summit of Mount Nittai. I myself identified approximately 400 caves on both sides of the valley as cliff shelters out of a total of 530 caves in Mount Arbel and Mount Nittai.

12 See Tepper/Shachar 1985:39; Tepper/Shachar 1992:33–38.
13 See Ilan/Izdarechet 1988:50–51.
14 Great lengths were taken to document the cliff shelters that could only be entered – for the first time – using abseiling and rock-climbing techniques. With thanks to the Israel Parks and Nature Authority for permitting us to abseil in Arbel Nature Reserve.

Fig. 32: Mount Nittai, surveyed cliff-shelters

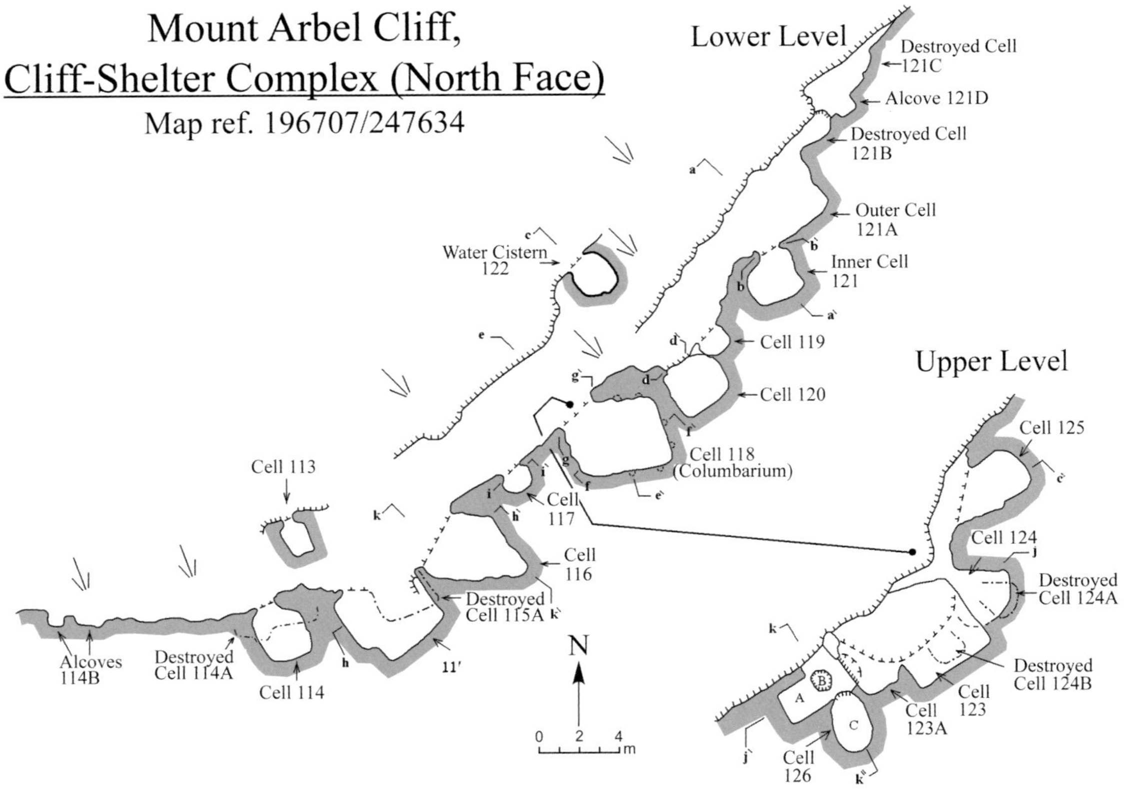
Mount Arbel Cliff,
Cliff-Shelter Complex (North Face)
Map ref. 196707/247634
Lower Level
Destroyed Cell 121C
Alcove 121D
Destroyed Cell 121B
Outer Cell 121A
Inner Cell 121
Water Cistern 122
Cell 119
Cell 120
Upper Level
Cell 118 (Columbarium)
Cell 125
Cell 113
Cell 117
Cell 116
Cell 124
Destroyed Cell 124A
Destroyed Cell 115A
Alcoves 114B
Destroyed Cell 114A
Cell 114
N
0 2 4 m
Destroyed Cell 124B
Cell 123
Cell 123A
Cell 126

Map 3

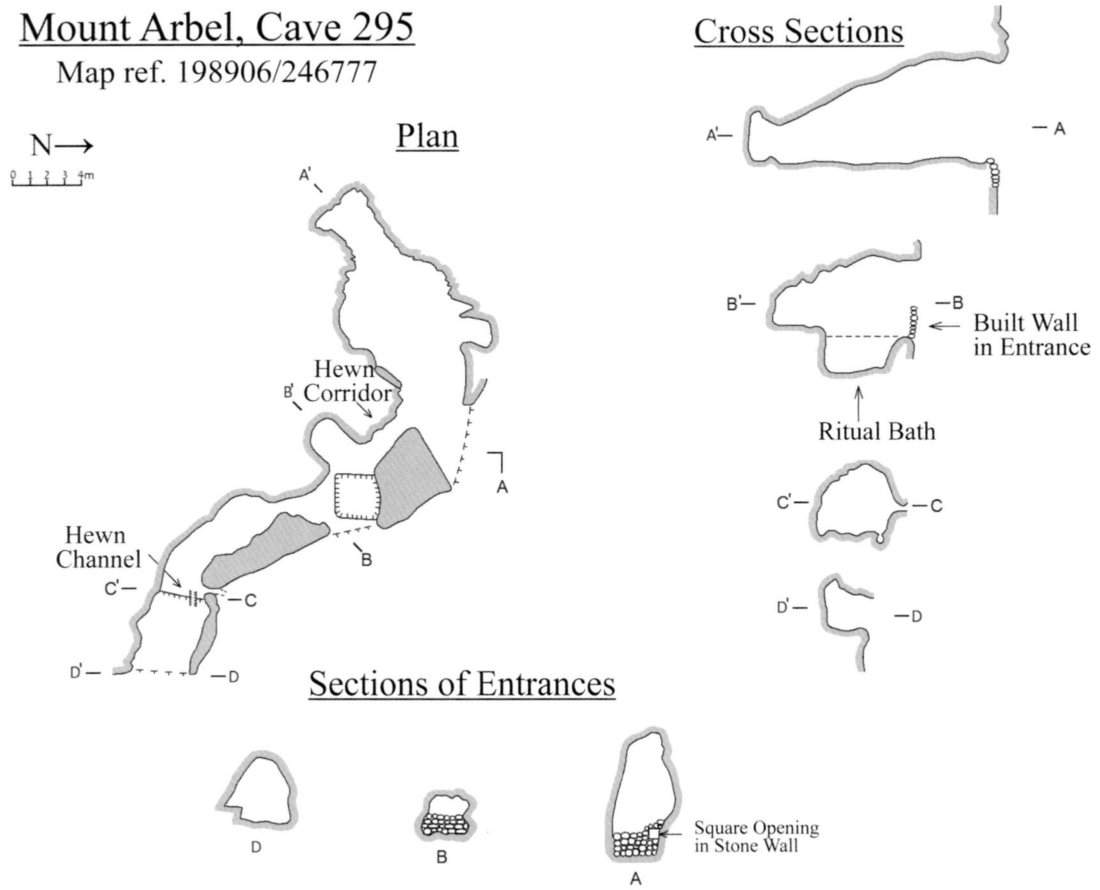
Mount Arbel, Cave 295
Map ref. 198906/246777
N→
0 1 2 3 4m
Plan
Cross Sections
Hewn Corridor
Hewn Channel
Built Wall in Entrance
Ritual Bath
Sections of Entrances
Square Opening in Stone Wall

Map 4

Mount Arbel Cliff

Map ref. 196707/247634

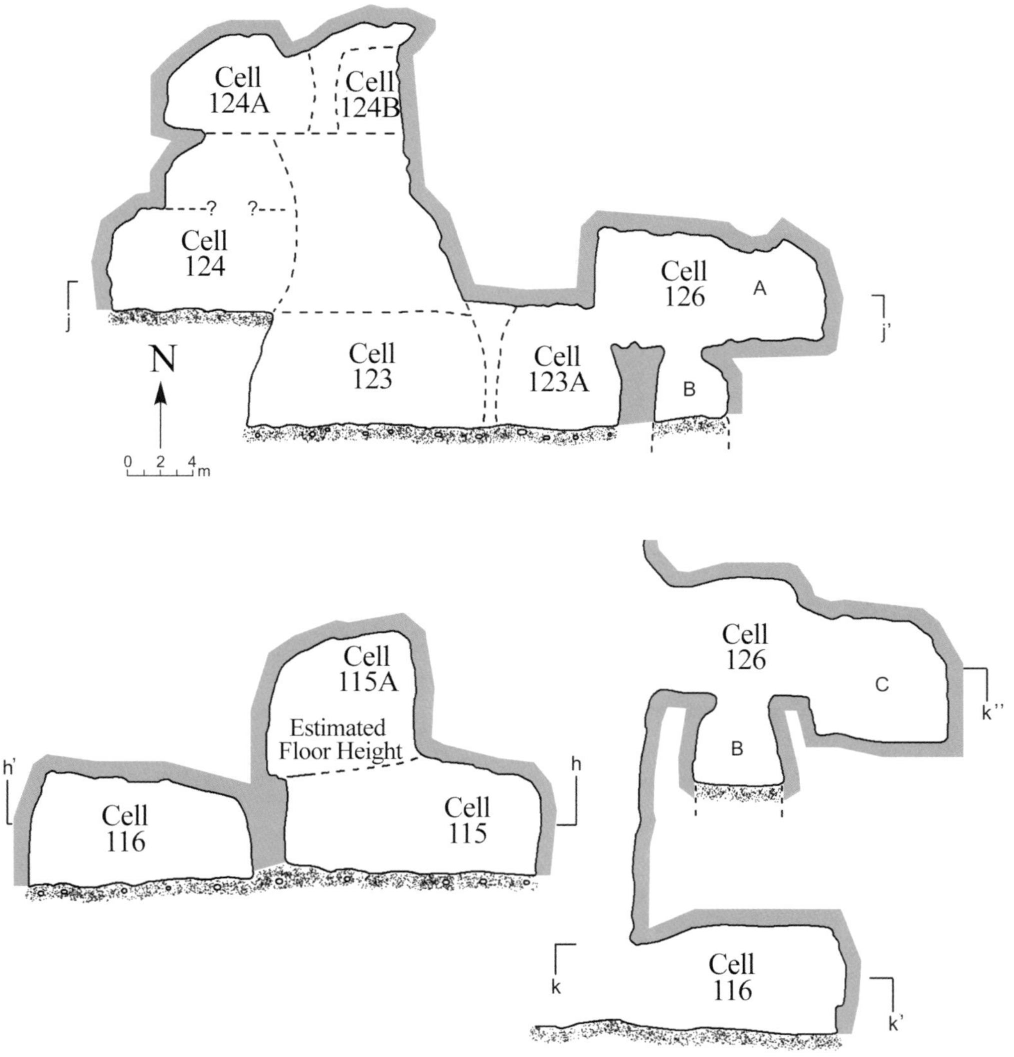

Map 5

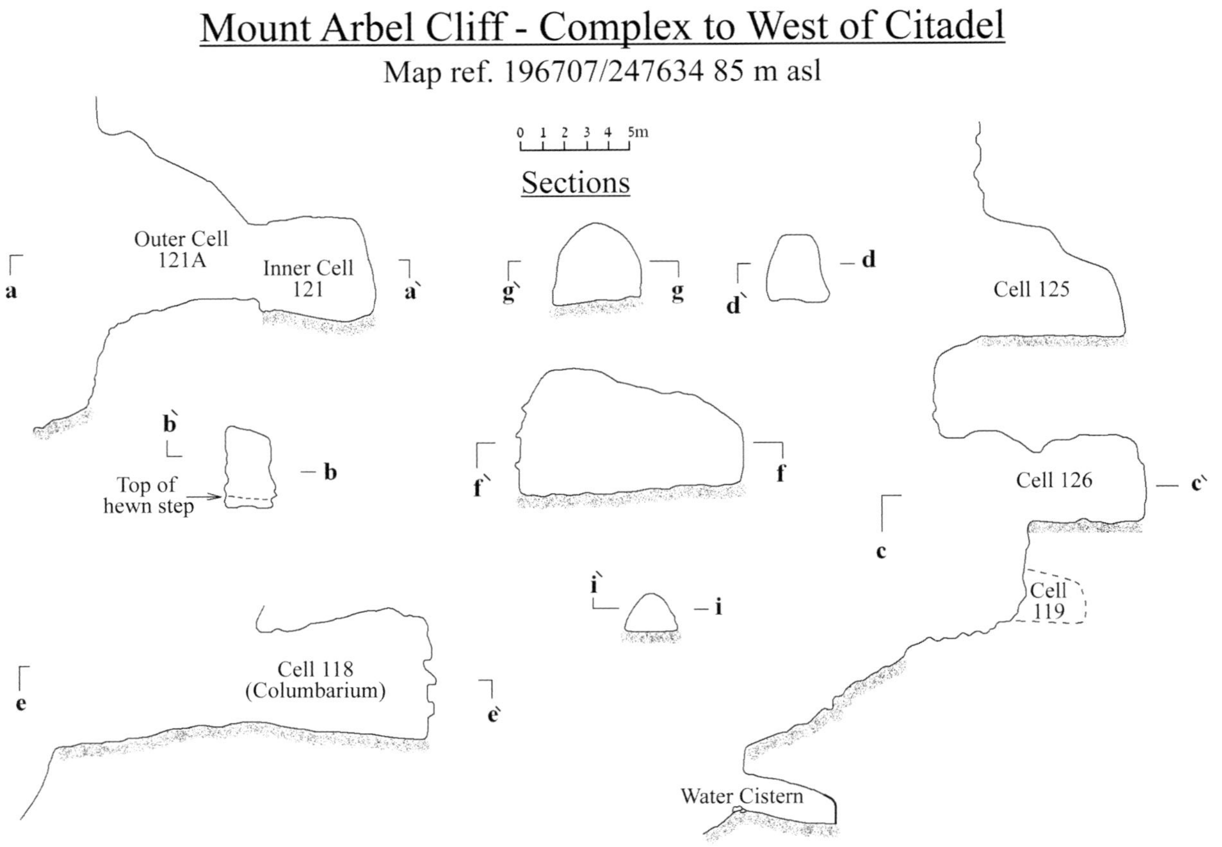
Mount Arbel Cliff - Complex to West of Citadel
Map ref. 196707/247634 85 m asl
0 1 2 3 4 5m
Sections
Outer Cell
121A
Inner Cell
121
Cell 125
Top of
hewn step
Cell 126
Cell
119
Cell 118
(Columbarium)
Water Cistern

Map 6

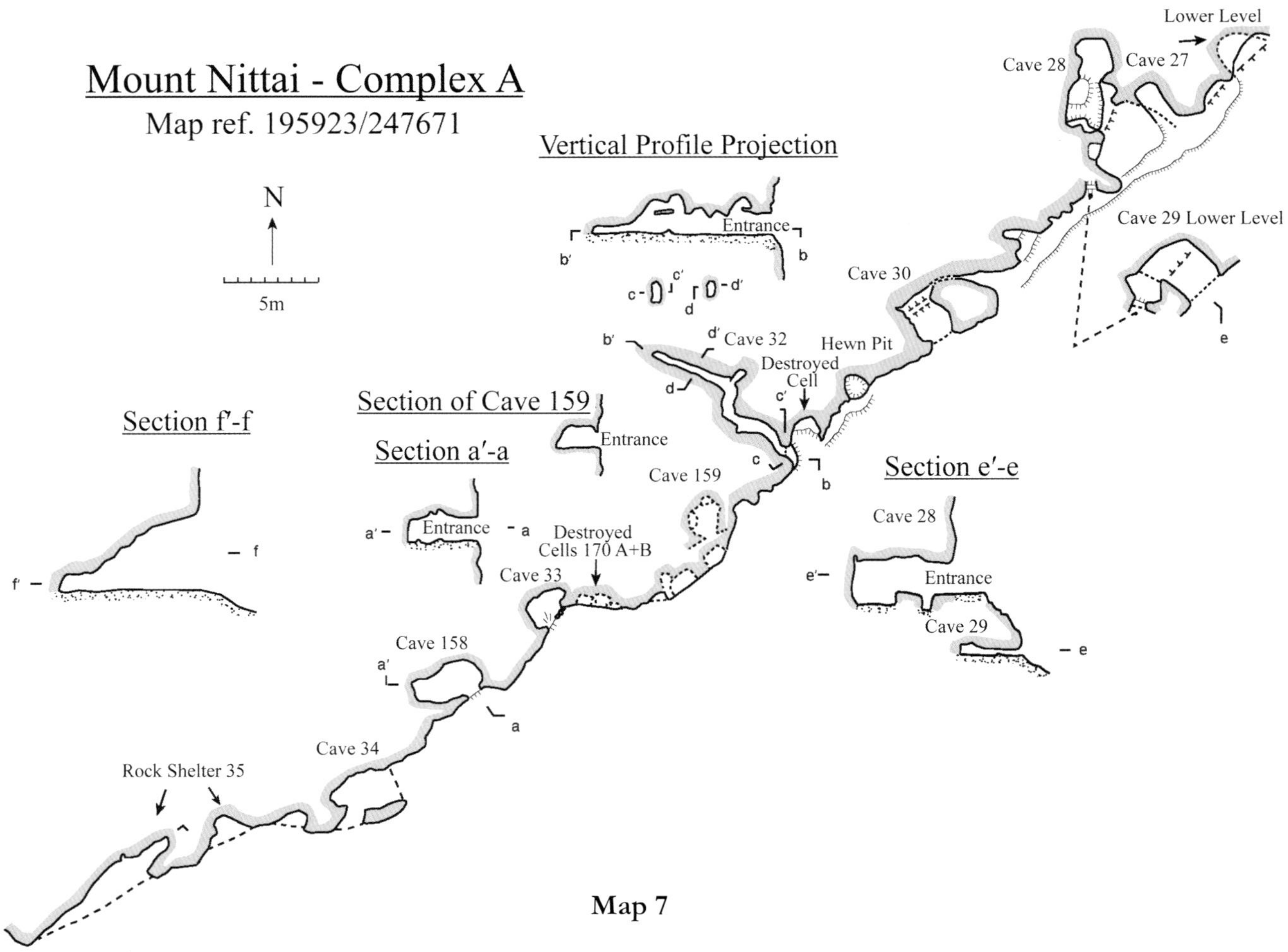
Mount Nittai - Complex A
Map ref. 195923/247671
N
5m
Vertical Profile Projection
Entrance
Lower Level
Cave 28
Cave 27
Cave 29 Lower Level
Cave 30
Cave 32
Hewn Pit
Destroyed
Cell
Section of Cave 159
Entrance
Section f'-f
Section a'-a
Entrance
Cave 159
Section e'-e
Cave 28
Entrance
Cave 29
Destroyed
Cells 170 A+B
Cave 33
Cave 158
Cave 34
Rock Shelter 35

Map 7

Fig. 33: Mount Arbel, hewn and plastered water cistern containing a channel cut to collect runoff water from the cliff top

Fig. 34: Mount Arbel, ritual bath (1)

Fig. 35: Mount Arbel, additional ritual bath (2)

The majority of the Arbel cliff shelters consist of clusters of between four and twelve caves. Each cluster is situated between two steep walls of rock, any access from the side is difficult and often it is impossible without using ropes or rock-climbing equipment to scale the cliff face. Based on the pottery finds, the caves were divided into two main periods: Small natural caves with signs of rough, undressed hewing that probably date from the Hellenistic period, and a second group of larger caves, all man-made and cut with straight sides, dated to the Early Roman period.[15] A few of the rock-hewn caves contain two or three chambers, some of which are long and narrow. In various cases passages were found between caves on different levels and some had shafts cut in them to move from one to another. Access ladders were probably erected inside chambers that were completely hidden from the outside.

Inside the cliff shelters approximately 30 water reservoirs were found, fed by hewn gutters that channeled the rainwater from the top of the cliff or by stalactites dripping directly into them (**Fig. 33**). The caves also contained five ritual baths dated to the Second Temple period (**Figs. 34–35**).[16] The slope below the caves yielded pottery from the Early Roman and Byzantine periods onward. A Hellenistic coin minted in Tyre under Antiochos VII (138–129 BCE), a coin of Antiochos IX (115–96 BCE), eight coins dating from the reign of Alexander Jannaeus and a 496 CE coin of the emperor Anastasius were also recovered from the caves. A 2011 survey of shelters located in exceptionally steep cliffs recovered another five coins: One of John Hyrcanus (129–104 BCE), two of Alexander Jannaeus from the ninth decade BCE and a Sidonian coin from the 1st c. BCE.

The seventeenth-century CE ruler of Zefat, Ali son of Emir Fakhr-al-Din, founded a citadel called Qal'at Ibn Ma'an in the center of the cave complex. The citadel was built across the entrances to caves used in the Hellenistic and Early Roman periods and one of the ritual baths was incorporated in it.[17]

The general orientation of the Arbela cliff is northward and the caves extend east and west from the cliff top. A survey of the central caves revealed that they are arranged on seven different levels with between four and nine caves on each level, some opening onto remnants of an interconnecting horizontal

15 Ilan also noted this in connection with the lower cave, see Ilan 1991–1992:11.

16 Three ritual baths were described by Roni Reich and Zvi Ilan, see Reich 1990:321–324; Shivti'el 2012a.

17 See Ilan 1991–1992:11–12.

Mount Arbel, Cave 144-145 with 'Hanging Ritual Bath' and Water Cistern

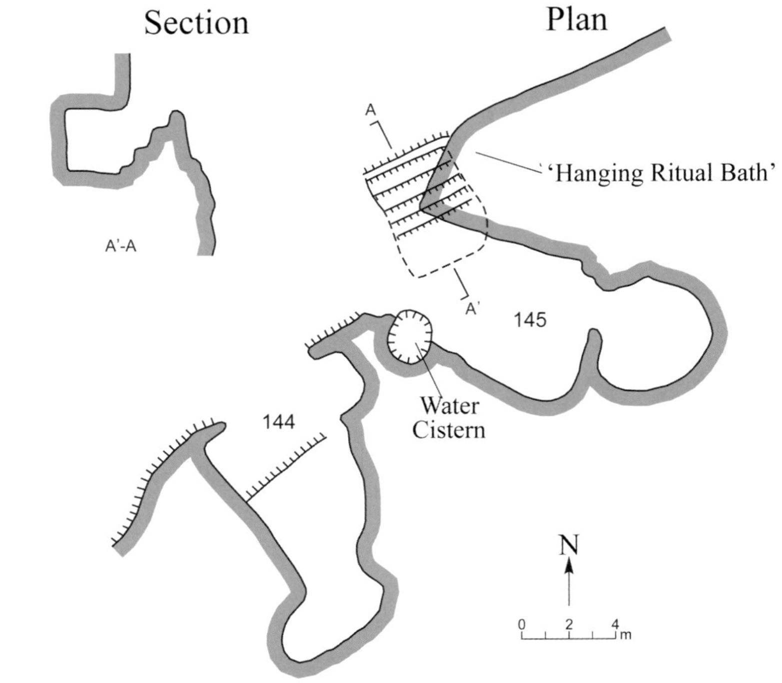

Map 8

Arbel, Ritual Bath 2

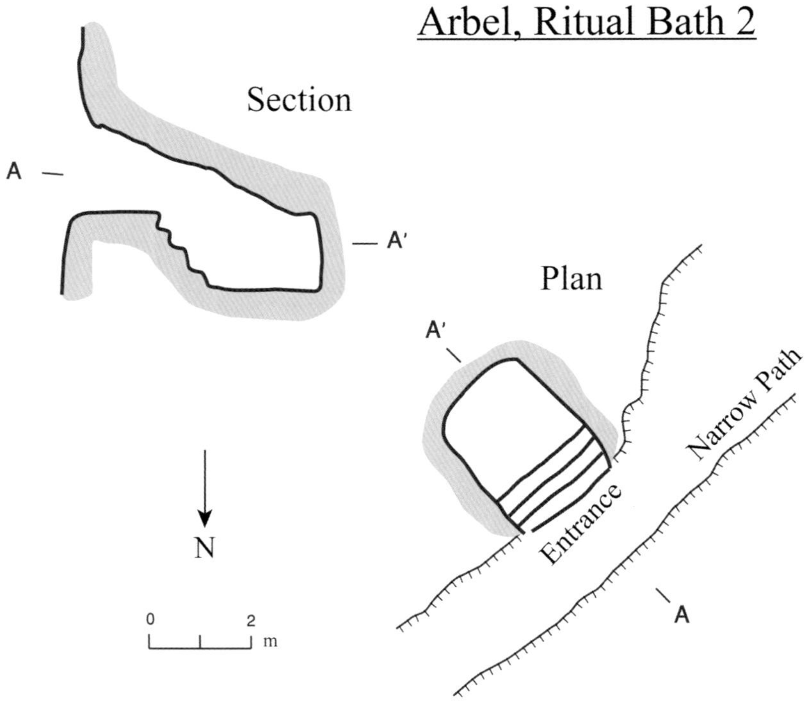

Map 9

Fig. 36: Mount Arbel, different levels of shelter

Fig. 37: Mount Arbel, abseiling to a cliff shelter

path (**Fig. 36**). A stairway with traces of 17 rock-hewn steps climbs diagonally up from Nahal Yonim to a number of caves adapted as dwellings and two caves converted into water cisterns. To the west of this cave series is a karstic fault now used by hikers to reach Nahal Yonim from Mount Arbel. Above and northeast of the fault is a group of caves resembling a dwelling complex. The caves have been enlarged and show clear signs of chiseling. The cavities are cut in the form of a square or rectangle and their average dimensions are 3 × 4 m and 2 m in height. One of the ritual baths, coated with traces of gray plaster, was found in a cave containing two chambers in the center of the complex. On the west side of the complex is a water cistern fed by rainwater channeled into it by a shaft hewn in the rock. The numismatic finds, pottery, and plaster show that the caves were first used in the Late Hellenistic (Hasmonean) period. Most of the pottery found inside some caves and scattered across the slope below them dates to the 1st c. CE. The caves continued to be used whenever the local population felt threatened, including in the Mamluk period. From this series of caves a path climbs eastward past other complexes and ending in a flight of built steps that forms part of the Qal'at Ibn Ma'an citadel. East of this staircase is a further cave complex containing another ritual bath. One more complex of rock-hewn caves is situated behind the citadel, inside a karstic fault. These caves are arranged on six different levels and require advanced rock-climbing skills to reach (**Fig. 37**). They contain multiple large chambers, some of which are meticulously finished. In some instances, the passages between the different caves and levels suggest that they would have allowed anyone hiding in them to pass from one chamber to another (**Figs. 38–39**). The pottery finds and plaster analyzed from these complexes also show that they were occupied in the Early Roman period. Uzi Leibner, who surveyed the area at the foot of the western and eastern groups of caves, recovered a large quantity of Hellenistic and Early Roman pottery of all types. The lower caves also yielded arrowheads (**Fig. 40**), ancient metal furniture nails, three Hasmonean coins, and an autonomous coin from the first century CE. Leibner believes that the caves may have been adapted for use by the local population as part of the preparations for the Great Revolt.[18]

The opposite side of the gorge, in the Mount Nittai cliff, produced complexes of the same kind as those found in Arbela. About 180 caves arranged along two

18 Leibner 2009:256.

Fig. 38: Mount Arbel, connecting shaft hewn between two levels in a cliff shelter

Fig. 39: Mount Arbel, view of the sea of Galilee from cliff-shelter complexes, north face

Fig. 40: Mount Arbel, arrowhead from a cliff shelter

Fig. 41: Mount Nittai, abseiling to a cliff shelter, south face

Fig. 42: Mount Nittai, abseiling to a hanging water cistern in a cliff shelter, half of which has collapsed

cliff terraces and only accessed with difficulty were surveyed in Mount Nittai. They can be reached from the southwest or via an arduous climb from the north-east. The climb would have been virtually impossible for a military force weighed down with weapons and armor. The caves have been badly damaged by rock falls; the cave complex was organized as a dwelling unit in which chambers were probably allocated for cooking, sleeping and storage. In another cave, at the north end of the cliffs, a karstic fault was extended to form an aqueduct for rainwater leading to a square, plastered room. The caves at the foot of the cliff were surveyed in the 1980s by Yigal Tepper and Yuval Shachar who reported finding "Galilean Coarse Ware" dating to the Herodian period and fragments of an oil lamp with a pared nozzle.[19] Another large complex of caves was quarried out in a natural depression in the center of the cliff. The caves are arranged on three levels and have concealed entrances.

19 See Tepper/Shachar 1992:34; also Rabani in his Survey of the Western Sea of Galilee 1958, in Tepper and Shachar 1992:27 n. 20.

Fig. 43: Mount Nittai, the wall

Fig. 44: Mount Nittai, watchtower

On top of Mount Nittai, various explorers over the years noted the presence of a wall with nine watchtowers.[20] Three sections of the wall were excavated in 2010 by Uzi Leibner who identified two distinct phases, one dating from the Early Roman period and the other from the Middle Roman period.[21] The wall is 286 m long and clear traces of its nine towers are visible in the field (**Fig. 43**). The tower walls are roughly 1 m thick and project about 1.3 m out beyond the line of the wall. The wall itself is 1.2 m wide and was further widened by another wall along most of its length, where it reached a depth of 4–5 m. The wall was built of dressed field-stones and is bow-shaped when viewed from Mount Arbel. Two clear features show that the wall was probably built to protect the cave complex to its east:

(1) all nine watchtowers project westward – the only direction from which a hostile attack could be anticipated (**Fig. 44**) – and (2), on the north side of Mount Nittai the wall terminates in a square tower with only a narrow pass between it and the cliff edge. This was the only place where the wall could be crossed above the steeply sloping cliff. In plan, the wall curves to encircle the cliff from the west; here too, this was the only side from which the cliff top could be reached. The wall was therefore built across the mountain's more moderate slope where an attacking force could try to approach the caves. The western part of Mount Nittai is a high plateau that is easily accessed from the west. The watchtowers therefore faced the direction most likely to be attacked by the Roman army. These two elements show that the wall was built to defend those hiding in the cliff shelters. I believe that it was part of the series of fortifications constructed just before the Great Revolt. An important related factor is the discovery of a Jewish settlement in Wadi Hammam at the foot of Mount Nittai. Leibner's excavations at the site exposed a 3rd c. CE synagogue. Probes beneath the synagogue's mosaic floor detected a deliberate fill dating to the Early Roman period. The pottery and numismatics show that the settlement already existed in the Late Hellenistic period.[22] There appears to be an obvious connection between the Jews who fled from

20 The wall was already identified in the 19th century. Publications of the Israel Antiquities Authority show that the extensive stretch of stones was identified as a wall by Bezalel Ravani in the 1950s and by Yosef Porat in 1970. Porat reported finding Early Roman potsherds there. Claire Epstein visited the site on 31 December 1972 and noted that the wall was no earlier than the Roman period; see IAA archives, File 80/Arbel 8/X 80/Mount Nittai/X.

21 Personal communication, with thanks to Uzi Leibner.

22 See Leibner 2010:39; Leibner 2015.

the village of Arbela and the Arbela cliff shelters, and between the Jewish fugitives from Wadi Hammam and the Nittai cliff shelters. The large number of cliff shelters at both sites (roughly 500) may also indicate that they were used by refugees from nearby Migdal as well.

The surveys conducted in the 1990s and in 2008–2010 located the entrances, measured the caves, and produced a written description of the cavities and photographs of the archaeological, biological and geological findings. Panoramic photographs of the entire cliff were taken on which the entrances were marked with serial numbers that included the caves discovered in Stage 1 of the survey.

Nahal Arbel (Yonim) forms a gorge between the cliffs of Mount Arbel and Mount Nittai but they are regarded geographically and geologically as a single cliff that was joined in the geological past. The name Mount Nittai was given to this part of Mount Arbel by Israel's Government Names Committee, but in the Second Temple period the name Arbela was used for both sides of the gorge. Two ancient Jewish settlements both containing impressive synagogues have actually been found in the region of Arbela. One was exposed in the 1980s on the summit of Arbela (north of the modern village of Arbel) by Zvi Ilan and Avraham Izdarechet and was excavated in 2012 by Benny Arubas.[23] Uzi Leibner excavated the other synagogue for several seasons beginning in 2006 at the foot of Mount Nittai south of the Arab village of Wadi Hammam. According to its excavator, the Jewish settlement in Wadi Hammam was at its height at the beginning of the Early Roman period.[24] It can therefore be assumed that the inhabitants of both these settlements converted the natural caves into cliff shelters.

The Settlements of Huqoq (Kapharcho?) and Horvat Kur: The Cliff Shelters in Central and Lower Nahal ʿAmud

The north bend of Nahal ʿAmud consists of limestone rock from the Eocene epoch. Geological faults exposed on the east bank of the channel and plentiful rainfall (450 mm per year) have led to the formation here of natural caves, some of which developed inside limestone "notches." A small group of caves along an easily accessible slope in the central part of the valley was surveyed in the 1950s by Bezalel Ravani, who was Inspector of Antiquities at the time. Ravani named two of them "Cave Group 25–26" and they are about 500 m away from Horvat Huqoq (Khirbet Yaquq). Ravani recorded that he retrieved potsherds from the Hellenistic, Roman, and Byzantine periods in and around the caves.[25] A survey of the site by Yigal Tepper, Gil Dar'in and Yotam Tepper in the 1980s recovered 15 bodkin arrowheads of a type known to have been used by the Roman army in the time of the Great Revolt.[26] The points of some have been flattened or bent by the impact on rocks or hard material like bone, showing that a battle was fought here during the Early Roman period. The surveyors also found coins, some dating to the first century CE, Tiberian coins, coins issued by Roman prefects and Nero, and Hellenistic and Early Roman pottery.[27] A survey documenting all the cliff shelters in Nahal ʿAmud includes all of central Nahal ʿAmud from Route 85 to lower Nahal ʿAmud where the valley meets the Huqoq-Migdal road (Route 8077). Within this region, 346 caves were surveyed of which about 250 were classified as cliff shelters. All the caves are clearly distributed northwest of the rock pillar that has given Nahal ʿAmud ("pillar") its name. The Nahal ʿAmud series of cliff shelters begins at a cave complex marked on footpath maps as Shovach Caves (map ref. 197425/253722) and the shelters continue northwest from there to the point where the river valley meets Route 65. Along this route three large complexes were prepared in an unusual manner: The first of these is the Lower Shovach complex; two kilometers further on is the Upper Shovach complex, and after about 500 meters comes the Wind Vane complex. Further shelters are dispersed between these three complexes; some were readied as lookout posts and rock shelters and are characterized by walls built at their entrances. The distribution of the shelters and their distinctive complexes reinforce the supposition that the cliff shelters were prepared by members of Jewish settlements known to have existed near this area, namely Huqoq (Kapharcho?), the ancient site known today as Givʿat Sheikh Nashi, and the Jewish settlement of Horvat Kur where a synagogue has recently been discovered.[28]

23 Forthcoming.

24 Leibner 2010:40; Leibner 2015.

25 Ravani's survey has not been published, results are cited by Tepper, Dar'in and Tepper 2000:38.

26 See Stiebel 2007:790–799.

27 See Shachar 1987:166; Tepper, Dar'in and Tepper 2000:87–99 with thanks to Yoav Fogelson for details of the arrowheads. In his doctoral dissertation, Stiebel published 36 arrows found by Tepper and Shachar but with no actual photos, see Stiebel 2007:90–99.

28 Zangenberg, Münger, Hakola, McCane 2013; Zangenberg 2016; Zangenberg 2017.

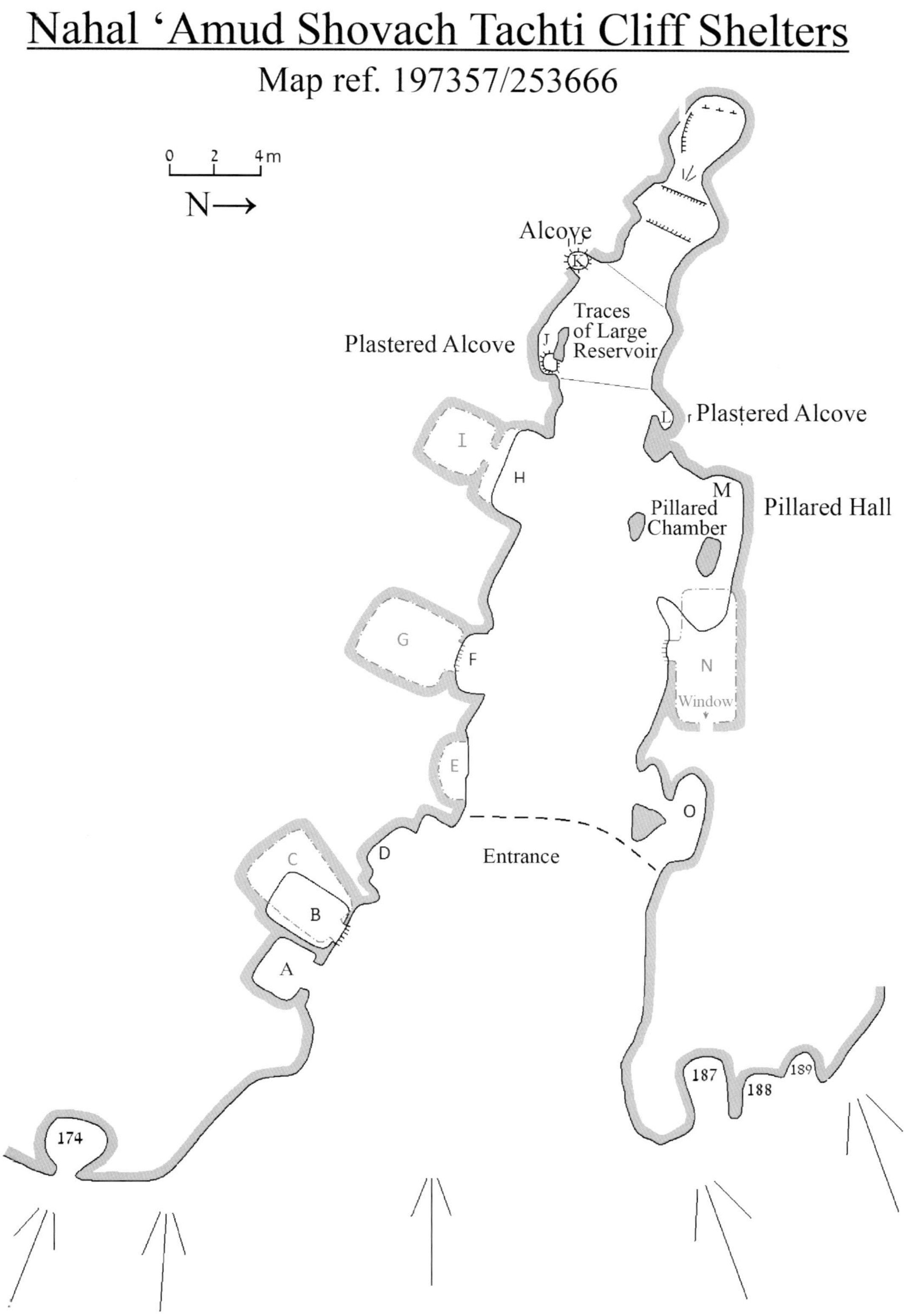
Nahal 'Amud Shovach Tachti Cliff Shelters
Map ref. 197357/253666
0 2 4m
N→
Alcove
K
Traces
of Large
Reservoir
Plastered Alcove
J
L
Plastered Alcove
I
H
M
Pillared
Chamber
Pillared Hall
G
F
N
Window
E
O
C
D
Entrance
B
A
187
188
189
174

Map 10

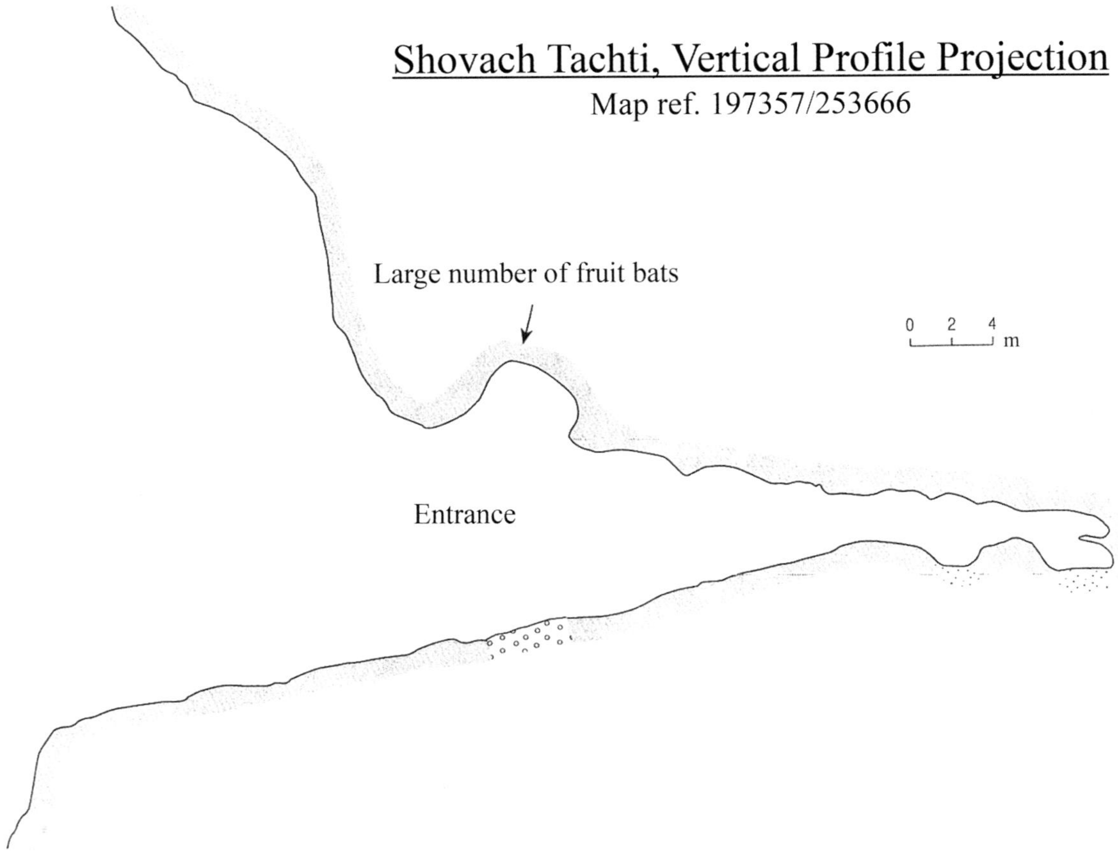
Shovach Tachti, Vertical Profile Projection
Map ref. 197357/253666
Large number of fruit bats
0 2 4 m
Entrance

Map 11

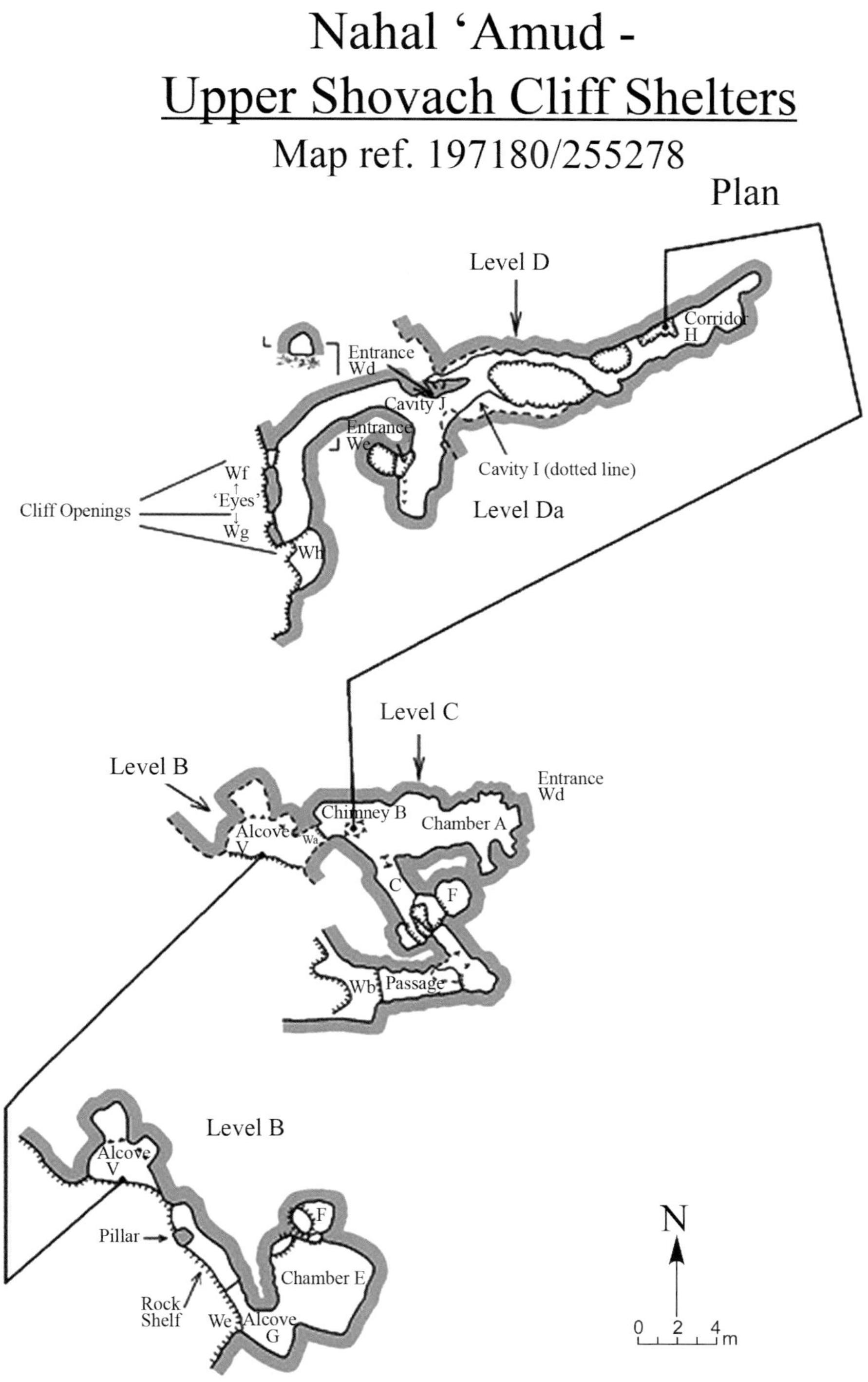
Nahal ‘Amud -
Upper Shovach Cliff Shelters
Map ref. 197180/255278
Plan
Level D
Entrance Wd
Corridor H
Cavity J
Entrance We
Cavity I (dotted line)
Level Da
Cliff Openings
Wf
‘Eyes’
Wg
Wh
Level C
Level B
Entrance Wd
Alcove V
Wa
Chimney B
Chamber A
C
F
Wb
Passage
Level B
Alcove V
Pillar
F
Chamber E
Rock Shelf
We
Alcove G
N
0 2 4 m

Map 12

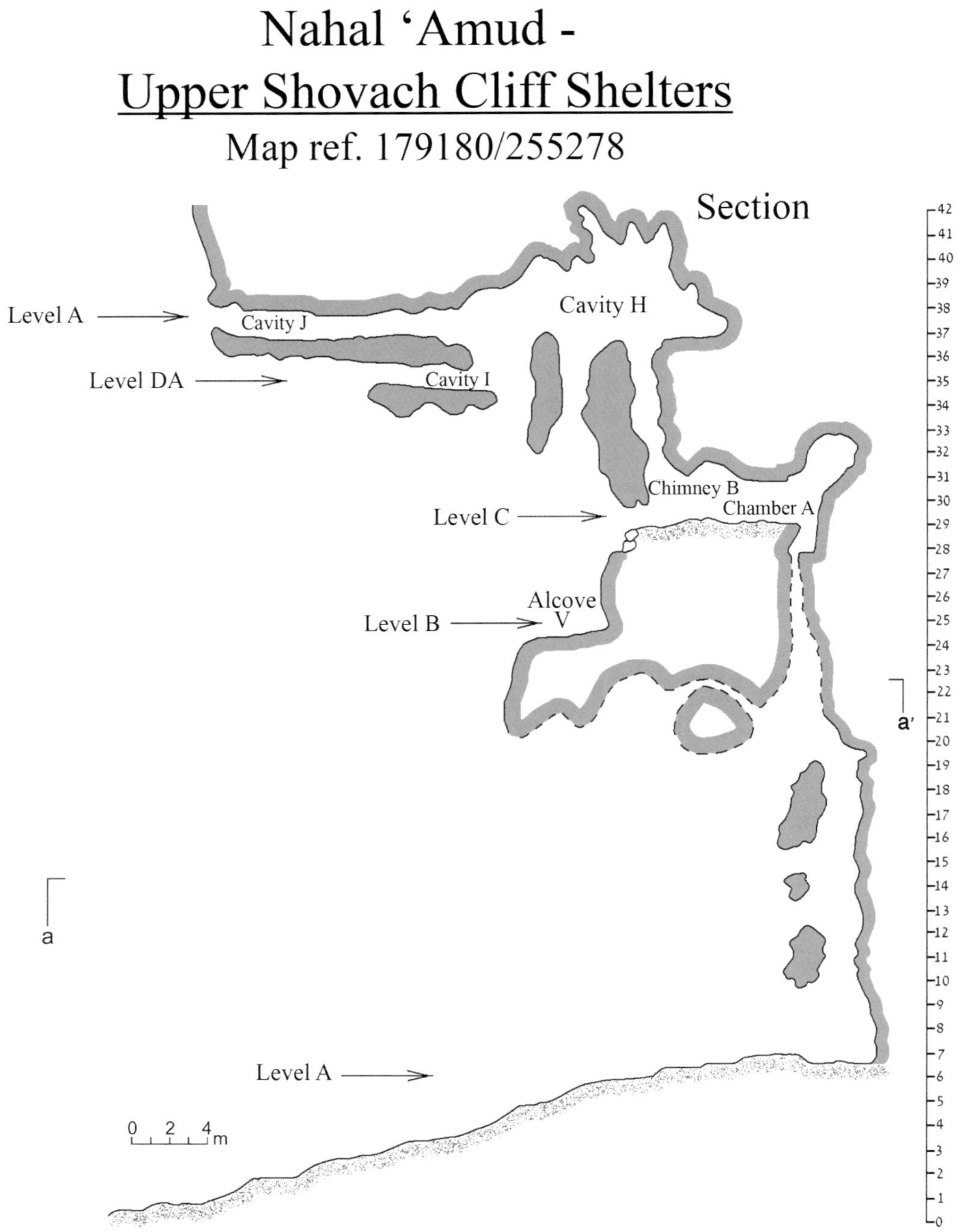
Nahal 'Amud -
Upper Shovach Cliff Shelters
Map ref. 179180/255278
Section
Level A
Cavity J
Cavity H
Level DA
Cavity I
Chimney B
Chamber A
Level C
Alcove
V
Level B
a'
a
Level A
0 2 4 m
42 41 40 39 38 37 36 35 34 33 32 31 30 29 28 27 26 25 24 23 22 21 20 19 18 17 16 15 14 13 12 11 10 9 8 7 6 5 4 3 2 1 0

Map 13

The ancient settlement of Kur is situated east of the village of Kahal and there is an ancient path to its south where the rock is particularly steep with a series of rock-hewn steps leading straight toward the main cliff-shelter complexes in Nahal 'Amud. The lowest caves in the Lower Shovach complex, which can be reached without ropes, were excavated in the 1960s by archaeologists from the University of Chicago. The expedition interpreted the complex as a prehistoric site from the Middle Palaeolithic Mousterian culture. In the highest caves in this complex, reached using abseiling and rock climbing techniques, we also recovered finds from the Hellenistic and Early Roman periods. The upper complex has about 30 rock-hewn caves that are also visible from the outside. They contain all the typical features of cliff shelters mentioned above. In the south rock wall of the complex, at a height of over 30 m above its base, a broad section of wall was coated with gray plaster that can clearly be seen when looking up from the bottom of the sheer rock face. Below it, four plastered channels hewn in a gradual slope to catch water running down the cliff are only visible if one climbs up the vertical wall toward the exposed plaster. The water ran down from the top of the cliff to the plastered section, draining over it and into the channels. These carried the water to a reservoir concealed between two clefts in the rock. The reservoir is hewn in an oval shape and is finely coated with gray hydraulic plaster. In the middle of the reservoir a kind of plastered seat was hewn. It is quite possible that this was a ritual bath although if that was the case, it is the only existing find of its kind. Above the exposed plaster section on the rock wall a concealed cliff shelter was discovered containing an almost intact jar (0.5 × 1.3 m, internal diameter 0.47 m). It is difficult to date the jar since its rim is missing. The general shape is however consistent with jars from the Hellenistic and Roman periods.

Fig. 45: Nahal 'Amud, Shovach Tachti (lower) cliff shelters near the settlement of Horvat Kur

Fig. 46: Nahal 'Amud, Shovach 'Aili (upper) cliff shelters near the settlement of Horvat Huqok

Fig. 47: Nahal 'Amud, 'En Shavshevet cliff shelters

The second complex is about 2 km northwest of the Lower Shovach complex. Since this feature has the same form and type as those of the cliff shelters we named it the Upper Shovach Complex. The Upper Shovach complex is in fact the most elaborate complex of cliff shelters found to date, both in Nahal 'Amud and at other sites examined in Galilee. It can only be reached using rock-climbing and abseiling techniques. To enter some of the shelters in both these complexes, it was first necessary to descend 60 m by rope, then find a rock with which to anchor a second rope, then traverse across the vertical rock face toward the complex at the bottom of a concealed cleft in the rock protected by a massive rock roof towering above the entrances to the caves prepared as shelters. Those who built the complex probably reached the caves by climbing up from the slope at the base of the cliff. The climbers used wooden wedges driven into cracks in the rock, some of which can still be seen *in situ;* the first climber fixed ropes to the wedges to secure himself and continued climbing in a similar manner. When the first climber reached the series of caves at the intermediate level, rock loops were cut in order to attach ropes that were then let down to the bottom of the cliff for others to grasp and scale using the wedges as footholds. Inside the intermediate level, connecting shafts were hewn to the upper levels where the main work on the caves as an impregnable refuge was concentrated.

Most of the inner series of caves at both complexes is totally concealed from anyone looking up from the bottom of the slope between the vertical cliff and the river valley. From the valley, there appears to be merely a network of natural cavities opening onto the slope. The Upper Shovach Complex is composed of three levels connected by shafts or narrow rock shelves that can only be traversed by leaning into the rock wall and clasping natural rock ledges to avoid plummeting to the bottom. The third level hangs between the rock roof and the vertical rock wall and is about 40 m above the river banks in this place. The cavities in the third level are connected by meticulously hewn passages and are very reminiscent of the underground hiding complexes discovered both in Galilee and in Judea. The longest passage leading from the deepest cavity to the one overlooking the valley measures no less than 17 m. This passage reaches three rock-hewn windows with views of Ramat Huqoq and Nahal 'Amud. The frames of the three windows are connected to the rock roof. On the sill of the middle window, next to the crawl passage, a step was hewn in the form of a triangle with a funnel-shaped apex over the gaping chasm. The roof of the third cavity at the end of the passage is covered in stalactites that are still active. Some of the water runs in a rock-hewn channel to a triangular step in the main cavity. The two cavities were probably used for water collection. A large grain-storage pit was hewn on the second floor with a window in its center that leads to an arched chamber measuring 8 × 8 m. At the south end of the chamber a frameless window was cut that provides a perfect view of Ramat Huqoq and Livnim Ridge. The height from the bottom of the cliff is about 30 m here. The first level serves as a kind of entrance leading to the cliff, below which wooden wedges remain fixed in the rock although they are extremely hazardous to climb. The entrance level contains four hewn cavities and a narrow chimney leading up to the second level above. The eight-meter squeeze through the chimney is perilous, requiring the climber to pull up with the arms using small protrusions left over from cutting the chimney while pushing up with the tips of the toes through the narrow gap between the rock walls. The complex is very reminiscent of one in Nahal Parat (Wadi Kelt) in Judea, where I also identified typical cliff shelter characteristics. The site in Judea was examined in the 1980s by Yossi Patrich, who suggested that it may have been Simon Bar Kokhba's headquarters. We cannot know who commanded the Galilean rebels here, but the tremendous amount of work invested in this complex shows that it was in all likelihood an important headquarters for rebels in the region. Apart from potsherds positively dated to the Early Roman period, it is worth noting that no other finds were recovered from the complex. This may indicate that those holed up here did not surrender and survived to come out of the complex alive, taking all their belongings with them.

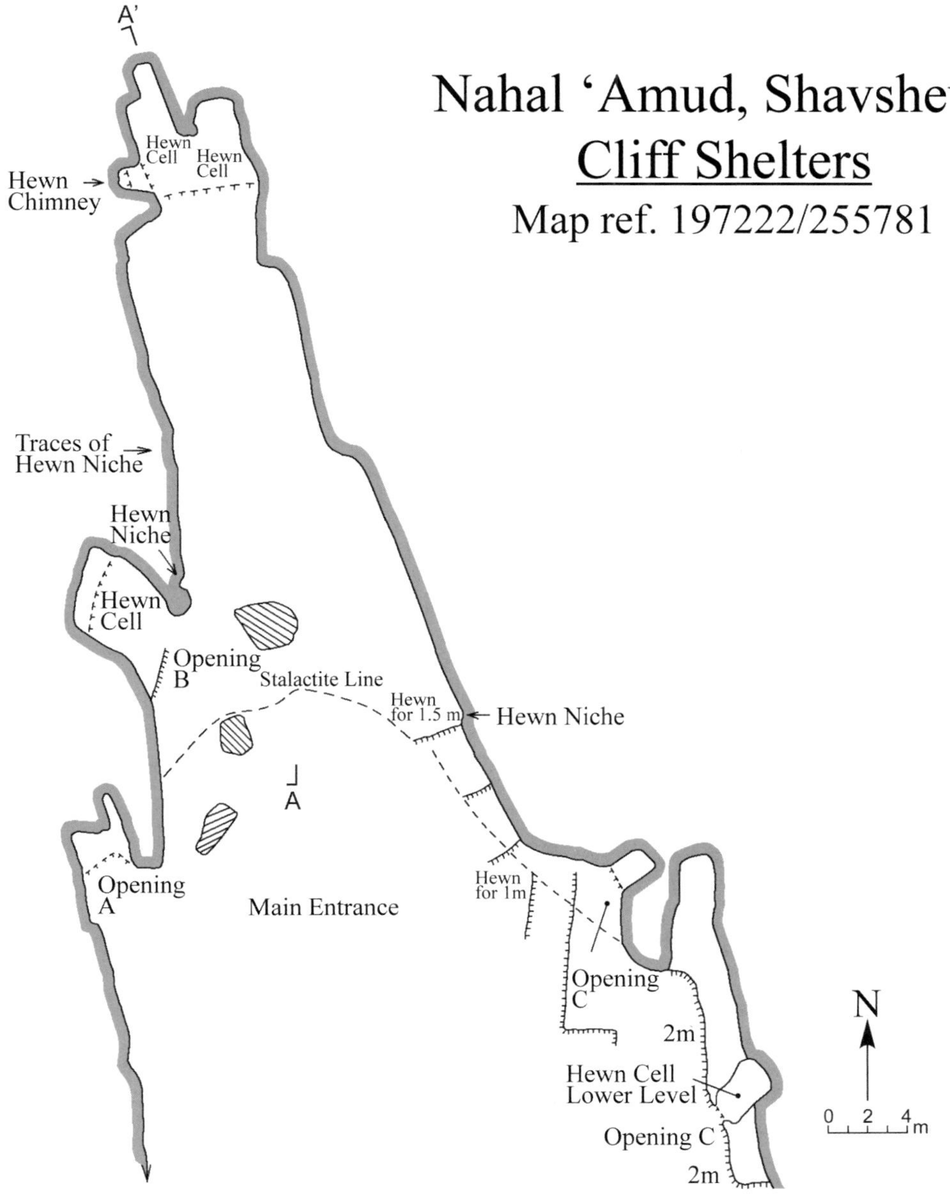
Nahal 'Amud, Shavshevet
Cliff Shelters
Map ref. 197222/255781
A'
Hewn Chimney
Hewn Cell
Hewn Cell
Traces of Hewn Niche
Hewn Niche
Hewn Cell
Opening B
Stalactite Line
Hewn for 1.5 m
Hewn Niche
A
Opening A
Main Entrance
Hewn for 1m
Opening C
2m
Hewn Cell Lower Level
Opening C
2m
N
0 2 4 m

Map 14

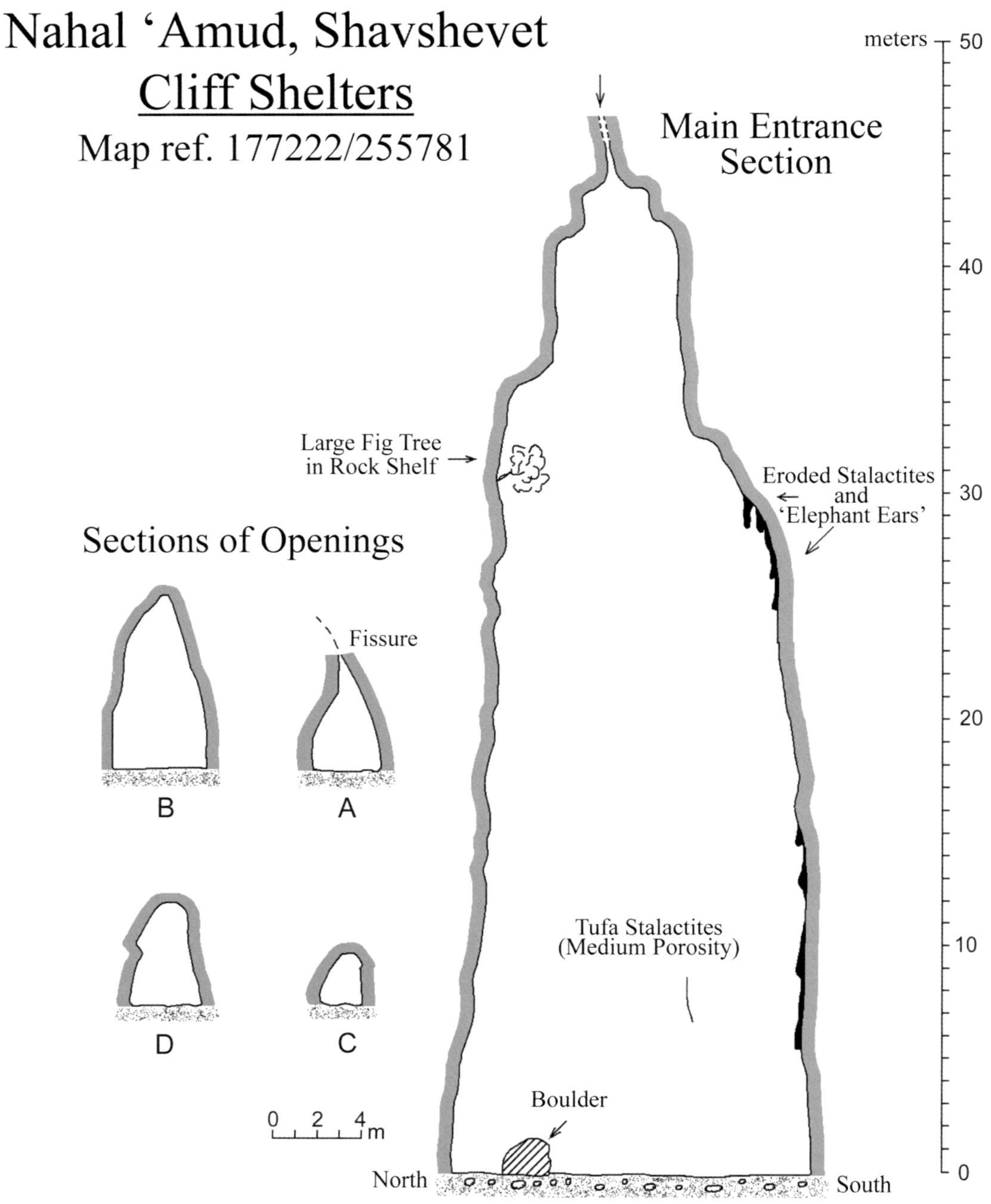

Nahal 'Amud, Shavshevet
Cliff Shelters
Map ref. 177222/255781
Main Entrance Section
meters
50
40
30
20
10
0
Large Fig Tree in Rock Shelf
Eroded Stalactites and 'Elephant Ears'
Sections of Openings
Fissure
B
A
D
C
Tufa Stalactites (Medium Porosity)
Boulder
0 2 4 m
North
South

Map 15

Cliff Shelters - Stalactite Cave
Lower Nahal ‘Amud
Map ref. 197380/255310

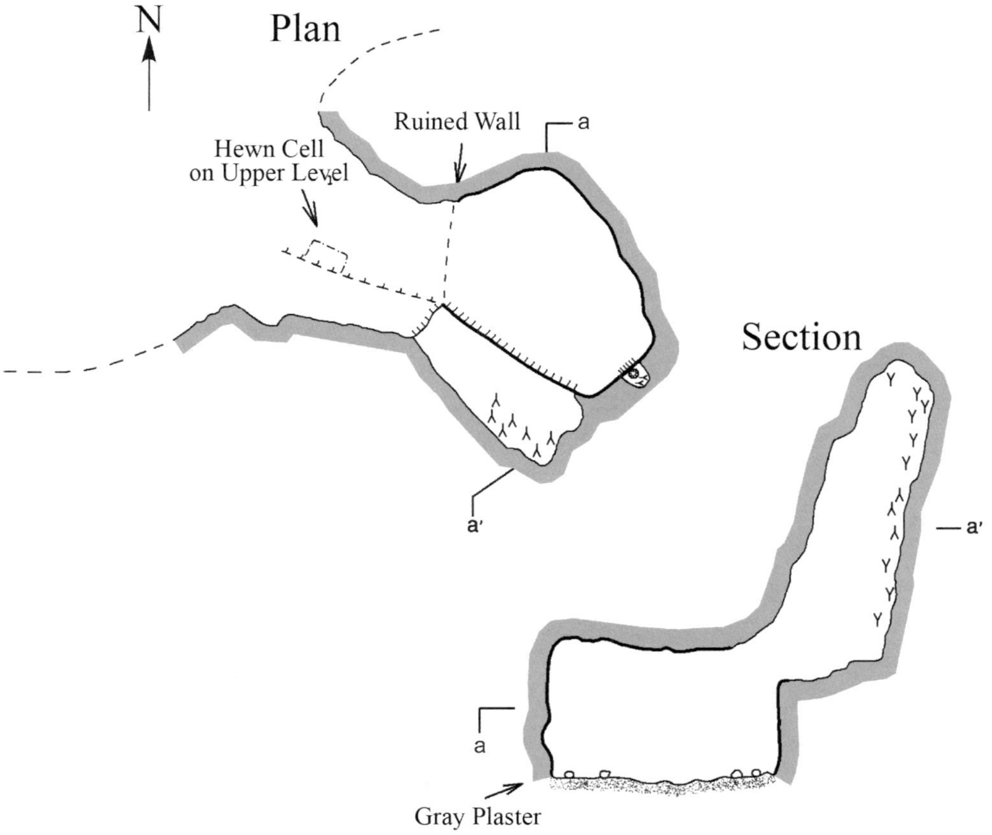

Map 16

Fig. 48: Nahal 'Amud, abseiling to a cliff shelter where a jar was discovered

Fig. 49: Nahal 'Amud, the jar

Fig. 50: Nahal 'Amud, pithos in cliff shelter beyond the plastered rock wall

We named the third complex the "Shavshevet ("Wind Vane") Complex" since it is situated exactly opposite the 'En Shavshevet spring marked on Nahal 'Amud trail maps. Shaped in the form of a bell, the Shavshevet Complex contains a network of twenty shelters hewn above a smooth, vertical rock wall about 20 m above a step in the valley slope that can only be scaled using climbing tackle. From the bottom of the north-facing vertical rock wall, one can still see long, deep grooves hewn horizontally along the face of the wall. They look like slots for scaffolding placed there while quarrying out the shelters in order to reach them. On the inner wall of the bell, a large water reservoir was hewn and coated with gray plaster; a 7 m long vertical channel cut above it leads from a group of stalactites inside a concealed karstic fault, carrying the dripping water to the reservoir. (**Map 16**) Above the channel is a narrow rock shelf and above this a number of rock-hewn rooms that can only be seen after climbing up the channel. South of the Shavshevet Complex and 15 m away, in the center of the large cliff and 20 m above ground level, a hewn alcove probably provided a lookout post for a single person. It yielded an intact jar dated to the Hellenistic-Roman period. In front of this cave, on the opposite side of the creek, we surveyed another cave. Inside of it we found a pithos of the Galilean Course Ware (GCW) type that was common in the Hellenistic period. (**Figs. 48–50**) Most of the finds from the Hellenistic and Early Roman periods recovered from and near to the cliff shelters represent the period when the Jewish settlements of Huqoq, Tel Nashi and Kur were occupied. It is important to remember that the shelters may have been started in the Hellenistic period when Jewish settlement was on the rise in these parts of Galilee. Uzi Leibner, who collected potsherds at the foot of two of the cliff-shelter complexes (the east and the west), noted that they both yielded mainly Early Roman specimens. Without knowing about the finds from the upper shelters, Leibner also believed that the caves were used mainly during the Great Revolt.[29]

29 See Leibner 2009:145.

The Settlement of ʿAkhbaraʿ: Akhbara Rock Cliff Shelters

Josephus clearly stated in his *Jewish War* that he fortified ʿAkhbara Rock and not the settlement of ʿAkhbara. In his *Life,* the historian mentions ʿAkhbara as one of the "very rocky" settlements (*War* 2:572–576; *Life* 187–188). ʿAkhbara Rock reaches a height of 132 m and is the highest vertical cliff in Galilee (**Fig. 51**). The settlement of ʿAkhbara, often mentioned from the Second Temple period to the Middle Ages as a Jewish settlement, is situated at the foot of the rock cliff. The lowest caves in ʿAkhbera Rock were first surveyed in the 1980s by Yigal Tepper and Yuval Shachar's survey team. Nine caves reached by abseiling were first surveyed by myself in the late 1980s during a trial survey I conducted at the site that was directed by Emmanuel Damati of the Israel Antiquities Authority.[30] In 2005–2006, Vladimir Boslov, teams from the ICRC and myself surveyed all the cliff shelters in ʿAkhbara Rock – a total of 127 caves described below (**Map 17**). The survey was conducted from south to north and the cliff was divided into six sections; each cave was described and marked on a panoramic photograph of the cliff. Plans were also drawn of some of the main shelters.

Most of the caves made into shelters are arranged in the steepest, northernmost part of the cliff and can only be reached by abseiling down from the cliff top. Because of its great height, it was sometimes necessary to abseil over 100 meters down to the cliff shelters (**Map 18**). The main complex in ʿAkhbara Rock is located in the center of the rock, where a number of caves were joined together by cutting chimneys and openings to create a complex on three levels. In the chambers of the upper complex, a water cistern was hewn beneath a cluster of stalactites that were still active when the caves were surveyed. The lower part of this complex can be reached by climbing up the rock wall holding on to natural protrusions in the rock. Coins minted in Sepphoris were also recovered from the upper level of this complex. Coins found in other cliff shelters date to Alexander Jannaeus and to Agrippa I.[31]

Fig. 51: ʿAkhbera Rock, abseiling down to cliff shelter

30 The results of the survey have not been published yet.

31 See Shivtiʾel and Zissu 2007–2008; with thanks to Vladimir Boslov for his valuable help in surveying the caves in ʿAkhbara Rock.

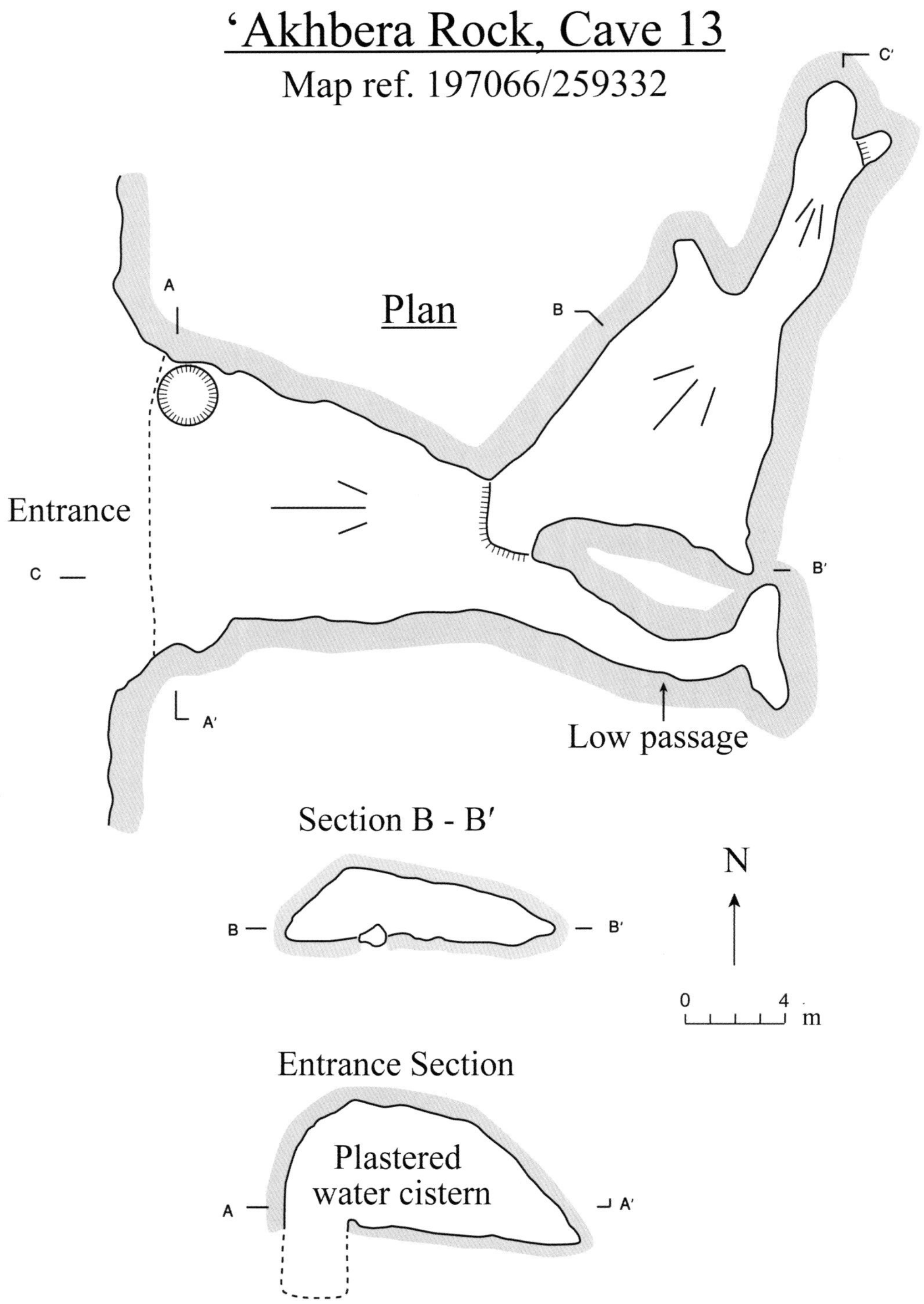
'Akhbera Rock, Cave 13
Map ref. 197066/259332
Plan
A
B
C'
Entrance
C
B'
A'
Low passage
Section B - B'
B
B'
N
0
4
m
Entrance Section
Plastered
water cistern
A
A'

Map 17

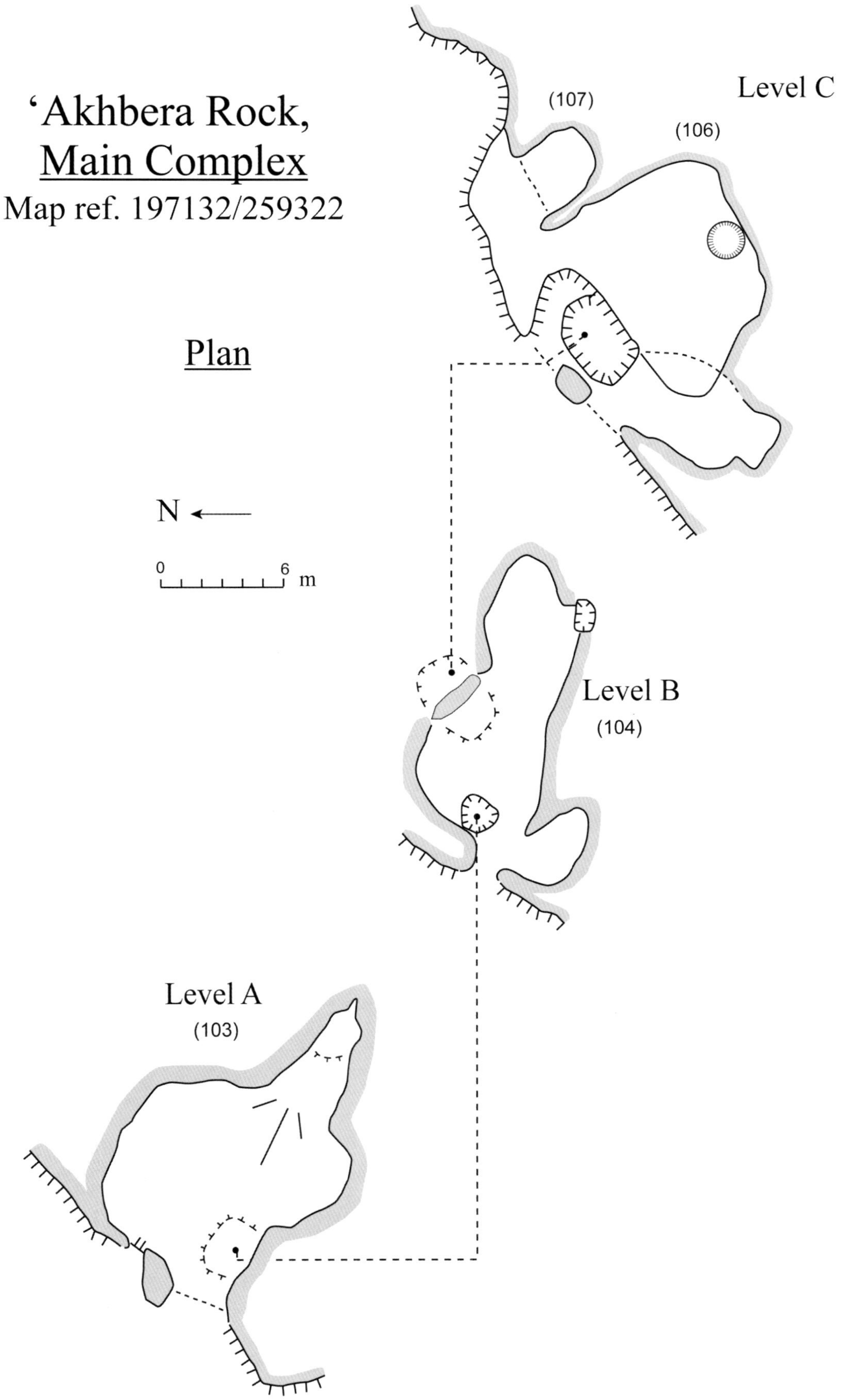
'Akhbera Rock,
Main Complex
Map ref. 197132/259322
Plan
N
0
6
m
Level C
(107)
(106)
Level B
(104)
Level A
(103)

Map 18

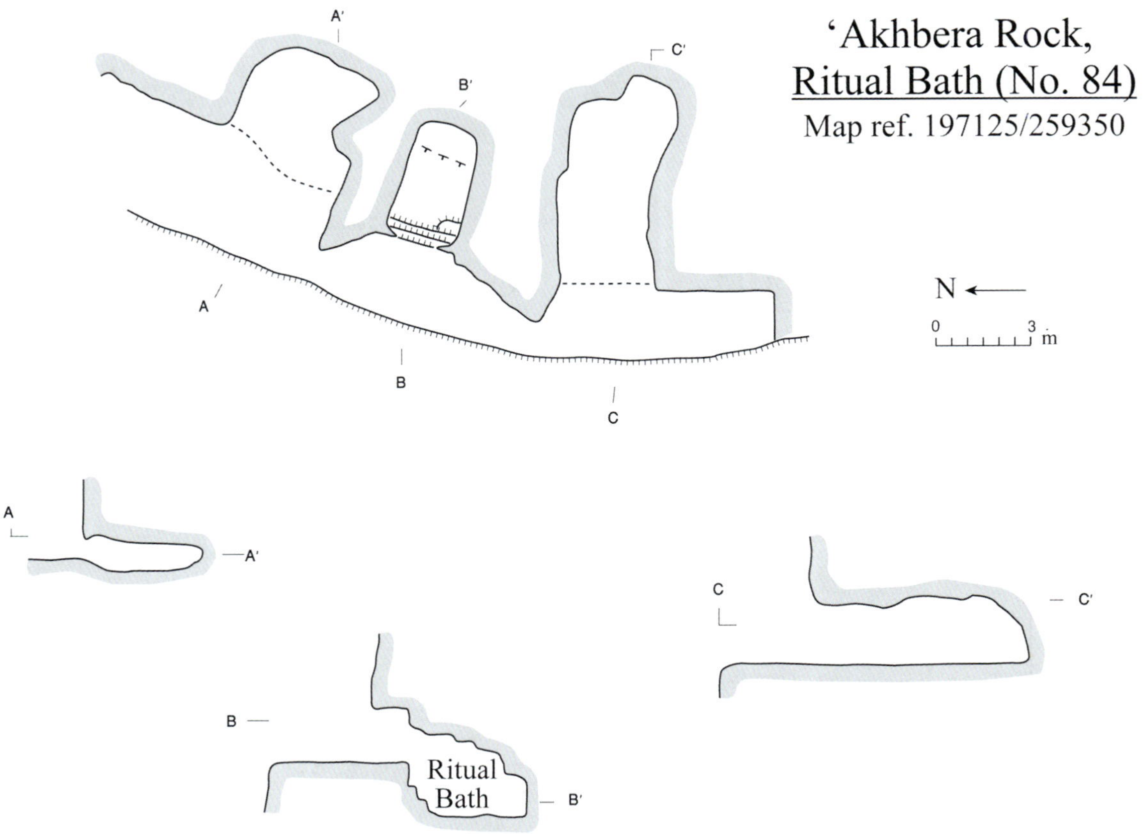

Map 19

Fig. 52: 'Akhbera Rock, ritual bath

Fig. 53: 'Akhbera Rock, a glass vial from Akhbara cliff shelter

The survey of ʿAkhbara Rock's 127 caves revealed that about 80 percent of them had been worked. Furthermore, there is a greater concentration of caves prepared as dwellings and water cisterns in the east section of the cliff. Hewn gutters, one on the summit of ʿAkhbara Rock, lead to two plastered caves. In one of the caves we found a ritual bath with a karstic crack in its back wall from which water was dripping, rendering it ritually pure.[32] (**Map 19**) (**Fig. 52**) Some of the water cisterns were quarried out beneath active stalactites inside the cave. Rafi Frankel and later Uzi Leibner surveyed a ruin at the foot of the cliff, which Leibner called East ʿAkhbara, in the ʿAkhbara Valley. It faced Horvat ʿAkhbara to the west of the rock, on a small hill on the west bank of ʿAkhbara Valley and about a kilometer away from ʿAkhbara Rock. The survey noted that most of the potsherds recovered from this site date to the Early Roman period.[33] Also attributed to the Roman period are a four-winged arrowhead found in a cliff shelter on the south bend and a small glass bottle (**Fig. 53**). It is worth noting that Josephus gives a precise description of his fortification of ʿAkhbara, stressing that he fortified ʿAkhbara Rock and not the settlement, unlike when describing the defenses built for other settlements (*War* 2:573). The fortification of ʿAkhbara Rock – namely the preparation or use of cliff caves as shelters during the Great Revolt – appears to be compatible with Josephus' description.

The Settlement of Meroth: Cliff Shelters in Mount Eviatar

Mount Eviatar, about 2 km southwest of the Jewish settlement of Meroth, is mentioned in Josephus' lists as having been fortified by him and also as marking Galilee's northernmost border (*War* 3:40). It consists of a rock cliff rising steeply up above the south bank of Nahal Hazor with dense vegetation covering its rocky slopes. Along a bare stretch of rock in the center of the cliff are forty caves hanging about 100 m above the valley floor, giving the cliff its Arabic name: El-Shbabik ("window") caves. The Mount Eviatar caves were surveyed in 1988 with the author's participation during Zvi Ilan's excavation season at Meroth.[34] Signs of hewing were clearly evident in thirty-five caves divided into two main complexes. The east complex consists of caves on five levels containing large rectangular halls. The chambers are approximately 10 m long, 6 m wide, and 5 m high. One of them contained a hewn pit with traces of plaster. The caves in the west complex measure 1.5 to 2.5 m and eleven of them are grouped together and interconnected. One of the caves is a 2 × 5 m rectangular and is coated with thick hydraulic plaster typical of the Herodian period. Another group of six caves is situated in a karstic fault. All the caves in both complexes had been adapted for human habitation (**Fig. 54**). A thick layer of bird droppings covering the cave floors meant that very little pottery was recovered. Seven of the caves explored in a preliminary survey yielded potsherds from the first century CE and the Early Islamic period. However, most of the potsherds found below the caves date to the Hellenistic and Early Roman period. The two complexes were probably used as shelters by the population of Meroth and perhaps also by the inhabitants of the ancient Jewish settlement of Dalton, which is only 1.5 km away from the Mount Eviatar cliff shelters.

Following the 1980s survey (including 35 cliff shelters), another eight sites were examined in the Mount Eviatar cliff-shelter survey completed in 2013, bringing the number of cliff shelters probably used by the Jewish population of Meroth here to 43.[35] The cliff refuges of Mount Eviatar are no different from the other refuges described above. It is extremely difficult to estimate the number of people who could have used them at any one time, but they would certainly have been able to accommodate hundreds of fugitives.

32 See Shivti'el 2012b.

33 See Leibner 2009:108; Frankel, Getzov, Aviam and Degani 2001:77, 82, 88.

34 See Ilan and Izdarechet 1988:50–51. The previous survey was carried out by the ICRC in 1984.

35 The relatively few cliff shelters attributed to the settlement of Meroth do not give any indication of the size of its population. It should be recalled that a synagogue was found at Meroth, as well as a number of hiding complexes in the vicinity (see below).

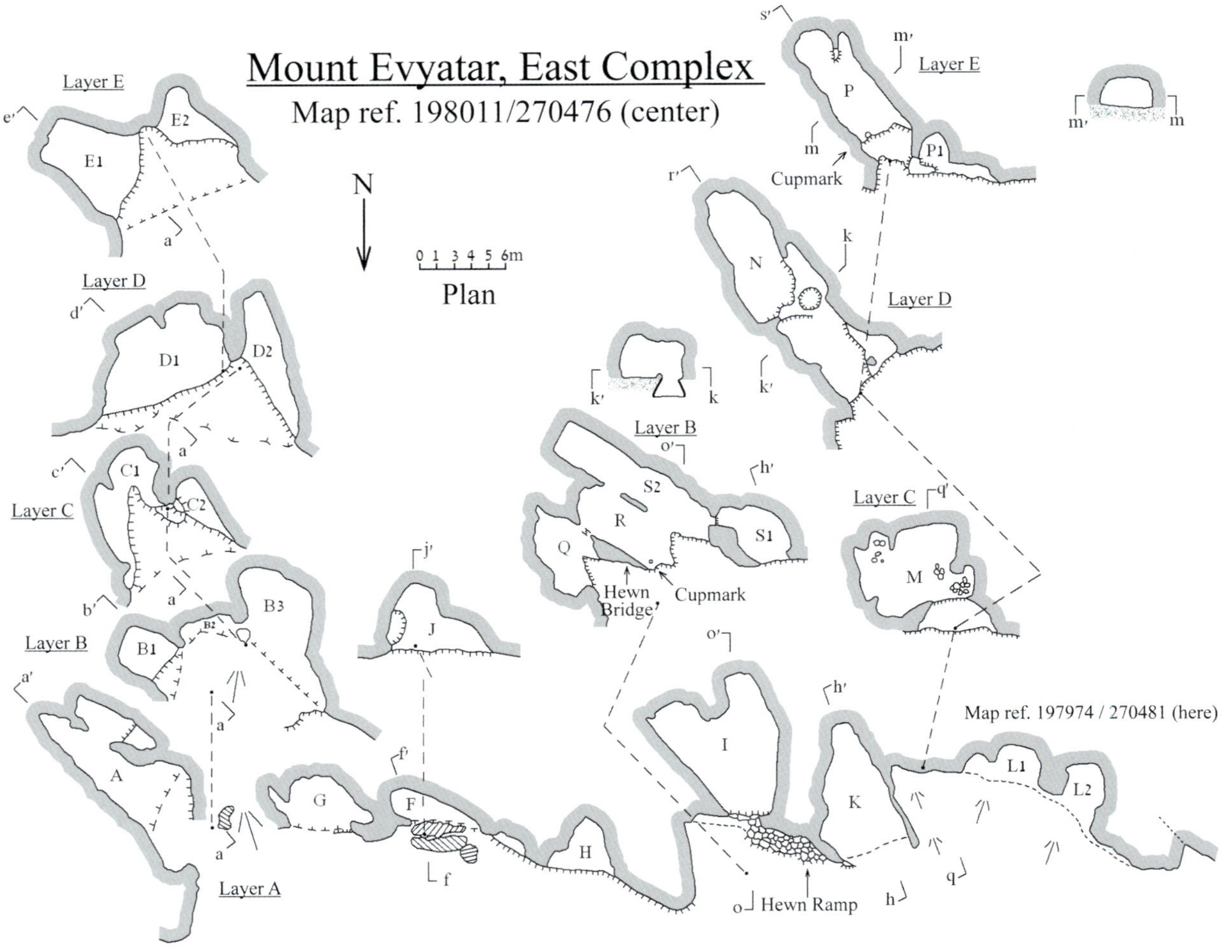

Map 20

Fig. 54: Mount Evyatar, cliff shelters

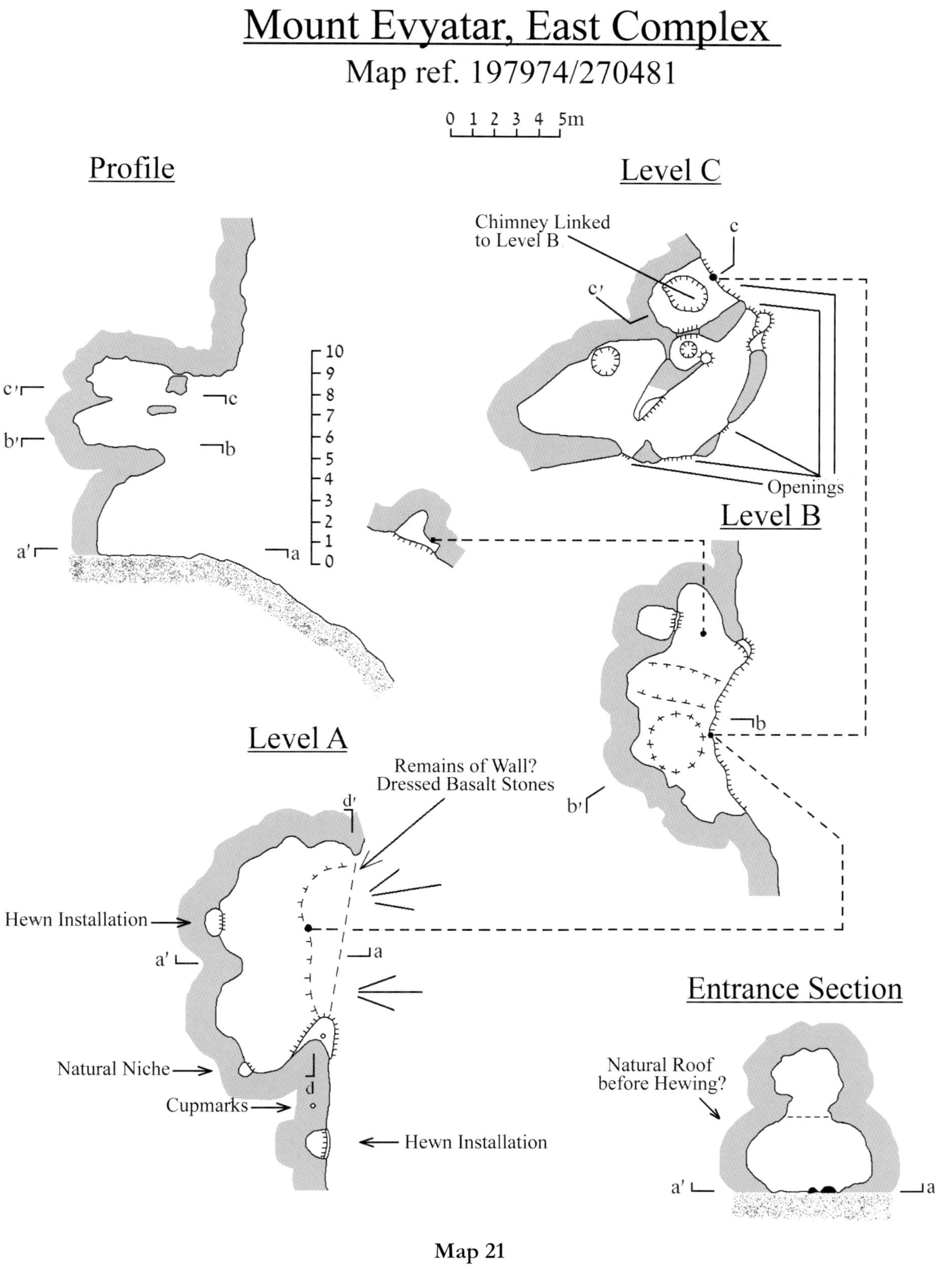
Mount Evyatar, East Complex
Map ref. 197974/270481
0 1 2 3 4 5m
Profile
Level C
Chimney Linked to Level B
c
c'
c'
c
b'
b
a'
a
10
9
8
7
6
5
4
3
2
1
0
Openings
Level B
b
b'
Level A
Remains of Wall? Dressed Basalt Stones
d'
Hewn Installation
a'
a
Natural Niche
d
Cupmarks
Hewn Installation
Entrance Section
Natural Roof before Hewing?
a'
a

Map 21

Mount Evyatar, East Complex

Map ref. 197974/270481

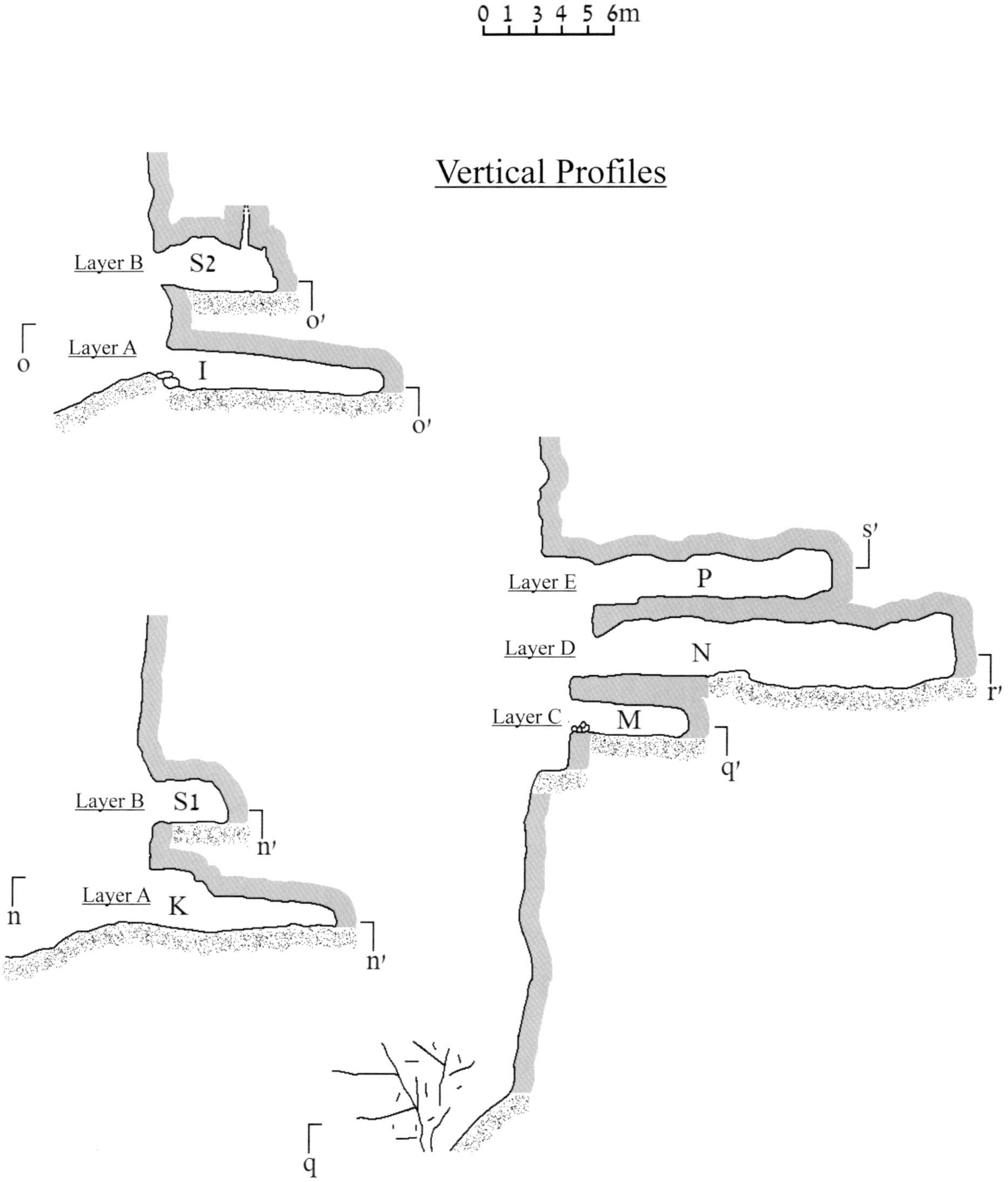

Map 22

Chapter 3:

"Cliff Shelters" at Sites not Recorded by Flavius Josephus

The previous chapter described the research and documentation of hundreds of cliff shelters found near five of the settlements Josephus claimed to have fortified. In our opinion, Josephus employed the term "fortification" to mean the adaptation of cliff shelters to provide the nearby population with a place of refuge from the wrath and might of the Roman army. The precarious method of accessing such shelters, demanding great skill and daring in order to descend via rope into the caves, could only have been prompted by extreme adversity. The Jewish population apparently believed that the Roman army did not have the sufficient tactical military response or specialized equipment (such as ropes and crates) and technical understanding of the anchoring places needed to send hundreds of soldiers into the cliff shelters. The following chapter reveals examples of other cliff shelters, discovered in Western Galilee and located beyond the area of Josephus' operations. This is a region that is not mentioned in Josephus' works and is not known to have had a large Jewish population, although it does contain some settlements that may have had Jewish inhabitants and that are adjacent to steep cliffs with similar cliff shelters. These sites exhibit signs of adaptation and finds that correspond with those from the Eastern Galilee cliff shelters. I shall here discuss the scope of the phenomenon and the resulting conclusions regarding the Jewish community in Western Galilee.

The phenomenon of shelters in steep cliffs extends beyond the borders of the Jewish Galilee defined by Josephus. This chapter discusses five cliff-shelter sites northwest of the region in which Josephus fortified Jewish settlements, in Nahal Dishon and its tributaries, Nahal Aviv and Nahal ʿAlmon, Nahal Namer, Nahal Bezet and Nahal Keziv in Western Galilee. It summarizes a preliminary survey of the sites whose historical context has not yet been authenticated.

Cliff Shelters in Nahal Dishon, Nahal ʿAlmon, and Nahal Aviv

Nahal Dishon rises as a stream to the northeast of the Meron mountain range and flows into the Hula Valley. It passes through a deep gorge containing a large number of natural caves. The walls of the gorge are at their most precipitous near the confluence of two of its main tributaries: Nahal Gush Halav, which flows into Nahal Dishon from the northern slopes of Ramat Dalton, and Nahal Aviv, which joins Nahal Dishon about 2 km east of Avivim.

A small valley by the name of Nahal ʿAlmon also enters Nahal Dishon from the west. The abundant rains gushing through Nahal Dishon in the winter months have carved out the valley and exposed numerous caves in its cliffs. Lower downstream, near the point where it joins Nahal Gush Halav, is a cave complex resembling those in Nahal ʿAmud. The caves lie halfway up the cliff and can only be reached by rope. Before Vladimir Boslov and myself surveyed the cliff, no archaeological record existed of the caves; the only known find from the Nahal Dishon caves was a jar recovered by two mountaineers in 1976.[1]

1 See Ravak 1976:11–12. Ravak, who removed the jar together with Yigal Sela, told me that he knew neither the date nor the present location of the jar which was not registered in the Israel Antiquities Authority archives.

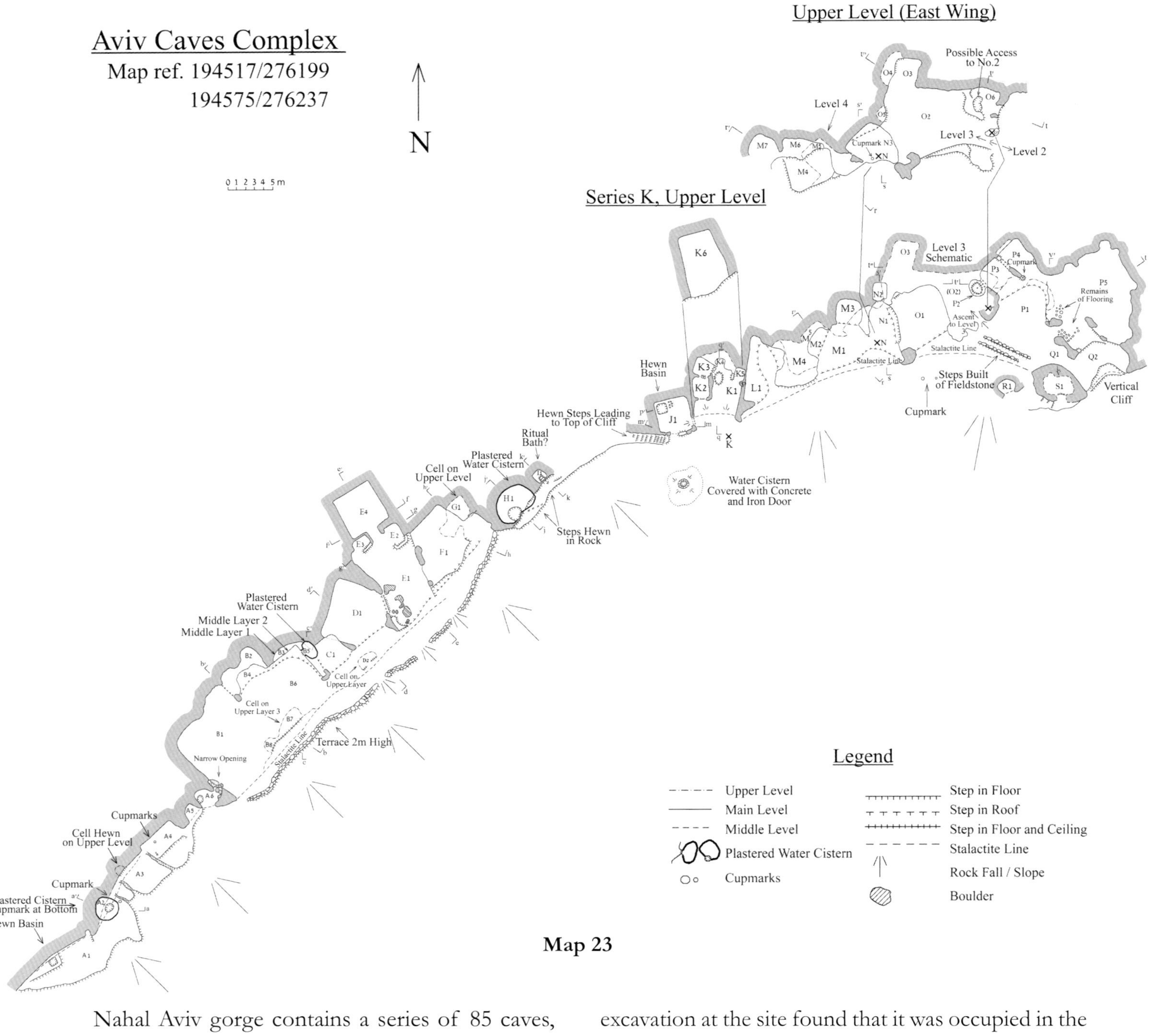

Map 23

Nahal Aviv gorge contains a series of 85 caves, niches and rock shelters, some of which exhibit all the typical features of cliff shelters. The caves stretch along both sides of the valley and have twice been surveyed.[2] Two cave complexes on the south cliff are particularly noteworthy. One is situated in the upper part of the stream and is marked as Nahalit Cave. The cave is about 10 m^2 in size and can be reached without special equipment. The cave was probably used by the inhabitants of nearby Horvat 'Avot. A salvage excavation at the site found that it was occupied in the Early Iron Age and in the Persian and Hellenistic periods.[3] Lower downstream, about 1.5 km before Nahal Aviv joins Nahal Dishon, a second cave complex was found on both sides of the valley and includes Haniya Cave. The large karstic cave extends over three levels that can either be reached by climbing a ladder or by rappelling down from the cliff top. Each level is divided into rock-hewn alcoves, some of them with windows overlooking the valley. This complex has all the typical features of cliff shelters and is similar to those in Nahal 'Amud. No pottery was found in the current survey, probably because the lower level had regularly served as a shelter for livestock, but Roman

2 The first survey was conducted in 1979 by a team from Achziv Field School. Partial results of the survey were published in an article entitled "An Archaeological Trip in Nahal Achziv," see Aviam and Ohel 1980: 249. A second survey was carried out by Erez Ben Nathan from the ICRC in 2003; its results are published in this volume.

3 See Aviam and Ohel 1980.

Fig. 55: Nahal Aviv, hewn cliff-shelter openings (from outside)

and Byzantine potsherds were recovered there in the mid-1980s.[4] In the north cliff, opposite Haniya cave, lies the main complex of refuge caves in Nahal Aviv, consisting of a series of 25 caves with entrances half-way up the rock face and about 30 m below the cliff top. Some have been meticulously hewn and finished and some are natural. The caves can only be reached using abseiling techniques. The current study found that both the hewn and the natural caves share identical features with those of the caves in Nahal 'Amud and at 'Akhbara Rock, since they consist of rock-hewn chambers built on different levels that were adapted for use as shelters. Small niches for oil lamps are hewn into the chamber walls. One contained two oil lamps, showing that the site was also used in the Mamluk period. Two of the caves contain cisterns coated with gray hydraulic plaster typical of the Early Roman period. In one, a rock wall contains a hewn, chimney-like gutter to channel runoff water from the rock wall outside into the cisterns. One of the cisterns had been built under a cluster of dripping stalactites. Another cave, hewn into a notch in the cliff, leads to a chamber measuring 5.5 m^2 from which a passage leads to a smaller chamber measuring 1.5 m^2. Three round pits dug at the end of the small chamber were probably used for storage. The south end of the chamber contains a rock-cut window overlooking the stream.[5] In another shelter, whose entrance is hewn beneath the roof of the notch, is a massive basalt stone that may have been used to seal the opening. The cave contains a rock-hewn water cistern that is still fed by water seeping through the adjacent rock wall. Looking down from its entrance to the point where the floor of the notch joins the cliff slope, a cupmark is

4 See Aviam and Ohel 1980:246; Aviam 2004:201 remarks that hermits lived in the caves in the Byzantine period.

5 This entrance is very similar to an entrance found at El-Aliliat cave in Nahal Michmash in the Land of Benjamin, a site whose cave typology, style of rock working and location near a Jewish settlement are consistent with a "cliff-shelter"-type site; see Shivti'el 2011b:45–58.

visible that gradually fills with water running off the notch walls. The cupmark may have been hewn below the entrance as a stand for some kind of vessel that the shelter's occupants could draw up with a rope. Defensive walls built at the entrance to three of these hanging shelters are made of three to four courses of dressed fieldstones placed on top of each other. In four shelters we found logs of wood jammed vertically between the lintel and the cave that were used to anchor climbing ropes. (**Fig. 55**) In other shelters we found loops for ropes hewn into the lintels. Almost all of these cliff shelters are interconnected; one can only move between the floors and levels by climbing up hewn ledges or natural crannies in the walls. The caves' occupants would probably also have used ladders in places where there were no holds in the rock. Potsherds found at the site date from the Early Roman to the Mamluk periods.

Another, particularly large series of hewn and natural caves is situated further downstream, east of the complex described above; it consists of three complexes separated by a series of rock-hewn steps leading to the cliff top. The complex to the west of the steps contains individual shelters hewn inside a wide, curved notch. About 4 m above the place where the notch meets the rock slope and is high enough to stand in, rings were cut for attaching climbing ropes. A distinctive feature here is the presence of twelve hollows cut in a line along the length of the notch, which may have supported scaffolding. To the east of the steps, a large water cistern about 7 m deep was cut into the rock. The cistern is fed by a channel designed to collect water running along the notch. About two meters east of the cistern, a square water reservoir has a step leading down into it. This kind of reservoir with an inner step, which would naturally reduce its capacity, is probably a ritual bath and this supports the theory that the Nahal Aviv shelters harbored Jewish occupants.[6]

6 However, the plaster taken from the cistern looking like a ritual bath was dated to the Middle Roman period according to an analysis by Dr. Elisabetta Boaretto from the Weizman Institute.

Fig. 56: Nahal Aviv, stepped and plastered water cistern (possible ritual bath)

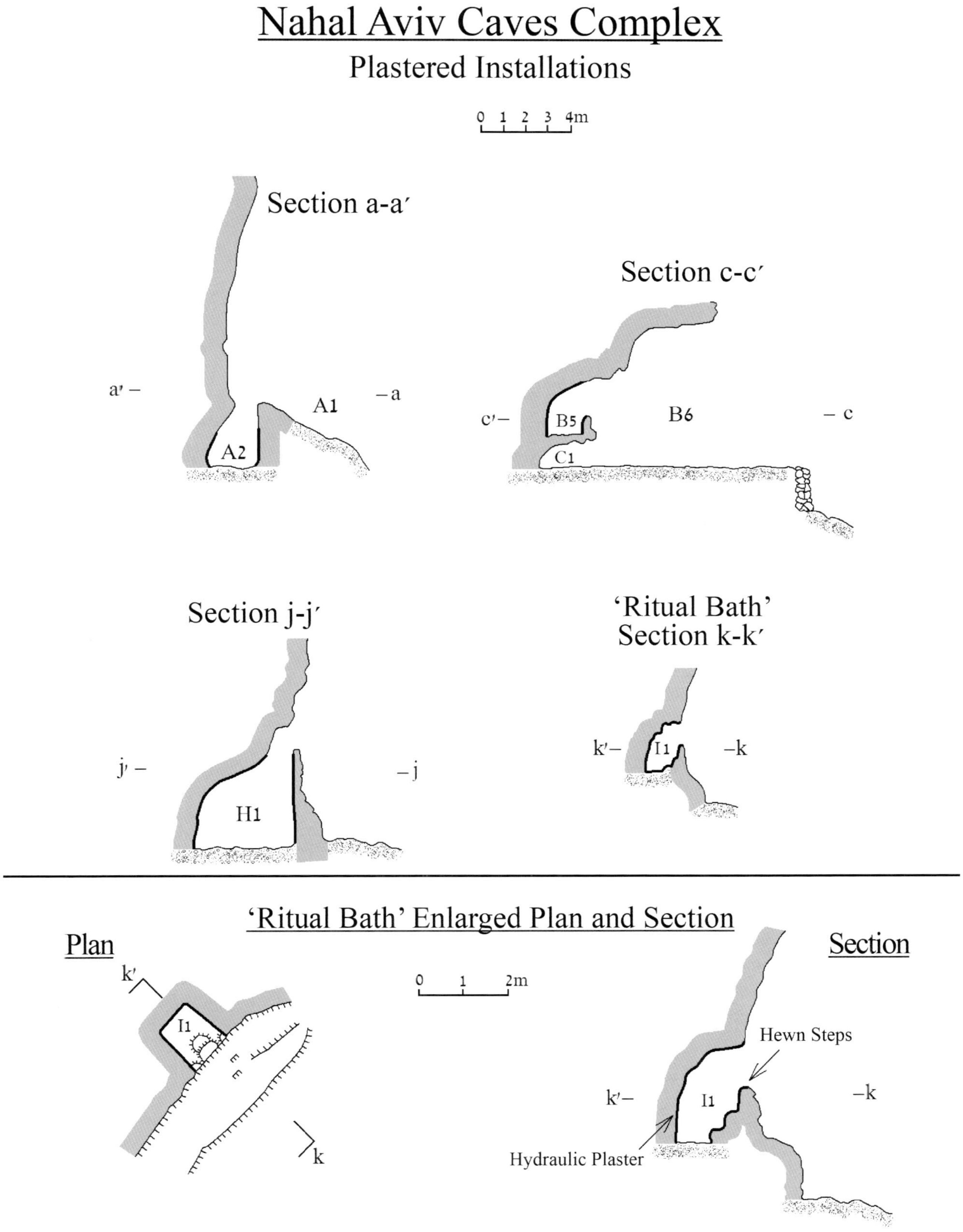
Nahal Aviv Caves Complex
Plastered Installations
0 1 2 3 4m
Section a-a′
a′ –
A1
– a
A2
Section c-c′
c′–
B5
B6
– c
C1
Section j-j′
j′ –
H1
– j
'Ritual Bath'
Section k-k′
k′–
I1
–k
'Ritual Bath' Enlarged Plan and Section
Plan
k′
I1
k
0 1 2m
Section
Hewn Steps
k′–
I1
–k
Hydraulic Plaster

Map 24

Only a few meters away from the large water cistern and the probable ritual bath, another cave complex extending several dozen meters consists of large, natural cavities with openings from which any movement in the valley can be observed. The complex has four different levels. The highest can be reached by abseiling down to it. This complex is charted on trail maps as Aviv Cave. It has none of the characteristics of a cliff shelter, since the caves can be reached with relative ease. Only a few are inaccessible without ropes. Facing the Aviv caves on the southern bank of the stream bed and near the edge of the cliff, the remains of an olive press, cisterns and various agricultural installations are hewn in the rock.

The Nahal Dishon Cliff Shelter Survey

The Nahal Dishon cliff shelter complex is located downstream from the point where Nahal Aviv runs into Nahal Dishon. This is in fact the location of the main cliff-shelter complex in Nahal Dishon, charted as Miglash Cave (**Maps 25–26**). We recorded approximately 100 caves that had been adapted for human occupation in the Nahal Dishon cliffs. Miglash Cave is a typical cliff-shelter complex consisting of 21 hewn cavities and is identical to the Dove Caves complex in Nahal ʿAmud, although on a smaller scale. The shelters lying northwest of the confluence of the Dishon and Aviv streams contain dozens more caves, 25 of which are described in this volume and have distinctive cliff-shelter characteristics.

The most important components of the Nahal Dishon cliff shelter complex are:

1. The Miglash Cave: The cave complex is located inside a concealed fissure in a cliff 30 m high and 500 m long. Inside the natural cleft, a bell-shaped cave formation is narrow at the top and wide at the base. The cave is about 25 m long and 12 m wide. Two stone walls divide the shelter into two levels. The wall on the upper level was founded on natural wooden logs placed horizontally from one side of the cleft to the other, while the wall on the lower level was built in a stepped manner, with two stones jammed into the cleft surmounted by four stones and increasing numbers of stones in each consecutive

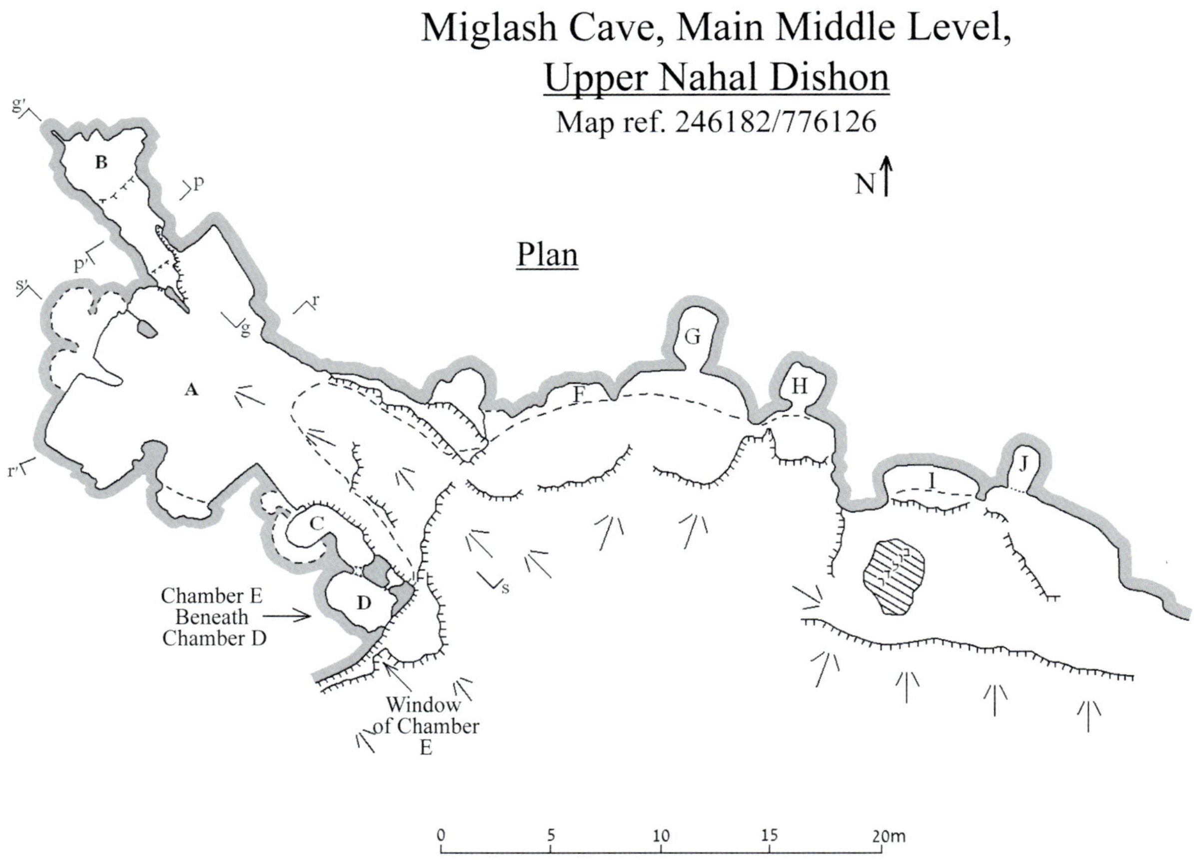

Map 25

course. The partition walls are about six meters apart. In the middle of the wall, the top of a long wooden beam protrudes toward the center of the complex. This shelter is accessible by rope and the fugitives it harbored may also have reached it by climbing up a long ladder. Potsherds dating from the Hellenistic to the Late Roman period were recovered from the two chambers on both floors. Further on in this complex is an elongated cave that can be climbed up to by foot. The cave penetrates deep into the rock and is concealed by it. Potsherds and fragments of a stone wall that probably blocked its entrance are scattered on the cave floor.

2. A round, southeasterly facing opening was hewn outside the entrance to the complex and 20 m above ground level. It is accessible by rope from the cliff top. It measures 1 × 1.2 m and leads to an elliptical chamber 1.5 × 5 m with a leveled bedrock floor. The roof of the shelter is blackened with soot.

3. Six other chambers can be reached by climbing from the base of the cleft. The chambers are hewn, some have windows facing onto the gorge and some have niches for oil lamps that retain traces of soot.

Fig. 57: Nahal Dishon, Miglash Cave cliff shelters

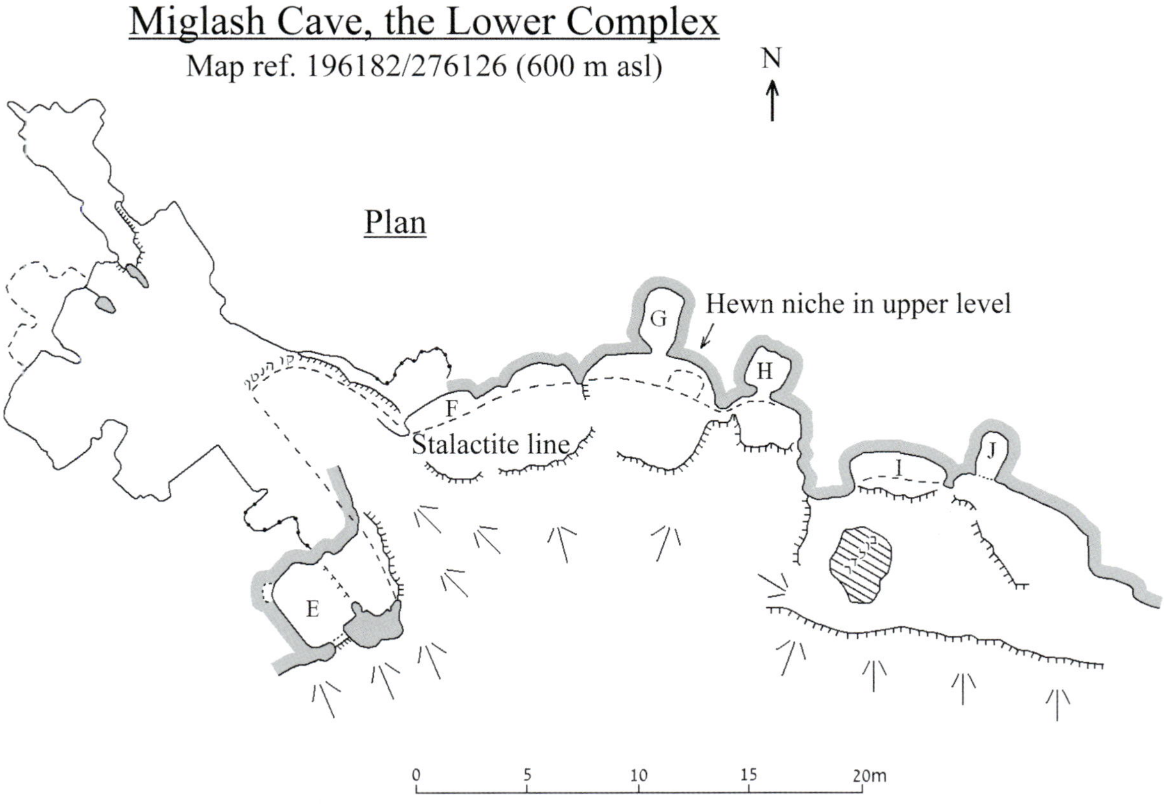

Map 26

4. Eleven other chambers were prepared deep in the cleft and on the two sides of the cliff. The finds and appearance of the Miglash cave complex in Nahal Dishon confirm that they belong to the category of cliff shelters. We have evidence of Jewish settlement in the Early Roman period at places such as Barʿam, ʿAlma and Ketzion (and possibly also at Dishon).[7] Furthermore, at Mount ʿAlmon – to the south of the Nahal Dishon cliff shelters – burial caves have been found that were probably used by Jewish inhabitants from the ancient site of ʿAlma.[8] Although they have still not been fully investigated, the remains suggest that the Nahal Aviv-Dishon cliff shelters were used by the inhabitants of nearby ancient settlements.

Fig. 58: The door of a burial cave near the wadi with a five-branched candelabrum (menorah)

The Cliff Shelters in Nahal Namer

The Nahal Namer gorge contains a number of karstic caves formed by large quantities of water that run off Hasulam ("Ladder") ridge. The river passes close by Upper and Lower Hanita, mentioned in rabbinic literature and in the Rehob inscription as places where produce cannot be farmed in a sabbatical year and where tithes must be given.[9] This interesting fact indicates that these villages were wholly or at least mainly Jewish. Rafi Frankel and Nimrod Getzov surveyed the two sites and remarked that Upper Hanita is today part of Kibbutz Hanita, while Lower Hanita can probably be identified as Khirbet el-Bich'a. At this site they discovered pithoi of the Galilean Course Ware (GCW) type that was common in the Hellenistic period; also recorded there was the find of a stone burial door engraved with a seven-branched menorah.[10]

Dozens of karstic caves are scattered along Nahal Namer, many on the west bank of the gorge, yet they remain unexplored because of the current security situation in the region. Midway down the valley is a large complex of karstic caves marked on trail maps as the "Kuchim" and "Adar" caves (**Map 27**) that are visible from the road leading up to the village of Admit. Many of the caves can only be reached by abseiling down from the cliff top (**Fig. 59**). The more easily accessible of them were surveyed by Frankel and Getzov who noted that the natural caves show signs of having been worked by man.[11] In our survey of the area we found three cave complexes extending along the cliff; a path built to the western complex leads to a rock-hewn water cistern with plastered walls. The present survey showed that the higher caves resemble the cliff-shelter complexes in Eastern Galilee, which also contain hewn and plastered water cisterns fed by gutters.

Another series of caves stretches along the east slope of Nahal Namer and also contains a type similar to the "Kuchim" cave complex. Its surveyors found Hellenistic and Byzantine potsherds. The third complex is marked on maps as the Adar Caves and extends along the north slope of Nahal Namer. In 29 June 2018 a survey of "Kuchim" cliff shelters was begun, led by the author and Dr. Danny Syon of the Israel Antiquities Authority. A number of intact jars, amphoras, a bowl, juglets and a cooking pot were

7 See for example Foerster 1972:1–7; Ilan 1991a:50, 56–57.

8 The site has not been fully explored, but we found that it contains ten burial caves. Mordechai Aviam, who knows the site well, identified the burial niches as belonging to the ancient site of ʿAlma with whose surface remains he is familiar (personal communication – with thanks).

9 See *tShevi'it* 4:9; Zussman 1981:117–190.

10 See Frankel and Getzov 1997:83.

11 Ibid:87.

Fig. 59: Nahal Namer cliff shelters

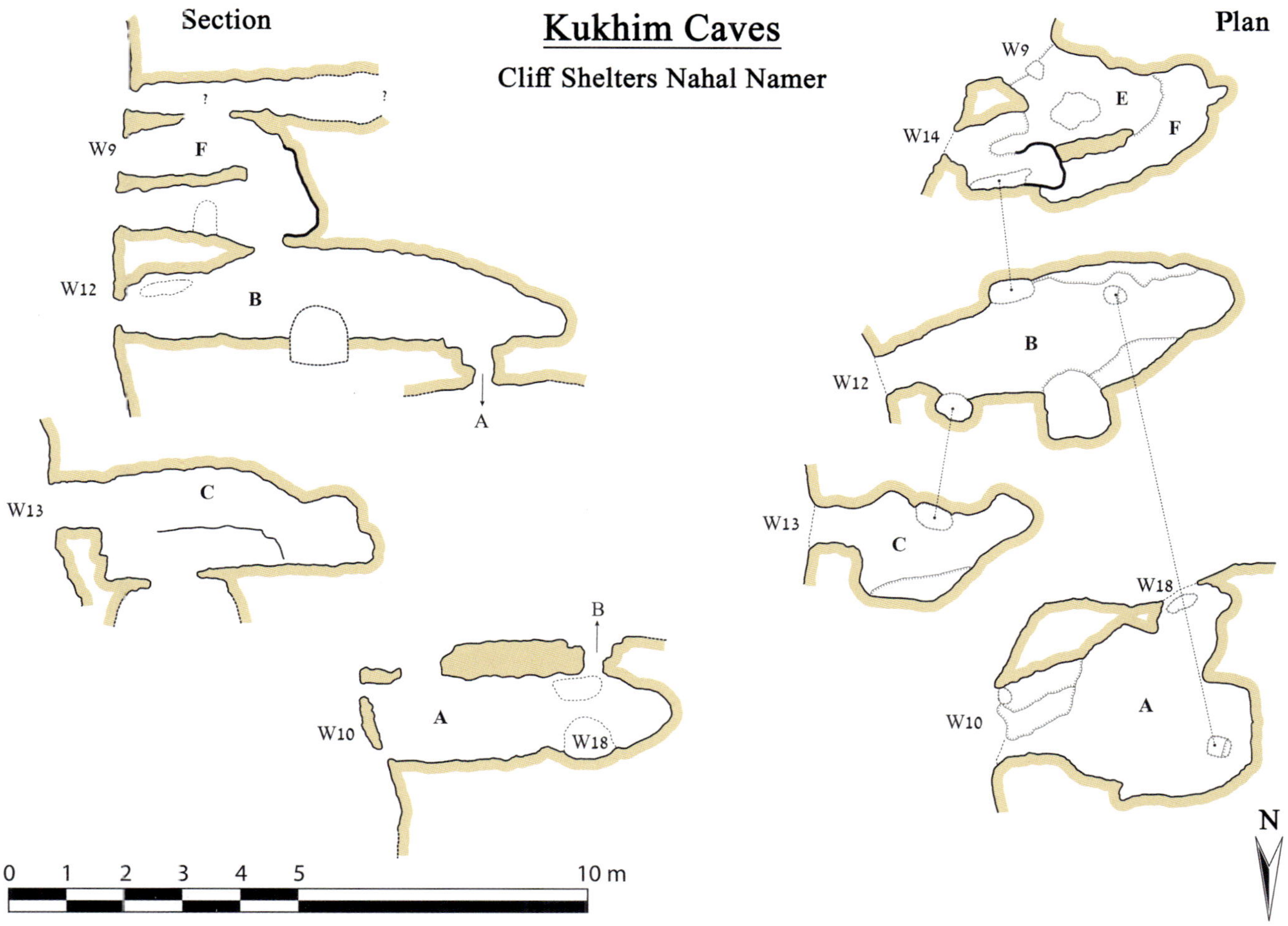

Map 27

discovered in one of the steepest caves. The finds have not yet been dated. Here too, there is evidence of caves hewn and adapted for human occupation. In the preliminary survey of Frankel and Getzov the potsherds found near the caves indicate extensive use in the Hellenistic and Byzantine periods. Early Roman potsherds have been found mainly in the ancient settlements surveyed by Frankel and Getzov[12] and especially at Horvat Mazzuva (Horbat Pi-Mazzuva), which is also mentioned in the list of "forbidden" towns.[13] At Horvat el-Bassa (Bezet or Shezet), Frankel and Getzov's survey found a burial monument bearing a still undated Greek inscription and the relief of a circle inside a square that may well be Jewish.[14] A lintel found at Kibbutz Hanita was identified by Moshe Prausnitz as that of a synagogue.[15] The survey also recovered numerous potsherds now recognized as Kefar Hananya Ware and dating from the Early Roman period, but since the survey was conducted prior to the publication of David Adan-Bayewitz's study on Kefar Hananya Ware they were not identified as such at the time. The numismatic finds in the area surveyed may also indicate a Jewish presence in the region during the Early Roman period. Out of 368 coins found at the site, Arie Kindler lists ten "Jewish coins" including one minted by Agrippa II (50–93 CE). Other coins from this period found by members of local kibbutzim have yet to be published.[16] At ʿEvron, an amulet with Hebrew lettering has been dated to the third–fourth centuries CE.[17] It is, therefore, highly likely that the inhabitants of Upper and Lower Hanita used the caves in Nahal Namer as refuge places in the Early Roman period (possibly during the Varus invasion), during the Great Revolt, and perhaps also in the Second Revolt, although I expand on this in Chapter 4.

The Cliff Shelters in Nahal Bezet

Nahal Namer flows into Nahal Bezet, which is one of the largest river courses in the Western Galilee and channels vast quantities of water from the Admit and Zarʿit heights and Mount Shomera ridge. A number of springs rising in the valley are marked on maps as "ʿEnot Kerkera." The northern slopes of the valley in the region of ʿEnot Kerkera are filled with hundreds of karstic caves. Above ʿEnot Kerkera, on the

12 See Frankel and Getzov 1997:86–87, 91, 108.
13 Klein 1945:159.
14 See Frankel and Getzov 1997:88, 91.
15 See Prausnitz 1986:461.
16 See Kindler 1961:15–16.
17 Kotansky 1991:81–87.

Fig. 60: Nahal Bezet, cliff shelters

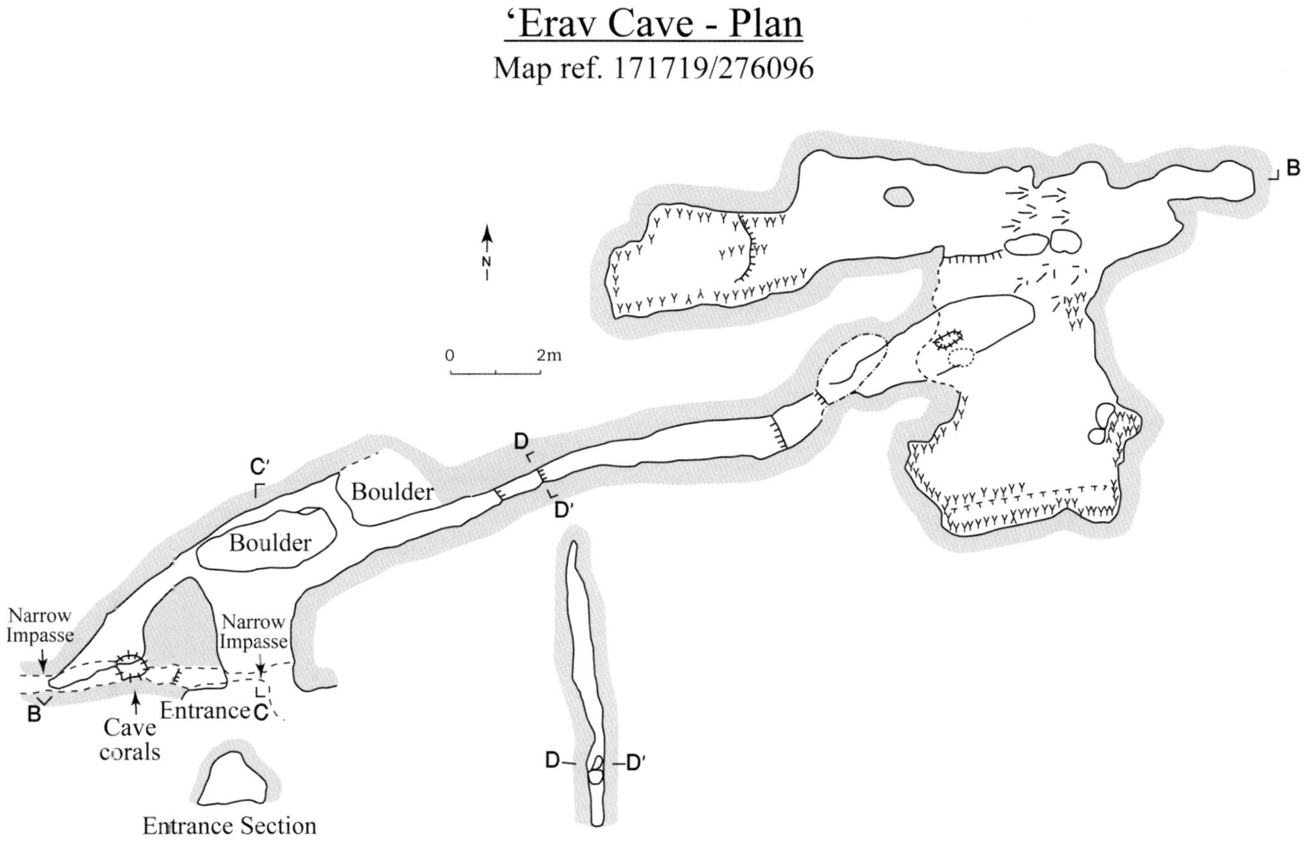
'Erav Cave - Plan
Map ref. 171719/276096
N
0 2m
B
C'
D
D'
Boulder
Boulder
Narrow Impasse
Narrow Impasse
B
Entrance
C
Cave corals
Entrance Section
D
D'

Map 28

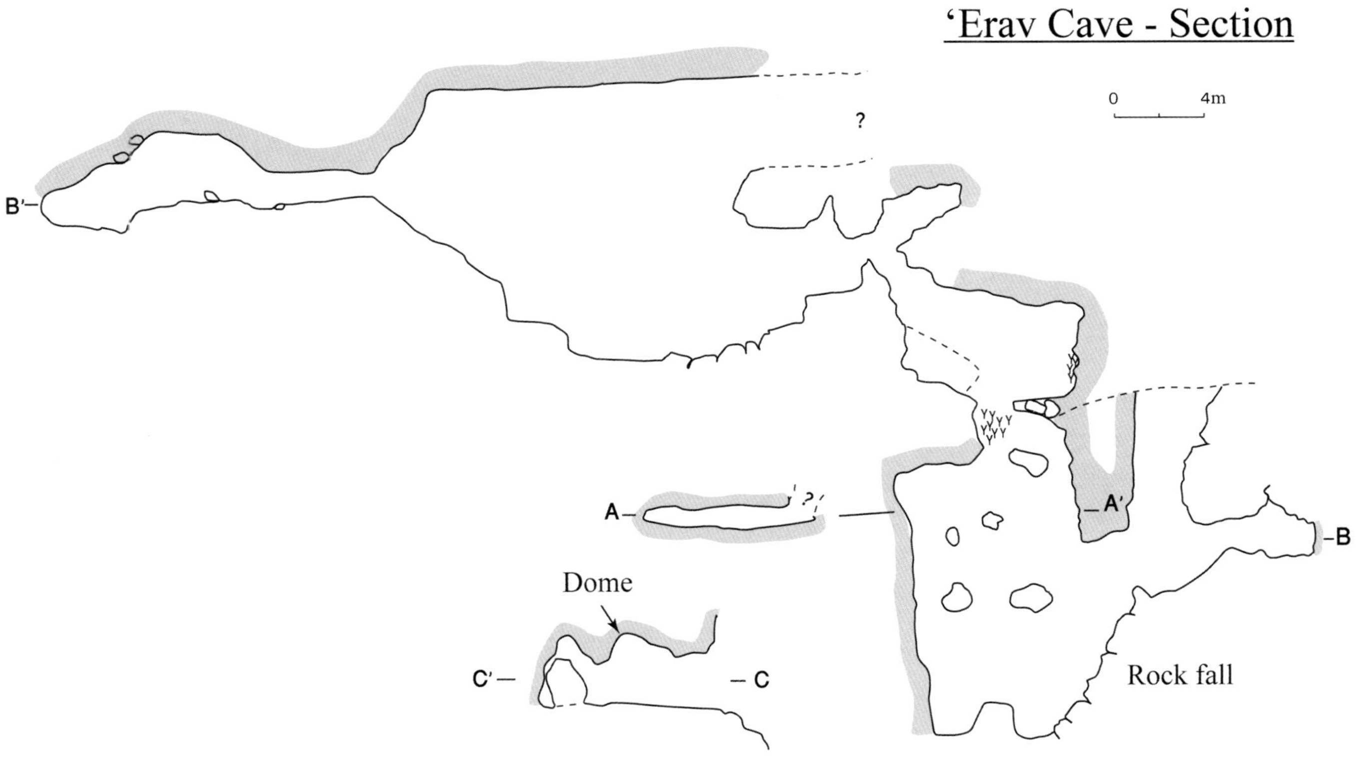
'Erav Cave - Section
0 4m
?
B'
A
A'
B
Dome
C'
C
Rock fall

Map 29

ridge of the northern cliff top, lie the ruins of Horvat ʽErav. Horvat ʽErav is generally identified as "Rish Mayya," mentioned in Tosefta (*Shevi'it* 4:9), as "Rosh Mayya" in the Jerusalem Talmud, or "Bet Bariya" or "Bet Badiya," which would place it correctly in the list of "forbidden" towns in the territory of Tyre (see above). These settlements appear immediately after Upper and Lower Hanita. Zvi Ilan, who excavated a Byzantine church at Horvat ʽErav, suggested that the site be identified with the Jewish Rosh Mayya and put forward the theory that, as Christian influence increased in the region during the Byzantine period, the Jewish population of Western Galilee was either pushed back by the Christian population or conceded lands to it. Possible evidence for this is provided at Horvat Galil, near Moshav Goren, which is usually identified with the Jewish site of "Castra ("fort") in Galilee".[18]

Nahal Bezet and its cave complex have not yet been surveyed or documented by archaeologists, apart from the series of five caves examined in the current survey in the middle of the cliff below Horvat ʽErav. A few Hellenistic and Early Roman potsherds were recovered at the foot of these caves together with more ancient artifacts. A juglet from the Mamluk period was also found in one of the caves (**Maps 28–29**). This cave is particularly large and contains a long corridor and numerous cavities, all of which have yielded potsherds and show evidence of human occupation. The thick layer of mud covering the floor of the cave has made it impossible to identify the potsherds, apart from the Mamluk juglet. The form of the cave is reminiscent of refuge caves in the Judean Desert. The Nahal Bezet cave complex may have been used by the inhabitants of Horvat ʽErav/ Rosh Mayya and Horvat Kerkera.

The Cliff Shelters in Nahal Keziv

Nahal Keziv is the largest river course in the Western Galilee drainage area. It rises in the Mount Miron range and flows about 20 km to its Mediterranean estuary. Its upper tributaries receive about 1000 mm annual rainfall and its main riverbed, near Ma'alot, is characterized by precipitous slopes and an abundance of natural caves. Several springs emerge in Nahal Keziv, the largest of which is ʽEn Ziv which discharges approximately 600 cubic meters per hour. West of and downstream from ʽEn Ziv is an imposing cliff marked on maps as Mount Ziv. Along the entire length of this cliff, which is about 150 m high, are dozens of natural caves, many of which have been adapted for use by man. On the opposite bank of the river, numerous similar caves are visible (**Figs. 61–62**). Eighty of the Nahal Keziv caves were surveyed in the early 1980s by Shmuel Be'er, who was the first to clamber through the dense vegetation to the caves halfway up the cliff, where he recognized signs of human activity in some of them. Be'er also collected potsherds from different periods in the caves.[19] His most exciting find was a relief in human form chiseled into the rock near a complex of four caves on the north bank of Nahal Keziv, opposite Mount Ziv. Frankel interpreted the figure as a Phoenician goddess but noted that the relief had no parallels to substantiate his interpretation. On the third floor of the cave complex and about 15 m west of the relief, Frankel recovered large quantities of potsherds from the Iron Age and Hellenistic periods.[20] The current survey examined the relief figure carefully and discovered the following:

(1) A well-made ancient path leads down to the cave complex from Ramat Abirim, ending at the cliff where the cave complex and the nearby relief are located;

(2) despite the previous report, the figure is not bald but is wearing a helmet or a crown;

(3) a kind of shield-shaped plaque is carved on its breast. As already observed, the figure wears a pleated skirt and a belted sword.

Together with the current observations, this suggests that the relief probably depicts a Roman soldier and was cut in the rock by Roman soldiers charged with looking out for fugitives in the Nahal Keziv cliff shelters.[21] Alternatively, it may portray a military figure symbolizing the sun-god *Sol Invictus.*[22]

Three surveys were carried out in the Nahal Keziv caves. One of these was conducted in the framework of Shmuel Be'er's research and the second by the author in 2004, including further examination of 11 higher caves in the middle of the northern and southern cliffs of Mount Ziv. All the caves produced signs of hewing and adaptation and some yielded Early and Late Roman potsherds. Defensive walls were built across four of the entrances and niches

18 See Ilan 1986a:503–515. The ruins at Kerkera yielded a coin of Herod Antipas and two coins from the city of Tyre, one from the 1st c. BCE and the other from the 2nd c. CE, see Getzov 1961:55.

19 See Be'er 1990:40–42.

20 See Frankel 1986:51–52.

21 Stiebel also reached this conclusion (2007:107).

22 Ovadiah and Shivti'el 2016: 351–375.

Fig. 61: Nahal Keziv – Mount Keziv, cliff shelters

Fig. 62: Nahal Keziv, cliff shelters, north face

for oil lamps were found in two of the caves. In 2009, Vladimir Boslov and myself conducted a comprehensive survey of all 300 caves in Nahal Keziv. The survey revealed that most of the caves, especially those only accessible by rappelling or skilled rock climbing, were typologically identical to the cliff shelters found near settlements in the lower and upper Eastern Galilee. Based on the ceramic finds, they were evidently occupied mainly in the Early Roman period and they produced no Byzantine finds. Some contain water reservoirs fed by dripping stalactites as well as connecting shafts between floors, niches for oil lamps, and rock-hewn chambers. During the current survey, 103 cliff shelters and over 180 alcoves were examined, some of which had been adapted for human use.[23]

Although it is not certain whether the above-mentioned sites in the list of "forbidden" towns were Jewish, extant historical sources prove beyond doubt that Achziv had a Jewish population. The town of Achziv has been located south of the Nahal Keziv estuary and is known by its Arabic name as Tel e-Zib. Achziv lay on the route between Phoenicia and the Land of Israel. In Josephus' writings, Achziv (Ἐκδίππον—Ekdippon) is mentioned as a town on the coast visited by Phasael, Herod the Great's brother, after its inhabitants warned him of a Parthian plot to ambush him (*War* 1:257; *Ant.* 14:343). Achziv is also mentioned in Rabbinic literature in connection with the territories subject to sabbatical laws (*mShevi'it* 6:1). The sages were divided as to whether or not Achziv marked the boundary where these laws were applicable (*tOhalot* 18:14) and even visited the town to resolve matters of religious law.

Excavations conducted at Tel e-Zib have uncovered public buildings from the Hellenistic and Roman periods.[24] Although Achziv is 12 km away from the Nahal Keziv cave complex, it is highly likely that the Jewish population from there or from other Jewish settlements close to the plentiful sources of water in Nahal Keziv – such as the Jewish settlement at Fassuta (Mifshata), seat of the Harim priestly order, or Castra in Galilee (Horvat Galil), which is mentioned in the *Baraita of Tehumim* as marking the boundary of the Land of Israel – used the cliff shelters in Nahal Keziv in the Early Roman period and during the Great Revolt.[25]

23 The survey is due to be published as part of the Survey of Western Galilee, led by Mordechai Aviam, and is therefore not duplicated here.

24 See Prausnitz 1992:28.

25 See *Shevi'it* 4:9; see Ilan 1986b:516–524 for the identification of Castra in Galilee.

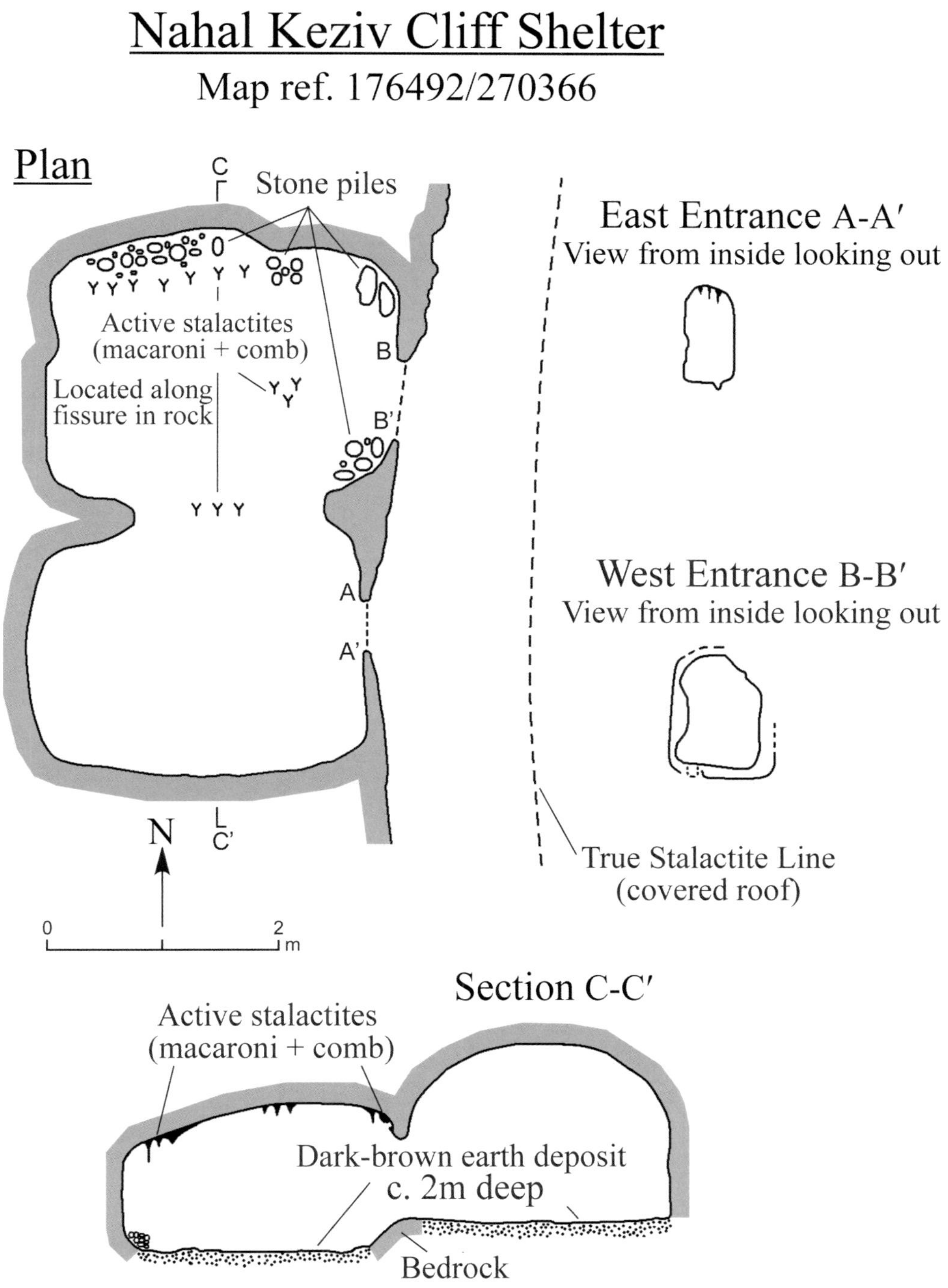
Nahal Keziv Cliff Shelter
Map ref. 176492/270366
Plan
C
Stone piles
Active stalactites
(macaroni + comb)
Located along
fissure in rock
B
B'
A
A'
N
C'
0
2
m
East Entrance A-A'
View from inside looking out
West Entrance B-B'
View from inside looking out
True Stalactite Line
(covered roof)
Section C-C'
Active stalactites
(macaroni + comb)
Dark-brown earth deposit
c. 2m deep
Bedrock

Map 30

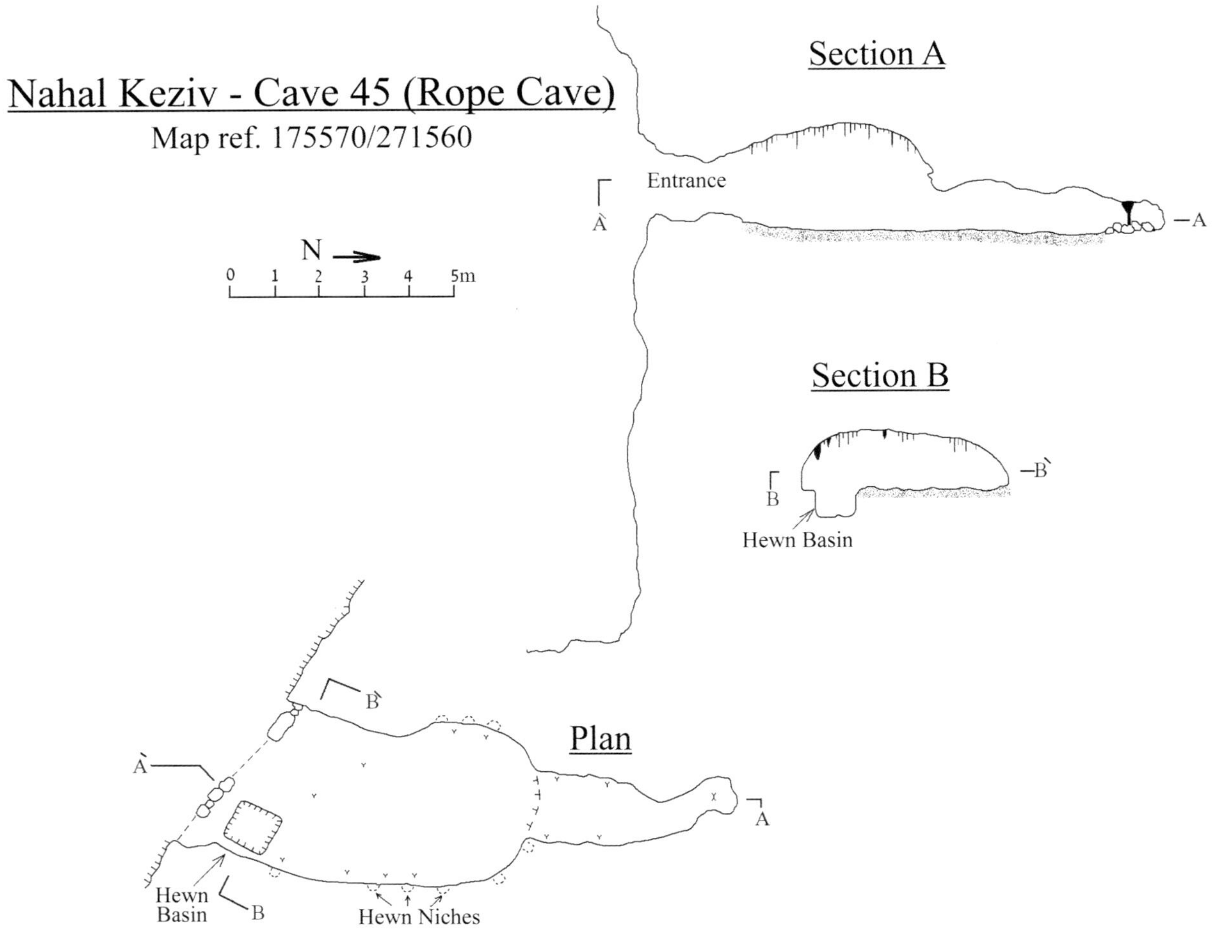
Nahal Keziv - Cave 45 (Rope Cave)
Map ref. 175570/271560
N
0 1 2 3 4 5m
Section A
Entrance
A`
A
Section B
B
B`
Hewn Basin
Plan
B`
A`
A
Hewn Basin
B
Hewn Niches

Map 31

Chapter 4:

Underground Caves and Hiding Complexes. Results of Systematic Surveys

Chapter 3 discussed the research and mapping of hundreds of cliff shelters at sites not mentioned in Josephus' records that are nevertheless very similar to the cliff shelters near settlements mentioned by the ancient historian. Exploration of the cliff shelters in Western Galilee has revealed that the population in this area, whether Jewish or not, used caves as cliff shelters. This chapter describes the exploration and offers the documentation of the most common defensive method used in the Galilee, as in Judea, namely the practice of hewing out underground hiding complexes under or near dwellings in settlements known to have had a Jewish population. Josephus records that some of these settlements participated in the Great Revolt. Some are mentioned in rabbinic literature or contain finds attesting to Jewish occupation such as ritual baths, Hebrew inscriptions, and architectural features engraved with Jewish symbols. The following summary reviews all the known hiding complexes of this type in Galilee and includes all the current data from historical sources and from archaeological finds. Interestingly, the findings from all these Galilean hiding complexes indicate that they were used during more than one period of crisis under Roman rule, as they were in Judea[1].

Since they [*scil.* the Trachonites] had neither city nor field of their own but only underground shelters and caves, where they lived together with their cattle. They had also managed to collect supplies of water and of food beforehand, and so they were able to hold out for a very long time in their hidden retreat. Moreover, the entrances (to their caves) were narrow, and only one person at a time could enter, while the interiors were incredibly large and constructed to provide plenty of room, and the ground above their dwellings was not high but almost level with the (surrounding) surface. The whole place consisted of rocks that were rugged and difficult of access unless one used a path with a guide leading the way, for not even these paths were straight, but had many turns and windings (*Ant.* 15:346–348).

The underground hiding complexes in Galilee were examined after their discovery in the 1980s by Amos Kloner, Yigal Tepper and Yuval Shachar as well as by the Israel Cave Research Center. Most of the underground cavities identified as hiding complexes in Galilee, including some that were previously unknown, have been re-examined and re-mapped by the author and colleagues.[2] Notably, although the Galilean hiding complexes have their own specific features, they are similar to the hiding complexes in the Judean foothills. (Tables 2–3)

The following tables show features identified in hiding complexes in the Judean foothills compared with features of hiding complexes in Galilee and the similarities between them.

1 Shivtiel 2013b.

2 Vladimir Boslov, the late Ahiakm Amichai, Boaz Langford, Shmuel Avidan, Nevo Fischtein and Elhanan Klienberg from the Israel Cave Research Center (ICRC) participated in the mapping.

Type of installation	Form	Use
Entrance shafts	Round or square cistern.	Used to reach or leave a complex.
Passages	Winding, with 90–degree angles; each section is only about two meters long, is hewn as wide as a body, and measures an average of 0.6×0.7 m in section.	Used as narrow access passages between cavities and between ancient installations and hiding annexes.
Chambers with entrances that sometimes bear hewn thresholds, lintels, door jambs, and bolt holes	The roof is as high as a person, sometimes hastily hewn and sometimes well finished.	Refuge dwellings or storerooms.
Locking mechanisms/bolts/seal stones	A narrower opening in the side of the passage has a stone slab fixed to it. The jambs of the opening have stone supports. The bolt holds the stone secure against the jambs and the roll-stone blocks the entrance.	Security mechanisms to stop hostile intruders.
Lighting	Hollows or ledges for lamps hewn along passages or elsewhere in the complexes.	Pottery oil lamps were the most common method of lighting the hiding complexes and their cavities.
Ventilation shafts	Utilizing openings from an existing installation, such as a water cistern, to provide ventilation.	Fresh air circulation for underground fugitives in case the entrances to the complexes had to be blocked or sealed.
Storage installations and silos	Bottle-shaped or irregularly shaped cavities capable of holding comparatively large quantities of storage vessels.	Rock-hewn cavities used to store food and grain before the hiding complex itself was built and to which the passages were connected, or storage places hewn while preparing the complexes.
Water storage	Hewn and plastered cisterns and reservoirs fed by water carried from the outside via hewn channels.	Ensuring a regular water supply.
Converted ancient installations	Oil presses, columbaria, livestock pens, and water cisterns.	Incorporating existing underground installations in hiding complexes.

Table 2: Features of Hiding Complexes in the Judean Foothills (according to Kloner and Tepper)[3]

3 Kloner and Tepper 1987:50–71.

Type of installation	Form	Use
Family storage complex	Begun as an underground storage cavity, without narrow winding passages, the complex consists mainly of a series of small chambers and bottle-shaped cavities or chambers for jars.	Readily accessible refuge for a family.
Family refuge and storage complex	An underground shaft tunneled from inside a dwelling house leading to a winding passageway that may be at different levels; along the passage and at the end of it are chambers and bottle-shaped cavities.	Prepared in advance as a hiding place; storage is not its main purpose.
Family hiding and storage complex with a reservoir	The complex includes all the typical early features with added access to an ancient water reservoir.	Prepared to enable lengthier stays underground.
Simple communal complex	A large hiding complex with many branches, also including ancient installations – some communal – that were rendered obsolete and concealed.	Since it is hewn into installations belonging to the communal infrastructure, it is a shared complex.
Communal complex expressly hewn as a hiding complex	Consisting mainly of passages and small chambers and incorporating no previous installations.	An extremely rare type of communal complex.
Escape complex	Its unique feature is a long passage via a small number of installations like those in the other types of hiding-complex.	May be private or communal. The escape complex provided a hidden exit route from within a settlement.
Hiding complex linked to a burial cave	Passages breaking through the wall of the entrance to a burial cave but not into the burial chamber itself. Alternatively, passages beginning inside the settlement and linking up with the burial cave.	Used for hiding or as a means of escape (this type is rare).
Hiding complex incorporating large natural cavities	Passages hewn inside natural caves.	Found at sites where the natural rock is especially hard.
Hiding/escape complexes linked to synagogues	Hewn beside or beneath synagogues, some using natural cavities that were widened and adapted as hiding places.	The link between the hiding complexes and the synagogues may indicate that they were used by those who attended the synagogue, although there is no proof of this.

Table 3: Typological Division of Hiding Complexes in the Judean Foothills (according to Zissu)[4]

To date, 74 underground cavities used as hiding complexes have been discovered in Galilee[5] and they can be classified into several types. For comparison's sake, the data is presented following typology used for sites in the Judean foothills

4 Zissu 2002:274–276.

5 Just prior to the publication of this book, further hiding complexes were discovered at Horvat Lubiya, Kabul, Mimlah, Daboria, and Tel Tsuffa (Ayelet Hashachar).

1. Simple hiding complexes (resembling complexes from the Second Temple period in the Judean foothills)	2. Sophisticated, meticulously hewn hiding complexes (resembling complexes from the Bar Kokhba Revolt in the Judean foothills)	3. Underground cavities hewn into installations used on a daily basis
Nevoriah	Gush Halav, in the center of the village, in the courtyard of a private dwelling	Gush Halav, at the highest point of the settlement, east of the upper synagogue
ʿIyei Meʿarot, Caves 70 and 71	Meroth, the synagogue	ʿIyei Meʿarot, Caves 28 and 28A
ʿIyei Meʿarot, Cave 83	ʿIyei Meʿarot, Cave 54	ʿIyei Meʿarot, Caves 74 and 74A
ʿIyei Meʿarot, Complex 97	Qeiyuma	ʿIyei Meʿarot, Cave 75
Huqoq, Horvat Huqoq	Har Hazon	Huqoq, beneath the synagogue
Ravid	El-Khirbeh	Bet Natofa
Mimlah, three complexes	ʿIbillin + four complexes	Turʿan, two complexes
Lubiya	Horvat Ruma	Kafr Kanna,
El-Khirbeh, the small complex	Kafr Kanna, Khirbet Khuwwkha, in the center of the village	Zippori, two complexes
Kafr Kanna, the northern residential area, Karm a-Ras, (Area W)	Nazareth, St. Joseph's Church	Shikhin, west of Jebel Qat.
Kafr Kanna, south of the village	Ilaniya	Kafr Kanna, Khirbet Khuwwkha (western complex)
Mushtah	ʿEnot Shoʿim	Horvat Dabbura
Horvat ʿAmmudim		
ʿIbillin, ʿIbillin Village		Horvat Tiriya
Shikhin, west of Jebel Qat (southern complex)		Bet Sheʿarim
Iotapata, lower slope		Iotapata, upper slope
Horvat Bina		Horvat Riv
Buleiq		Migdal Haʿemeq
Evtsam		Kabul
Horvat Dabbura B		Horvat Qisi
Horvat Nurit		Usha
Rushmya (Rosh Maya) Fortress (Citadel)		Maskana 1+2
24	16	23

4. Underground cavities hewn into burial caves	**5. Escape passages (similar to hiding complexes found in Nahal Yattir and Horvat ʿAqad in Judea)**	**6. Underground cavities that were probably not used as hiding complexes**
Meroth, east of the settlement	Gush Halav, on the east slope of Nahal Gush Halav	Jebel Qat
ʿIyei Meʿarot, Cave 9		ʿEilabun
ʿIyei Meʿarot, Cave 69		Nahal ʿAmal passages
ʿIyei Meʿarot, Cave 88		Tel ʿAmal tunnel
Kafr Kanna, north of Zipporit industrial estate		
Shunam		
6	1	4

Table 4: Classification of the Galilean Hiding Complexes in this Volume (according to Shivti'el)

Total number of hiding complexes: 74.

Below is a list of all the underground cavities found so far in Galilee according to type. The subsequent discussion refers only to sites that can definitely be identified as hiding complexes, while the following list also includes underground cavities that cannot conclusively be identified as hiding complexes.

Both cliff shelters and hiding complexes were the main methods of defence employed by the Jewish population of Galilee during the Early Roman period and probably also in subsequent periods.

List of Galilean Sites and Underground Cavities Identified as Hiding Complexes.[6]

1. Gush Halav, at the highest point of the settlement, east of the upper synagogue.*
2. Gush Halav, in the center of the village, in the courtyard of a private dwelling.*
3. Gush Halav, on the east slope of Nahal Gush Halav.*
4. Meroth, within the compound of the ancient synagogue.
5. Meroth, 2 km east of the settlement (inside a burial cave).*
6. Qeiyuma, north of the Meron-Zefat highway.
7. Nevoriah, Biriah Forest near Amuka, south of the synagogue.

8–17. ʿIyei Meʿarot, Hazor Ha-Glilit (ten complexes).*

18. Mount Hazon.
19. Huqoq, Horvat Huqoq (in the synagogue compound)
20. Huqoq, water cistern at Horvat Huqoq.*
21. Mimlah, on the west side of Horvat Mimlah.
22. Mimlah, approximately 500 m south of the complex on the west side of Horvat Mimlah.*
23. Mimlah, approximately 170 m north of the dirt track leading to the summit.*
24. Horvat Ravid.
25. 'Eilabun, east of the town of Eilabun.
26. Mushtah, a hill overlooking the village of 'Arʿabeh.
27. Yodefat, on the lower slope of the site.
28. Yodefat, on the upper slope of the site.
29. Kabul, in the center of the ancient village

30–33. ʿIbillin, inside the Crusader citadel in the village of ʿIbillin (four complexes).

34. ʿIbillin, in the village of ʿIbillin.
35. Bet Natofa, Tel Bet Natofa.
36. Lubiya, near Kibbutz Lavi (east of the Golani Junction).
37. El-Khirbeh, on a hill west of Lubiya, the large complex.
38. El-Khirbeh, east of the hill summit, the small complex.
39. Ruma, in Bet Rimon Valley
40. Kafr Kanna, north of Zipporit industrial estate, on the edge of the village of Meshhed.*

6 An asterisk denotes a hiding complex discovered during the current survey. The list also includes complexes that were formerly identified as such, but whose re-examination has cast some doubt on their classification.

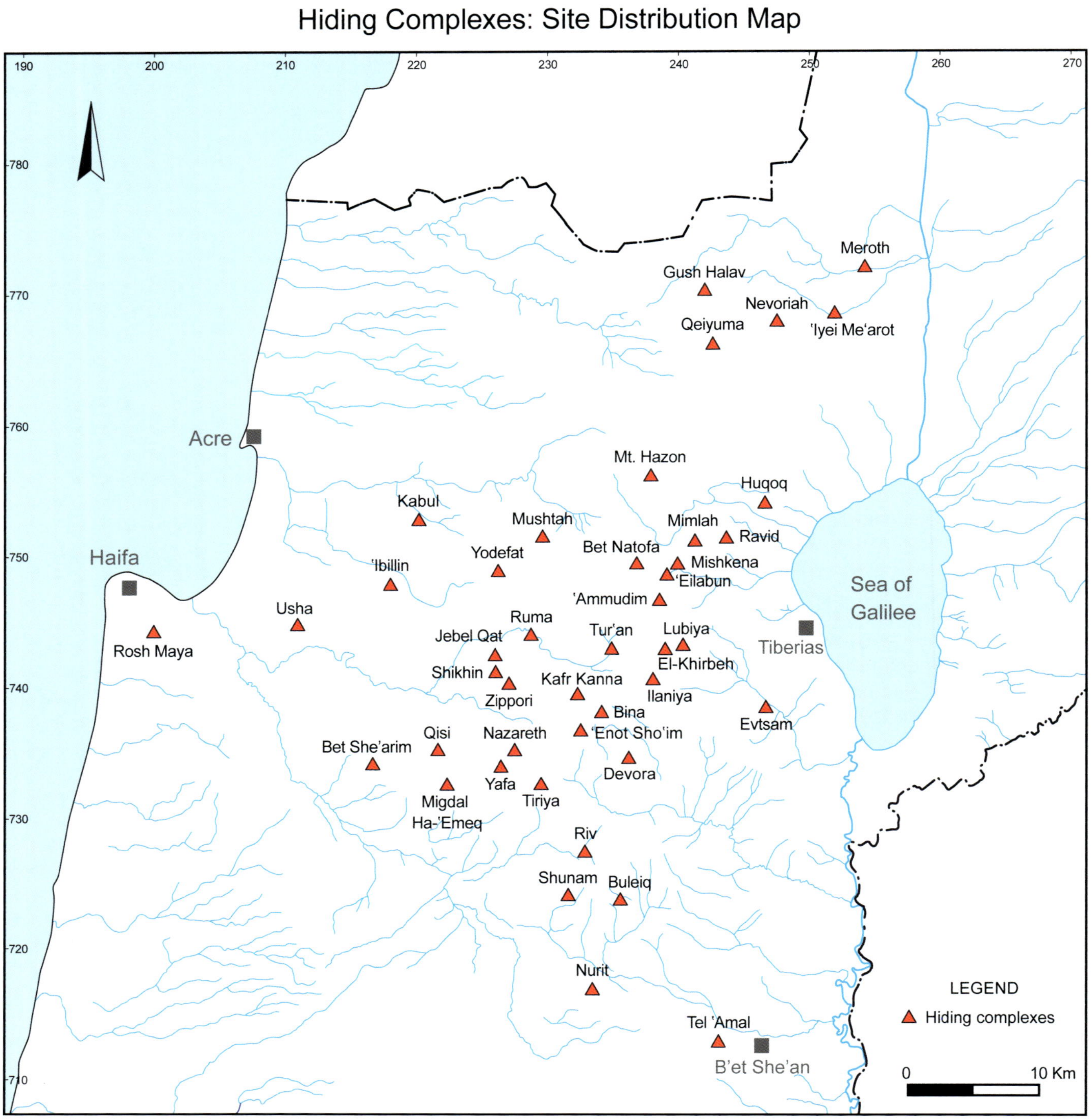

Fig. 63: Distribution of the Hiding Complexes in Galilee

41, 42. Kafr Kanna, the northern residential area of the village, Karm a-Ras (two complexes).
43. Kafr Kanna, in the center of the village (at Khirbet Khuwwkha).
44. Kafr Kanna, c. 40 m west of the complex in the center of the village (at Khirbet Khuwwkha).
45. Kafr Kanna, ʿEn al-Jouza, one kilometer south of the village.*
46. ʿEnot Shoʿim (ʿEn Mahel).
47, 48. Turʿan, in the village of Turʿan, next to the Golani Junction (two complexes).*
49. Ilaniya, at Khirbet Sejera.*
50. Evtsam, in Yavniʿel Valley.
51. Jebel Qat, north of Zippori.
52, 53. Shikhin, west of Jebel Qat (two complexes).*
54. Zippori, on Zippori Hill.*
55. Zippori, c. 80 m west of Zippori Citadel.*
56. Horvat Bina, north of ʿEn Mahel.*
57. Horvat Tiriya, on a hill southeast of Nazareth.*
58. Nazareth, St. Joseph's Church.
59, 60. Horvat Dabbura, one kilometer northeast of Daburiya village (two complexes).*
61. Bet Sheʿarim, in the courtyard of Bet Zaid, near the synagogue.
62. Migdal Ha-ʿEmeq.
63. Horvat Riv, on the south bank of Nahal Tabor.*
64. Shunam, on the south slope of Givat Ha-Moreh.
65. Horvat Buleiq, near Ein Harod.*
66. Horvat Nurit, on Mount Gilboa.*
67. Tel ʿAmal tunnel, at Horvat Tel al-ʿAsi, on the south bank of Nahal ʿAmal.
68. Nahal ʿAmal passages, in Gan Ha-Shlosha National Park on the north bank of Nahal ʿAmal.
69. Horvat ʿAmmudim (Khirbet Umm el-Amad).
70. Horvat Qisi.*
71. Horvat Maskana 1.*
72. Horvat Maskana 2.
73. Romema, Haifa (Rosh Maya, Rushmya).*
74. Usha.*

Distribution of Sites with Hiding Complexes in Galilee (Fig. 63)

This map completes the list of underground cavities identified as hiding complexes in Galilee.

Gush Halav (Gischala)

Three underground cavities were discovered at Gush Halav, which lies on a summit 840 m above sea level and about 7 km northwest of Zefat. To the east of the summit is Nahal Gush Halav, to the north is Nahal Dishon, and to the west is an alluvial plain below the slopes of Mount Meron. Josephus mentions the site several times as one of the Jewish settlements that participated in the Great Revolt under the leadership of John of Gischala, with whom Josephus shared a deep-seated personal animosity. Josephus records that in preparation for a Roman offensive, John of Gischala fortified Gush Halav and built a wall around it (*War* 2:575–576, 632; *Life* 189). Gush Halav, according to Josephus, was the last settlement in Galilee to remain defiant against the Romans during the Great Revolt. He describes how John of Gischala and many of its residents abandoned the town in the dead of night after John of Gischala persuaded Titus that he would deliver the town to him without resistance, if Titus would allow him to wait until the end of the Sabbath without desecrating it (*War* 4:84–120). Gush Halav is mentioned in the Mishnah as a Jewish town surrounded by a wall from the time of Joshua Ben Nun (*m.Arachin* 9:6) and in Rabbinic sources it is famous for its fertile lands, vines, olives, and fine oil. Various sources record that Jews occupied the place until the Middle Ages.[7] The ruins of ancient Jewish Gush Halav are today covered by the Arab town of el-Jish whose population consists of Maronite and Greek Orthodox Christians and a few Muslims. Two ancient synagogues and a mausoleum dating to the 4th c. CE have been excavated at Gush Halav.[8]

7 See Stepansky 2000a:67–80.
8 See Meyers et all, 1990; Shivti'el, 2004; Strange 2015b:389–403.

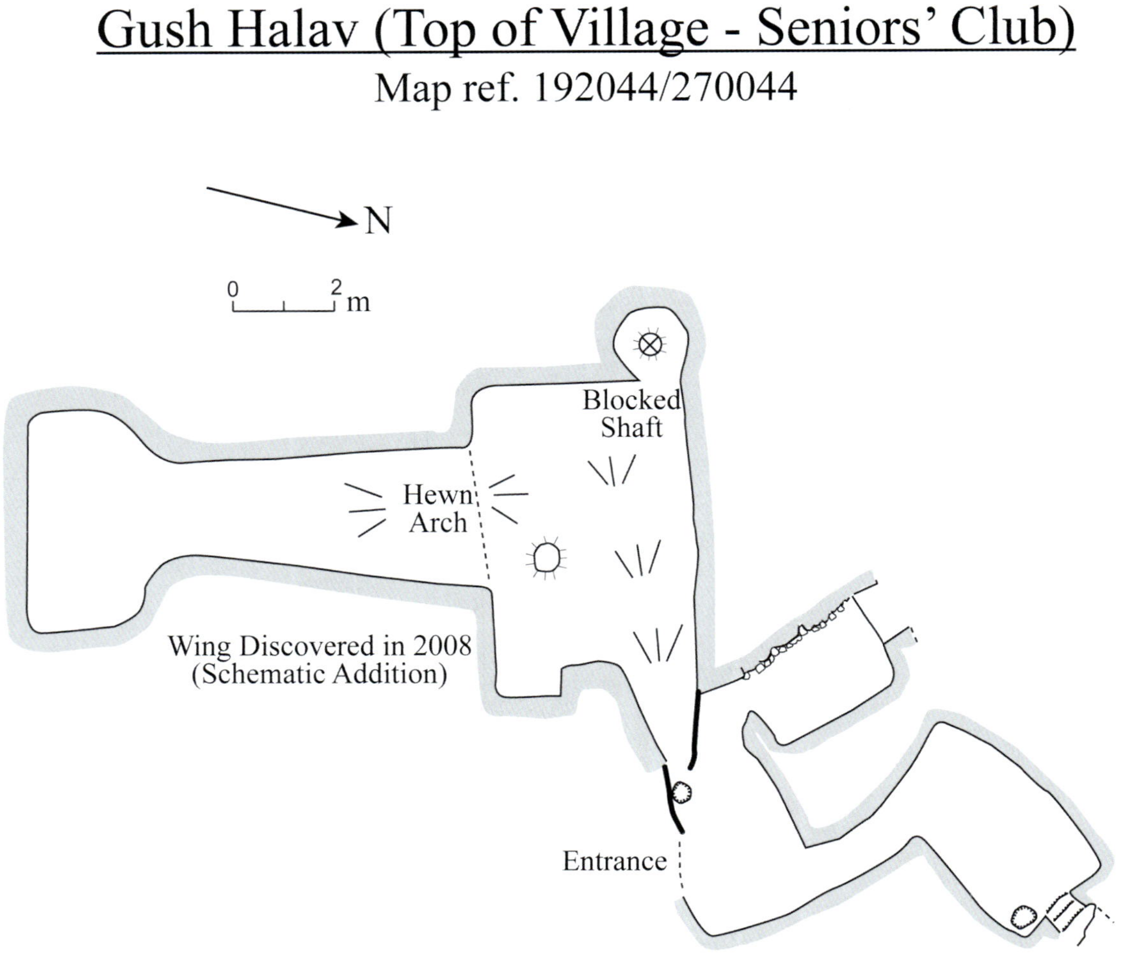

Map 32: Gush Halav, the highest point (summit of settlement, seniors' club)

1. Gush Halav: The highest point of the town, east of the upper synagogue (beneath a senior citizens' club) (Map ref. 192044/270044)

Fig. 64: Gush Halav, Hiding Complex at the highest point of the settlement

A salvage excavation was conducted at the site in 1989.[9] The original entrance to the hiding complex is near the wall of a modern building and was still open when the building was completed. The entrance leads to a rock-hewn cavity with an arched roof. On removing the debris, it became clear that the complex was hewn into the soft rock of the hillside to a depth of about 6 m. It is reached by crawling through an opening in the south wall, as are six more hewn chambers with interconnecting passages. The south chamber of the complex has a stairway leading to another chamber (2.3 × 4.4 m) with an arched roof whose walls contain rock-hewn niches for oil lamps that retain traces of soot, two of which are triangular. Three groups containing 41 incised lines were found on the walls and the Greek letters **Ne** were carved above the entrance to the passage. A hewn depression in the southeast corner of the chamber contained fragments of the base of a jar and four pottery jar lids, which the archaeologists

9 See Damati and Abu-'Uqsa 1991.

identified as resembling 1st c. CE lids. The hewn steps probably led to other chambers that are now blocked with earth. A gap in the southern wall of the third room leads to another chamber measuring 2.5 × 3.5 m and 1.4 m high. The chamber has rounded corners and a vaulted roof. The walls of this chamber also contain triangular niches for oil lamps. From here, a small chamber was hewn with steps leading to a fifth chamber where another blocked passage is unexcavated. There is a water cistern near the entrance to the complex.

The site probably began as a series of underground storerooms converted into a hiding complex by the addition of passages between the chambers. The passages themselves have narrow crawl-ways leading off in further directions. On examining the complex, the chambers were found to contain additional hewn passages that are now blocked with earth. These were probably the underground storerooms of one of the ancient houses of the village of Gush Halav. Since the floors of the passages were clear of earthen debris, they were probably hewn from the outset as low, narrow passages rather than a corridor providing easy access from one chamber to another, as one would expect from a place used only for storage. The site was later dug by robbers, who exposed a 4 m deep plastered water cistern in its southern part with a 1 × 9 m entrance. In the floor of the cistern, the entrance to a hewn passage is visible; its opening measures 0.1 × 0.2 m, but its continuation is blocked.

2. Gush Halav: An underground cavity in the courtyard of a private home in the center of the village (Map ref. 192001/270075)

The current survey discovered the cavity in the courtyard of a house in the center of the north part of the village. The entrance lies a few meters away from the east wall of the house, where an ancient stairway descends to a depth of 4 m and into a hewn chamber (2.3 × 4 m). A square niche is hewn in the roof of the chamber and a narrow passage 5 m long leads to a small chamber (2.5 × 3 m) whose walls contain niches for oil lamps. The small chamber has two rounded openings; the south opening ascends to a hewn chamber with an

Fig. 65: Gush Halav, Hiding Complex, Miriam's House

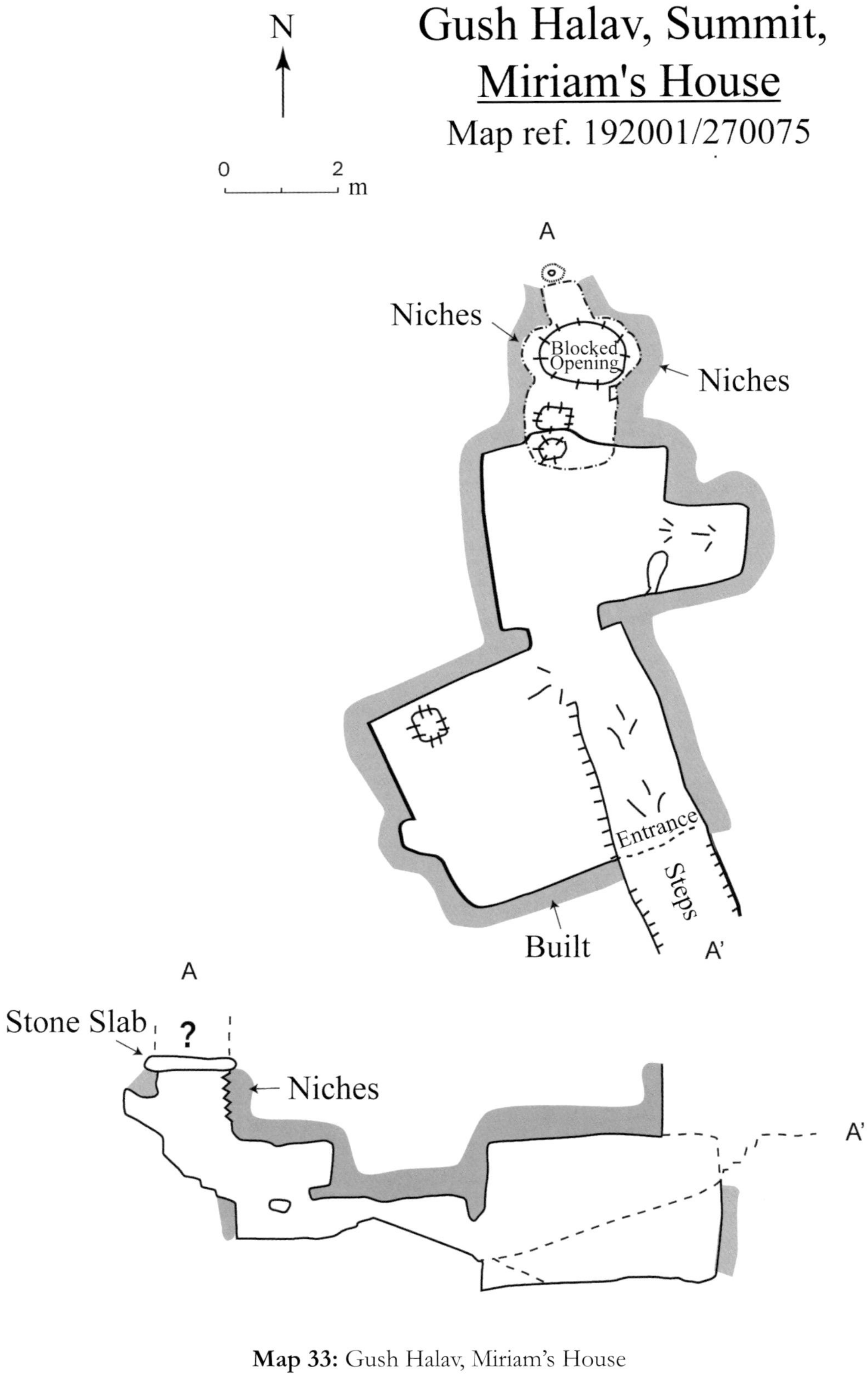

Map 33: Gush Halav, Miriam's House

arched roof measuring 2 × 3 m. From here, an opening leads to another chamber containing a series of oil-lamp niches. A symmetrically dressed step was hewn in this chamber leading to a fourth chamber with a round opening in its roof that is now blocked but was probably used as a ventilation shaft. Five niches hewn one above the other in this chamber were apparently climbing holds. The rock above the highest niche is filled with earth that probably accumulated there when the modern house was built. On the north side of the above-mentioned chamber, at a height of 0.5 m, an arched opening leads to another passage that is now blocked with earth. This seems to have been a family-hiding complex hewn on a number of levels beneath an ancient dwelling house. The climbing holds found in the complex are similar to those found at al-ʿAliliat cave in Nahal Michmash, in the Judean Desert.[10]

10 See Patrich 1985:21–26; Shivti'el 2004; Shivti'el 2011b:51–52.

3. Gush Halav: Escape passage on the east slope of Nahal Gush Halav (Map ref. 192607/270963)

The passage is on the north bank of the Gush Halav gorge and to the west of its lower synagogue. Two natural caves are located one above the other and halfway up the cliff. The entrance to the lower cave (5 × 5 m) is 15 m above the base of the slope and can be reached by scaling the rock. Karstic dissolution processes are evident in the smooth rock, as shown by the traces of travertine in the notch formed in the lower part of the cave. The cave can be entered standing up for the first 9 meters, after which it can only be crawled into for a further 18 meters. A natural karstic process at the end of the passage formed two branches. The northeast branch, which is 4 m long, leads to a shaft 1.5 m deep and 2 m in diameter. The shaft descends to the lower level and terminates in a small chamber (c. 4 × 4 m) containing a

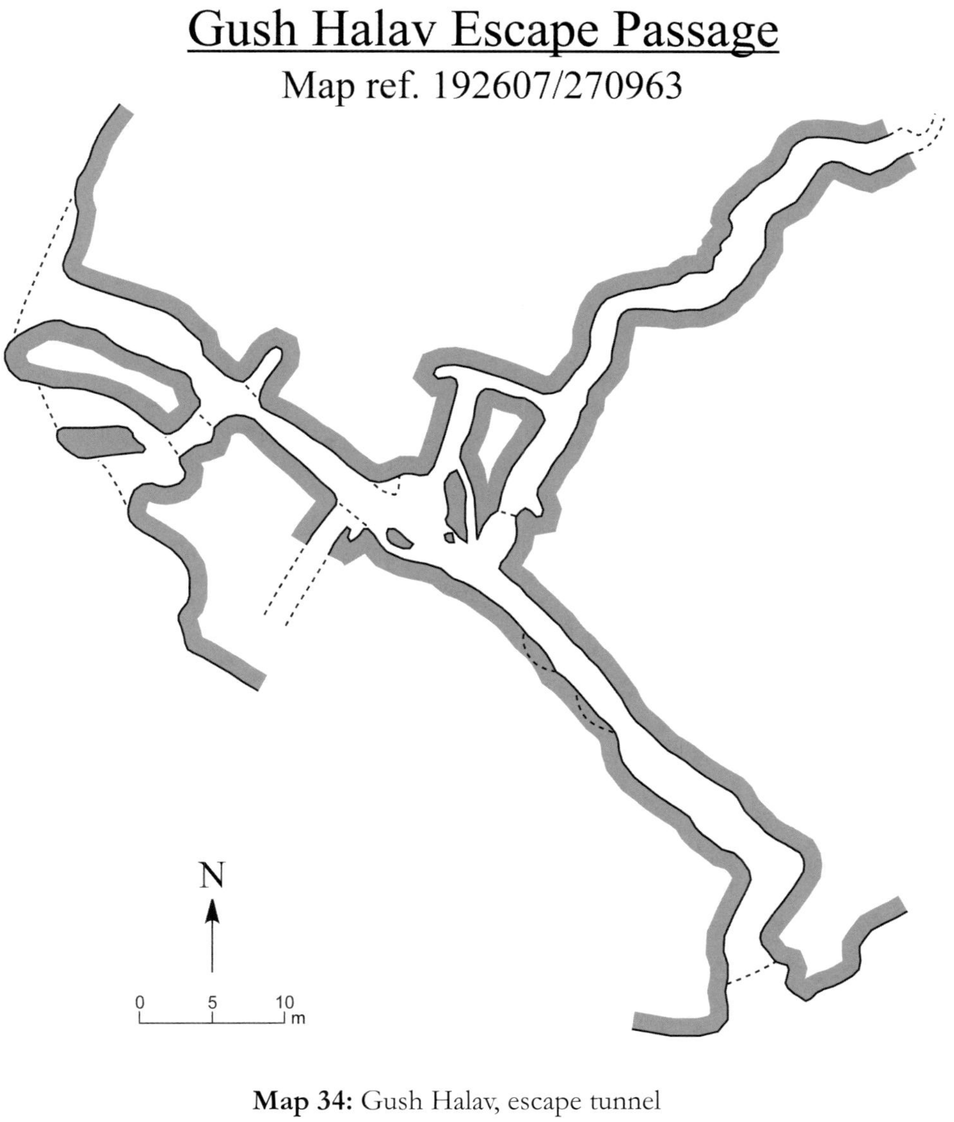

Map 34: Gush Halav, escape tunnel

pool of water. The second branch continues north into the hillside. The passage contains signs of hewing and produced non-diagnostic potsherds. Further on, the passage has been blocked by collapsed earth and is now impassable. The accessible section of the passage is 157 m long and bends northward. On the north slopes of the cliff, near the point where the 'Ein 'Alva spring emerges, a cave measuring 5 × 8 m is now used as a pen for sheep and goats. On its inner, west-facing wall the other end of the passage leading to the lower cave was discovered. After crawling for 5 m through this passage, one encounters the blocked section. The passage crosses through the cliff from the lower cave, emerging at 'Ein 'Alva spring northeast of the neighboring cave. Although it is not a typical hiding passage, it was most probably used by the inhabitants of Nahal Gush Halav below the settlement as a concealed access to the spring. Notably, Josephus records that those besieged at Iotapata crawled out of the town through a narrow channel (passage?) to convey messages and bring food in a similar manner (*War* 3:190–192).

Fig. 66: Gush Halav, entrance to escape tunnel

4. Meroth (Kh. Marus), inside the compound of the ancient synagogue (Map ref. 199935/270753)

Meroth synagogue is located in the center of the ancient Jewish town of Meroth, on whose ruins the Arab village of Marus was built. Meroth lies on a high plain in the foothills of the Mount Naftali Ridge west of Mount Ayelet, 3.5 km west of Tel Hazor and c. 7 km northeast of Zefat. Victor Guérin visited Kh. Marus and his journal describes a deserted and ruined Arab village whose ancient architectural remains included ashlars, column fragments and Doric capitals.[11] Zvi Ilan discovered Meroth's synagogue late in 1981 while surveying the ruins at Marus. He later conducted archaeological excavations at the site with Emmanuel Damati and exposed a synagogue and finds attesting to continuous Jewish occupation there from the 3rd c. BCE to the 6th c. CE.[12] The discovery of the synagogue at Meroth led to the identification of the ancient Jewish town mentioned in Josephus' works as "Mero" (Μηρώθ) in *War,* or as "Ameroth" (Ἀμηρώθ) in *Life.* Meroth is one of the settlements near which cliff shelters have been found (at Mount Aviatar) and it also contains hiding complexes. The entrance to a hiding complex was discovered in the center of the floor in the synagogue's main hall. Exploration of the underground cavity beneath the synagogue revealed that the hiding complex connects the synagogue to an existing ritual bath that became obsolete when the underground complex began to be used as a hiding complex. Based on the direction of the chiseling, it seems that the hiding complex was hewn from inside the ritual bath near the south wall of the synagogue and it is an example of the type that eliminated previous installations. The complex consists of five large hewn cavities: A catapult stone found in the eastern cavity may attest to the site's capture by the Romans. Zvi Ilan and Emmanuel Damati believe that the synagogue was built above the hiding complex and that interconnecting passages were hewn between the various underground complexes near the synagogue. In the tunnels of the hiding complex, Ilan and Damati reported pottery from the 2nd to 5th c. CE. The main passage emerges from the east wall of the ritual bath and leads to two cavities measuring c. 4 × 5 m. A pit hewn in the center of the first cavity leads down to another underground chamber that is now filled with earth. On the north side of the cavity, the main passage leads to a junction of two passages. The southern

11 See Guérin 1880,7:255.
12 See Ilan and Damati 1988:8–15, 52.

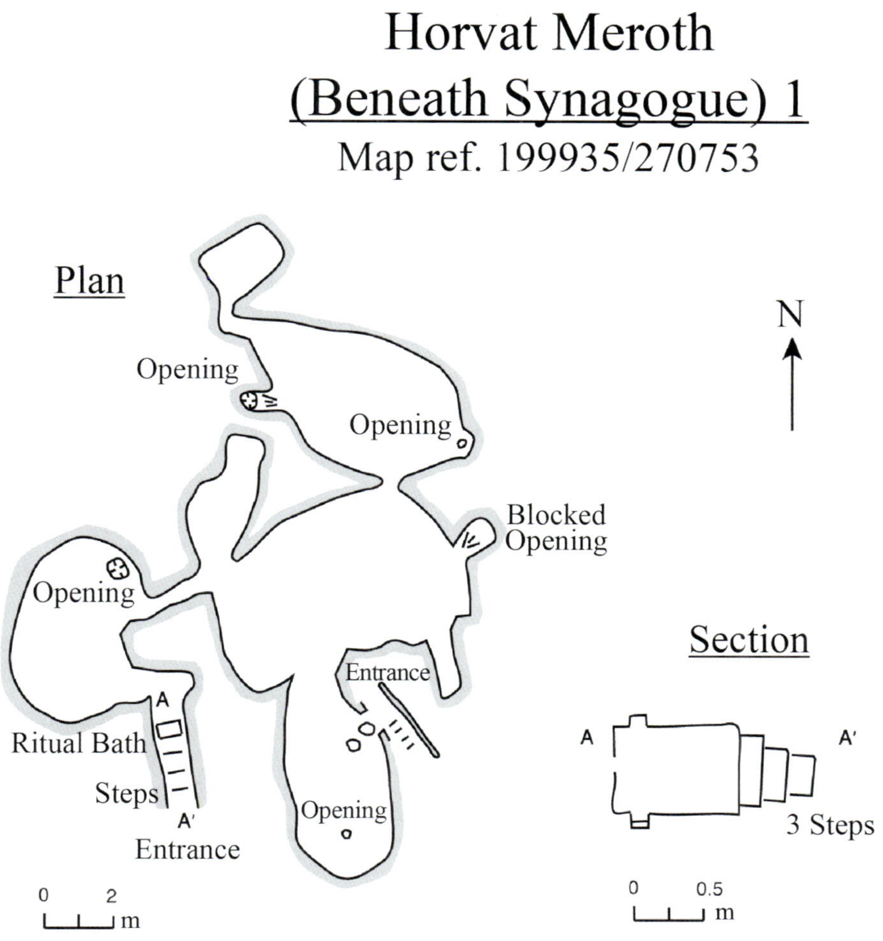

Map 35: Meroth synagogue Hiding Complex

Fig. 67: Meroth, synagogue Hiding Complex, under the hall floor, going into a ritual bath whose wall has been breached

passage leads to a cavity (c. 3 × 4 m) and the northern passage leads to one measuring c. 5 × 7 m. In the east wall of this cavity, the passage continues to another, elongated cavity whose end is blocked and where an opening leads out of the complex. Three passages were hewn in this cavity, one of which has an arched entrance and was never completed. To the left of the alcove is an oil-lamp niche retaining traces of soot. This is probably another passage that was never completed. The two other passages are not dressed and appear to have been hastily worked. One is hewn in the south wall of the cavity and into a water cistern with traces of plaster and narrow steps that appear to be have been worked later than the cistern and emerge outside the synagogue. The passages contain hewn niches for oil lamps, but they are free of soot, either showing that they were not used or indicating preparations for the Second Revolt. The third passage leads to another cavity with direct access to the middle of the synagogue hall. This is the first hiding complex to be found in Galilee beneath a synagogue that renders a ritual bath obsolete, indicating that the population preferred to use the underground cavity for hiding rather than for purification purposes. Other instances of the same phenomenon are discussed below. In Judea, hiding complexes dug beneath synagogues have been found at Susya and Eshtemoʿa, and possibly also at Maʿon in the southern Hebron foothills.[13]

5. Meroth, 2 km east of the settlement (inside a burial cave) (Map ref. 200590/270742)

During the excavation of the synagogue at Meroth in 1986, the burial caves at Horvat Meroth were surveyed. The survey covered 159 burial complexes across an area covering 300 dunams (c. 75 acres). Some of the burials had been dug into and a number of the caves had interconnecting passages. The surveyors believed that the burials had been disturbed by grave robbers. In the current survey, one of the burial caves was found to have features consistent with those of a hiding place. It is located about 2 km east of the synagogue, on the other side of a valley separating it from the settlement. The burial cave was hewn on the western-facing slopes of a rocky hill with a smooth surface where there are ancient rock-hewn industrial installations. The hillside contains a level terrace, into which the burial cave was hewn. The fifth burial cave has hewn and beveled openings that are now all blocked with earth. The main entrance to the cave is filled with a dressed seal-stone c. 1 m high. Exploration of the site revealed an opening above the smooth rock surface, near to one of the industrial installations. This cave entrance leads directly to a complex of seven chambers connected by hewn passages. We counted 84 burial niches in this cave. Some are hastily hewn and roughly finished, but are always found behind the burial niches or chamber wall and cause no damage to pre-existing burial niches. The passages in the Meroth necropolis are c. 0.5 m high and reach a length of c. 30 m. They form a labyrinth between the niches and in some places, small chambers are hewn. The working is simple and crude. Since the passages wend between the burials, the complex appears to have an elaborate plan. Some of the chambers contain openings blocked with dressed stones. Between Chamber 4 and Chamber 3, a passage is hewn in the southeast wall of the chamber roof and 1.3 m above the silt covering the floor. Strenuous climbing is required to enter the passage, which is 2 m long, 0.32 m high and 0.4 m wide. It leads to a chamber containing more burial niches whose western entrance is now blocked. The niches were found intact and undisturbed. Two are still sealed by fieldstones bearing traces of plaster. A passage 4.4 m long is hewn in the west wall between Chamber 6 and Chamber 7. The passage (0.4 × 0.4 m in section) emerges from the back wall of a burial niche and after 1.4 m makes a right angle turn to the north. After about three more meters, the passage cuts into the facing wall of a burial cavity in Chamber 7. The obvious care taken to avoid breaking into the burial niche, the way in which some of the passages were hewn with 90-degree angles, and the fact that the burial complex has openings from different sides providing easy access to all of the complexes without the rough hacking typical of grave robbers

Fig. 68: Meroth, Hiding Complex with entrance to passage from inside a burial niche

13 See Kloner and Zissu 2006:129.

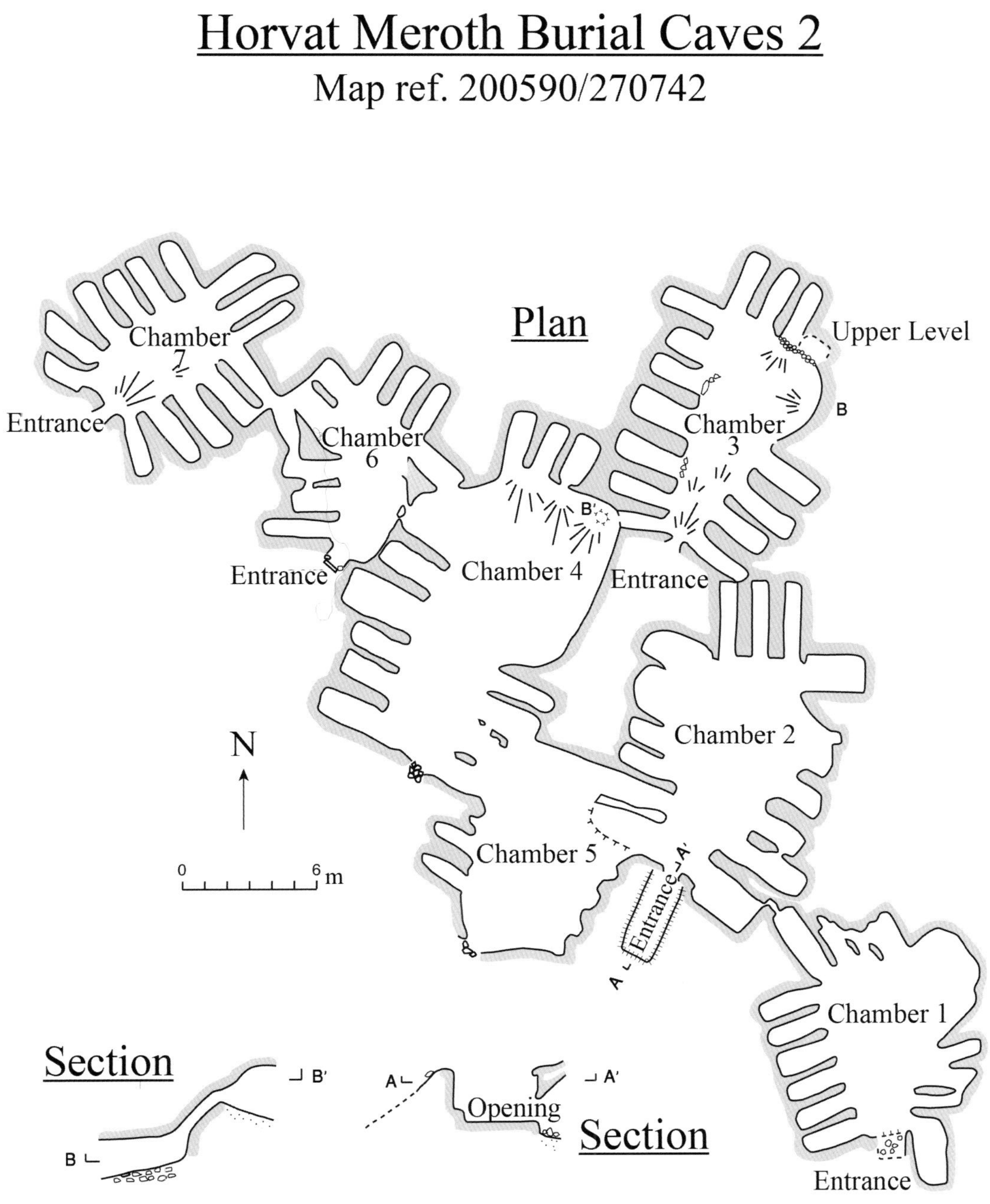

Map 36: Meroth, the burial chambers

all indicate that the site represents a burial complex converted into a hiding complex. Yigal Bar Yehuda, who first surveyed the burial cave in 1986, noted that it was blocked with earth debris, dense vegetation and fallen rocks.[14] Amos Kloner and Boaz Zissu noticed a similar phenomenon at the burial caves at Horvat Benaya and Horvat Burgin in the Judean foothills.[15]

6. Horvat Qeiyuma: North of the Meron-Zefat highway (Map ref. 193972/266495)

The ruins of an ancient settlement located north of the Meron-Zefat highway, about 2 km east of the Meron Junction. The remains are concentrated over an area of high land looking out over the northern Mount Meron ridge, with Qadita Valley spread out to the north. The origin of the site's name is obscure and may derive from the Arabic for 'eternal site'. It may also preserve the ancient name of the burial place of the 2nd to 3rd c. CE sage R. Jose of Yokereth.

14 Bar Yehuda and Pesach 1988:155.

15 See Kloner and Zissu 2006:129.

Tepper and Shachar cite Aviam's survey of the site, which recovered potsherds and coins from the Hellenistic to the Mamluk periods. They also surveyed the ruined settlement and discovered an oil press, ruins of buildings, and a public building. They found the underground cavity that may be a hiding complex beneath the remains of the public building.[16]

The hiding complex is entered via an opening formed by the collapse of its roof. This leads to a hewn passage ending in a round chamber with a ventilation shaft. Opposite the entrance is a round opening descending to a hewn chamber. From this chamber, the passage ascends to a higher level with a third chamber, where an opening cut in the wall leads to a bell-shaped chamber sealed with a round stone cap in its roof. In the west wall of this chamber is the entrance to another chamber, reached via a short passage. It contains incised marks that are impossible to decipher. A passage leading from the chamber links the complexes on the two levels.

16 See Tepper and Shachar 1987b:304.

Fig. 69: Qeiyuma, stone cap placed over entrance to Hiding Complex

Qeiyuma
Map ref. 193972/266495

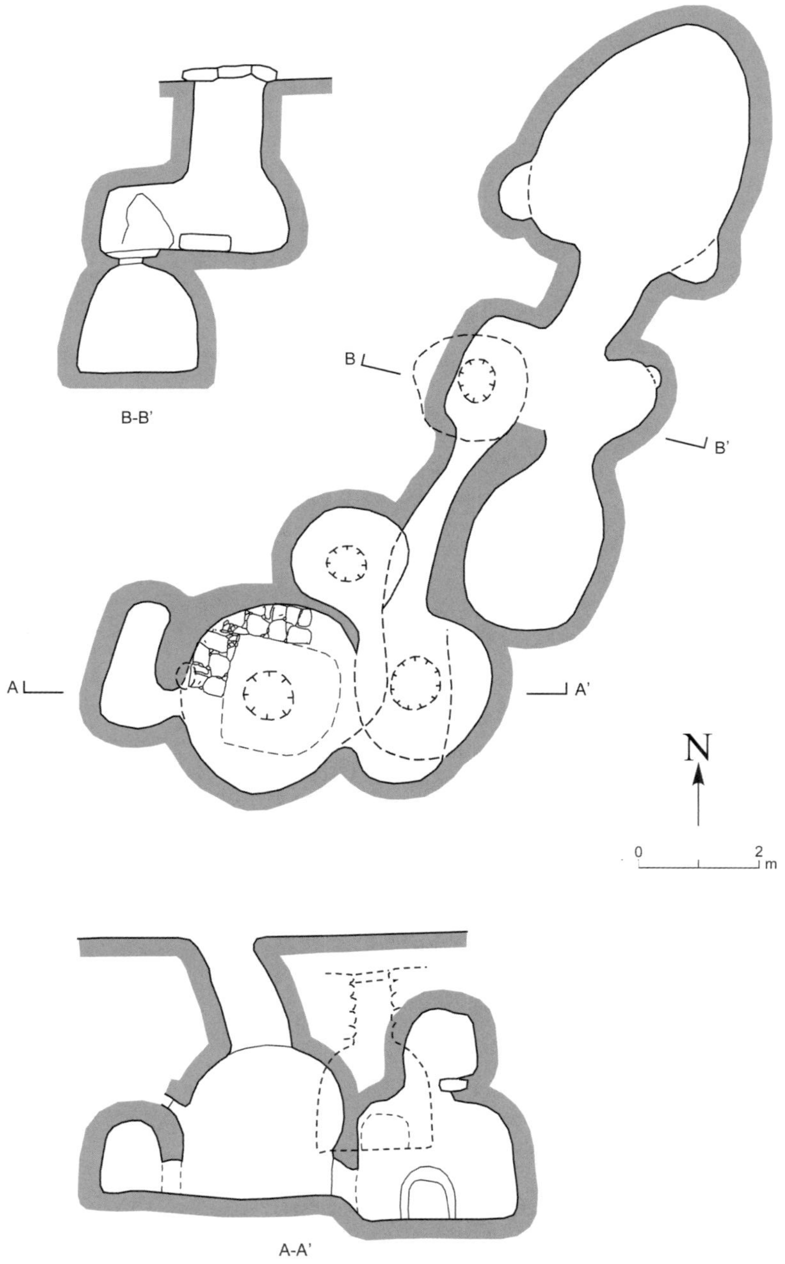

Map 37: Horvat Qeiyuma, Hiding Complex

7. Naburaya (Nabratein): Biriya Forest near ʿAmuqa, south of the synagogue (Map ref. 197966/267763)

The settlement of Naburaya lies in the middle of Biriya Forest, on the southern slope of Nahal Dalton, c. 1.5 km northwest of the settlement of ʿAmuqa and c. 8 km northwest of the city of Zefat. Naburaya was a Jewish town in Mishnaic and Talmudic times. It is mentioned several times as the home of Jacob of Naburaya, a fourth-generation Amoraim sage.[17] Victor Guérin described the place as a hill covered with various ruined building stones. North of the site, on a high hill where there is an ancient synagogue, Guérin found a lintel containing a seven-branched menorah and a dedicatory inscription in Hebrew. Nahman Avigad deciphered the inscription as reading, "Built four hundred and ninety years after the destruction of the Temple under the leadership of Hanina Ben Lizer and Luliana Bar Yudan."[18] Eric Meyers and his team excavated the synagogue in the early 1980s.[19]

During preservation work on the synagogue and to the south of the synagogue itself, a square pit measuring 4 × 5 m was discovered with an arched opening on its west side. The opening leads to a passage that is now blocked with earth. Above the opening, one can make out the remains of chambers whose floors have collapsed into the underground chambers. Mordechai Aviam identified the passage as a hiding complex,[20] but the place was blocked off before we were able to explore and map it.

17 See *yYebamoth,* 2,1:6; *Bereshit Rabah* 7.

18 See Avigad 1960:140.

19 See Meyers, Strange and Meyers 1981; Meyers 2015.

20 See Aviam 2004:127.

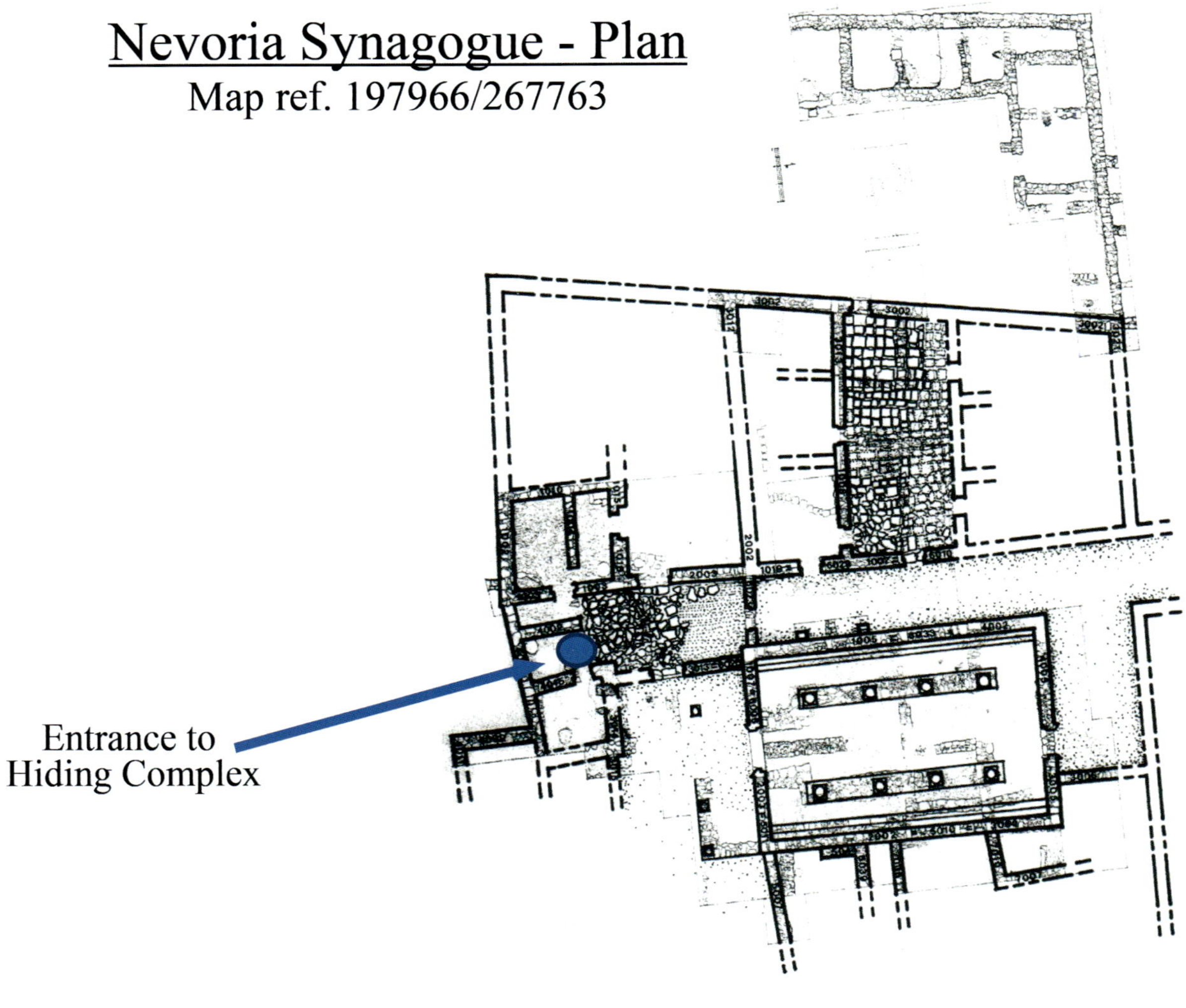

Map 38: Naburiya, the ancient synagogue

Fig. 70: Naburiya, hiding-complex entrance near synagogue

8–17. ʿIyei Meʿarot, Hazor Ha-Glilit (10 complexes) (central map ref. 200800/266060)

The site of ʿIyei Meʿarot is located northwest of the town of Hazor Ha-Glilit and contains the remains of numerous ancient structures extending over c. 70 dunams (17 acres) on a high ridge.[21] Guérin remarked on the large number of caves in the village.[22] Among the remains of the Arab village are ancient walls made of dressed limestone and basalt rock as well as architectural elements, plastered water cisterns, dwelling caves, burial caves, and agricultural installations. In his survey of the site, Ilan reported on the clearly visible architectural remains of a synagogue and recorded a hiding complex to its south. [23]

Fig. 71: ʿIyei Meʿarot, 1

The site has over 100 different kinds of caves spread along four to five topographical terraces. The majority of the caves – some of which are natural although most are man-made – were used as the inner rooms of buildings built in front of them. The buildings were sometimes constructed over the roof of a cave on a lower terrace, accessed via an entrance hewn in the cave roof. A few caves in the settlement have hewn burial niches, but most of the burial caves lie outside the village (see below). Some of the caves have plastered roofs showing that they were used as water reservoirs; in others, interconnecting passages were cut between the various chambers. Sometimes there are passages between different caves and some were clearly used as hiding complexes. An archaeological survey conducted in 1966 to the west of the settlement discovered a few burial caves; one of these contained a number of broken alcoves and two of them may have been converted into hiding complexes. Howard Smithline conducted an archaeological excavation in one of the burial caves, where he retrieved a stone vessel.[24] Quarried installations are located in the area surrounding the caves; of particular interest is a large rock-hewn installation coated with hydraulic plaster enclosing an area measuring 4 × 4 m and 2.5–3 m deep. A small alcove with an arched opening was hewn in its west wall. Near the northeast corner of the main installation, steps provide easy access to the bottom and it was probably used as a ritual bath or a pool. ʿIyei Meʿarot is the largest known site in Galilee where caves were adapted as dwellings, for water storage, as industrial installations, for burial and as hiding complexes. The current survey explored 104 caves in the area extending northwest of the Beit Ha-Galil hotel, above the Hazor Ha-Glilit industrial park and as far as the Bustan Ha-Galil neighborhood southeast of Hazor Ha-Glilit. The southern boundary of the survey was set at as the spot reputed to be the burial place of Honi Ha-Maʿagel ("Honi the circle-drawer," a 1st c. BCE Jewish scholar). Dozens of underground cavities were documented; thirty exhibit the characteristic features of hiding-complexes while seven others lack some of these features. The entrances to most of the cavities are hewn from inside water cisterns or burial caves. They include narrow passages typically found in hiding complexes. In most cases, the original purpose of the cavities was discontinued when they were converted into hiding places. Prominent examples of this are the plastered cisterns rendered obsolete by passages hewn in their walls. The same is true in the burial caves, cut into with absolutely no regard for their original purpose. The important discovery of numerous underground cavities at ʿIyei Meʿarot, some of which were used as hiding complexes, shows that the phenomenon extended to this part of Upper Galilee as well. Below is a detailed description of the ten hiding complexes at ʿIyei Meʿarot (8–17).

21 See Shivti'el and Stepansky 2013:241–266.

22 See Guérin 1880, vol. 7:252.

23 See Ilan 1991a:50.

24 See Smithline 2006 [accessed 21 June 2016].

‘Iyei Me‘arot Cave Survey

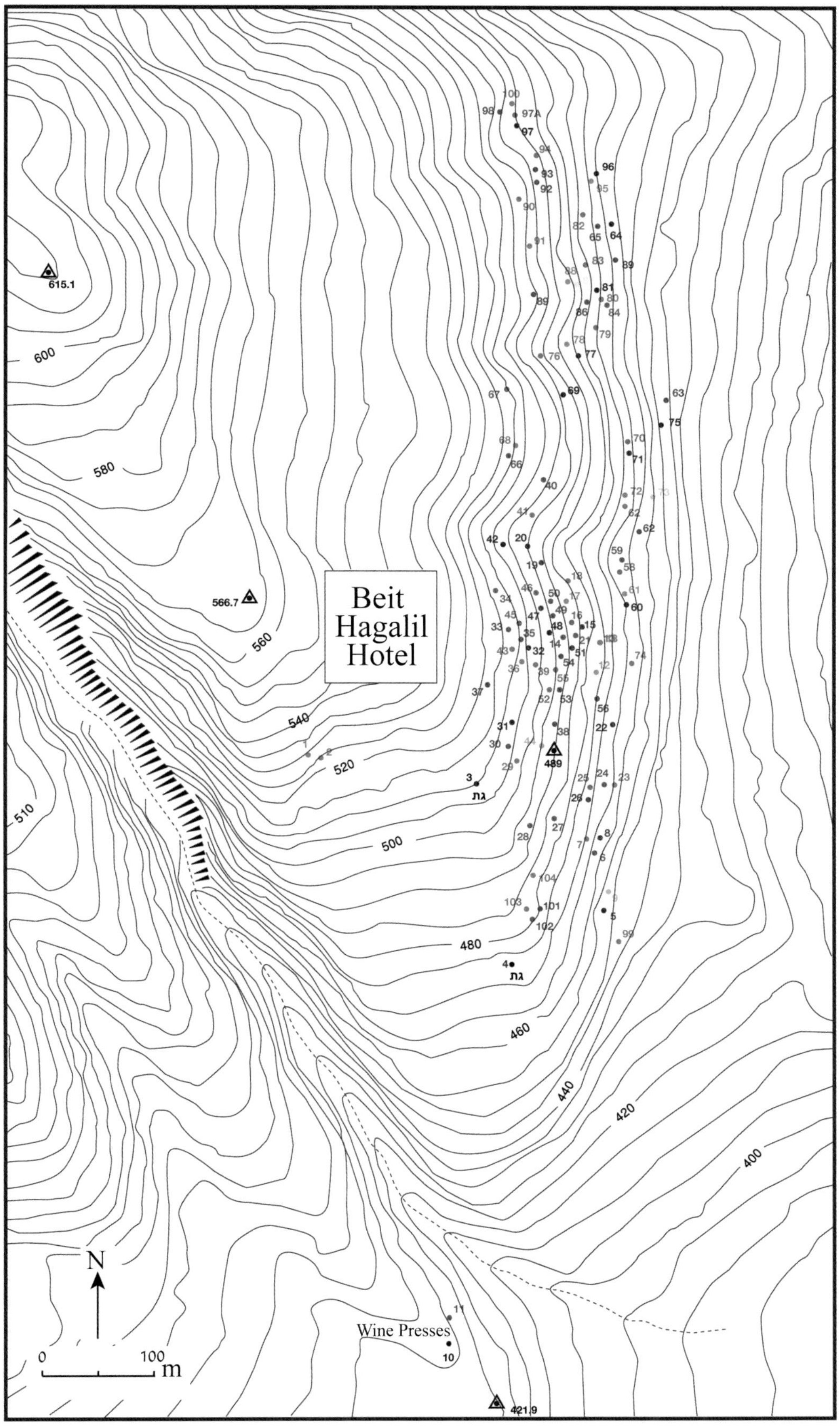

Map 39: ‘Iyei Me‘arot, distribution map of caves

8. 'Iyei Me'arot, Complex 1 (Cave 9) (map ref. 200855/265750)

Fig. 72: 'Iyei Me'arot 2

A survey conducted on behalf of the Israel Antiquities Authority in 1966 noted the discovery of a passage entrance in one of the caves. Tepper and Shachar tried unsuccessfully to identify this complex in 1983.[25] They did however discover another complex leading out of a cave with an arched entrance containing a door. In the walls of the cave, five hewn openings are now blocked by modern construction. One of these leads to a passage 2.2 m long. Beside the first cave is another cave, hewn in the form of a square chamber and containing a number of alcoves and openings that lead to blocked passages. Two of the openings lead to parallel passages about 3 m long that meet at the end. A third opening leads to a passage that was only explored from its other end and is about 3.5 m long. The current survey identified the underground cavity and measured it again. The entrance is rectangular (1.8 × 2 m) and a mortise is carved on the outside. The walls and arch of the entrance suggest that it is a burial cave. The cave is joined via a passage to another burial cave, which is full of earth. Each cave has a hewn passage leading to the surface. The passages were cut behind the alcoves, forming a kind of continuation of the burial niche that predated the hiding complex. This structure, therefore, probably represents a burial cave converted into a hiding place. The arched entrance and the deep frame hewn beneath it were designed to hold a square seal-stone similar to those in burial caves in Jerusalem and Judea.[26]

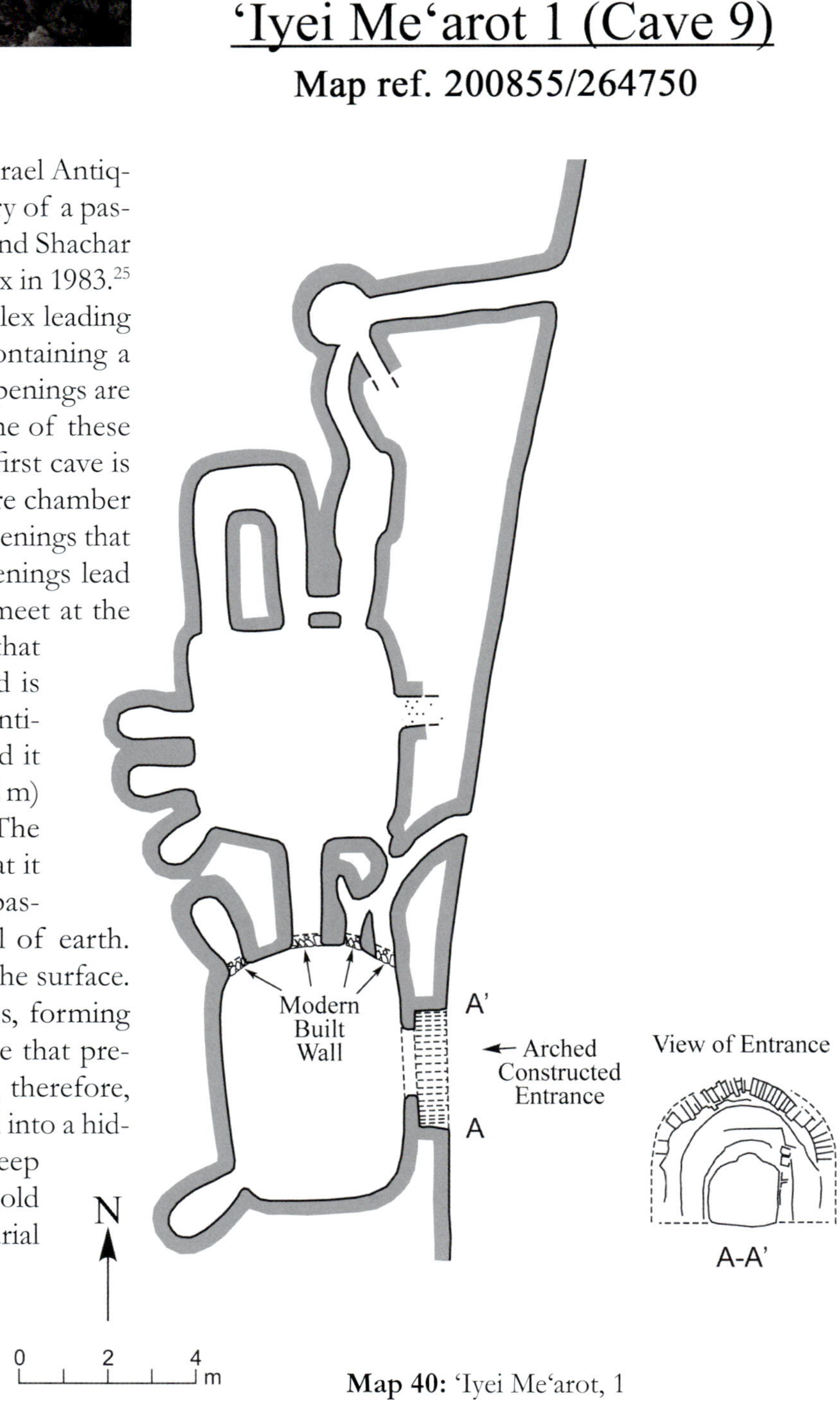

Map 40: 'Iyei Me'arot, 1

25 See Tepper and Shachar 1987b:299–300.
26 Kloner and Zissu 2005:129.

9. 'Iyei Me'arot, Complex 2 (Caves 28–28A) (Map ref. 200770/265833)

The cavity is entered through a roughly hewn arched opening 1.5 m high and 0.5 m wide. The cave consists of a chamber measuring 5 × 7 m and up to 2.5 m high. A blocked passage with an exposed entrance (0.35 × 0.55 m) was discovered in the south wall of the chamber. The form and dimensions of the entrance are characteristic of hiding passages. A passage with a 0.8 × 1.7 m entrance was found in the west wall of the chamber and can be crawled along for about 7 m, where six niches for oil lamps are visible. The passage, sloping upward at 25 degrees, leads to another cavity (5 × 9 m). An arched opening reaches another cavity (3 × 3 m) leading out to the south-facing side of the hill (28B). Although this complex lacks some of the characteristic features of a typical hiding complex, it does appear to have been used as one.

10. 'Iyei Me'arot, Complex 3 (Cave 54) (Map ref. 200803/265944)

This underground cavity bears typical characteristics of a hiding complex although it is far from sophisticated since the entrance is directly via a gap cut in the northwest face of a rock wall. The entrance, which has been enlarged by a rock fall, is 2 × 5 m and 2 m high and leads directly into an irregularly shaped chamber (4 × 5 m, height 2.5 m). The chamber is covered with collapsed rocks and its north end contains a wall (width 1 m) built of dressed fieldstones that reaches the roof of the chamber. Beside the wall, at the north end of the chamber, an entrance was hewn (0.4 × 0.5 m, length 6 m). After the entrance, the passage widens, makes a 70-degree bend, and leads to a small rectangular chamber measuring 3 × 4 m and 1.5 m high. A round, 0.6 m diameter opening hewn in the floor of the chamber provides access to a bell-shaped pit 2 m in diameter and 1.7 m deep. A few potsherds were recovered from the bottom of the pit, four of which date to the Early Roman period. Another passage, now blocked with earth, is visible on the south side of the pit.

Fig. 73: 'Iyei Me'arot 3

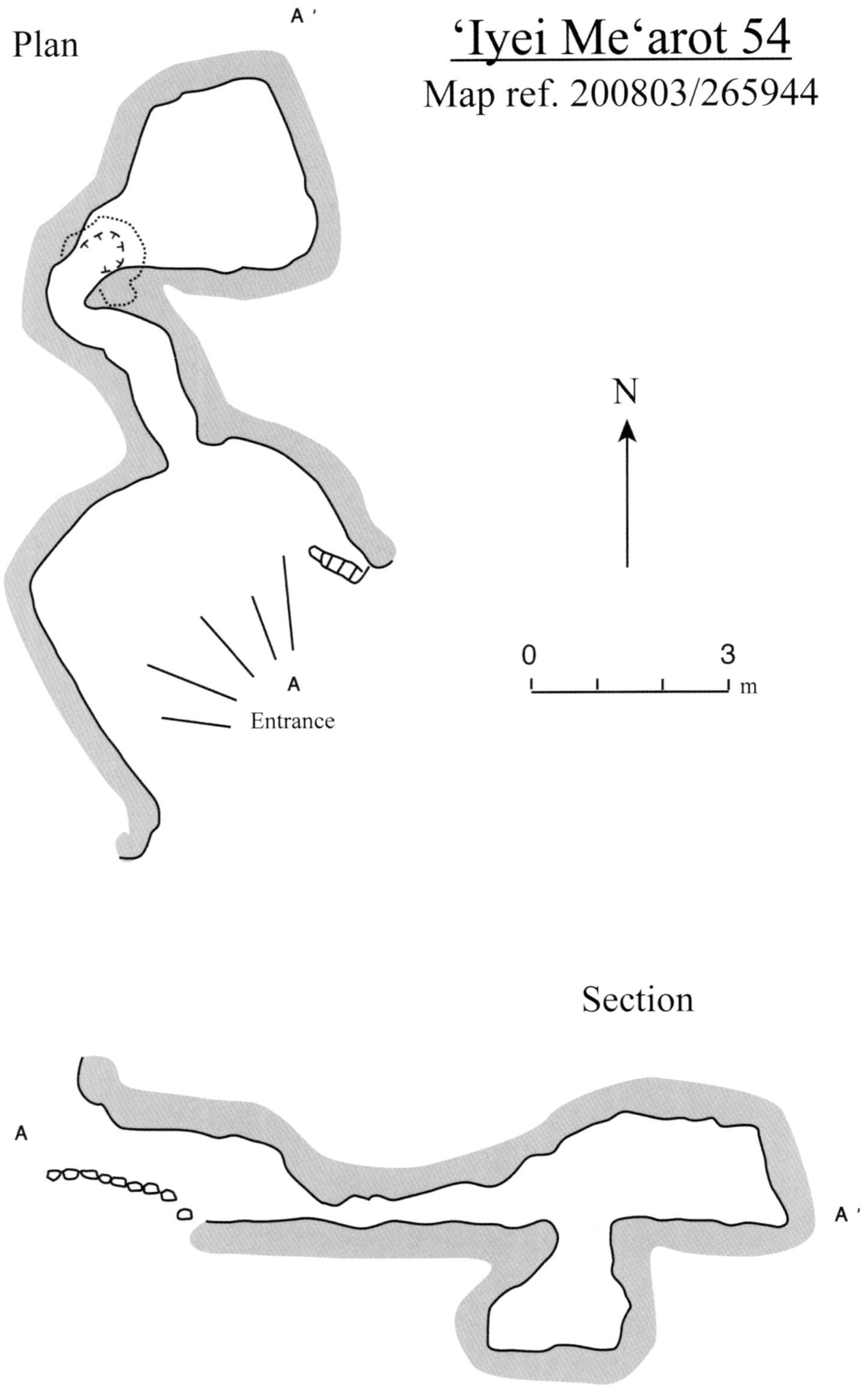

Map 41: 'Iyei Me'arot 2

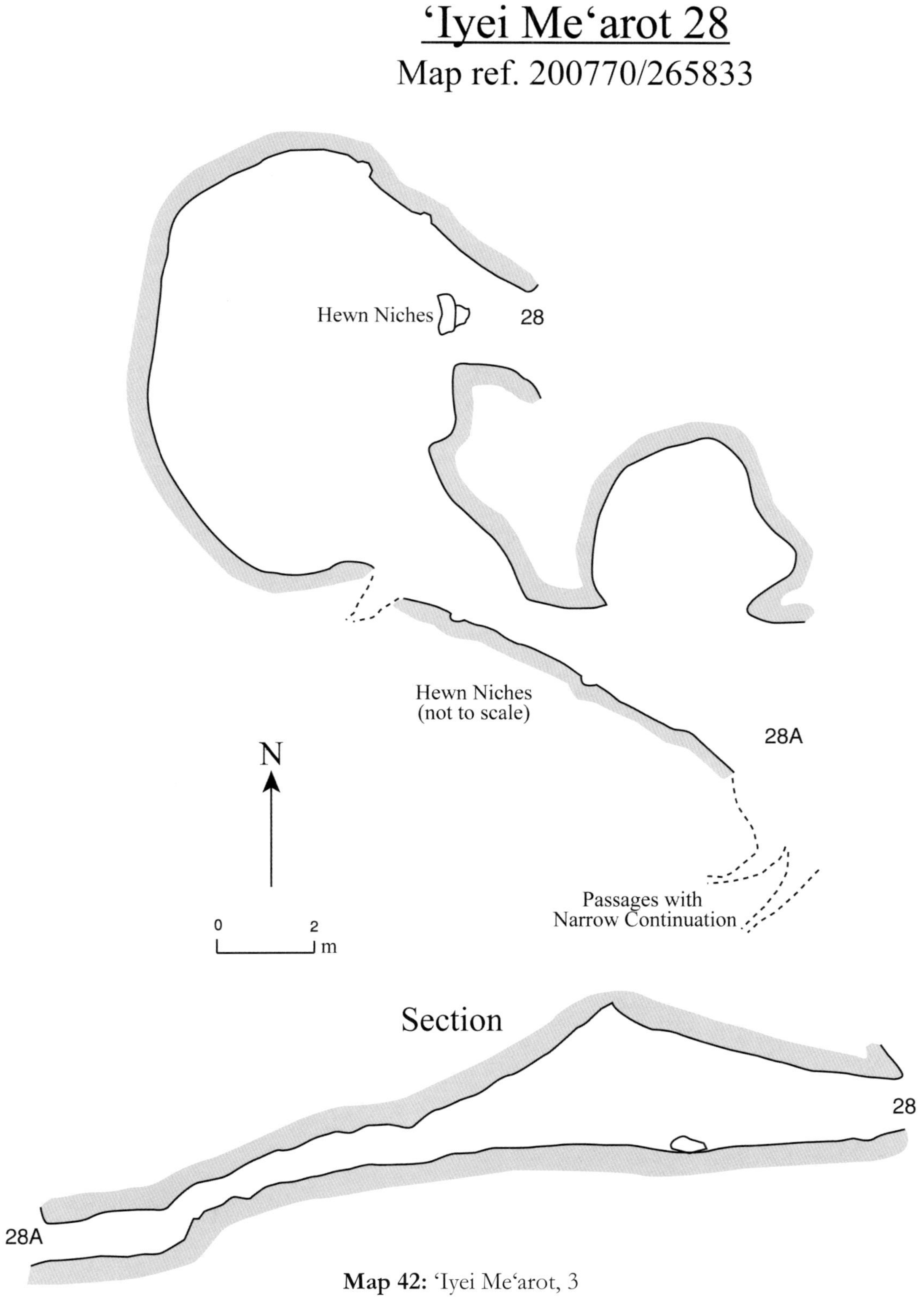

Map 42: 'Iyei Me'arot, 3

11. 'Iyei Me'arot, Complex 4 (Cave 69) (Map ref. 200814/266246)

This is a burial cave with six hewn niches. The cave entrance is square (0.6 × 0.6 m) and meticulously finished. The cave includes a rock-cut cavity (3.5 × 4 m, height 1.5 m) with burial niches hewn on all four sides. A rounded opening (0.50 × 0.55 m) hewn above the south niche leads to a passage about 1 m above the current level of the burial chamber's silted-up floor. The passage is roughly 4 m long and leads to a 4 × 7.5 m cavity. Human skeletal remains were discovered scattered along it. Two more unfinished burial niches are located at its south end. The passage continues west and branches into two after about 9 m. One branch continues for another 2.5 m until it is blocked by a collapse of stones and earth and the other (0.4 × 0.5 m in section) continues for c. 3 m until it too becomes blocked with earth. A gap cut in the side of one of the unfinished niches in the north wall opens into an eastward-leading passage. Its entrance measures 0.30 × 0.35 m and the 3 m long passage leads to a central cavity. This is probably an example of a necropolis that was subsequently converted into a hiding complex, since it is unlikely that robbers would have made the effort to cut such a long passage. It should be emphasized that the west hiding complex was cut in such a way as to leave the burial complex intact, but broke into the unfinished burial cavity when the cavity was converted into a hiding place. In contrast, the north passage may have been hewn by robbers; its dimensions are different and it was hewn with no consideration for the burial niche.

Fig. 74: 'Iyei Me'arot 4

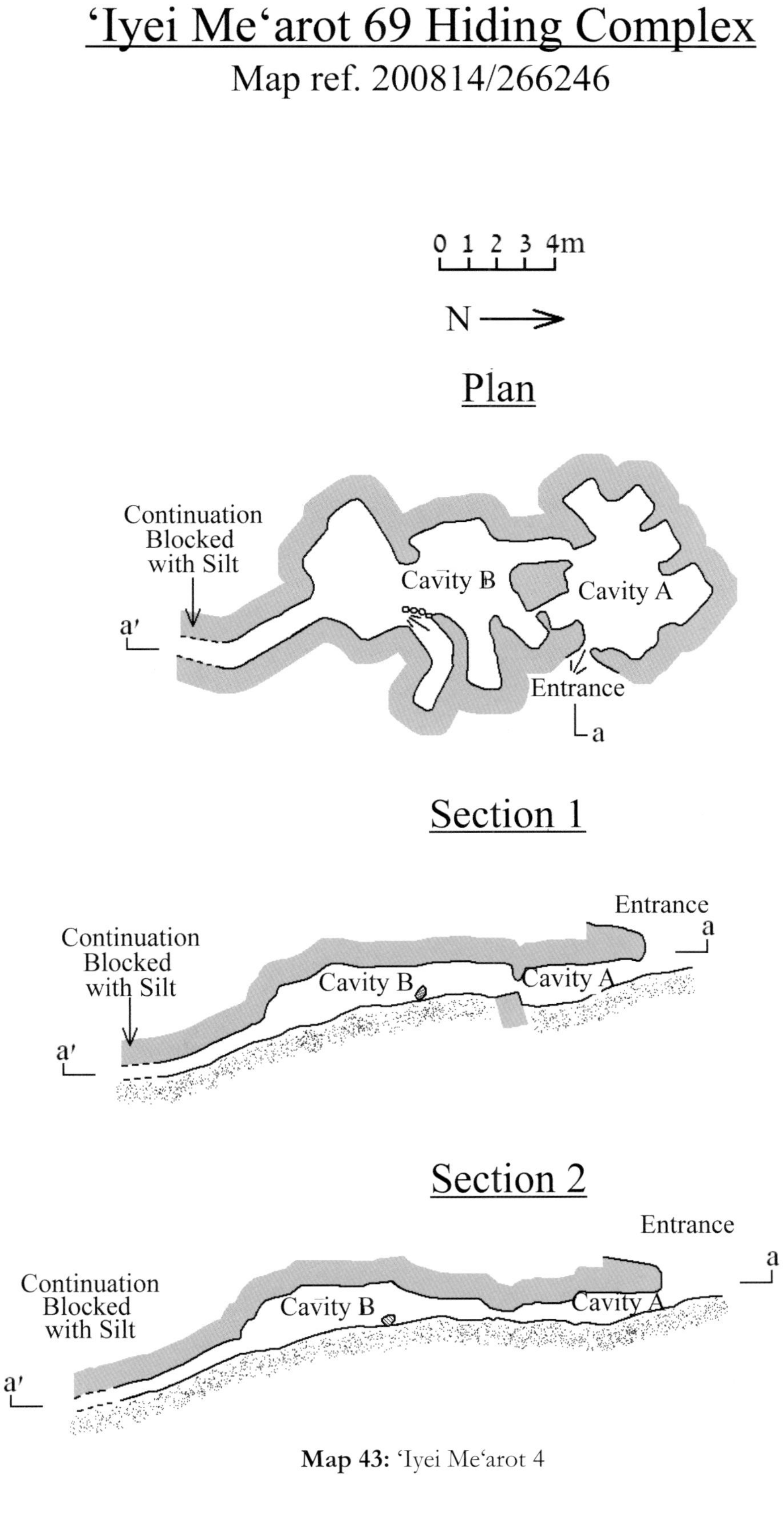

Map 43: 'Iyei Me'arot 4

12. ʽIyei Meʽarot, Complex 5 (Caves 70, 71) (Map ref. 200864/266191)

Cave 70 is a large dwelling cave with an entrance that either collapsed or was cut at a later stage. Based on the quantity of potsherds and installations it contains, it was probably last used during the Late Islamic period. The cave has an irregularly shaped entrance (1.6 × 3.3 m, height 2.6 m; leading to a rock-hewn chamber of 9.5 × 11 m) with a natural opening in its roof that can only be reached with difficulty. Three niches that are not burial niches are hewn in the south wall of the chamber. The dimensions of two of these are 0.50 × 0.55 m wide and 0.6 m deep, and the third niche measures 0.5 × 1 m wide and 0.2 m deep. A hewn passage entrance (0.3 × 0.35 m) is visible in the west wall leading to a 3.5 m long passage that is blocked by a rock fall. The passage probably continues toward another cave (Cave 71) located directly to the south of this one and consisting of two hewn and plastered dwelling chambers and two entrances. The north entrance (0.8 × 1.4 m) appears to have been the original entrance. The south entrance (0.9 × 1.6 m) is made of ashlars and leads to the southern chamber (7 × 8 m, height 2.1 m). The chamber walls are plastered and it was obviously used as a dwelling; two niches of identical size (0.5 × 0.9 m) are hewn in its south corner and a Muslim tomb is built in the center. A gap cut in the north wall of the chamber leads to a second room (6 × 7 m) whose west wall is plastered with a trough built beside it. This room contains a narrow, cupboard-shaped feeding trough that was probably used by local farmers in recent times. A passage in the north wall of this chamber has a 0.5 m square opening and continues north for 2.5 m, where another passage branching off to the east is blocked. The main passage continues north for 11 m until it encounters a stone collapse. Despite the collapse, the passage obviously links up with a passage coming from the dwelling cave.

This would appear to be a hiding complex joining the two caves together. The caves were used in the Islamic period, but it is not clear whether the interconnecting passage was also used at this time. Although the complex does not exhibit the typical characteristics of a hiding complex, the crawl passage between the two chambers and the breach made by the second passage suggest that hiding complexes were cut into these caves.

Fig.75: ʽIyei Meʽarot, 5

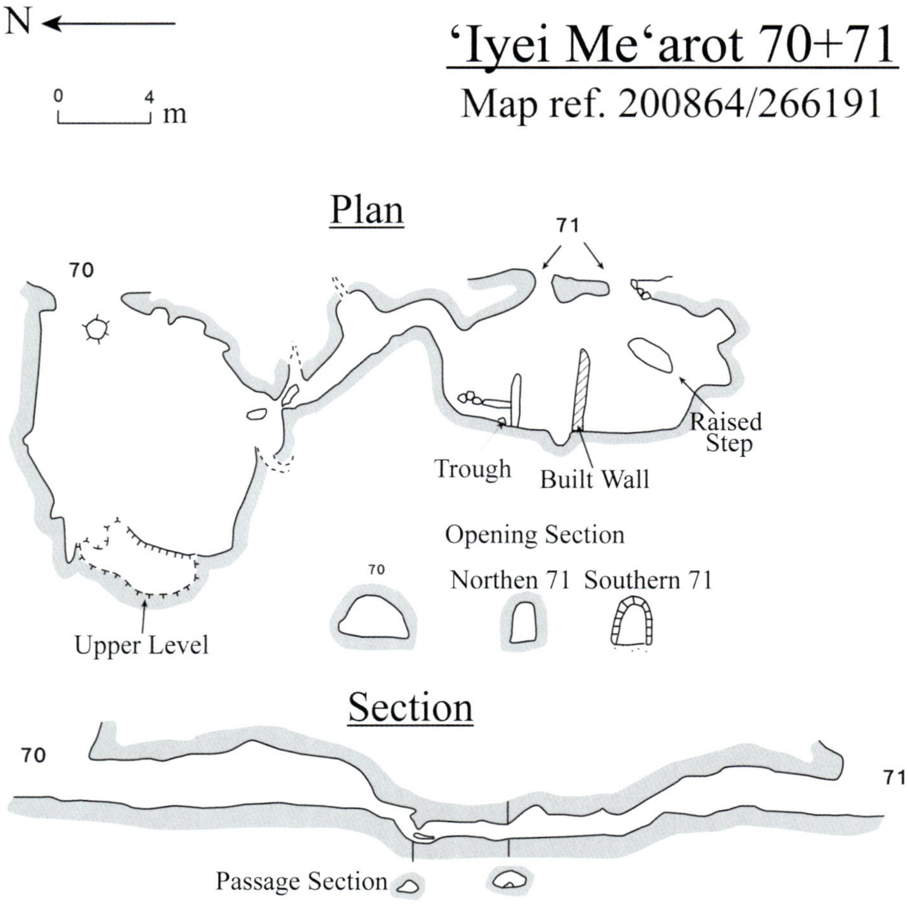

Map 44: ʽIyei Meʽarot 5

13. 'Iyei Me'arot, Complex 6 (Caves 74, 74A) (Map ref. 200876/265967)

This complex was hewn into a notch-shaped rock slope, at the bottom of which is an irregularly shaped arched entrance (0.9 × 3 m, height 1 m). The opening leads to a large chamber (8 × 12 m, height 2 m). The chamber's south wall contains a built stone wall in front of an arched opening. A gap cut in the chamber's west wall leads to a large water cistern (c. 6 × 7.5 m, c. 4 m high) coated with light plaster. The bottom of the chamber is covered with rocks that have fallen through the hole. Early Roman potsherds are embedded in the plaster in the southeast part of the cistern. The upper part of the chamber has four openings; three are blocked with basalt slabs and an entrance to additional chambers is visible through the fourth opening (0.5 × 1.3) which is 3 m above the silted-up floor. Climbing to the upper chamber, we discovered that it measures 2 × 3 m and is 1.8 high. An arched opening (0.4 × 0.6 m) hewn in the west wall of the chamber leads to a 3 m long passage until it becomes blocked with earth. By squeezing through a 0.5 m diameter opening hewn in the south wall of the chamber, it is possible to reach a hewn shaft filled with earth and collapsed stones. Scaling the collapse for about two meters, one reaches another hewn cavity measuring 5 × 10 m. In the west wall of this cavity (Cave 74A), 2.5 m above the floor, is a round hewn opening 0.5 m in diameter that can be reached with a ladder, thus entering another plastered water cistern (2.8 × 3 m). The lower third of the cistern is coated with small stones covered in plaster. Two holes in its roof are sealed with basalt slabs. This is probably a hiding complex that was built in two stages: In the first stage, a concealed passage leading to the water source was hewn from a dwelling house. In the second stage, a passage was cut that rendered the water cistern obsolete and an opening hewn in the floor of the cistern led to a large chamber. Another opening from this chamber descends to the floor of an additional water cistern. Both cavities were no longer used to store water and were probably used as hiding places (a similar phenomenon is found at Horvat Mishtah, Tur'an, and Zippori). The present exit to the surface was probably made at a later stage.

Fig. 76: 'Iyei Me'arot, 6

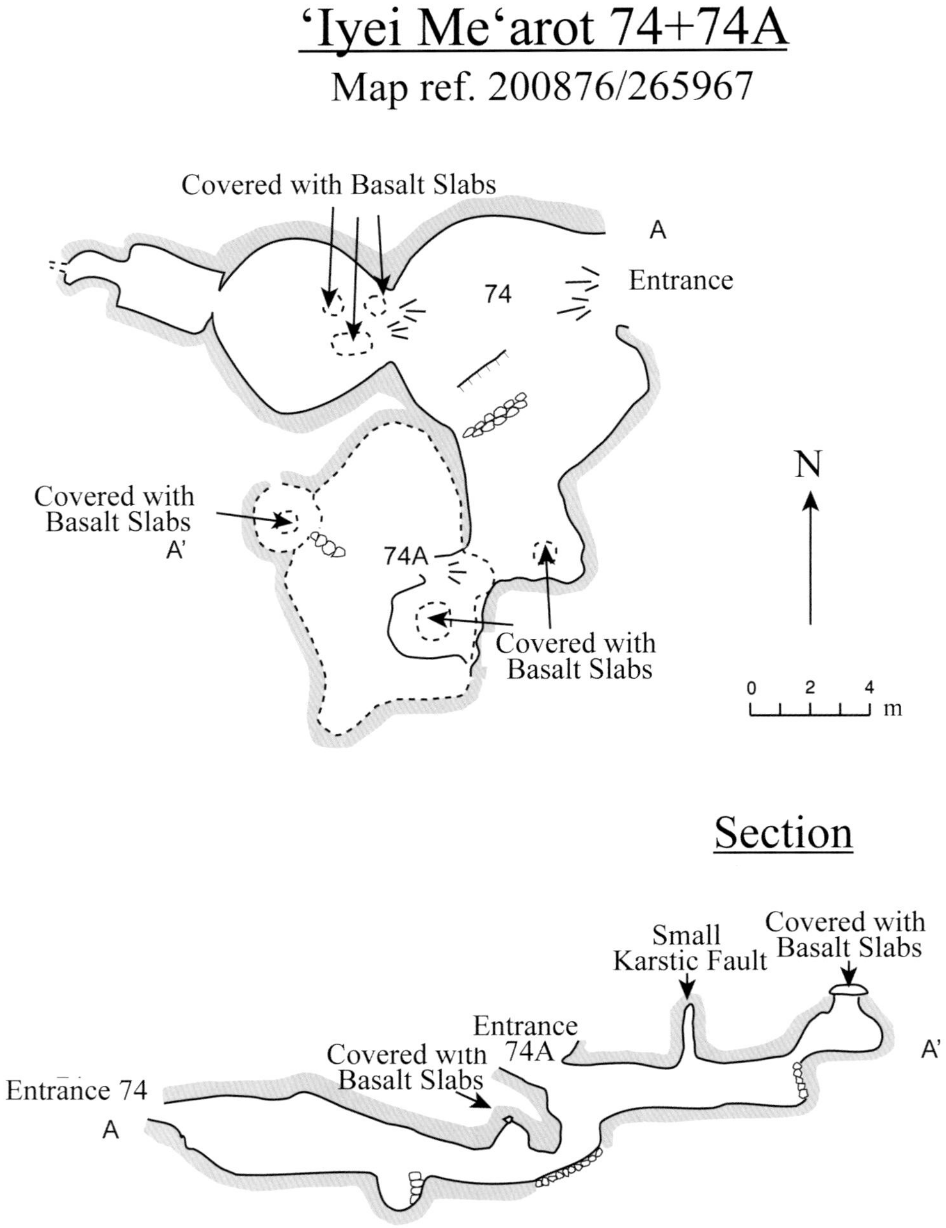

Map 45: 'Iyei Me'arot 6

14. 'Iyei Me'arot, Complex 7 (Cave 75)
(Map ref. 200905/266204)

This hiding complex is on two levels. Today, the entrance is via a trapezoidal opening (0.5 × 0.8 m) hewn in the east slope of the hill flanked by carved mortises in the rock face. A short entrance leads to a hewn chamber measuring 6 × 9 m. An alcove (2 × 3 m) hewn in the chamber's north wall has another, vaulted alcove beside it (4 × 5 m). In the center of a rectangular alcove (1.3 × 1.7 m) hewn in the south wall, an opening was cut (1.6 × 1 m) to provide access to the lower level where another chamber measures 12 × 15 m. A 12 m long passage (0.35 × 0.35 m in section) hewn into the west wall bends east and leads to another chamber (5 × 7 m). Another passage cut in the north wall of this room is now blocked with earth and measures 0.2 × 0.3 m at its entrance. Despite the multiple niches this is probably not a burial cave; built as a dwelling or underground storage complex, it was later converted into a hiding complex.

Fig. 77: 'Iyei Me'arot 7

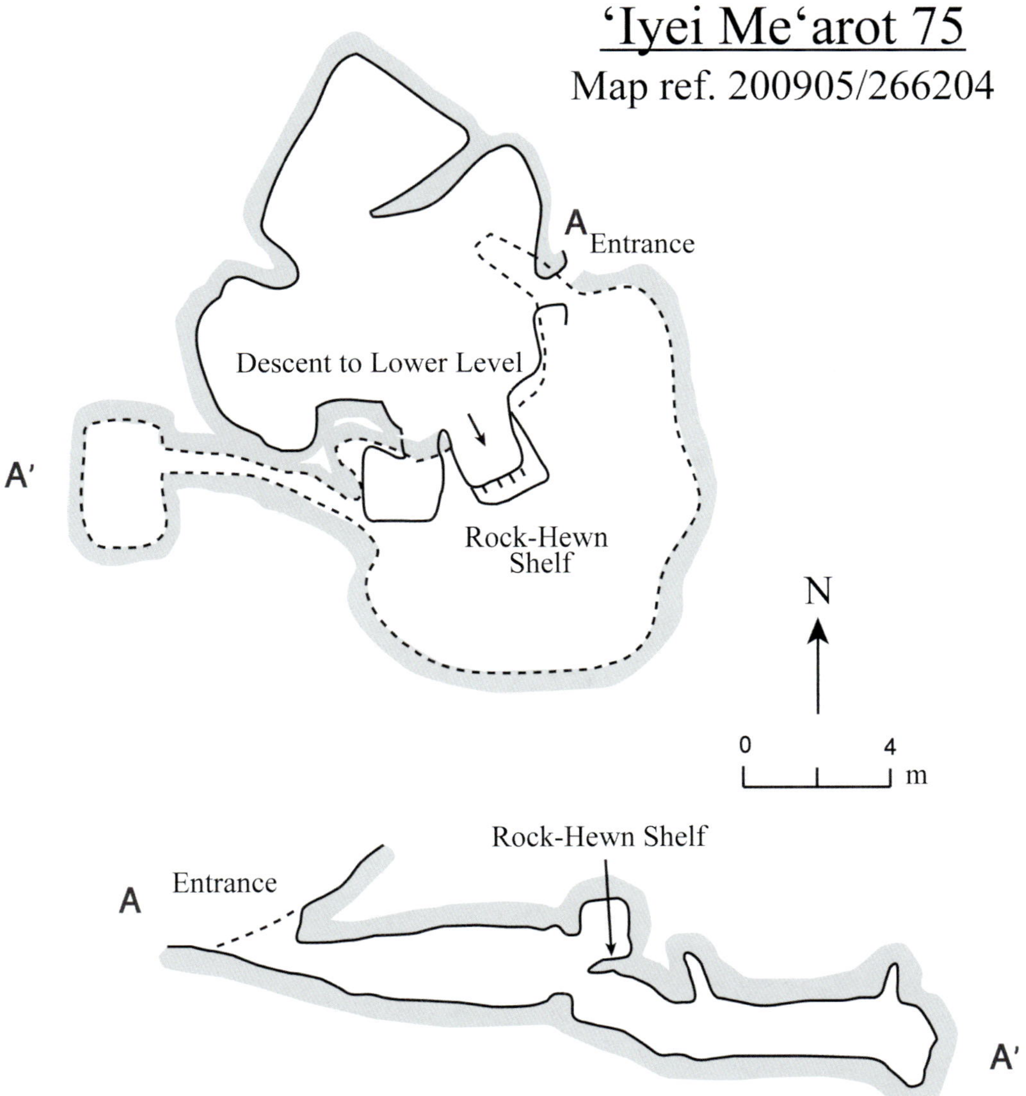

Map 46: 'Iyei Me'arot 7

15. 'Iyei Me'arot, Complex 8 (Cave 83)
(Map ref. 200829/266364)

This was originally a natural cave that was converted into a dwelling. The hewn entrance measures 0.43 × 0.62 m and a vertical channel 0.9 m long and c. 0.7 wide was cut in the rock face to its east. The channel reaches the entrance to the cave and was probably used as a gutter. The entrance leads to a large chamber (12 × 16 m) and from its east wall there is a passage (height 1 m, width 2 m) leading to a 7 × 9 m chamber, from where there is an exit to the surface via its collapsed east wall. A passage cut in the west wall of the chamber (0.35 × 0.35 in section, length c. 8 m) leads to a third chamber (5 × 8 m) that can now be reached via a narrow opening (0.3 × 0.45 m in section) about 10 m north of the original entrance to the hiding complex. Fragments of pottery and glass vessels were found in this cavity. The passage was evidently not designed to provide easy access between the chambers since, although it is exposed down to the natural rock, the third chamber can only be squeezed into on the stomach. This is probably another example of a dwelling cave containing a passage to a chamber used as a hiding place.

Fig. 78: 'Iyei Me'arot 8

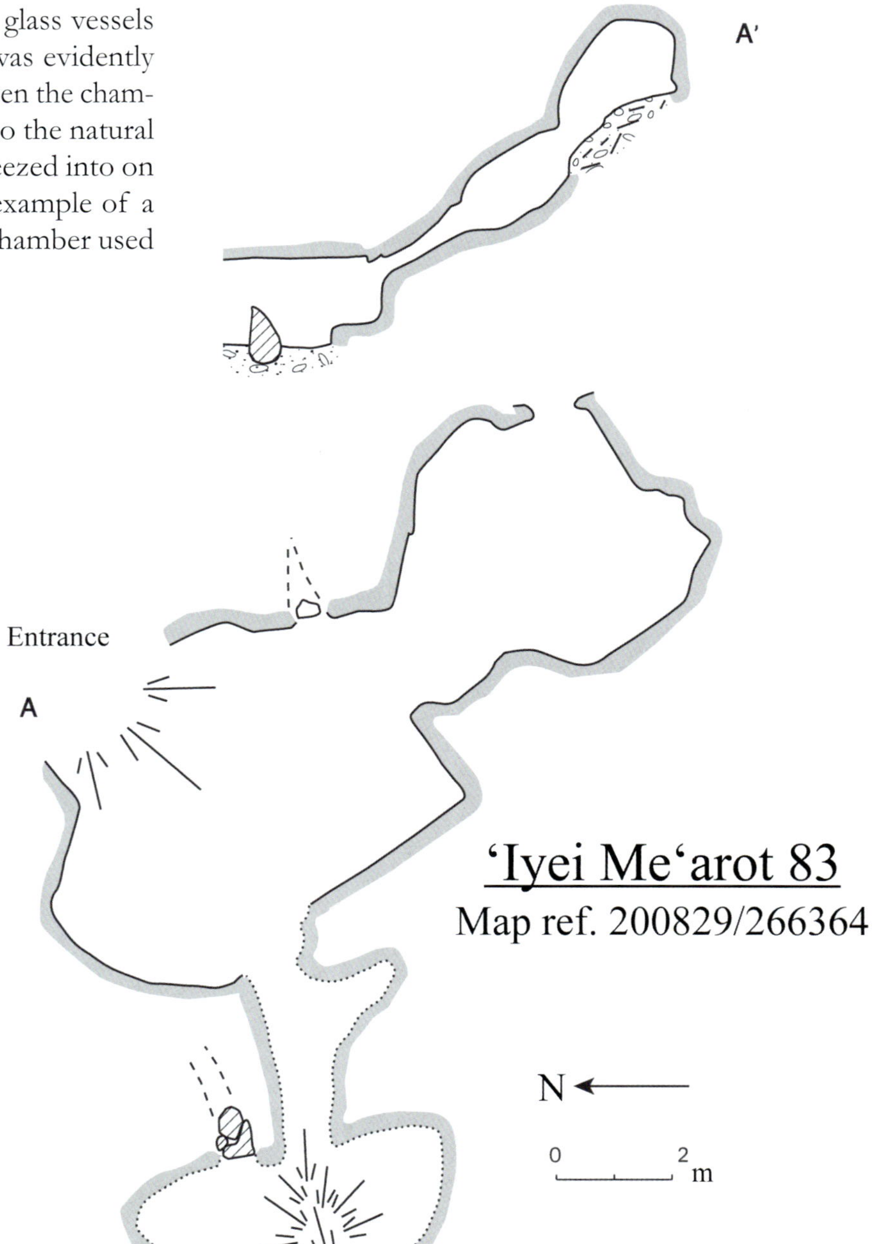

Map 47: 'Iyei Me'arot 8

16. 'Iyei Me'arot, Complex 9 (Cave 88)
(Map ref. 200815/266349)

This is another example of a burial cave possibly converted into a hiding complex. The entrance is not the original burial-cave entrance since it is very small (0.4 × 0.55 m). It is crudely hewn and leads to an irregularly shaped cavity measuring 5 × 7 m. The original entrance to the burial complex is located on the east side of the cave and is now blocked by a stone wall. The irregularly shaped cavity is not part of the burial cave either, and was probably added when the cave was converted into a refuge. In the north wall of the cavity, a hewn opening (0.35 × 0.5 m) leads to a 2.5 m long passage. The passage cuts into a burial niche (0.7 × 2 m). The main cavity of the burial cave (5 × 8 m) is entered via this niche and has six more hewn niches of the same size as the first. In the south wall of the burial chamber, the entrance to a hewn passage is blocked and an arched opening in the east wall is sealed with dressed building stones. Over the northwest burial niche, c. 0.5 m above the rock shelf, a hewn passage measures 0.4 × 0.4 m in section and 3 m long. The passage is simply finished and bends eastward, crossing above the burial niche before bending north to link up with a small chamber that is now inaccessible because the roof has caved in.

The conversion of burial caves into hiding complexes is discussed above. The passage over the west niche, which was obviously not hewn by robbers, suggests that this burial cave was also probably used as a hiding place.

Fig. 79: 'Iyei Me'arot 9

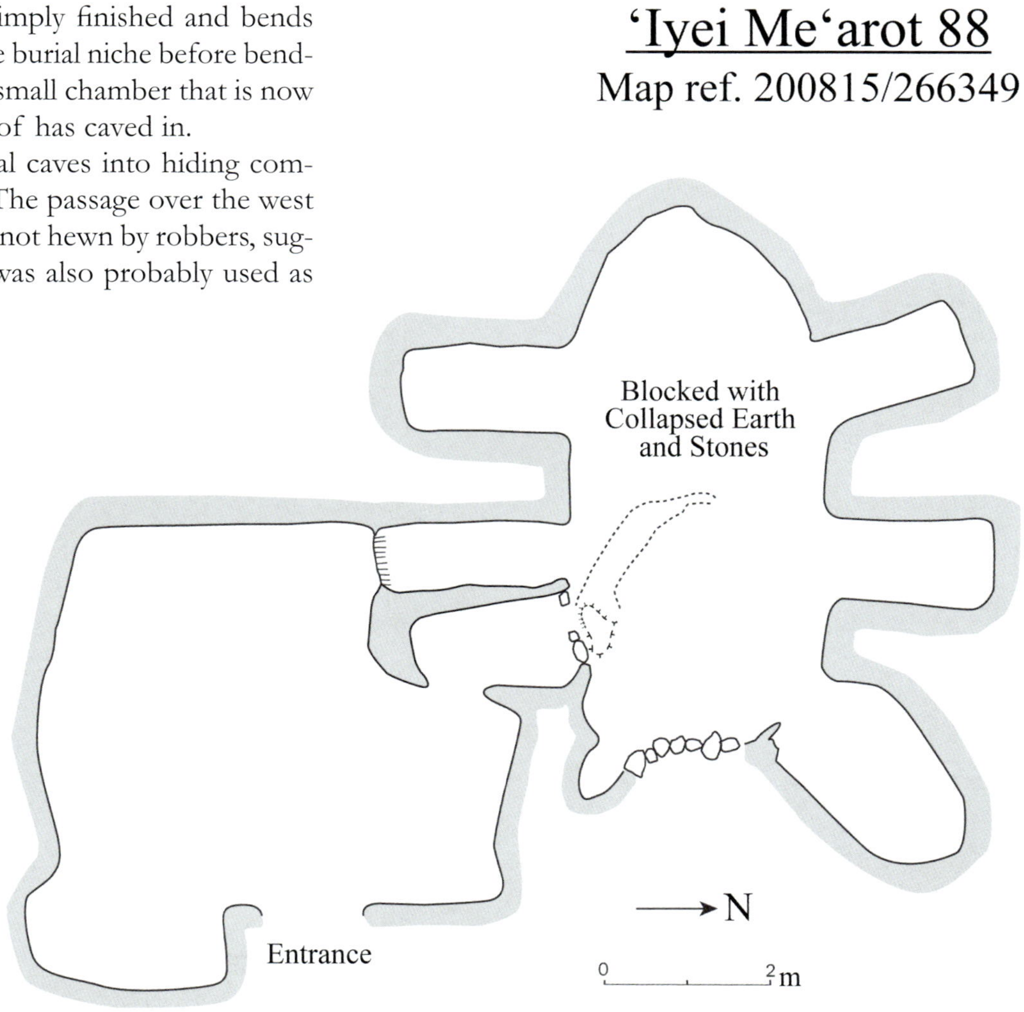

Map 48: 'Iyei Me'arot 9

17. ʿIyei Meʿarot, Complex 10 (Caves 97, 97A, 100) (Map ref. 200763/266505)

The entrance (0.6 × 0.6 m) is arched and expertly hewn and surrounded by a carved frame containing two boltholes at the sides. Based on the finely finished entrance, it may have been the start of a planned burial cave, or it may have been intentionally cut in this way to camouflage its true purpose. No burial niches were found in the cave, whose natural rock is fragile and crumbly and forms piles of white dust throughout the entire complex. The entrance leads to a small hewn chamber measuring 0.9 × 2.5 m and c. 1 m high. Four passages lead out of this chamber. One, cut in the northwest wall, is 7 m long and 0.2 × 0.8 m in section, branching off into another passage just beyond the entrance. The main passage turns north, while the side passage continues east and then north. The second passage (0.30 × 0.35 m in section) is a tight squeeze. The two passages reach another cavity (Cave 97A) that is 5.5 × 7.8 m in size and has an exit to the surface. A niche was hewn in its east wall and a passage cut into its northwest wall is impassable but leads north and evidently reaches another small cavity (Cave 100) that is accessible via an opening formed when the rock above it collapsed. The third passage, hewn to the southwest of the main cavity, is 0.3 × 0.35 in section and its entrance is blocked by a collapse. The fourth passage begins near the north side of the entrance to the complex. It measures 0.2 × 0.5 m in section and can be crawled along for about 5 m before it is blocked by a collapse.

Summary of the Hiding Complexes at ʿIyei Meʿarot

Ten underground cavities resembling hiding complexes were surveyed at ʿIyei Meʿarot; three of them (Complexes 2, 5, 8) lack the usual characteristics of hiding places. The find of such a large number of hiding complexes at ʿIyei Meʿarot shows that the conversion of caves into hiding complexes here was part of an extensive and organized operation involving the entire local population. Stone vessels found at the site, together with its proximity to the Jewish settlement of Farʿam near Hazor Ha-Glilit, show that it was a Jewish community. The rough and hastily hewn nature of the complexes, the elimination of existing installations and burials, and the pottery recovered indicate that most of those surveyed date from the Roman period.

Fig. 80: ʿIyei Meʿarot 10

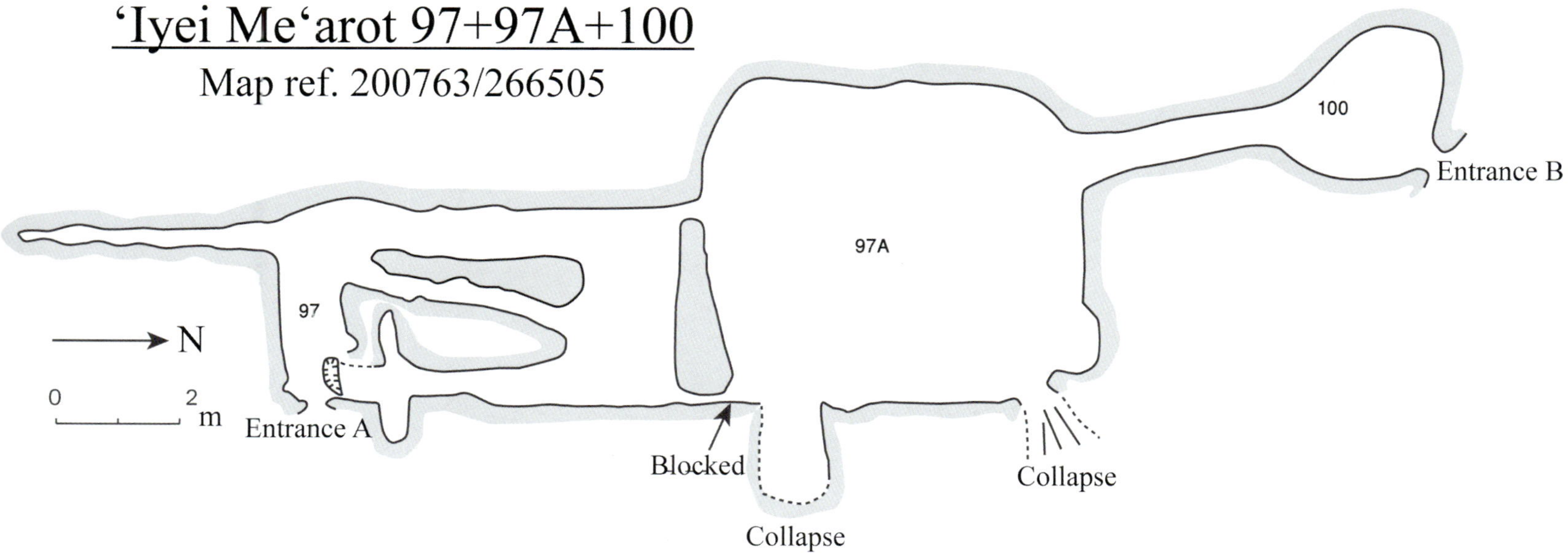

Map 49: 'Iyei Me'arot 10

18. Mount Hazon (Hazzur) (Map ref. 187472/256837)

The settlement of Hazon (Hazzur) was built on the upper third of the western slopes of Mount Hazon. The site has views of the northern rim of Beit Ha-Kerem Valley, Hananiya Valley and Kefar Hananiya. Near the top of the hill, the remains of the ancient settlement are visible and include water cisterns and caves. Victor Guérin identified the site as Khirbet Hazzur and recorded a square watchtower on its summit made of roughly dressed stones with no bonding material and traces of a wall.[27] Parts of the wall encircling the summit were re-discovered in the current survey. The hill contains ancient water cisterns and various installations; a hiding complex was discovered on its southern fringes. The complex was excavated in 1968 by Dan Bahat before the hiding complexes in the Judean foothills had been studied.[28] The structure begins inside a water cistern where numerous pottery vessels dating to the Great Revolt were recovered. Another breach cut in the side of the cistern and rendering it obsolete leads to an 8 m long passage terminating in a small pit, which Bahat did not finish excavating. A pottery roof-tile found on the passage floor bears the stamp of the Sixth Legion. Although Bahat found first-century CE pottery, he proposed dating the complex to the 2nd c. CE

Fig. 81: Mount Hazon

27 See Guérin 1880, vol. 7:225.
28 See Bahat 1974:165–167.

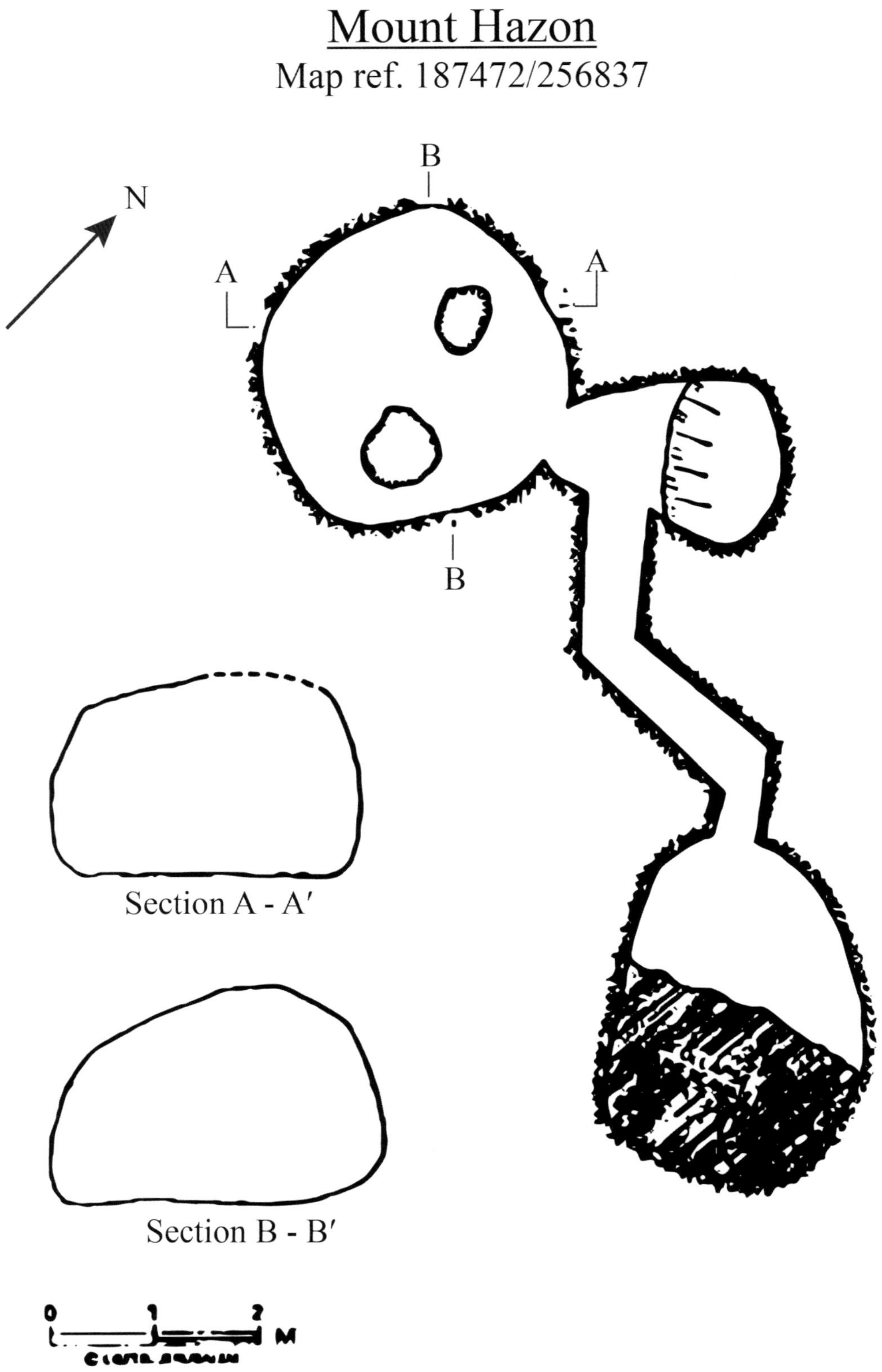

Map 50: Mount Hazon

19. Horvat Huqoq 1, Yaquq (Map ref. 195328/254600)

The ruins of the Arab village of Yaquq, built over the remains of the ancient Jewish settlement of Huqoq, are spread over two adjacent hillocks. Traces of an ancient settlement cover c. 30 dunams (c. 7.5 acres) and include a synagogue with a unique mosaic floor. The site also houses ritual baths, architectural elements, burials, and a large number of agricultural installations. Cliff refuges have also been found nearby.[29]

The first hiding complex was discovered at Huqoq in 1982 by Gil Darin – a youngster from Kibbutz Huqoq – and it was surveyed and mapped in 1986.[30] I myself surveyed the site and re-mapped the complex, discovering another hiding complex described below. The first complex is roughly hewn and is entered via a round vaulted pit c. 1.4 m in diameter; an opening at the bottom of its west wall leads to a rock-hewn chamber containing entrances to two more chambers. A passage hewn in the south chamber leads to a third chamber, from where a narrow passage makes a 90-degree turn toward a round water cistern coated in gray plaster and about 1.5 m deep. From its silted-up floor, one can crawl into two parallel passages. One of these climbs up until it is almost at the surface and the other leads to the first hewn chamber where there is a way out of the complex. The passages are equipped with oil-lamp niches. The hiding complex also produced a few Byzantine potsherds.[31]

29 On Huqoq see Chapter 2. Thanks to Prof. Jodi Magness for permission to use unpublished data.

30 See Tepper and Shachar 1987b:311 n. 51.

31 See Tepper and Shachar 1987b:311–312.

Fig. 82: Huqoq, Hiding Complex 1

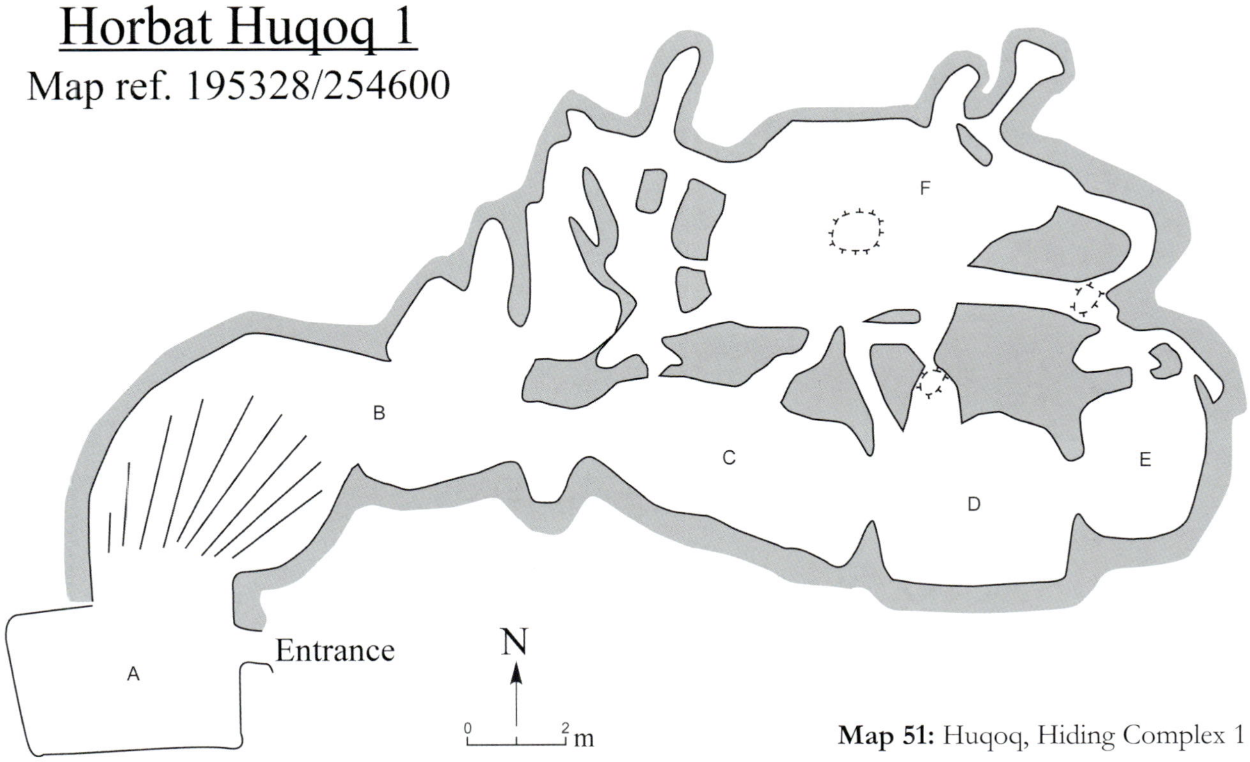

Map 51: Huqoq, Hiding Complex 1

20. Huqoq, Horvat Huqoq water cistern:
The synagogue system, 2 (Map ref. 195250/254527)

The complex was discovered in the center of the ancient ruined settlement of Huqoq, about 150 m northwest of a lone date palm on Huqoq Hill. It was discovered by myself and the late Ahikam Amichai of the ICRC in 2006 and is hewn from inside a plastered water cistern c. 8 m deep and 1.5 m in diameter. During the first archaeological excavation here in 2011, directed by Jodi Magness, the late David Amit and Shua Kisselevitz, the water cistern was discovered next to the excavation area where the remains of a public building had been exposed. A subsequent excavation season in 2012 uncovered a synagogue with a unique mosaic floor. I took this opportunity to excavate the water cistern and clear the earth fill from the complex. Four passages were found at the bottom of the cistern: The west passage, hewn in the middle of the cistern, is plastered and can be crawled along for 17 m until it becomes blocked up with earth. The northwest passage is 8 m long and leads directly underneath the floor of the synagogue, ending in a shaft with steps that climb up to emerge in the center of the synagogue's main hall, exactly beneath the mosaic floor. From the middle of this passage, another passage was hewn that turns south and is 7 m long, also leading to the surface. The 5 m long southeast passage reaches another large water cistern whose roof is deliberately blocked with a large stone. This water cistern evidently ceased to be used to store water when the hiding complex was made. The plaster in the west complex shows that there was a later attempt to reuse the water cistern. In this instance, there are two likely assumptions: Either the hiding complex was hewn before the synagogue's construction – at the time of

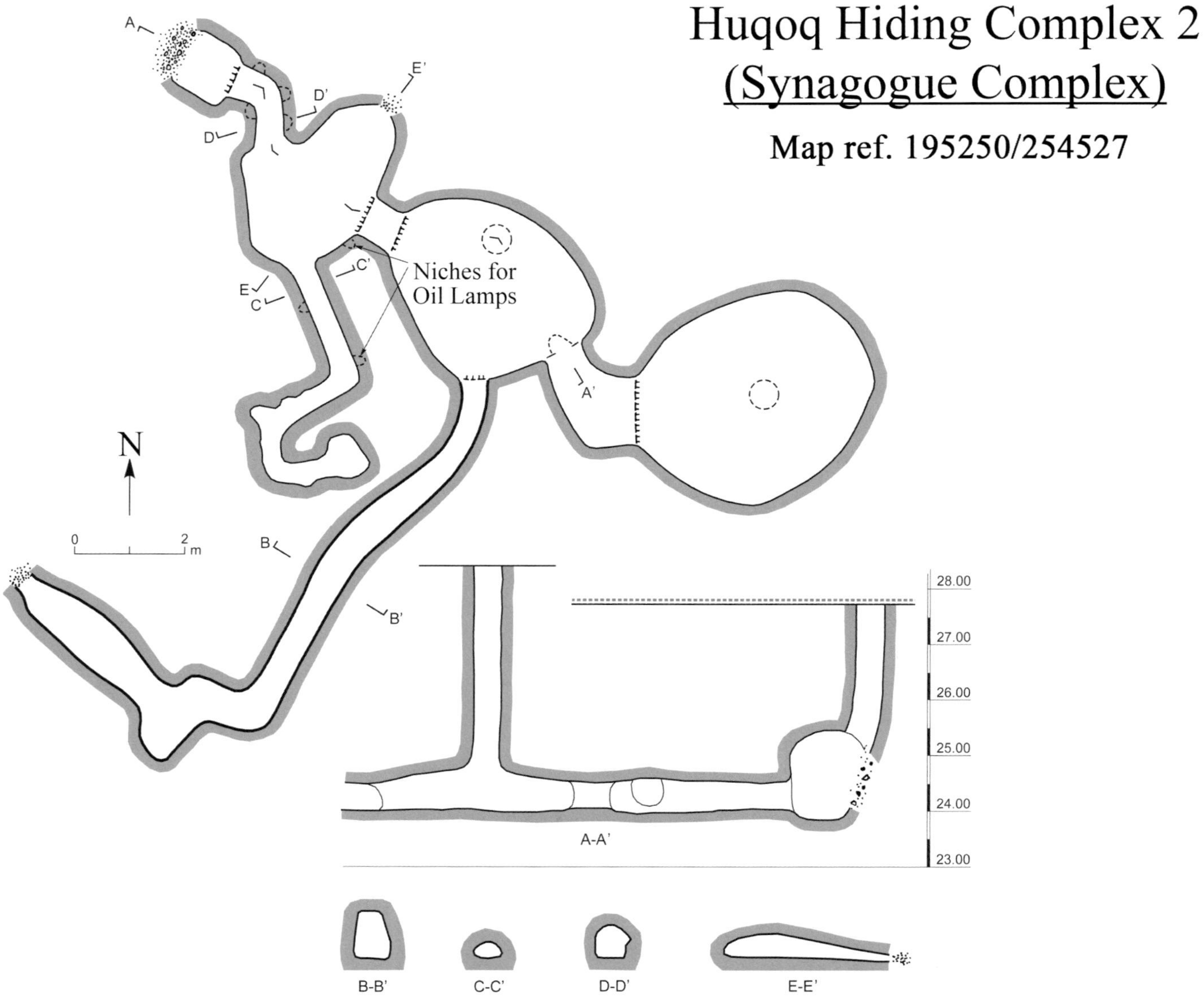

Map 52: Huqoq, Hiding Complex 2, synagogue complex

the Great Revolt or afterward – and the synagogue was built over it with the intent of using the hiding complex as a refuge, should it be needed. Alternatively, the hiding complex may have been made at the same time as the synagogue as part of the settlement's emergency defenses, continuing into the Byzantine period. Plaster traces found in some of the passages need to be analyzed in order to establish the use made of the cistern and the hiding passages in later periods. A similar phenomenon is known both from the settlement of Meroth and from synagogues at Eshtamo'a, Horvat Susiya and Ma'on in the southern Hebron hills. David Amit, who has studied hiding complexes in the southern Hebron hills, believes that they predate the synagogues there and were incorporated in the architectural complex in case of subsequent defensive needs.[32]

32 See Amit 2003:186.

Fig. 83: Huqoq, Hiding Complex 2, synagogue complex

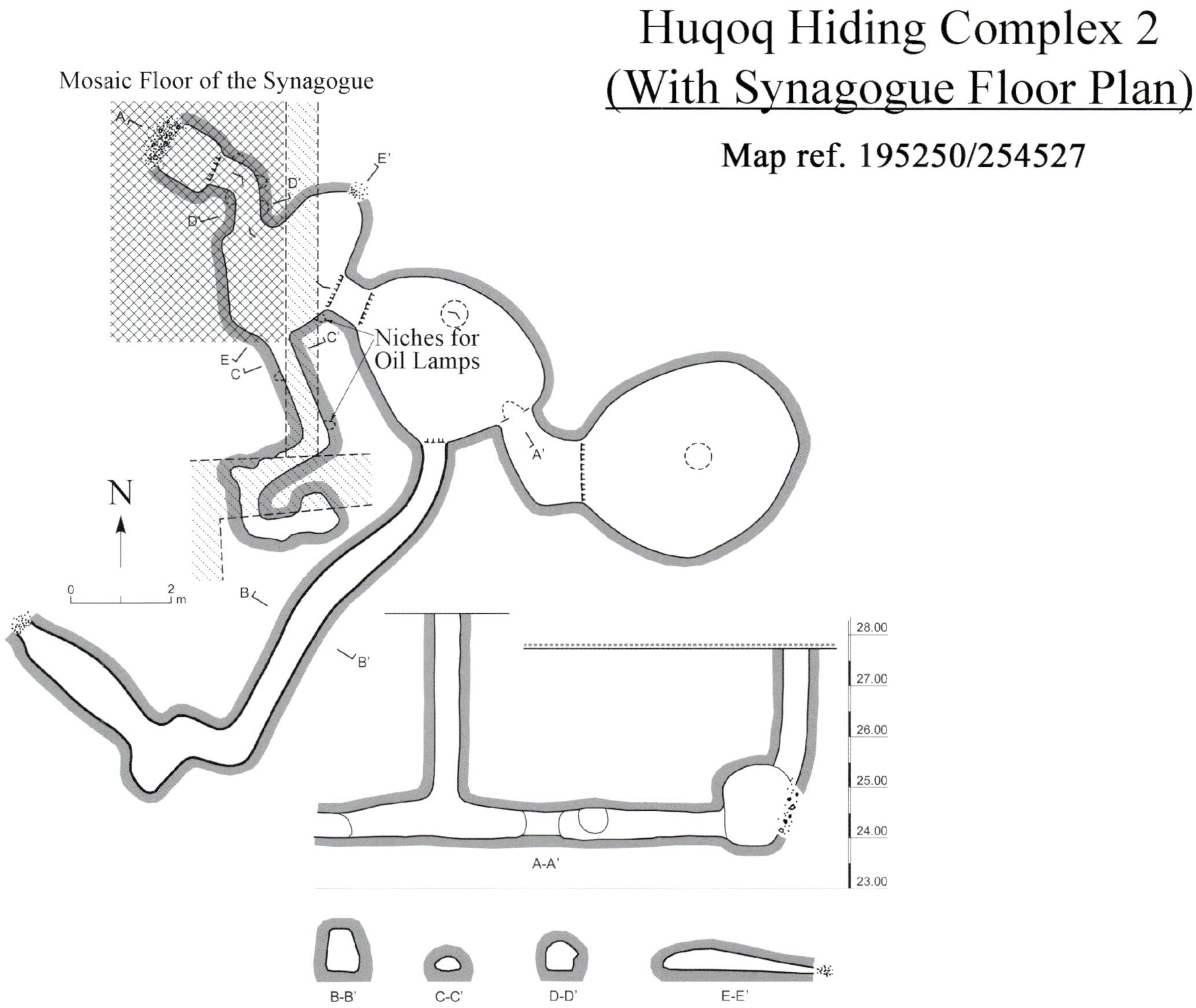

Map 53: Hiding Complex, with synagogue floor plan

21. Mimlah, 1 on the west side of Horvat Mimlah (Map ref. 191725/251422)

Horvat Mimlah lies on a spur c. 4 km southeast of the village of Maghar. The spur is isolated on three sides – to the north, east, and south – while on its west side it is joined by a saddle leading up to Mimlah Ridge. The summit has good views to the east, toward the northern Sea of Galilee, the village of Arbel and its cliffs, and the northern Golan Heights; to the north, Mount Canaan ridge and the city of Zefat are visible. The northern Galilee ridges stand out on the west side of the spur. A group of springs lies to its south. Mimlah is mentioned in rabbinic sources as a Jewish settlement and its name has several versions: Mimla, Mamlia, and Malhia.[33] According to the external Mishna of priestly divisions, it was the seat of the Hezir priestly order.[34] Concentrated particularly in its western part, the site contains the remains of buildings, water cisterns, burial caves and possibly also a synagogue.[35] In 1985, earthworks on the west side of the ruins uncovered the entrance to a hiding complex, hewn into layers of crumbling calcareous rock and therefore poorly preserved.[36] The entrance is inside a rock-hewn cave beneath the ancient ruined buildings. An opening in the east wall of the cave leads to an elliptical chamber (3.5 × 6.2 m, height 1.80 m) whose roof has a circular opening (diameter c. 2 m). The north wall of the chamber opens onto a passage with unclear dimensions, since its floor is covered with collapsed rock. The passage (c. 6.5 m long) is narrow at first but gradually widens out, ending in another chamber that is filled with earth. An opening hewn in the east wall of the cave leads to a small plastered bell-shaped chamber c. 2 m in diameter and 1.7 m high. In the south wall of the cave is a hewn opening that leads to another small bell-shaped chamber (1.6 m high) that is also plastered and has a 1.8 m diameter hole in its roof that is blocked with building stones. A breach in the southwest wall leads via a passage to another, irregularly shaped cavity that is connected to all four chambers and to further passages that were found to be blocked. The surveyors recorded no pottery or other finds.

33 See Klein 1939:105.
34 Klein 1939:163.
35 See Ilan 1991a:162.
36 See Tepper and Shachar 1987b:300–301.

22. Horvat Mimlah 2, c. 500 m south of the complex on the west side of Horvat Mimlah (Map ref. 191833/251469)

In the south part of Horvat Mimlah, several hundred meters south of the first complex, the present survey discovered another hiding complex. The complex begins inside a water cistern 4 m deep with an opening (0.66 × 0.80 m) lined with fieldstones bearing traces of gray plaster and silted up with earth. A cavity (2.7 × 7.6 m) hewn in its north wall stretches to the west. A 1.5 m long passage hewn in its north wall is 0.50 × 0.75 m in section. The passage leads to a small, finely hewn chamber measuring 2.15 × 3.50 m. In the north wall of the small chamber a passage hewn to the north measures 0.38 × 0.50 m at its entrance, but is blocked with earth. In the west wall of the small chamber, the opening to an additional passage also measures 0.38 × 0.50 m and is blocked with earth. In the east wall two holes are drilled to form a loop to which to attach large storage vessels to prevent them falling over. Since the entrance to the complex is via a water cistern, the loops cannot be tethering loops such as those known at Horvat ʿAmuda in the Judean foothills, since the chamber is not large enough for animals.

Fig. 84: Horvat Mimlah, Hiding Complex 1

Fig. 85: Horvat Mimlah, Hiding Complex 2

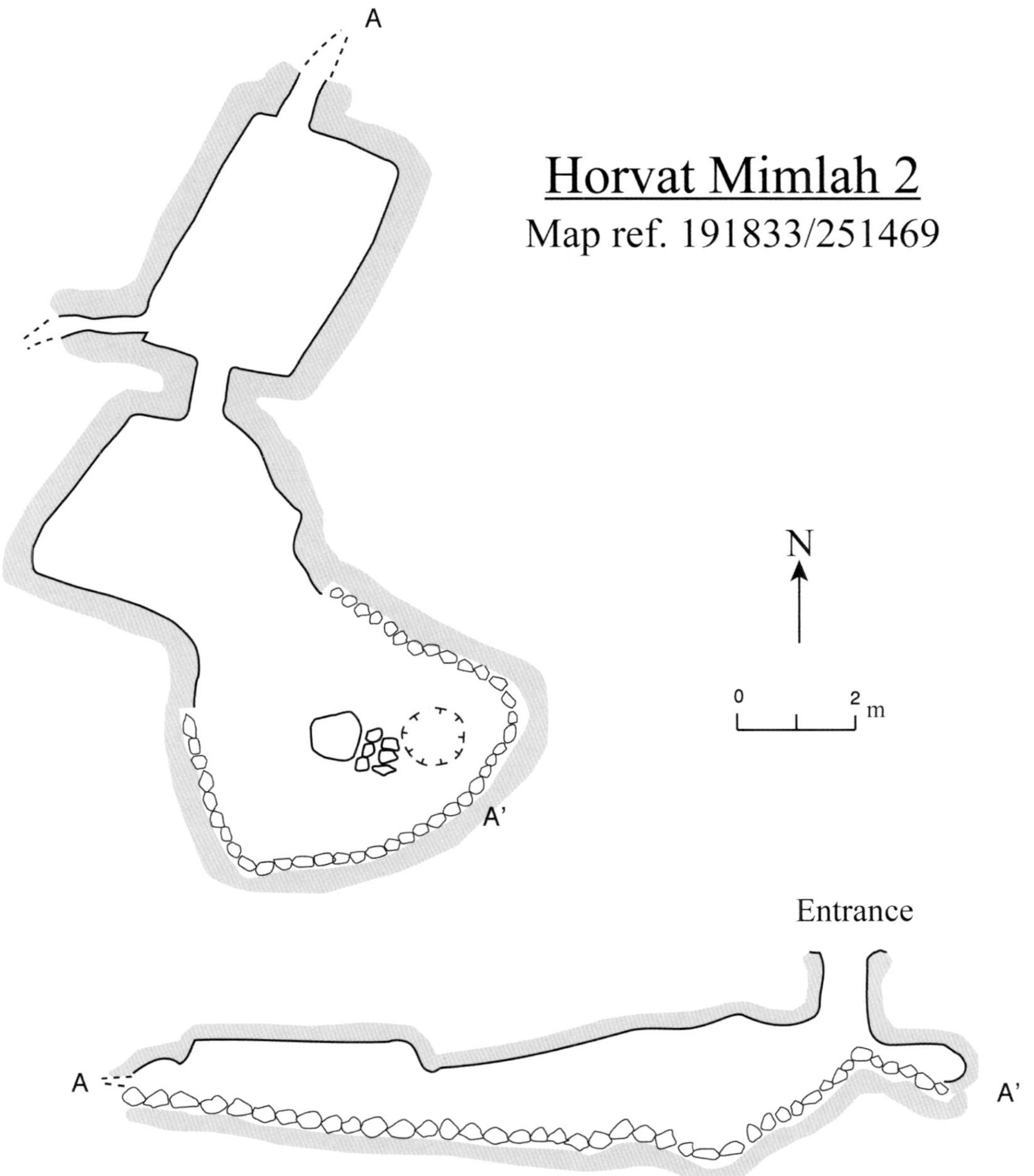

Map 54: Horvat Mimlah, Hiding Complex 2

23. Horvat Mimlah, c. 170 m north of the dirt track leading to the top of Horvat Mimlah, 3 (Map ref. 191899/251509)

I discovered the hiding complex in November 2012 while visiting the site with antiquities inspector Gilad Cinamon prior to development work by the Jewish National Fund. The complex is hewn from inside a natural cave formed on the wall of a rock ledge at the northern summit of the hill. The vaulted cave entrance measures 1 × 3 m. Near the entrance, we found the fragment of a nether stone from an ancient olive press. The irregularly formed cave measures 15 × 19 m. Three openings hewn in the north-west wall of the cavity measure 0.7 × 0.8 m each. After crawling for 5 m around a passage hewn from the entrance, one emerges from the third entrance to rejoin the large chamber. The central opening only reaches a depth of c. 0.5 m. Those who made the passage in this part of the cave encountered some kind of difficulty that caused them to shift to its north-east section. On this side of the cave, where the roof slopes down to the floor, a 7.5 m long hewn passage leads to another irregularly formed man-made cavity measuring 4 × 6 m; two openings that are identical in section (0.35 × 0.50 m) on its north side lead to two passages hewn in opposite directions, both now blocked with earth. Another opening is hewn

Fig. 86: Horvat Mimlah, Hiding Complex 3, north of the track leading up to the ruins

in the east wall of the cavity and from here, a passage continues in line with the main passage from the entrance. The 4.5 m long passage in this section has a sharp, right-angled bend after 3 m and opens onto a rock ledge leading down into an irregularly formed water reservoir coated in gray plaster. A round hole in the reservoir roof is blocked with a fill of earth and rocks. Another arched opening in the south wall of the cave leads to another passage that is blocked by an earth fill. A plastered water cistern, now only 2 m deep, lies 18 m to the south of the hiding complex. At the north end of the cistern, in a direct line with the hiding complex, a hewn passage is inaccessible due to a wall built to block it. A flashlight shone through the right-hand side of the wall reveals a passage leading directly toward the hiding complex.

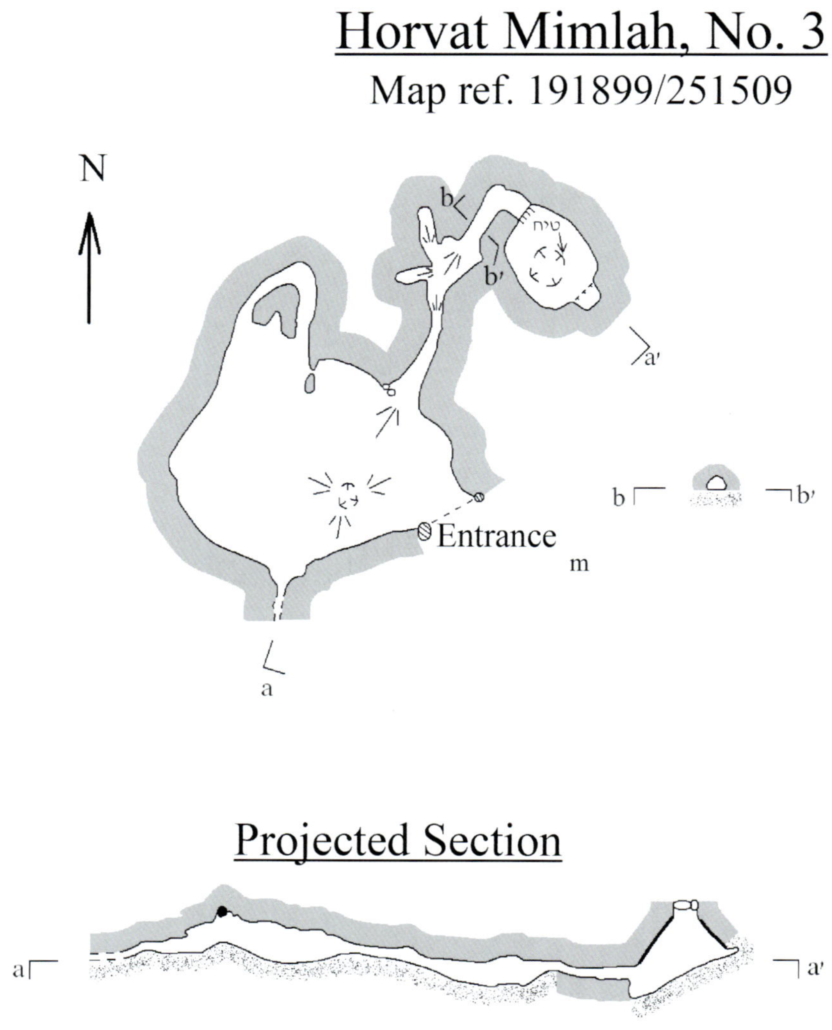

Map 55: Horvat Mimlah, Hiding Complex 3

24. Horvat Ravid, Kh. Rubadiya (Map ref. 194686/252062)

Horvat Ravid is situated on the south bank of Nahal Zalmon, c. 2 km east of Nahal Zalmon Junction and c. 5 km east of the ancient settlement of Migdal (Tarichaea) with Mimlah Ridge and Mount Ravid to its south. The site's ancient name is not known. Tepper and Shachar surveyed the ruin in 1986 and dated it to the Hellenistic, Early Roman, and Medieval periods.[37] Their survey records a hiding complex hewn from deep inside a natural cave. From the cave, a passage climbs steeply up into a square cavity reached by passages from different directions. One of the passages leads to the original entrance shaft of the complex. Another passage leads to a hewn chamber and yet another descends to a lower level and reaches an additional chamber with a ventilation shaft, beneath the entrance shaft. From this chamber, a further hewn passage contains a sealed stone door that was found *in situ*. The surveyors believed that a niche hewn in the wall of the passage was for a *mezuzah*. Apart from this, niches for oil lamps were installed along the passages. Significantly, Horvat Ravid is not far from the ruins of Huqoq and Eilabun, where hiding complexes were also discovered. Tepper and Shachar believe that these hiding complexes, together with the Bet Natofa refuge, represent a cluster of settlements where hiding complexes were hewn in the eastern Lower Galilee.

37 See Tepper and Shachar 1987b:314.

Fig. 87: Horvat Ravid

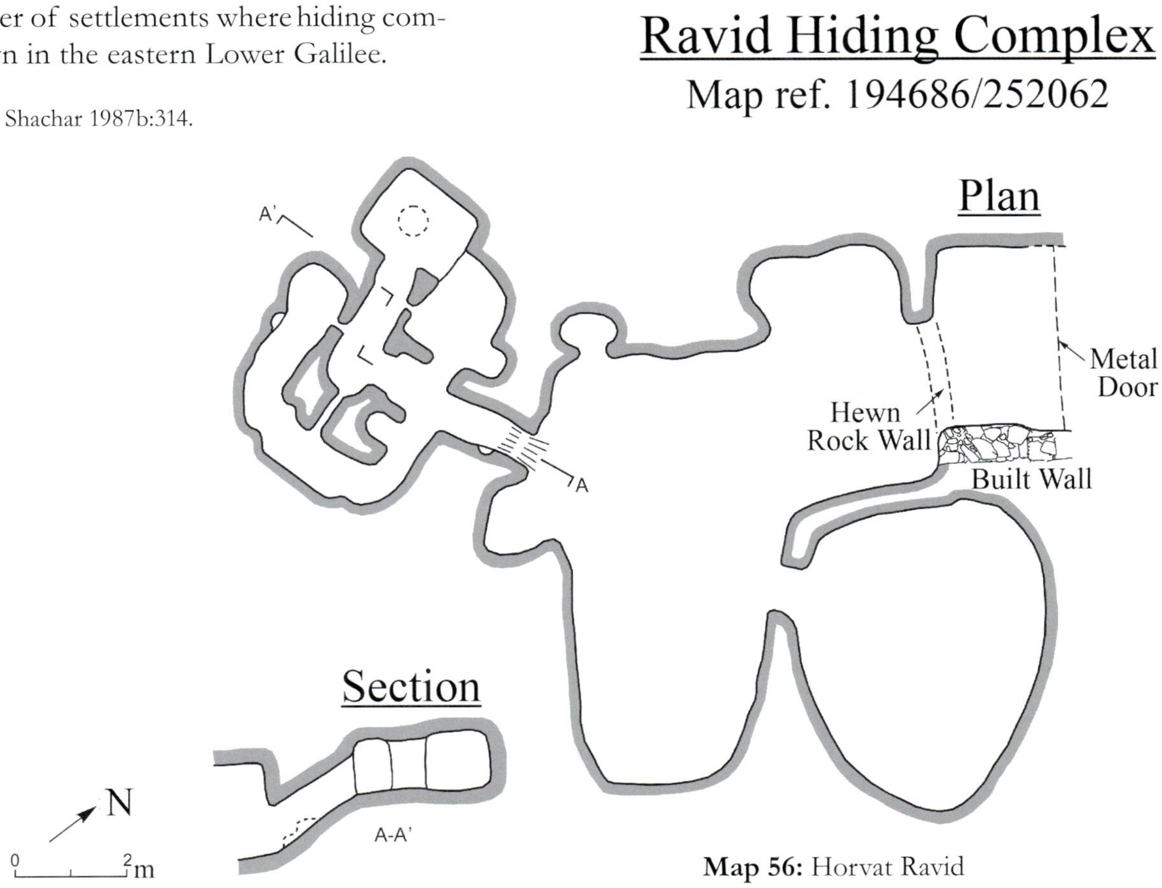

Map 56: Horvat Ravid

25. Eilabun, east of the village of Eilabun (Map ref. 187134/248752)

Fig. 88: Eilabun, entrance to Hiding Complexes as photographed in 1964

The Arab village of Eilabun lies on the northeast fringes of Bet Natofa Valley, c. 13 km northwest of Tiberias, along the elongated spur of a prominent topographic saddle. Eilabun is identified with the ancient Jewish village of Eilabun or Eilabo, the seat of the Hakkoz priestly order according to the *Baraita* of the 24 priestly divisions.[38] Guérin identified "sparse remains of a building with pillars that may have been a synagogue" at the site and medieval tradition holds that the second-century CE rabbinic sage Matteya ben Heresh was buried here.

When excavated in 1962, the complex was initially identified as an ancient tunnel.[39] It is 65 m long, c. 1 m wide and 1.75 m high and descends steeply into the hill. Two hewn pits were found in the complex. The few pottery finds collected from the tunnel date to the 2nd to 4th c. CE. A second tunnel found nearby was not excavated, but its unblocked section is 10 m long. Tepper and Shachar succeeded in locating the entrance to the complex and went c. 18 m down its sloping passages. The dimensions and height of the passage are not typical of hiding complexes and its location outside the settlement shows that it should probably not be identified as such.

38 See Klein 1939:165; Klein 1945:66–67, 192.

39 See Tfilinski 1983:49.

26. Horvat Mishtah, Kh. Mushta, a hill overlooking the village of 'Arr'aba (Map ref. 180066/250656)

Fig. 89: Horvat Mushtah, hiding complex entrance from inside a water cistern

An ancient ruin on top of a high hill rising between the village of 'Arr'aba and the town of Sakhnin. The hill is surrounded by ravines and is isolated on all sides. The hilltop has an excellent view of the Sakhnin Valley and the Yotvat hills. Victor Guérin visited the place and described the ruins as an ancient village.[40] He remarked that some of the hill slopes had large supporting walls and that he saw dressed stones at the site, together with traces of numerous buildings. He also noted rooms used as basements, water cisterns, and a pressing installation. Klein suggested identifying this site with the settlement of Mifshata recorded in the list of priestly divisions as the seat of the Harim order.[41] The current survey found a hiding complex in the center of the ancient village hewn from inside the ruins of an ancient building and reaching the entrance to a water cistern c. 2 m in diameter and c. 4 m deep. It is now only accessible via the water cistern by climbing from the floor of the cistern into a hewn passage about 2 m below surface level. The entrance (0.6 × 0.8 m) is c. 1.5 m below the water-cistern entrance. The hewn passage is 6 m long and c. 0.6 m high. It was roughly hewn in a straight line toward a cavity measuring 2 × 4 m and 1.2 m high. A shelf about 1.5 m wide was hewn in the west wall of this small chamber. From the north wall, the passage continues for 1.5 m and bends east for a further 1.7 m to a point where it is blocked with earth. The present overall length of the passage is c. 13 m. A chan-

40 See Guerin 1880, vol. 6:322.

41 See Klein 1945:67.

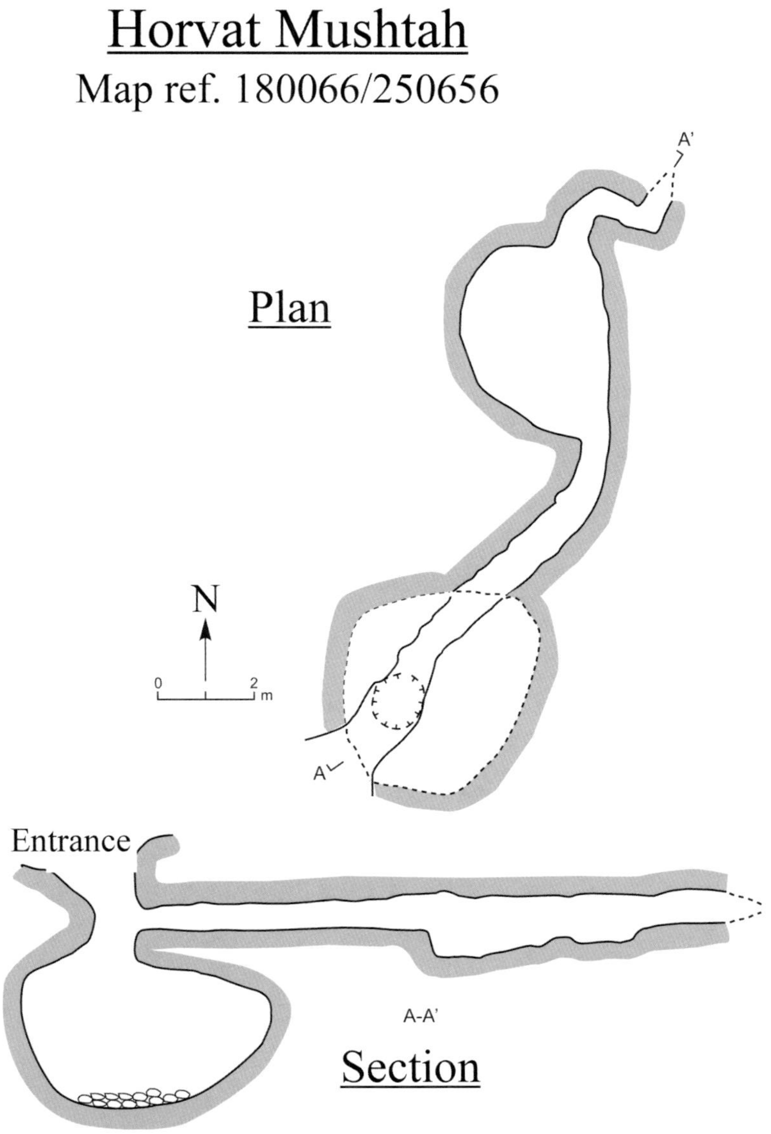

Map 57: Horvat Mushtah

nel cut in the north wall of the water cistern continued to supply it with water, so that in this instance the cistern could still be used even after the hiding complex connecting the building to the cistern was made. Some of the pottery finds at the site date to the Early Roman period.[42]

27. Yodefat, 1 (Iotapata); Kh. Shifat, the lower slope of the site (Map ref. 176250/248379)

The ancient settlement of Iotapata is situated on an isolated hill in the heart of the Yodefat hill ridge and is surrounded on three sides by ravines. Only its west side has a saddle linking it with the east slope of Mount Miyamin. South of the tell, Mount Azmon rises to a height of 547 m asl. Nahal Yodefat cuts a gorge between the mount and ancient Iotapata, its steep slopes providing the ancient hilltop settlement with the appearance described by Josephus as a hill "surrounded on three sides by ravines so deep that sight fails in the attempt to fathom the abyss" (*War* 3:158). The settlement of Iotapata is first mentioned in the list of settlements fortified by Josephus in preparation for the Great Revolt. It was here that Josephus surrendered to the Romans in July 67 CE (*War* 3:141–398).

During Mordechai Aviam's excavations at the site,[43] an underground cavity was identified as a hiding complex. The cavity was only partially preserved and, if it does indeed attest to the existence of a hiding complex at Iotapata, it should undoubtedly be dated to

42 See Aviam 2004:129.

43 See Aviam 2005:48, 60; Aviam 2015.

the Great Revolt. The complex was discovered in the southern enclosing section of the Iotapata casemate wall, in the lower part of the slope and c. 30 m above the streambed. It includes a finely hewn shaft measuring 0.70 × 0.87 m and c. 2 m deep, through which one descends to a tunnel on three levels. The shaft reaches a step leading to a chamber roofed with triangularly-laid stone slabs at a height of 2.5 m, from where a passage continues north for c. 2 m and reaches a low opening (0.95 × 1.10 m) that can be entered crouching down for about 15 m more, up to the point where it becomes blocked. The lower level is reached via the step and leads to a cavity (1.0 × 1.3 m, height 1.8 m) hewn in the rock toward the southwest. From this chamber, three more hewn steps lead down to a third chamber (3 × 5 m, height 1.4 m). The opening in the vertical passage, which was probably the original exit that emerged outside the walls, could be blocked with a stone door. Bolt holes are cut in the wall near the north side of the passage. Aviam remarked that the finds from the three chambers included 25 coins; seven of these were silver coins dating to the rule of Nero and the latest was minted in 64 CE. The chambers also produced Early Roman pottery, human and animal bones, a catapult stone, and an arrowhead. On examining the complex, Aviam found that it had been hewn earlier than the construction of the enclosing wall. The pottery and coin assemblages show that it was used as a hiding place during the battle of Iotapata in the Great Revolt, in the summer of 67 CE. Aviam noted that the find of a hiding complex at Iotapata contradicts Tepper and Shachar's theory that the phenomenon of underground refuges in the Galilee began only after the Great Revolt. Aviam remarked that even though Josephus did not describe the use of hiding complexes in his description of the siege of Iotapata, this does not mean that such complexes did not exist.

Fig. 90: Yodefat, lower slope

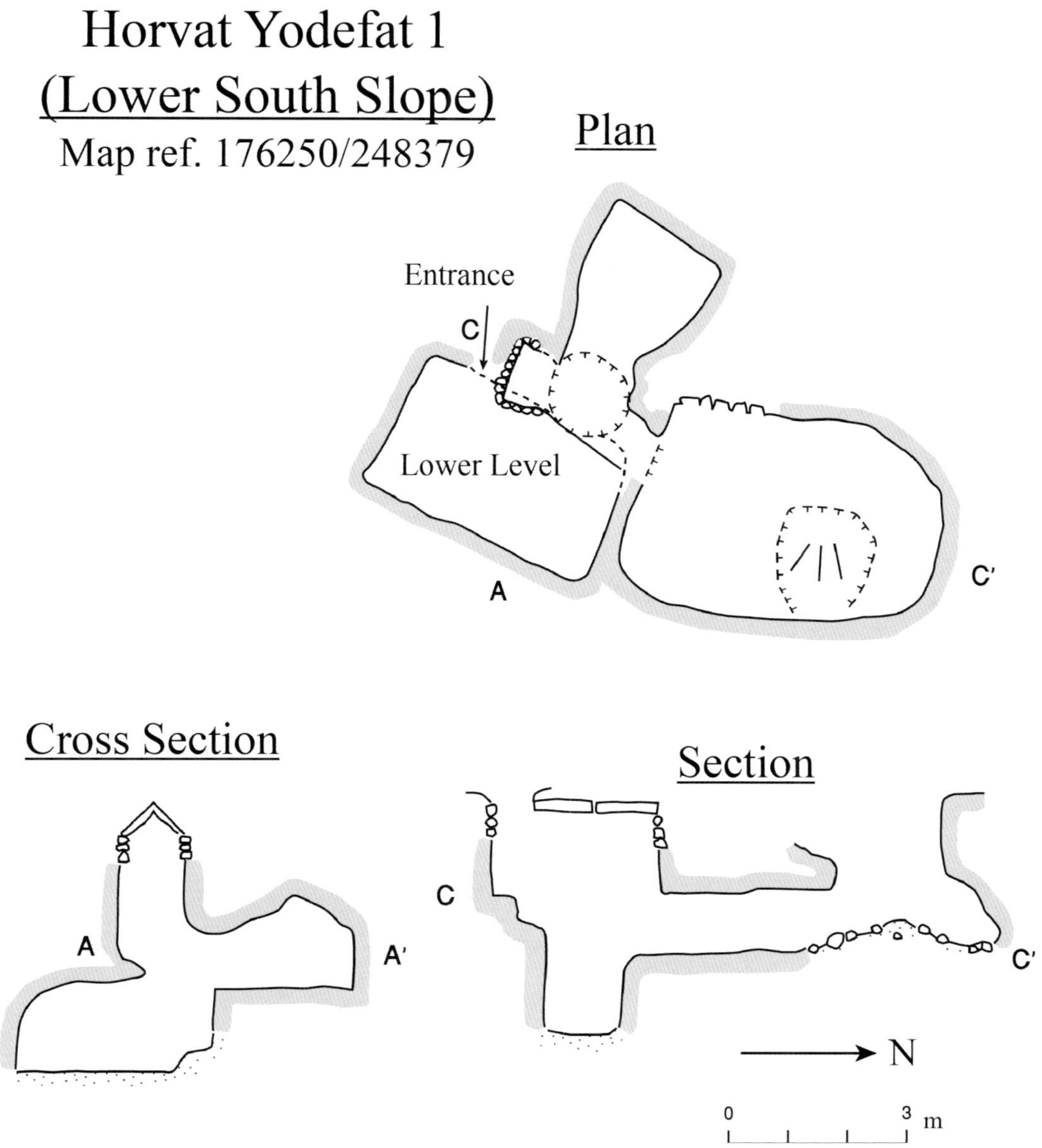

Map 58: Yodefat, lower slope

28. Yodefat, 2 on the upper slope of the site (Map ref. 176281/248557)

This underground cavity is located in the upper part of the south slope, near one of the top steps leading to a water cistern.[44] The cavity has not been excavated, but during the current survey we entered the opening to the complex, most of which is blocked. The rectangular opening is hewn into the rock at the top of the slope and measures 0.75 × 1.20 m and 0.60 m high. A gap hewn in its north wall measures 0.8 × 0.8 m. This leads to a hewn cavity with a short passage at its east end, opening onto another cavity 1 m further down. From here, there is access to another cavity (2.00 × 3.25 m) containing traces of plaster and a hewn niche. Its southwest wall bears the remains of a built wall that is now covered with earth. A passage hewn in the east wall is blocked with earth. Located 12 m northeast of this cavity, at the top of the tell, is an 8 m deep water cistern where a blocked passage appears to have been connected to the hiding complex from inside the water cistern. This was probably a second hiding complex at Iotapata whose construction rendered ancient installations obsolete.

44 See Aviam 2005:60.

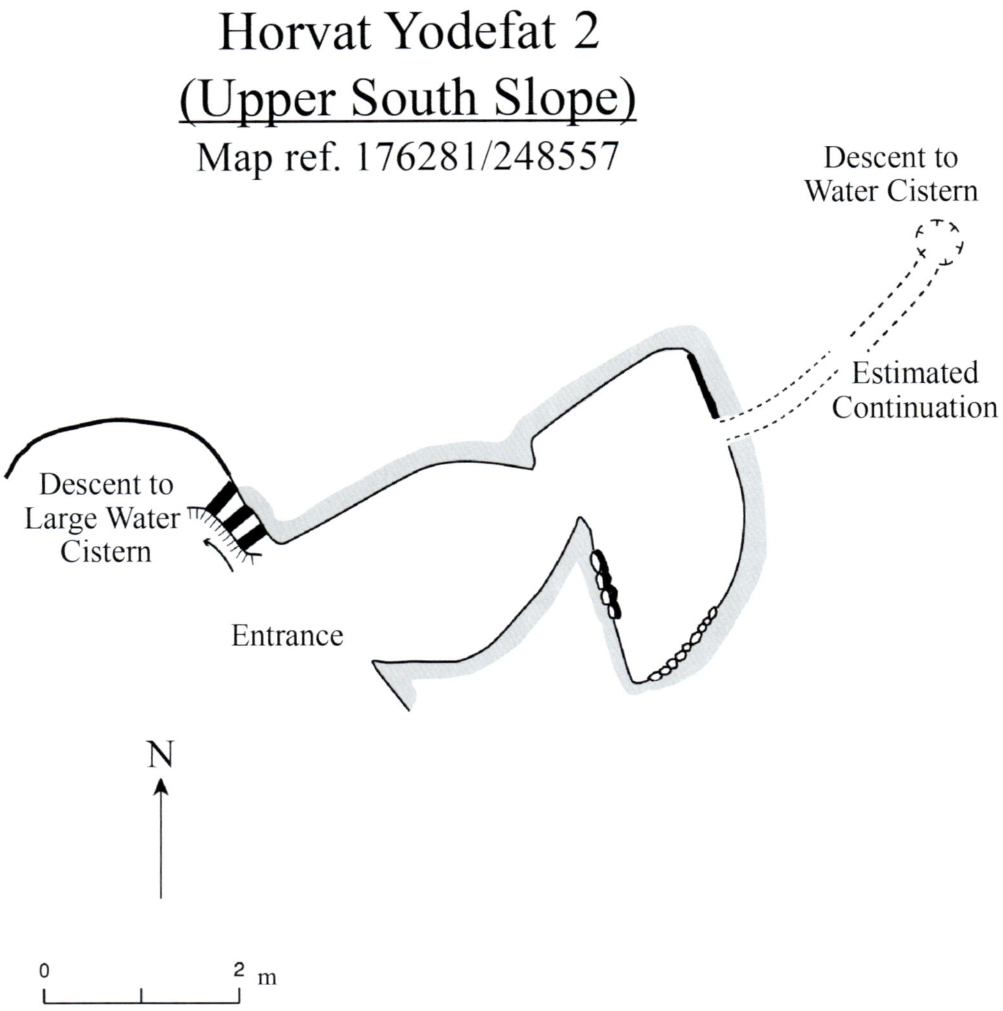

Map 59: Yodefat, upper slope

Fig. 91: Yodefat, upper slope

29. Kabul, the center of the ancient village in the Arab village of Kabul (Map ref. 170157/252492)

The ancient settlement of Kabul (Kabulon) appears in the Bible as a town in the territory of the tribe of Asher on the eastern border of the territory of Naphtali (Joshua 19:27). Zvi Gal conducted an archaeological excavation in the 1990s at the neighboring site of Horvat Rosh Zayit, located on a hill sloping down to 'Akko Valley, where Kabul is mentioned in the Bible. On the basis of his finds, Gal identified the Rosh Zayit site with the biblical Kabul. He uncovered a large fortress enclosed by a wide wall with guard towers. Finds from the fortress include dozens of storage jars, pottery stoppers, iron tools and arrowheads, and traces of a large fire. The finds date to the 10th to 9th c. BCE. The archaeologist believes that at some time in the second half of the tenth century BCE the Phoenicians conquered the area called Kabul in the Bible, which was probably part of the 'Akko Valley, in the region of the present-day village of Kabul. There they built a Phoenician fortress that served as their administrative center.

The Phoenician fortress was burnt down in the late 10th or early 9th c. BCE. Gal believed that the destruction of the fortress was linked to the end of Phoenician control in the region, begun when Solomon gave the area to Hiram, King of Tyre. Kabul was probably re-occupied under the rule of the northern kingdom of Israel, split after the kingdom of David and Solomon and in the time of Rehoboam. The Israelite village of Kabul was destroyed by fire in the 8th c. BCE, apparently during the campaign of Tiglath-Pileser III. Gal believes that the fortress and its finds prove that the biblical story is based on historical events.[45]

45 See Gal 1990:74–84.

Fig. 92: Kabul, Hiding Complex entrance

A large olive press containing oil-production installations was discovered in the village, which is twice mentioned by Josephus. In his second reference, he states that it marks the division between the two Galilees: "On the north Tyre and its dependent district mark its limits. Lower Galilee extends in length from Tiberias to Chabulon" (*War* 3:38). Josephus refers earlier to the settlement as a fortified town "on the frontiers of Ptolemais" (*Life* 214). According to Josephus, all the Jewish inhabitants of Chabulon fled to the hills when Cestius' army marched against the town. Although he admired the town's beauty, Cestius pillaged its riches and torched its houses (*War* 2:503–504). In *Rabbah Lamentations,* the town is described as being so wealthy that its taxes had to be carried to Jerusalem in a wagon (*Eichah Rabbah* 2,2). After the destruction of the Temple, members of the priestly order of Shekheniya settled in the town. In the 16th c., a number of Jewish families expelled from Spain probably moved to Kabul. An Ottoman census from 1533 records that the village had five Jewish families and seven Muslim families. In the census of 1555/6, the number of Jewish families in Kabul had risen to fifteen and there were ten Muslim families.[46] Victor Guérin recorded that when he visited the village in the mid-1880s it had four hundred inhabitants, all of whom were Muslim. Inside the village, he noticed many rock-hewn water cisterns, ashlars scattered or incorporated in the walls of houses, and monolithic pillars deriving from some kind of public building.[47] Excavations in the village in the early 2000s uncovered ornamented stone sarcophagi from the Early Roman period, identified as Jewish sarcophagi.[48] An archaeological excavation of the ancient village was conducted by Omar Zidan and Yardenna Alexandre in 2012 on behalf of the Israel Antiquities Authority and exposed a hiding complex hewn into domestic bell-shaped storage pits.[49] One (Pit 109) has a maximum diameter of 2.55 m and a depth of 1.5 m with a round opening 0.65 m in diameter. In the south wall of the pit, 0.3 m above its floor, a passage was hewn measuring 0.6 m in diameter and 0.5 m long. The passage led to another bell-shaped pit (Pit 107) with a maximum diameter of 2.35 m and a depth of 1.38 m. In the north wall of the pit, 0.6 m above its floor, two adjacent round openings were hewn with an oil-lamp niche between them. The beginning of

46 See Louis 1956:177.
47 See Guérin vol.6: 1880:286
48 See Aviam 2004:132.
49 See Zidan and Alexandre 2012.

a passage in the south wall of Pit 107 was left unfinished. The passage and the east part of this pit were blocked with a built wall five courses high (1.38 m) and 1.8 m long. In the west wall of this pit, 0.5 m above its floor, another passage was found, 0.6 m wide and 0.3 m long. The passage led to a rock-hewn shaft (No. 106). The shaft is 1.2 × 1.8 m in section and over 2 m deep. The archaeologists did not reach the bottom of the shaft. A passage cut in the south wall of the shaft branches into two: The east branch (0.95 m wide) was not excavated but the west (0.7 m wide) led to a third pit (No. 108). This pit was only partially excavated. Another shaft (No. 105) found 1.5 m east of the entrance to Pit 109 leads to a water cistern. This shaft was also not excavated. In the south wall of the cistern, 0.3 m above the floor, is the entrance to another passage that was not explored. A large number of pottery vessels were recovered from the pit floors: Cooking pots, jars, jugs and two oil lamps. The archaeologists dated the pottery recovered to the Early Roman period. All cooking pots belong to types known to have been used in the Early Roman period in Galilee, i. e. Kfar Hananiya types A3, A4, B1 and B4 ware.

Zidan and Alexandre believe that the complex underwent two phases: In the first, the storage pits were used to store farm produce beneath a dwelling house, which also had a domestic water cistern. In the second phase, as part of the Jewish population of Kabul's preparations for the Great Revolt, the storage pits were converted into an underground hiding complex that was accessible from inside the house. The archaeologists believe that the abundance of vessels from the Early Roman period on the pit floors shows that those hiding in the complex left in a hurry and were unable to take their possessions with them.

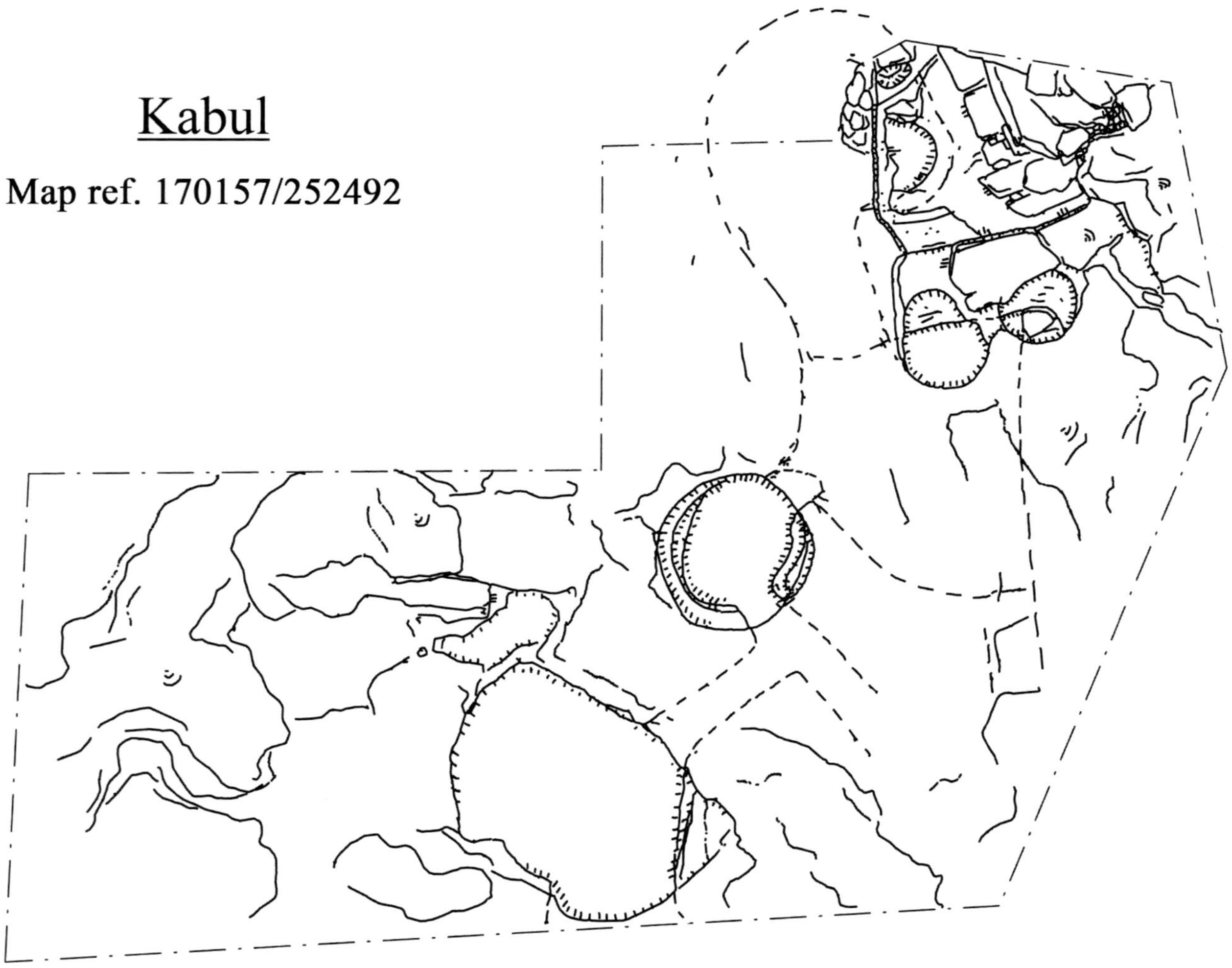

Map 60: Kabul, hiding complex

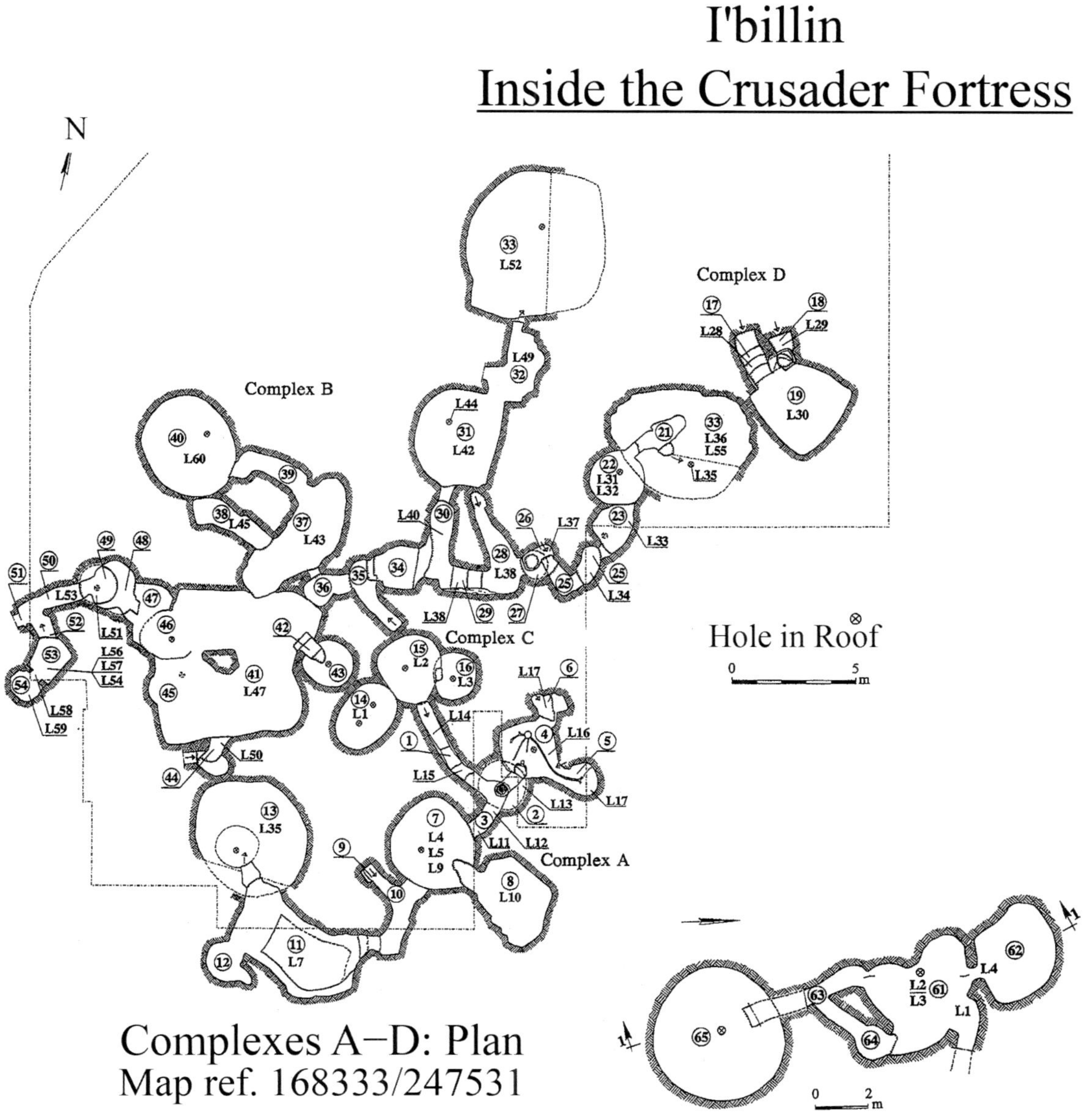

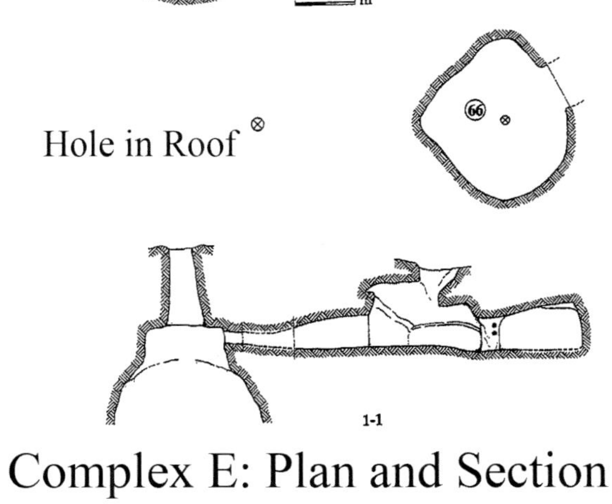

Map 61: ʿIbillin

30–33. ʿIbillin – The Crusader Fortress in ʿIbillin Village (Map ref. 168333/247531)

The village of ʿIbillin is situated in central Lower Galilee, 2 km north of Shefarʿam. It lies on a high hill near the route of the Roman road that once linked ʿAkko Valley with Bet Natofa Valley. Its name probably preserves the ancient Arab name Eblim, or Eblin, also recorded in other versions as Evilin, Evulin, Ivlim, and Ovlin.[50] The site is mentioned in the *Tosefta* and other rabbinic literature. A stone inscribed with an Aramaic inscription of a kind found in synagogues and a relief of a seven-branched candelabrum discovered in the past attest to the existence here of a Jewish community.[51]

50 See Klein 1945:61.
51 See Braslavsky 1954:277–282; Nave 1978:43.

Five underground cavities excavated at ʿIbillin can be identified as hiding complexes:

One complex (A) is reached via a passage with a round pit hewn in its floor that was concealed by a stone cover. Inside the pit, a passage leads to two more pits that were joined together by dismantling a rock partition between them. An industrial installation, possibly an olive press, was built in the resulting chamber. From the first pit, another passage leads in a southwesterly direction to a round chamber with a circular ventilation shaft cut in its roof. From here, a hewn step leads to an underground cavity where an exit shaft ascends to the surface. In the middle of this shaft, a corridor leads to a large chamber with cupmarks hewn along its walls. Another passage leads to a plastered water cistern. A second hiding complex (B) located a few meters north of Complex A has four entrances. One of these is blocked and a second is via a built shaft (1.26 × 1.50 m) from where a 3 m long passage leads out through a 0.6 m square shaft with a protruding climbing hold. A third access is via a water cistern that linked the entire complex, while a fourth was via an entrance that is blocked with large dressed limestone blocks. The complex included further halls, chambers, and pits linked by narrow entrances and passageways. The third hiding complex (C) is located between the first two complexes, although it is not connected to either of them. It was hewn around three pits whose partition walls were removed and it yielded a large quantity of jars, showing that it was a storage area. The excavators noted the numerous stone vessels found in all three complexes, attesting to their use by a Jewish population. The pottery vessels date to the 2nd to 3rd c. CE. In addition to the vessels, Early Roman pared-nozzle oil lamps were also recovered. The ancient water cisterns cut into by the passages also yielded Hellenistic stamped handles from Rhodes. The third complex, which was initially built as an underground storeroom, is similar to hiding complexes found in Galilee (and Judea) that show that underground storerooms, water cisterns, and even burial caves were sometimes converted into hiding complexes. The fourth hiding complex (E) was found c. 500 m to the south of the others and is entered via a 6 m diameter water cistern. After 2 m, a 4 m long passage hewn in its north wall branches into two: One branch turns east and the other turns west. The two passages meet in a large chamber originally used as a water cistern. A short passage cut at the north end of the cistern leads to another cavity. This was a sophisticated and meticulously hewn complex whose oil-lamp niches bear traces of soot. A feature marked as Complex D by the site's excavators is not a hiding complex, since it has merely a single chamber reached via a stairway.[52]

34. ʿIbillin, ʿIbillin Village (Map ref. 168333/247531)

This hiding complex was excavated near complexes A–C, next to a water cistern 5.5 m in diameter and 5 m deep.[53] The entrance is 0.6 m wide. To the east of the cistern, on a level rock surface, a wall 3.5 m long and 0.3 m wide was exposed and an entrance (0.5 × 0.6 m) discovered in its south corner leads to an underground chamber (diameter 4 m). At the east end of the chamber, a hewn opening leads to a blocked passage. The archaeologists identified the find as a hiding complex and noted that pottery found nearby indicates that it was used in the Second Temple period.

35. Bet Natofa, Horvat Bet Natofa, Tel Bet Natofa, Kh. Natif (Map ref. 186327/248747)

Horvat Bet Natofa lies on the northeastern fringes of Bet Natofa Valley, c. 2 km south of ʿIbillin Village, on an elongated, south-sloping hill. Its summit has a southeasterly view of the agricultural plain of Bet Natofa Valley, toward Mount Turʿan and the villages of Buʿeine and Nujeidat. The Arabic name of the valley, Sahl el-Batuf, may preserve the name of the Jewish village of Natuf whose olives and lands, grown in the valley, are mentioned in rabbinic writings as being of high quality.[54] Victor Guérin called the site "Khirbet

52 See Mokari 1999:24–26.
53 See Yitach 2000.
54 See Klein 1939:24, 108; Klein 1945:24.

Fig. 93: Horvat Bet Natofa

Nathif" and noted that the hill contained ancient ruins "eroded by the teeth of time."[55] Safrai recorded that Horvat Natuf was the main settlement in Bet Natofa Valley in Mishnaic and Talmudic times and that it covered 35–45 dunams (c. 8–12 acres).[56] The current survey found traces of the ancient settlement including remains of a wall built of dressed fieldstones, potsherds from different periods, water cisterns – most of which are blocked – and rock-hewn agricultural installations. To the south of the ruins, the entrance to a hiding complex was discovered and mapped,[57] resulting in a new plan of the complex. The entrance (0.9 × 0.9 m, depth 3 m) is coated with gray plaster. A chamber hewn in the south wall of the pit measures 5.6 × 6.4 m and is about 1 m high. An entrance hewn in the southeast wall measures 0.6 × 3.0 m and leads to another chamber. This chamber (3.2 × 6.0 m) is only accessible by crawling. The north wall of the chamber is adjacent to the wall of the main pit, which can be rejoined via an irregularly shaped opening (0.45 × 0.65 m) cut between the two. The south wall of the chamber contains another opening (0.3 × 0.5 m) providing access to a third cavity (c. 2 × 2 m) that is now blocked with earth. In the south wall of this cavity, a narrow hewn passage 1 m long is blocked with earth. In the south corner of the north wall of the main cavity, another passage is hewn to the east, making a 90–degree turn before it is blocked by earth after 1.5 m. On the surface, about 8 m away from the turn in this passage, are the remains of a public building measuring 8 × 15 m. Based on the direction of the chiseling, the hiding complex probably continued underneath the public building, from where a passage was cut to the water cistern rendered obsolete by the hiding complex.

55 See Guerin 1880,6:317–318.
56 See Safrai 1981:79.
57 See Eshel 1983:51.

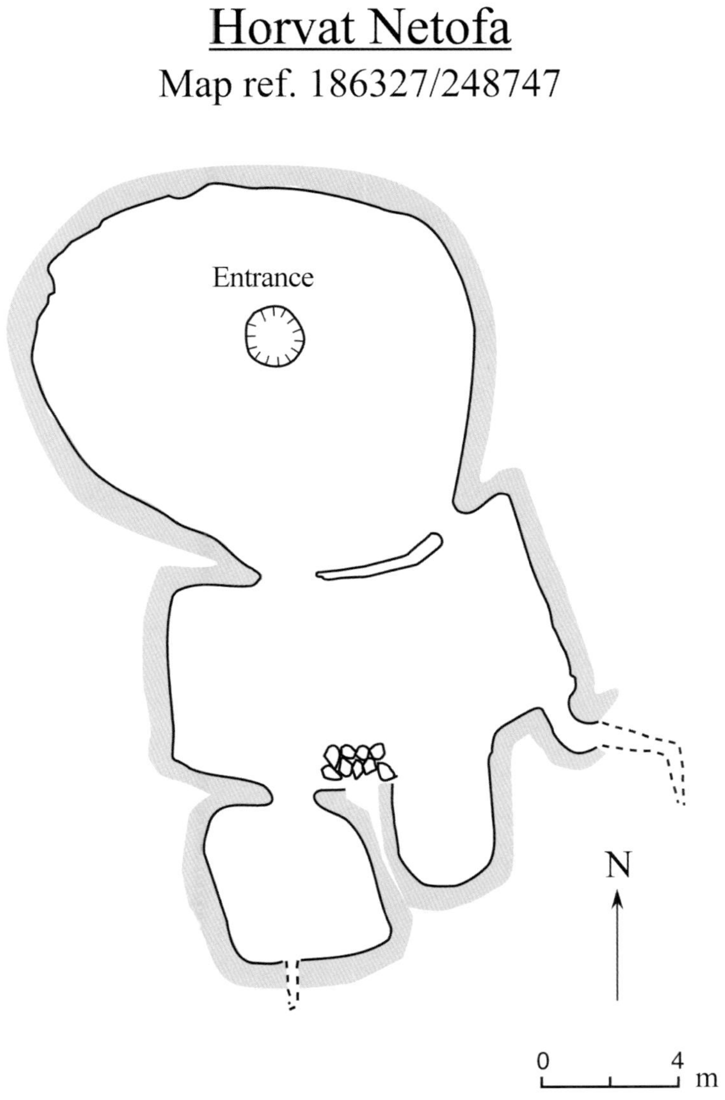

Map 62: Horvat Beit Netofa

36. Lubiya, Horvat Lubiya, near Kibbutz Lavi (east of Golani Junction) (Map ref. 190418/242587)

An ancient settlement situated on an elongated spur of Cretaceous rock, c. 3 km east of the Golani Junction. To the southwest of the ruined Arab village are the remains of an ancient settlement containing traces of buildings, cisterns, installations, and potsherds from various periods. This was most probably the site of the ancient Jewish settlement *Punduqa Da-Lavi* ("Lavi Inn") or a way station with a similar name used by passing travelers.[58] It appears in the Jerusalem Talmud (*y.Shekalim* 7:50,3) and in various other manuscripts as *Pundika Da-Labiya.*[59]

Tepper and Shachar discovered a hiding complex on the eastern fringes of the site,[60] beneath the remains of a building (3 × 6 m) with a vaulted roof. A shaft climbing up from the southern wall of a cave narrows to a gap 0.3 m in diameter. A channel cut to the surface through its northern wall was probably used to collect rainwater. The remainder of the complex has a narrow entrance c. 1 m long leading to a hewn, elongated underground chamber (1.3 × 6.0 m). A passage cut in the west wall of this chamber terminates in a built shaft. Hewn steps descend from the shaft to another passage 2.2 m long, which leads to

58 See Klein 1945:120 n. 25.
59 See Klein 1939:99.
60 See Tepper and Shachar 1987b:294–295.

Fig. 94: Horvat Lubiya

another chamber (3.0 × 4.5 m). Two rounded openings hewn in the center of the chamber floor lead to another underground complex. An unfinished niche is cut in the north wall of the cavity. Signs of daylight are visible through a 5 m long passage leading off the chamber's east wall. From the west wall of a small room, another passage was cut measuring 0.6 × 1.0 m in section that is now filled with earth.

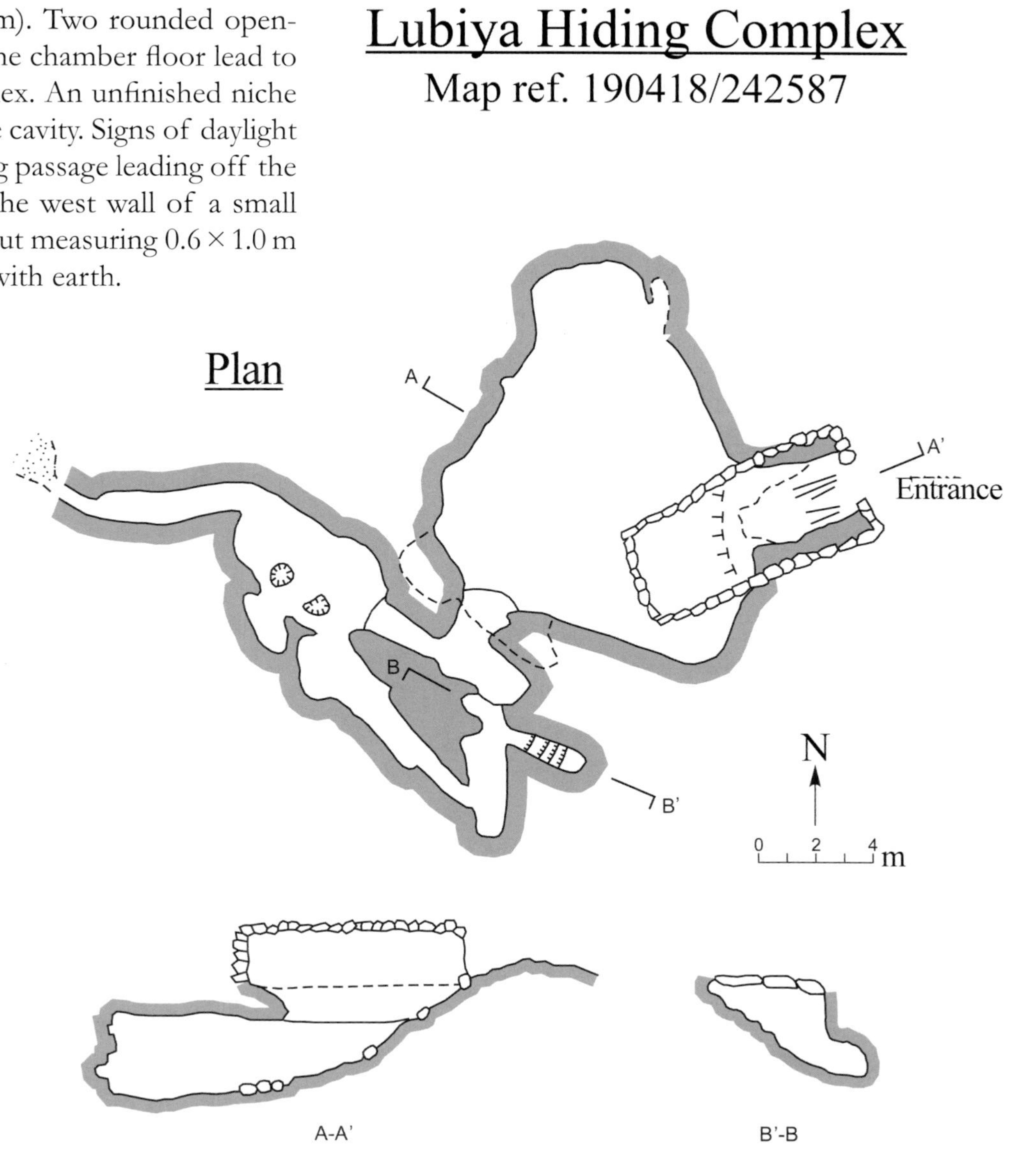

Map 63: Horvat Lubiya

37–38. El-Khirbeh 1, on a hill west of Lubiya, the large complex; El-Khirbeh 2, east of the hilltop, the small complex (Map ref. 189893/242089)

The site is on a hill overlooking Golani Junction and c. 2 km west of the village of Lubiya. Two hiding complexes were found at the site. One includes a hewn cave measuring 9.3 × 11.0 m with a bench built along its western and southern walls; in the center of the cave is an olive-crushing basin (1.6 m diameter).[61] Three passages are visible in the cave. Tepper and Shachar identified it as a hiding complex hewn from inside an ancient olive press that underwent several phases.[62] Three entrances to a large hiding complex are hewn in its west wall. The northern passage (0.6 × 0.7 m in section) leads to an elongated chamber (1.5 × 3.0 m) terminating in a blocked entrance to a passage. Another passage, identical in section, was hewn for 12 m. Five niches for oil lamps were cut along its southern wall and four niches were cut along its north wall. The passage reaches a rectangular chamber (4.2 × 7.0 m). An opening cut in the chamber's south wall was probably the original entrance to the complex and is now blocked with earth. Two more chambers were hewn to the north of the rectangular chamber. A blocked passage in the east wall of

61 See Shenhav 1984:18.

62 See Tepper and Shachar 1987b:295–299.

the entrance cavity is identical in section to the other two passages. The marks of a hewn upward shaft that was probably used for ventilation are visible next to the opening. Two circular interconnected openings are hewn in the floor of the central chamber in the complex. A breach in the north wall of the chamber leads to a round chamber about 4 m in diameter. A passage hewn in its north wall is blocked after 2 m. A round opening in the floor of the passage has a rounded hewn frame for a stone cover. In the south wall of the main chamber (No. 5 in plan) is the entrance to a 20 m long passage terminating in a rectangular hewn chamber (2.4 × 4.0 m). A passage hewn in the north wall of this chamber ascends to a round cavity 2 m in diameter. A round hole in the roof of the cavity (0.6 m diameter) contained a stone door designed to seal the passage. A vertical passage in the middle of the round chamber floor descends to a lower level where there is a passage whose dimensions are identical to those of the other passages leading to a rectangular chamber measuring 3 × 7 m. In the northeast wall of the chamber is a large opening (diameter 1.6 m) and there is a round blocked hole in its roof (diameter 0.5 m). A passage ascending to the southeast in the east wall of the chamber is blocked after c. 4.5 m. Another upward passage leads from the south wall of the same chamber and is also blocked after c. 3.5 m. A gap in the north wall of the chamber leads to another round chamber (diameter 3 m) with a round opening (diameter 0.8 m) that is now blocked. At the north end of the round chamber is a narrow entrance 0.5 m wide that ends in another round chamber (diameter c. 3.8 m). In the roof of this chamber is a round opening (diameter c. 1.2 m). A stone door beside it was probably used to seal the passage between the chambers. A 1 m long passage climbs upward from the south end of this chamber.

Fig. 95: Horvat El-Khirbeh Hiding Complex 1

Fig. 96: Horvat El-Khirbeh Hiding Complex 2

To the east of El-Khirbe, Tepper and Shachar discovered a second hiding complex.[63] It is smaller than the previous one and its entrance measures c. 0.45 × 0.50 m. Six poorly preserved round openings are hewn in the entrance floor. A square opening cut in the upper end of the south wall of the chamber is now blocked with stones. A passage c. 2 m long is hewn in the east wall; its roof is built of dressed fieldstones and its continuation is blocked. At the north end of the main chamber, a corridor-like entrance leads to a circular chamber c. 2 m in diameter. A west–east passage with a vaulted roof is hewn from this chamber. After about 3 m, a round niche (diameter 0.75 m) was found to be blocked by a stone door. On opening the door, another stone door was discovered on the far side. The rest of the passage was filled with earth.

Potsherds collected from this complex include cooking pots, jars, and pottery lids dated to the 2nd c. CE. Two salvage excavations were conducted at the site; in one, a building from the Roman period was exposed and Hellenistic potsherds and an imported Byzantine bowl were recovered;[64] the second excavation has not yet been published.

63 See Tepper and Shachar 1987b:299.
64 See Alexandre 2003.

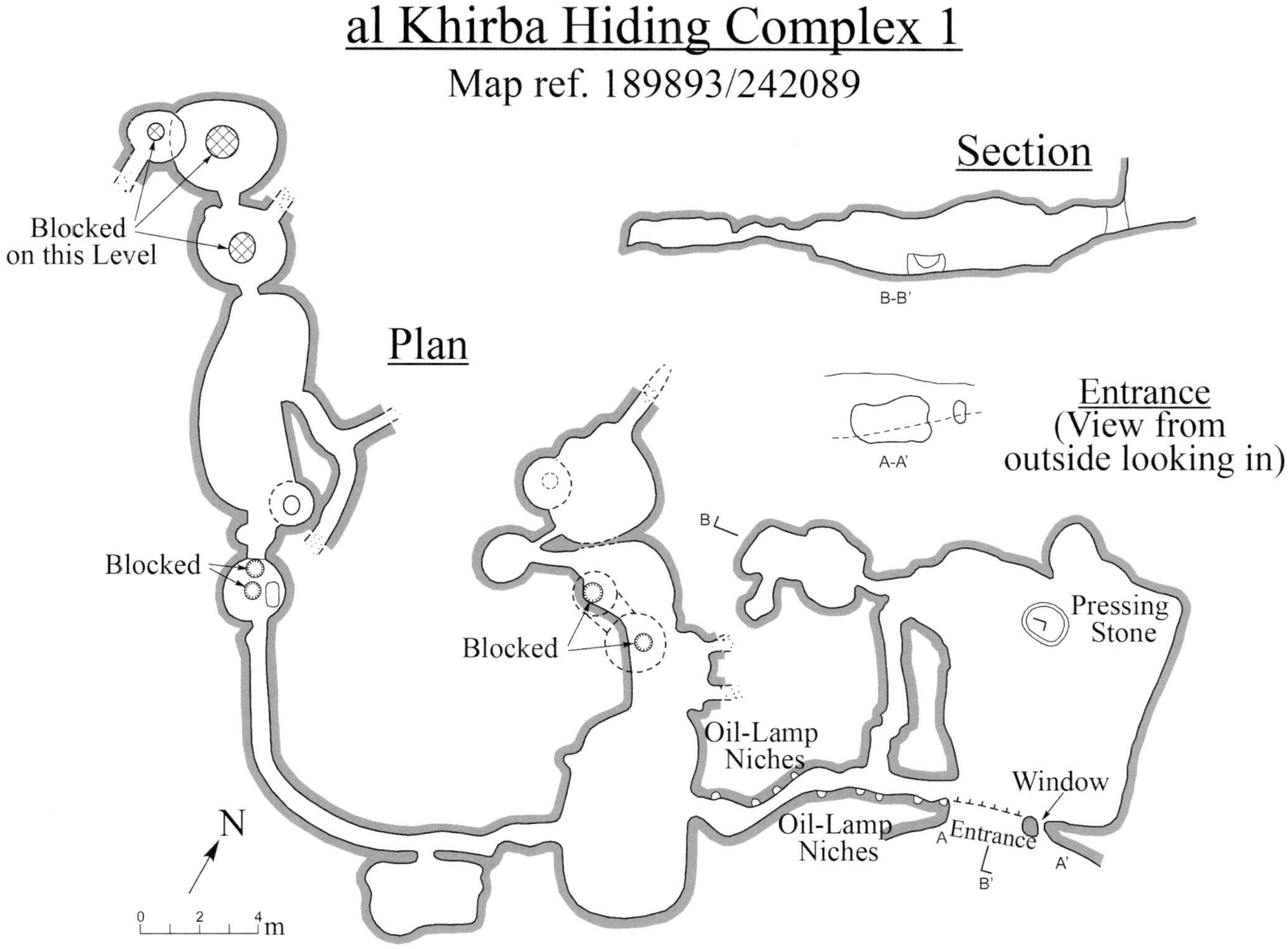

Map 64a: Horvat El-Khirbeh Hiding Complex 1

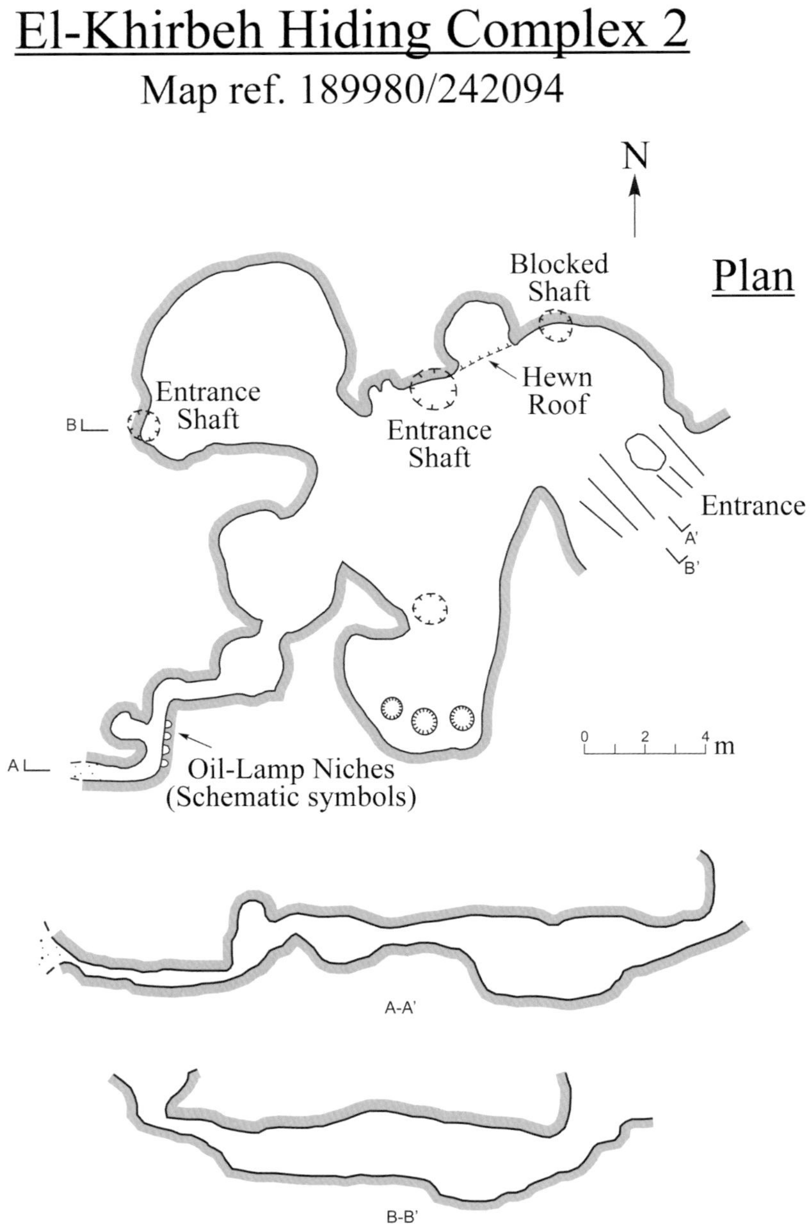

Map 64b: Horvat El-Khirbeh Hiding Complex 2

39. Ruma, Horvat Ruma, in Bet Rimon Valley (Map ref. 177765/243833)

Horvat Ruma covers an area of c. 40 dunams (c. 10 acres) on a low hill on the southern fringes of Bet Natofa Valley, c. 4 km northeast of Zippori. Today, the Bedouin village of Rumat al-Heib preserves the site's ancient name. About 1.5 km north of Horvat Ruma is the site of Horvat Rumana and both contain the remains of ancient Jewish settlements.[65] Horvat Ruma has a view of Zippori Hill, the mountain ridge of Nazareth to the east, and the Yodefat mountain ridge to the west. The site has been identified as the Jewish village of "Ruma," home of Netir and Philip who fought to defend Iotapata during the Great Revolt (*War* 3: 233). On its summit, Victor Guérin saw the ruins of buildings, water cisterns, the walls of a small structure aligned from east to west, and column drums. He noted that the slopes of the hill contained the remains of numerous ancient buildings, most of which had rock-hewn water cisterns or underground chambers. On the east slope, Guérin saw a fine, monolithic burial door.[66]

The hiding complex surveyed by Tepper and Shachar and mapped by the ICRC is located in the southeastern part of Horvat Ruma.[67] The complex includes all the typical features of hiding complexes in the Judean foothills and consists of hewn chambers with interconnecting passages. Access is via a water cistern rendered obsolete by the complex. Another water cistern found at the bottom of the complex bears marks made by water. The total length of its passages is c. 100 m and all are hewn horizontally.

65 See Safrai 1981:69–76.

66 See Guérin 1880,6:247.

67 The complex was first discovered by Michael Even-Esh, see Tepper and Shachar 1987b:290 n. 27. The ICRC map is published in Cohen 1983:39; Tepper and Shachar 1987b:292.

Fig. 97: Horvat Ruma

The height differences were overcome by using ladders. Niches for oil lamps were found along the passages. A salvage excavation in the hiding complex in 1983 focused on one of the chambers and part of a passage between two chambers whose northern wall was adjacent to the water cistern at the bottom of the hiding complex.[68] The archaeologists discovered that this passage had been roofed with rectangular stone slabs and its rock-hewn floor had been coated with two plaster layers dating no earlier than the 1st half of the 1st c. BCE. The excavation produced pottery from between the 1st c. BCE and the 2nd c. CE, as well as some potsherds from later periods.

68 See Rochman 1986:35.

Kh. Ruma
Hiding Complex

Map ref. 177765/243833

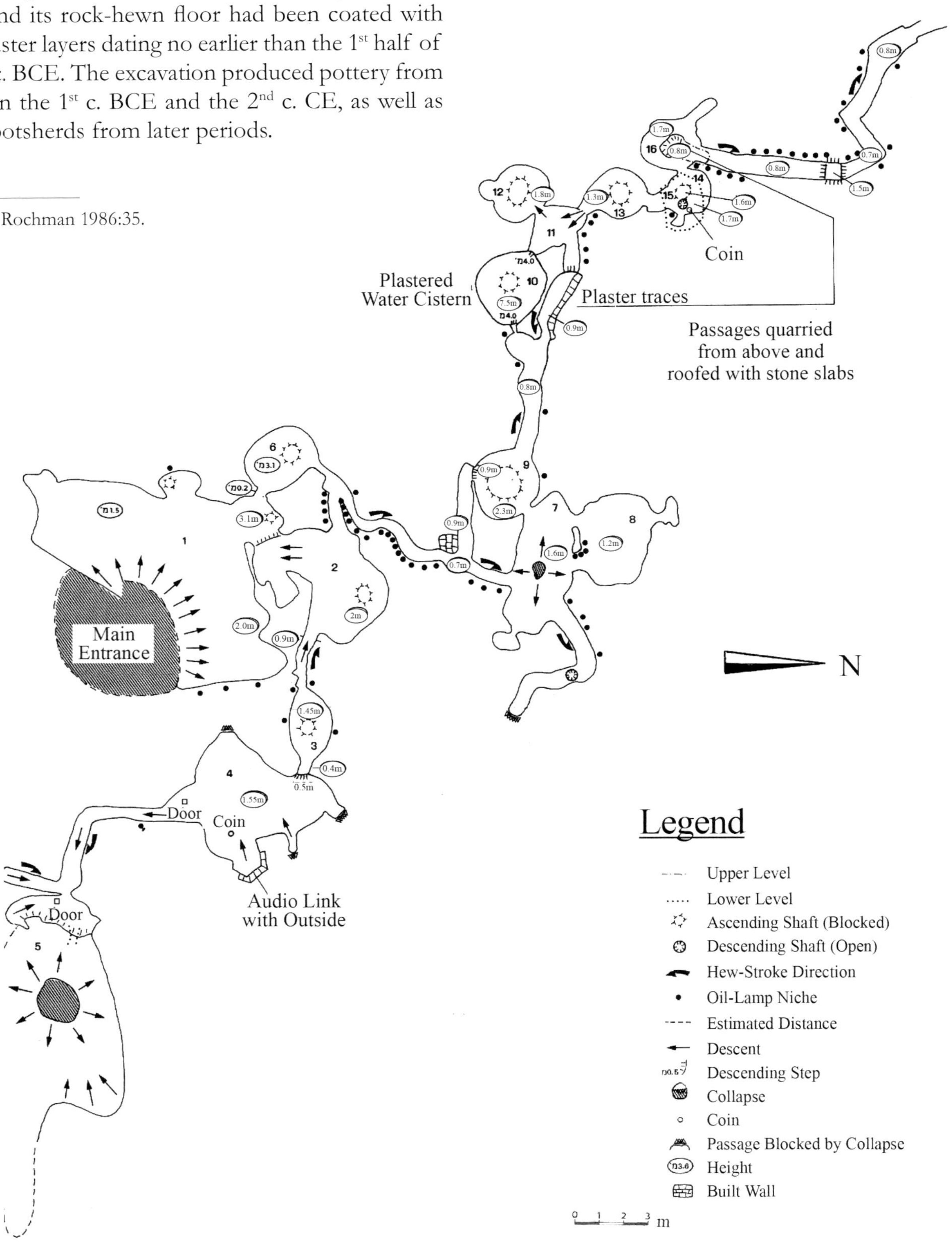

Map 65: Horvat Ruma

40–45. Kafr Kanna, Khirbet Qana and Karm er-Ras (6 complexes)

In the Gospel of John "Cana of Galilee" is mentioned as a Jewish village and the site of Jesus' first miracle converting water into wine (John 2:1–12 Κανά). The village of Cana is cited by Josephus as his headquarters at the time of the preparations for the Great Revolt (*Life* 86).

The question of where to locate "Cana of Galilee" is old. Some identify the Roman-period Jewish village of Cana of Galilee at Karm er-Ras or in the village nucleus of Kafr Kanna, whilst others identify it at Khirbet Qana, a site located on the slopes of Mount Azmon, about 10 km northeast of the Arab town of Kafr Manda and 13 km north of Nazareth.[69] Victor Guérin identified Cana of Galilee at a site near Nazareth, extending over a high hill with abundant traces of water cisterns, hewn underground chambers, remains of walls of a rectangular building, and an ancient tower. Guérin also surveyed another hill called Khirbet Kanna southwest of Kafr Qana.[70]

Kafr Kanna lies 4 km northeast of Nazareth in the Lower Galilee. Several archaeological sites with some Roman-period remains have been identified within the area of the present-day village, including Karm er-Ras, a low hill at the western edge of the village, the ancient village nucleus area in the center of Kafr Kanna and Jebel Khuweikkha, a chalky limestone hill lying above and at the eastern edge of the village. In the past, a section of mosaic flooring was found here containing two dedicatory inscriptions in Aramaic of the type found in ancient synagogues.[71] Recent explorations have produced substantial archaeological evidence at Khirbet Qana, Karm er-Ras and Kafr Kanna.[72] Among these remains are five hiding complexes discovered at Kafr Kanna and Karm e-Ras which we will now describe.

40. Kafr Kanna, north of Zippori Industrial Estate, on the edge of the village of Meshhed (Map ref. 180800/239600)

The first hiding complex to be discussed is located on a prominent hill where the northwest houses of Meshhed village are located. The top of the hill looks out over Tur'an Ridge, Kibbutz Bet Rimon, and Zipporit Industrial Park built to the south of Hoshaya. A hiding complex explored during the present survey was hewn from inside a water cistern with two openings, thus rendering the cistern obsolete. From here, one of the entrances cuts into a burial chamber, skirting around the burial niches and taking care not to damage them. This hiding passage continues in a southerly direction for 26 m and four chambers of various sizes are hewn along its length. It eventually cuts into a burial chamber with seven niches. From here, the main passage continues to the southeast and reaches a dressed stone door that is now mostly blocked with earth. Another passage in this complex is filled with earth. The hiding complex yielded four Early Roman potsherds.

69 See Schwartz 2008:83 n. 134; Douglas 2002:101–102.
70 See Guérin 1880:216.
71 See Ilan 1991a:218.
72 See McCollough 2015 discussing Khirbet Qana or Luca 2015 summarizing the finds from Kafr Kanna, on recent explorations on Karm er-Ras see Alexandre 2015; Alexandre 2017.

Fig. 98: Kafr Kanna, Zipporit

Kafr Kanna (near Zipporit)

Map ref. 180800/239600

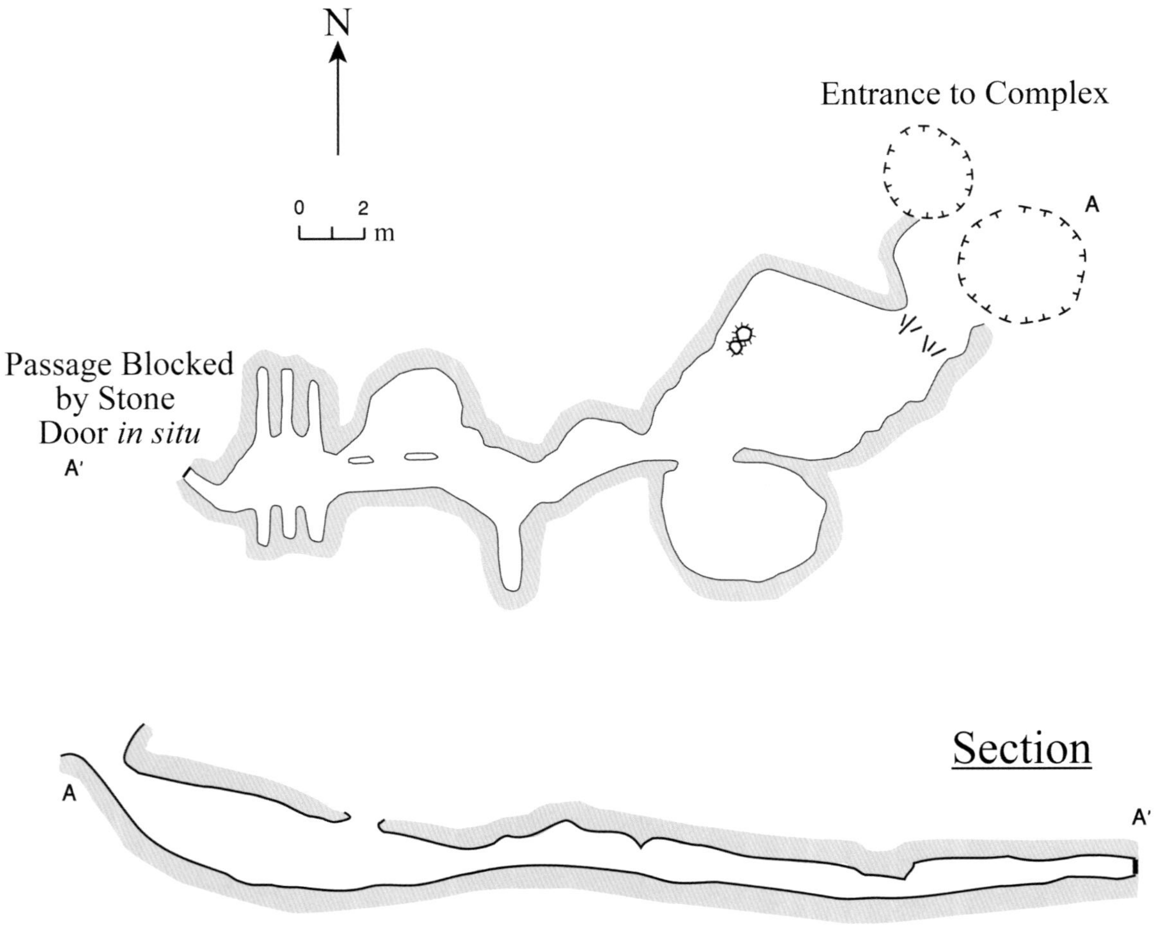

Map 66: Kafr Kanna, Zipporit

41–42. Kafr Kanna, northern residential area, Karm er-Ras (Area T: Map ref. 181646/239411; Area W: Map ref. 181554/239558)

The remains of Karm e-Ras lie on the western fringes of Kafr Kanna, c. 5 km west of Nazareth, on the upper western slopes of the large ridge where the Arab village of Kafr Kanna is situated (213 m asl). From the ruined settlement, which is now covered by a modern house, one can see Tur'an Ridge and Kibbutz Bet Rimon to the west and Yodefat Ridge and Zipporit Industrial Park to the southwest. From the top of Karm er-Ras hill and 1.8 km away one can see the hill near Sepphoris (Complex No. 38). Zvi Gal identified Karm e-Ras with the biblical city of Jotbah (*2 Kings* 21:19). Yardenna Alexandre exposed traces of the settlement, dating from the Iron Age onward, in a salvage excavation conducted in 2007 in the northern residential area of Kafr Kanna. The excavations exposed two hiding complexes dating to the Early Roman period; one complex was marked as Area T and the other as Area W.[73] The excavation uncovered a small house, beneath which three bell-shaped cavities (maximum height 1.4 m) were found to be roofed with vaults made of small stones and covered with a stone slab. Two of these bell-shaped chambers (B and O) are adjacent to each other, whereas the third (A) is 5 m away and linked to them via an underground passage. From Chamber C, a short underground passage was meticulously hewn in the rock with a roof and floor built of large stone slabs. A small round hole was exposed in the rock floor (diameter 0.8 m) through which it is possible to peer down into a bell-shaped chamber with a level floor (diameter 2.5 m, height 2.5 m). Inside this chamber, eleven intact pottery jars were found *in situ* lying on their side and on top of each other. The jars are of a type used during the Great Revolt and were produced at Shikhin near ancient Sepphoris. The chamber appears to have been a storeroom inside an underground hiding complex built beneath a private home and it was doubtless the most important chamber in the underground complex, to which the other elements were built to provide access. Other, smaller pottery jars were exposed in this chamber and were probably placed there during the construction of the hiding complex. Chamber A also yielded two bronze coins minted in Jerusalem in the second year of the Great Revolt. These provide a precise date for the last use of the hiding complex, i. e. in the summer of 67 CE.

73 See Alexandre 2008:73–79. With thanks to Yardenna Alexandre for permission to use this information prior to the publication of her report.

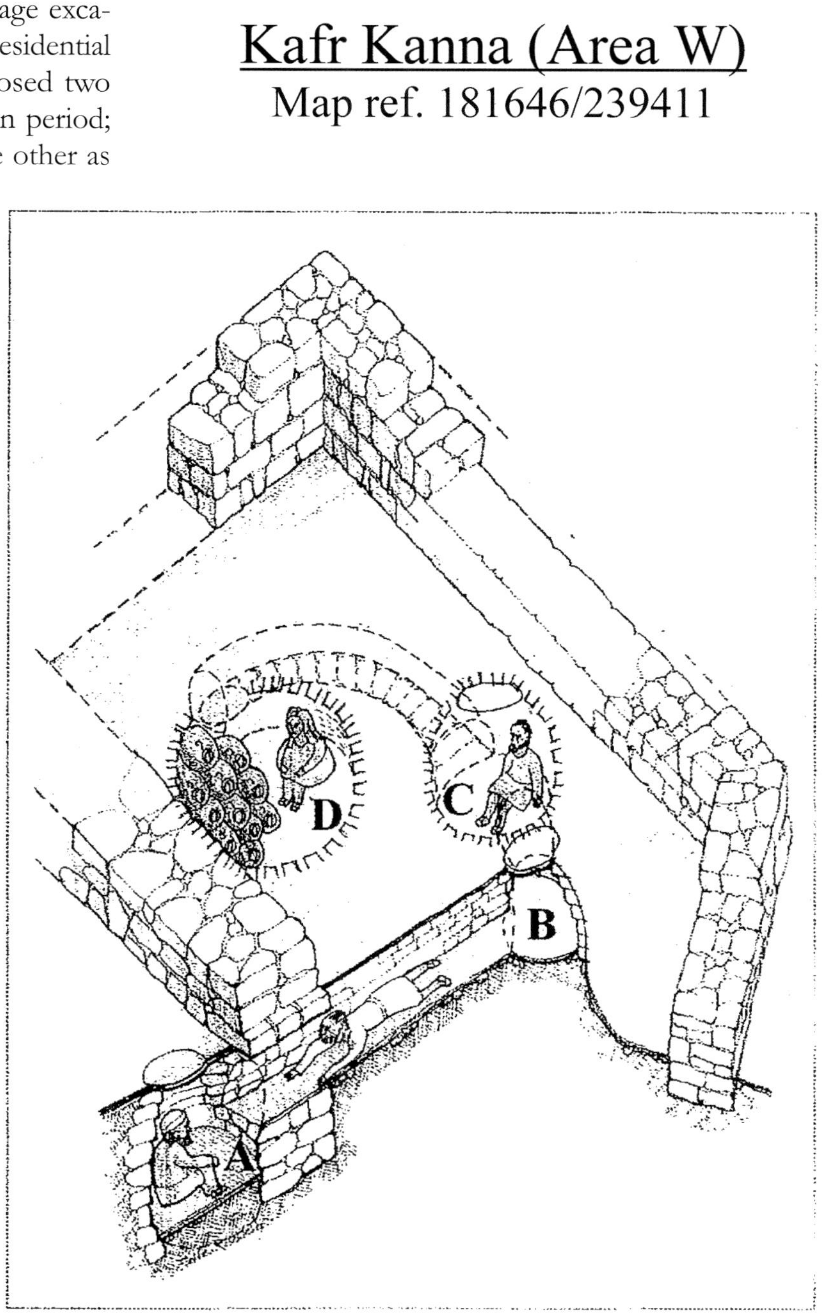

Map 67:
Kafr Kanna, Karm a-Ras Area W

Fig. 99: Kafr Kanna, Karm a-Ras Area W

43. Kafr Kanna, Kh. Khukha (A) (Jabel Khuwweikh), in the center of the village (Map ref. 182897/238949)

Although this hiding complex was excavated in the 1990s, the results remain unpublished. The only information about the finds discovered in the hiding complex was provided by Aviam who described the discovery of some sealed loci from the mid-second century CE, among them an ostracon engraved in Hebrew.[74] The hiding complex was mapped by the ICRC and is published for the first time in this volume. The complex had three entrances, only one of which has been preserved. The round opening (diameter 0.9 m) is blocked with stones and concrete. The hiding complex is meticulously hewn and its passages are about 70 m long. It contains water cisterns and passages. The entrances were blocked long ago by the occupants of nearby houses.

Fig. 100: Kafr Kanna, Khirbet Khukha in center of village

74 See Aviam, 2004:125.

Kafr Kanna - Kh. Khuwweikh (Jabel)

Map ref. 182077/237760

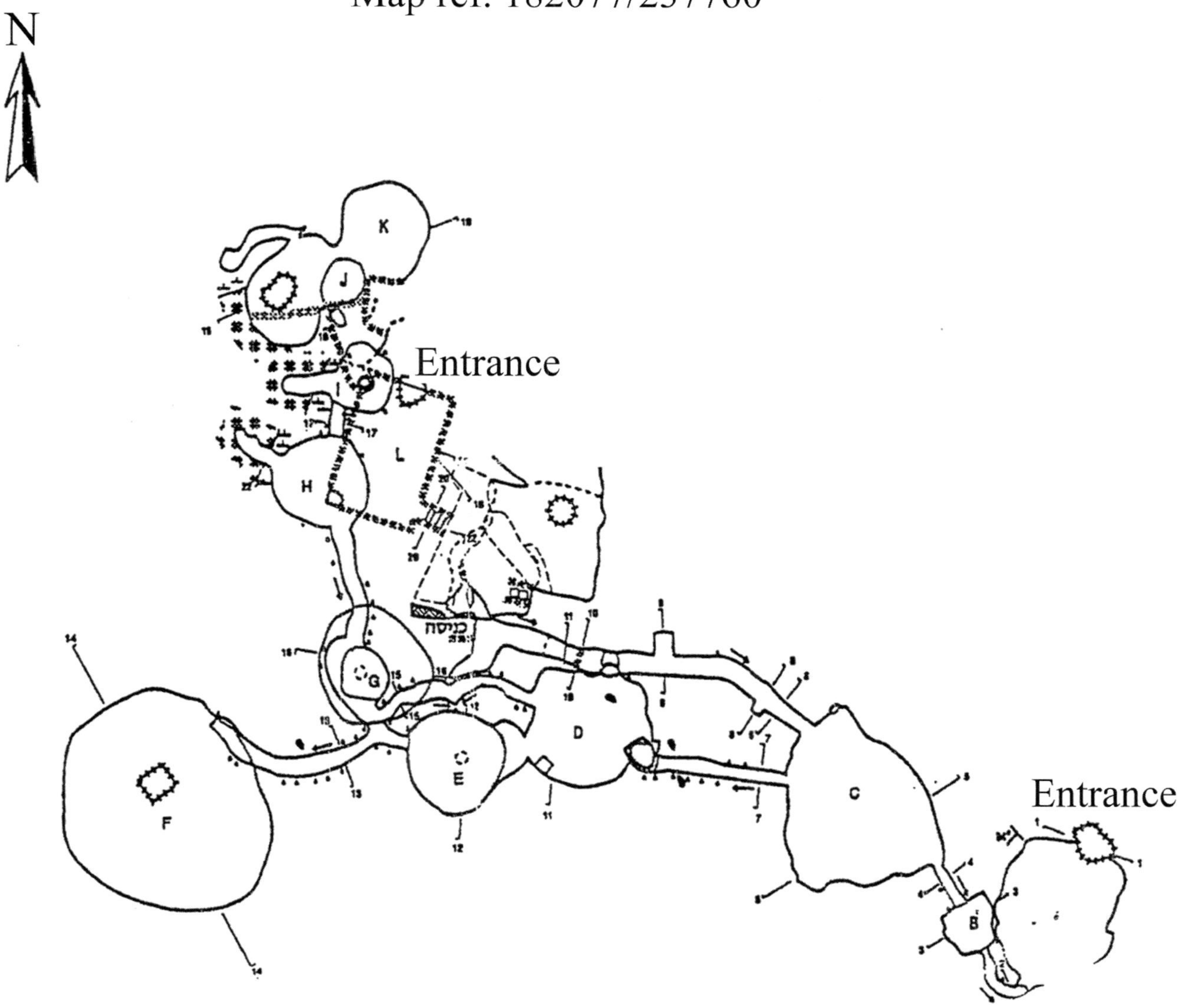

Map 68: Kafr Kanna, Khirbet Khukha in center of village

44. Kafr Kanna, Kh. Khukha (B) (Jabel Khuwweikh)
(Map ref. 182899/238978)

This complex was discovered by the ICRC while mapping the first complex and lies about 40 m to its west. It could be entered from inside a dwelling house, probably via an ancient olive press, and it too has been blocked off.

Fig. 101: Kafr Kanna, Kh. Khukha, location of the Hiding Complex

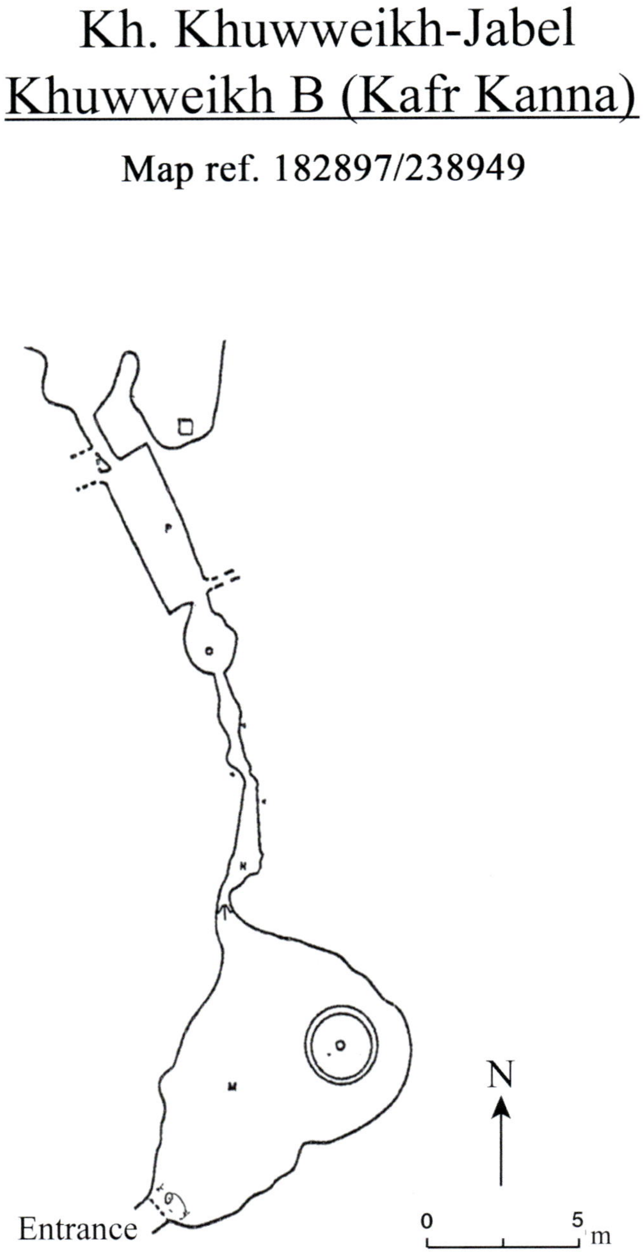

Map 69: Kafr Kanna, Kh. Khukha, (Jabel)

45. Kafr Kanna (Ein el-Jozeh)
(Map ref. 182077/237760)

This hiding complex was discovered c. 1 km south of Kafr Kanna at a site called Ein el-Jozeh.[75] Its entrance is hewn from inside a natural cave formed in the Bi'ina Formation limestone rock. The cave consists of a large chamber (20 × 60 m; height 6 m) and the overall length of the complex is 80 m. The chamber contains stream deposits, stalactites and stalagmites and has two openings. One leads to a chamber and is deliberately blocked, suggesting that the entrance was sealed off to prevent hostile elements from reaching the hiding complex. The other leads to a hewn passage c. 20 m long. The horizontal passage is linked at the end to the main cave by a 2 m high shaft. The hewn passage is a very tight squeeze, exposing anyone emerging from it into the main chamber and enabling those hiding in the chamber to deal with hostile intruders gaining access to the complex.[76]

75 See Frumkin 1984:95.

76 See Frumkin 1984:94–96.

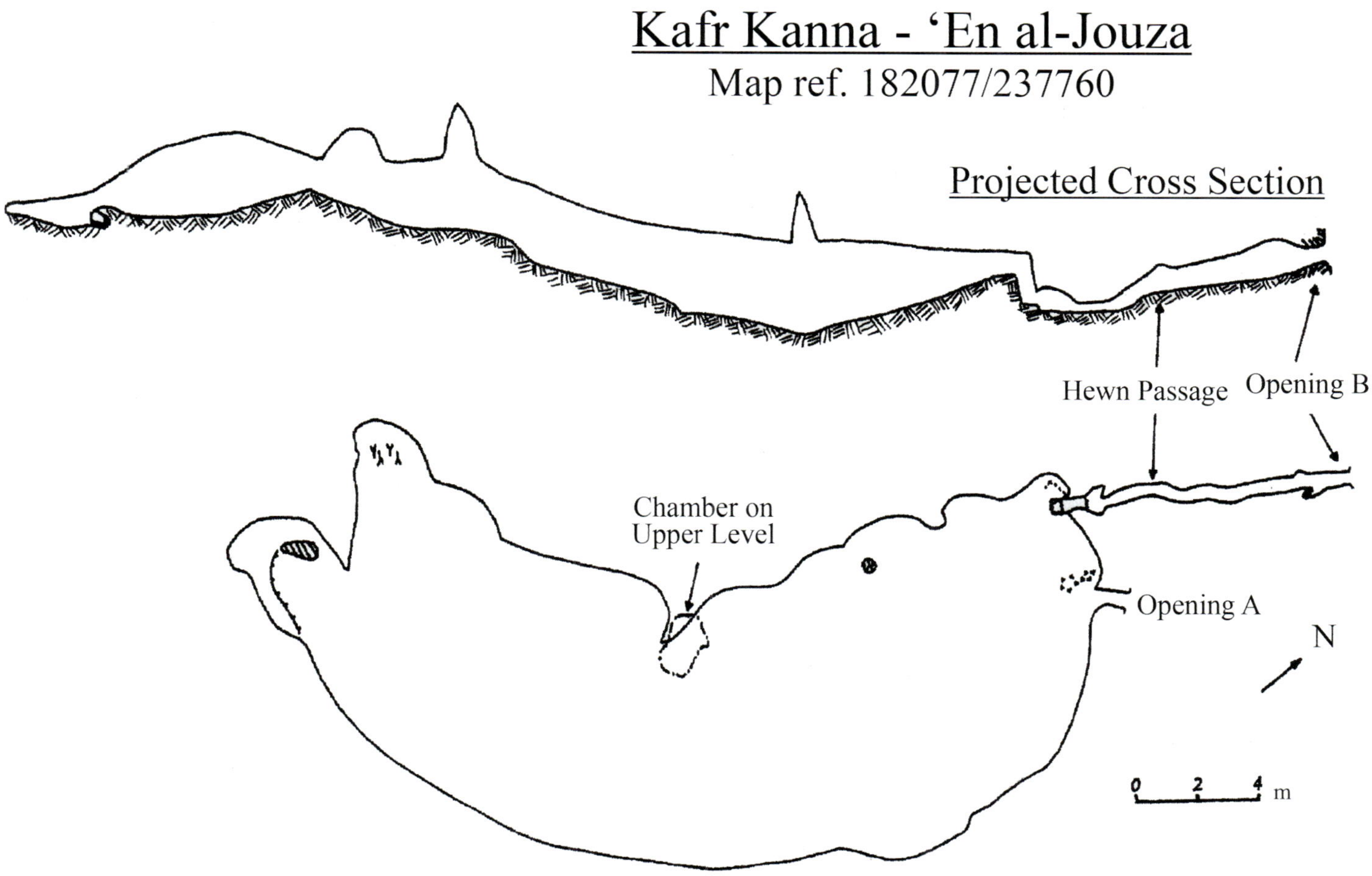

Map 70: Kafr Kanna, 'En al-Jouza

Fig. 102: Kafr Kanna, 'En al-Jouza

46. ʿEnot Shoʿim (ʿEn Mahel)
(Map ref. 182767/235550)

ʿEnot Shoʿim is a large site located on the eastern slopes of the Nazareth mountain ridge, c. 0.5 km south of the village of ʿEn Mahal, with an impressive view overlooking Mount Tabor and presently farmed and planted with olive groves. An abundance of pottery is scattered on the surface and building stones are incorporated in the terrace walls. The site was surveyed in the past by Nehemiah Zori, who reported the presence of Persian, Byzantine, and Arab pottery, and later by Zvi Gal as part of the Mount Tabor Map Survey, which recorded three adjacent sites containing flint tools and pottery from the Palaeolithic to the Ottoman eras.[77]

The site with the hiding complex is located at the bottom of a spur descending southward, toward Nahal Barak ben Avinoam, and is separated by a deep ravine from the main site of ʿEnot Shoʿim c. 300 m to the west. Based on the survey and surface finds, it covers c. 6 dunams (c. 1.5 acres). A coin of Constantius II (351–354 CE) and a Mamluk coin were found on the surface. Above the spur on which the site sits, Zvi Gal documented a concentration of agricultural installations and a necropolis containing cist tombs, shaft tombs with *arcosolia,* and a burial cave with *loculi.* This area yielded pottery from the Roman and Byzantine periods.[78]

The hiding complex, located in the upper part of the site and explored by Leibner, Shivtiʾel and Distelfeld,[79] begins with two passages that branch out to the north and west from the bottom of an unplastered bell-shaped pit (diameter 3 m, height 3 m), probably originally used for storing dry produce. Chisel marks are easily discernible on the walls and ceiling of the complex, which is meticulously hewn and contains about

77 Tsuri 1977:104–105; Gal 1998:39–40.

78 Gal 1998:35.

79 Leibner, Shivti'el and Distelfeld 2015.

Fig. 103: ʿEnot Shoʿim

20 oil-lamp niches cut near the roof in the walls. Movement within the tunnels is difficult, as they measure only c. 0.6 m wide and 0.6–0.8 m high. Tunnel A is c. 25 m long and links five rooms of various sizes. Tunnel B is c. 30 m long and has four rooms. Tunnel B is currently blocked at its entrance and access to this part of the complex is from above, where the roof was breached by a tractor that also exposed remains of a surface dwelling with a wall preserved to a height of five courses (1.5 m), a small section of floor covered by a burnt layer containing finds, and a threshold in secondary use.

Three of the rooms, located deep within the hiding complex and with no trace of disturbance by robbers, were excavated down to the bedrock and the soil from two of them (A2 and B3) was brought out and sieved. Since neither the rooms nor their environs had entrances or shafts descending from surface level, we could eliminate contamination by finds originating outside the complex.

Room B3 (2 × 4 m, maximum height c. 1.1 m) is located at the end of a short tunnel branching off from Space B2. A small bell-shaped pit (c. 1 m deep) is hewn into the floor of the room, near the east wall.

Room A2 is located along Tunnel A, c. 7 m from the entrance. The room is elliptical (c. 2.5 × 3.5 m, height 1.3 m). The bedrock lay beneath a 40-centimeter layer, the upper part of which contained dark-colored soil that may have come from Pit A1 and the lower part contained light-colored soil eroded from the walls. A bell-shaped pit was exposed near the center of the room and was excavated to a depth of c. 1 m without reaching bedrock. An entrance to another tunnel, blocked after about 2 m, was discovered in the north wall. Room A5, deep inside the complex, is rectangular (1.5 × 2.5 m, maximum height 1.3 m). The quality of the hewing and preservation of the room is better than in the two above-mentioned rooms.

This complex yielded a coin, a ring, fragments of glass vessels and dozens of identifiable pottery sherds as well as several restorable pottery vessels found *in situ*. All date to the Early and Middle Roman periods with no later finds, so that the conclusion that the

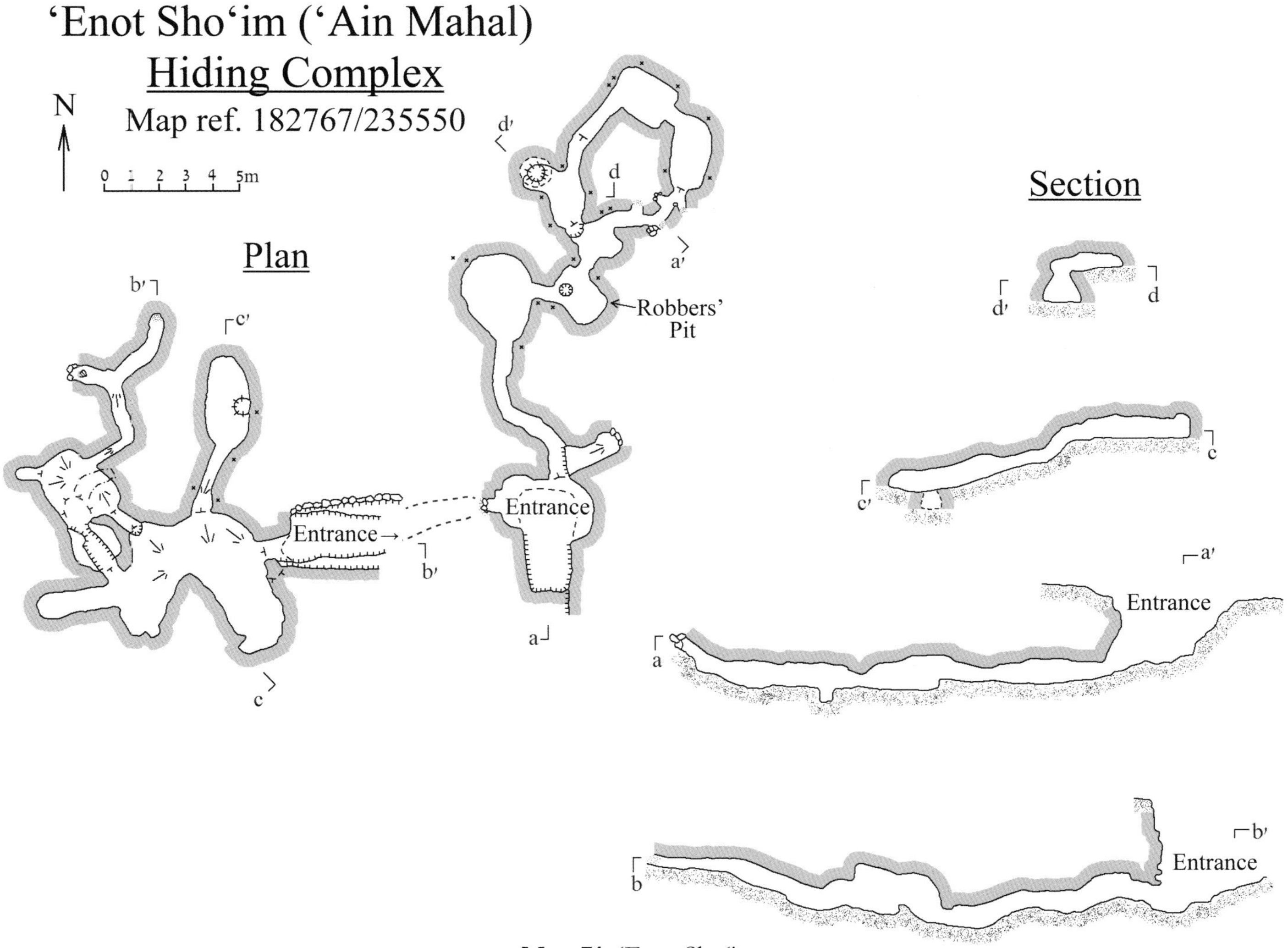

Map 71: 'Enot Sho'im

complex was already sealed in antiquity is plausible. This is of special importance since the dating of such hiding complexes is usually problematic owing to the presence of later intrusive finds. Most of the pottery vessels discovered are jars and the minority are small vessels such as bowls, jugs, and a juglet. Interestingly, neither cooking pots nor casseroles were found. Most of the vessels are of types produced in the famous workshop at Shikhin, only 8 km away, from where they probably came.[80] Recent pottery retrieved from an extensive destruction layer at Khirbet Wadi Hamam in Eastern Galilee helps date the finds. On the basis of two hoards, the destruction was dated to c. 125–135 CE and it appears that the entire village was damaged and perhaps even abandoned for several decades. The rich assemblages in the destruction layer provide new evidence for the pottery types found in the Galilee in the early 2nd c. CE and enable us to determine which vessels found in contexts of the Great Revolt, such as Iotapata and Gamala, no longer existed at the time of the Second Revolt in c. 130 CE.[81]

The only coin from the complex itself was found at the entrance to Room A2, at the end of the tunnel leading from Pit A1. The coin, dated to Trajan (98–117 CE), is a *quadrans* minted in Rome.[82] Two more coins can be associated with the dwelling above. One is a rare coin of Trebonianus Gallus (251–253 CE) and the other probably dates to the rule of Caracalla (198–217 CE). The pottery finds from Room A2 are homogeneous and are characteristic of Early Roman assemblages. Especially noteworthy is a fragment of a Herodian knife-pared oil lamp (Type IV, common from the mid-first century CE onward and found mainly in first-century CE assemblages)[83] and a jar with a simple rim and ridged neck. Similar lamps have been found in Judea in a few 2nd c. contexts; most noteworthy are those from Shuʿfat, where they are dated to the period between the First and Second Jewish Revolts.[84] To date, however, no such lamps are known from clear 2nd c. contexts in the Galilee, and this type is also absent from the rich assemblages in the destruction layer at Khirbet Wadi Hamam. The jar, Type T1.3 in Díez-Fernández's classification, is one of the most common types in Early Roman Galilean assemblages. While Díez-Fernández dates its appearance to the mid-1st c. BCE,[85] the excavators of nearby Sepphoris date it to the end of the 1st c. BCE.[86] Both date it to no later than the second third of the 1st c. CE. This jar was also present in the assemblage found with the boat at Ginnosar which Adan-Bayewitz dates to the mid-1st c. CE.[87] Evidence for the production of this type was found in pottery kilns that apparently operated until the Great Revolt at both Iotapata and Karm er-Ras.[88] It seems to disappear after the Great Revolt, is absent from the early 2nd c. destruction layer at Khirbet Wadi Hamam and, in general, no examples are known from 2nd c. contexts. Another jar from room A2 has a rounded everted rim and a relatively short neck with a ridge at its base (Type T1.5).[89] It appears in large quantities in 1st c. CE assemblages such as those from Iotapata and Gamala.[90] Eleven complete jars of this type were recently found in a simple hiding complex in Karm er-Ras together with two coins from the second year of the Great Revolt.[91] The type was also found in Middle Roman assemblages in Sepphoris and Capernaum.[92] Large body fragments found at the entrance to room A2 and in the bell-shaped pit in its center apparently belong to both these jars.

The only indicative find from Room A5 is the base of a mold-made oil lamp. In light of its small dimensions, round contours, and shallow ring-base it appears to be a local imitation of a Roman discus lamp common in second-century CE assemblages, although the type appeared in the second half of the first century CE and continued into the third.[93]

The finds from Room B3 include two restorable jars (Types T1.3 and T1.5). Other fragments of Type T1.5 vessels were found but they have a thick wall and higher neck; they are characteristic of the Middle Roman period and are prevalent in the destruction layer at Khirbet Wadi Hamam. Also noteworthy from this room are jar lids typical of the 2nd–3rd c. centuries CE[94] and a flat round lid carved of soft chalk that was probably used to cover a jar. Similar lids, usually lathe-made, were found in Second Temple-period assem-

80 Adan-Bayewitz and Wieder 1992:196.
81 The pottery from Khirbet Wadi Hamam has not yet been published but see Leibner and Bijovsky 2014.
82 Scholars opine that this type was minted before 103 CE and was originally intended for distribution among the army's legions; see Leibner and Bijovsky 2014:115–116 and references there.
83 Barag and Hershkovitz 1994:47–50.
84 Sklar-Parnes 2004:38; see also Rapuano 2013:87–88.
85 Díez-Fernández 1983:135.
86 Balouka 2013:37.
87 Adan-Bayewitz 1990:92.
88 Aviam 2005:196; see also Avshalom-Gorni and Getzov 2002:78.
89 See Díez-Fernández 1983:107.
90 Aviam 2005:126, Fig. 75; Berlin 2006:48, Fig. 2:26–27.
91 Alexandre 2008:77.
92 Balouka 2013:37–38; Loffreda 2008:118.
93 Rosenthal-Heginbottom and Sivan 1978:85
94 See Balouka 2013:52.

blages in Jerusalem, and one similar hand-made lid was found at Sepphoris.[95] Another interesting find from this room is an iron finger-ring of a type common in the Roman world mainly in the second half of the 1st c. and the 2nd c. CE.

The finds discovered in the hiding complex date to the Early and Middle Roman periods, but no stratigraphic sequence could be identified and, therefore, the artifacts were found mixed. Apparently, the finds are not all concurrent, a point that suggests prolonged use of the complex rather than a single specific period. Some of the finds are of types belonging primarily to the 1st c. CE, and it is therefore hard to imagine that they are all residual and were brought here only in the 2nd c. CE. These finds, especially the two Type T1.3 jars found in Rooms A2 and B3, indicate that the complex existed before the end of the 1st c. CE since the types found do not appear in later assemblages. Most of the pottery, however, belongs to types that were common in the 2nd c. (although some also continue into the 3rd). These finds, such as the high-necked jars and the coin of Trajan, indicate continuous activity here into the Middle Roman period, in the 2nd, maybe even 3rd c. CE. It is important to emphasize that the complex is located beneath a Roman-period dwelling at a site located in the heart of Roman and Byzantine Jewish Galilee. The complex, which was undoubtedly prepared as a hiding place, dates to the Early and Middle Roman periods. It seems likely that its quarrying and preparation are connected to the turbulent events of the two Jewish Revolts against the Romans.[96]

47 and 48. Tur'an, in Tur'an village, near Golani Junction (Map ref. 184824/242800)

Tur'an village is situated c. 3.5 km west of the Golani Junction. Klein proposed identifying the place with the Jewish village of Tur'an referred to in the Song of Songs and in rabbinical literature.[97] Guérin detected ancient threshing floors and rock-hewn water cisterns at the site.[98]

95 Magen 2002:24, 31; Zilberstein and Ben Efraim 2013: Fig. 9.6.4 and 217.

96 During the study of hiding complexes that exist at present, ceramic finds were found in many other types of hiding complexes dating to the first and second revolts. A comprehensive article on this issue will be published in the Israel Exploration Journal by Yinon Shivti'el and Mechael Osband, entitled "The Meiron Valley Cave Survey and the Discovery of a New Type of Refuge Cave in the Galilee" (in print).

97 See Klein 1945:218; Vilnay 1981:8159–8160.

98 See Guérin 1880,6:123.

Fig. 104: Tur'an, courtyard of private house

The hiding complex was discovered in the courtyard of a private home at the west end of the village.[99] The complex is hewn into the north wall of an ancient water cistern or public reservoir (12 × 25 m, height 6 m) The cistern is now accessible via the collapsed east wall, but the wall may be a later addition. The cistern has an oval hole hewn in its roof that is now blocked with stones and a stone wall is built along its south wall. In the cave wall beside it is a partially finished hewn passage that was not completed, for some reason. The passage opening measures 0.45 × 0.60 m. A hiding complex hewn near the southwest wall of the water cistern continues westward. The hewn complex would have rendered the water cistern unusable. The entrance to the complex is 0.6 × 0.6 m in section and the 12.5 m long passage is crudely cut in a straight line with occasional wider sections and terminates in a hewn chamber (2.0 × 2.1 m). The passage continues for another 0.5 m into the east wall of the chamber, but this has recently been blocked off. From local neighbors, we learned that the hiding complex reaches a water cistern in the middle of the ancient village, estimated to be 400 m away.

We were informed of a second hiding complex in Tur'an village, located in the center of the ancient village (map ref. 184873/242378), where a 7 m long passage was discovered, and another hiding complex in Tur'an whose passages are now filled with debris.[100]

99 With thanks to Yossi Moshe and Dror Barshad for information about the hiding complexes in the village.

100 With thanks to Dror Barshad, regional archaeologist for northern Israel, for this information.

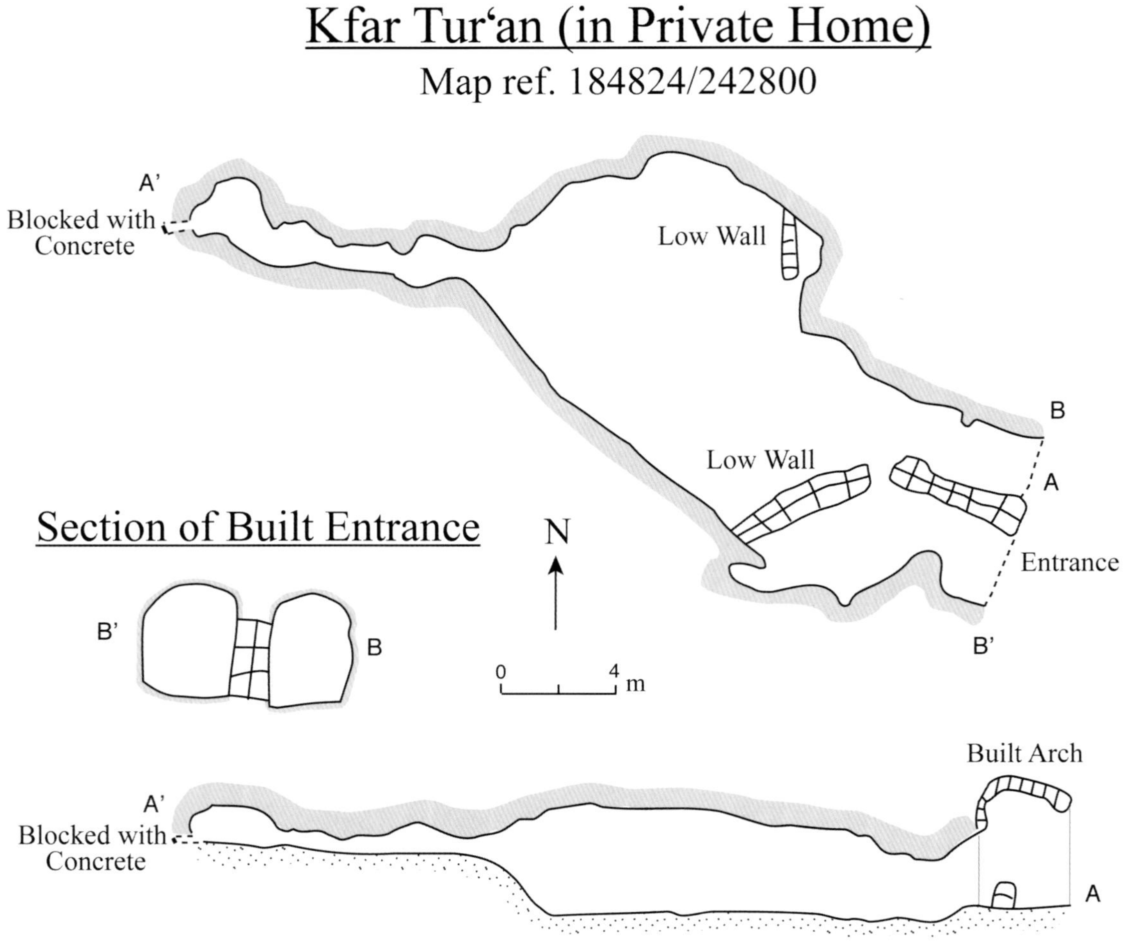

Map 72: Tur'an, Hiding Complex in private house

49. Ilaniya, Khirbet Sejera (Map ref. 187733/239921)

The ruins of Sejera village are about 3 km south of the Golani Junction and cover two mounds with numerous ancient remains, including agricultural installations, water cisterns, and rock-hewn burial caves. The surface finds suggest that Sejera village was built over a ruined Jewish settlement that has not yet been identified. Victor Guérin found traces of a rectangular building here made of ashlars, aligned on a west-east axis and measuring 6 × 10 m.[101] Gideon Foerster identified a synagogue from the many architectural elements found in the courtyards of local residents. My survey revealed that the site contains a large complex of approximately 200 dunams (50 acres). In the north of the mound, where there is a kind of natural arena, are the remains of a mosaic floor. Throughout the site there are dozens of burial caves, some of which are shaft burials and some niche-burial caves. Some burials show evidence of breached and connected niches resembling the complexes discovered at 'Iyei Me'arot. A fragmentary Greek inscription is engraved on the wall of one of the caves. Traces of an olive press found in another cave contain an entrance to a hiding complex. The olive-press cave (c. 14 × 18 m) has a central crushing stone with two stone weights beside it. Passage entrances hewn into two large niches in the southern wall are now blocked with earth. In the eastern wall is a passage measuring 0.45 × 0.65 m in section. In the early 1990s, the author and volunteers from Ilaniya cleaned out a 50 m long section of passage to discover that it leads to a plastered water cistern that can be reached by climbing 4 m down a rope.[102] In the east wall of the cistern is another passage that is blocked with earth. The main passage skirts around the cistern and terminates in a chamber measuring 2 × 3 m.

101 See Guérin 1880, vol. 6:124.

102 With thanks for permission to clear the passage from Gideon Avni of the Israel Antiquities Authority. Erik Gold, Esti Yankelevitch, Atalia Truah from the Sejera Preservation Site and Azrieli Reikin from the ICRC participated in the work. With thanks to Erik Gold for information about the many finds from Sejera.

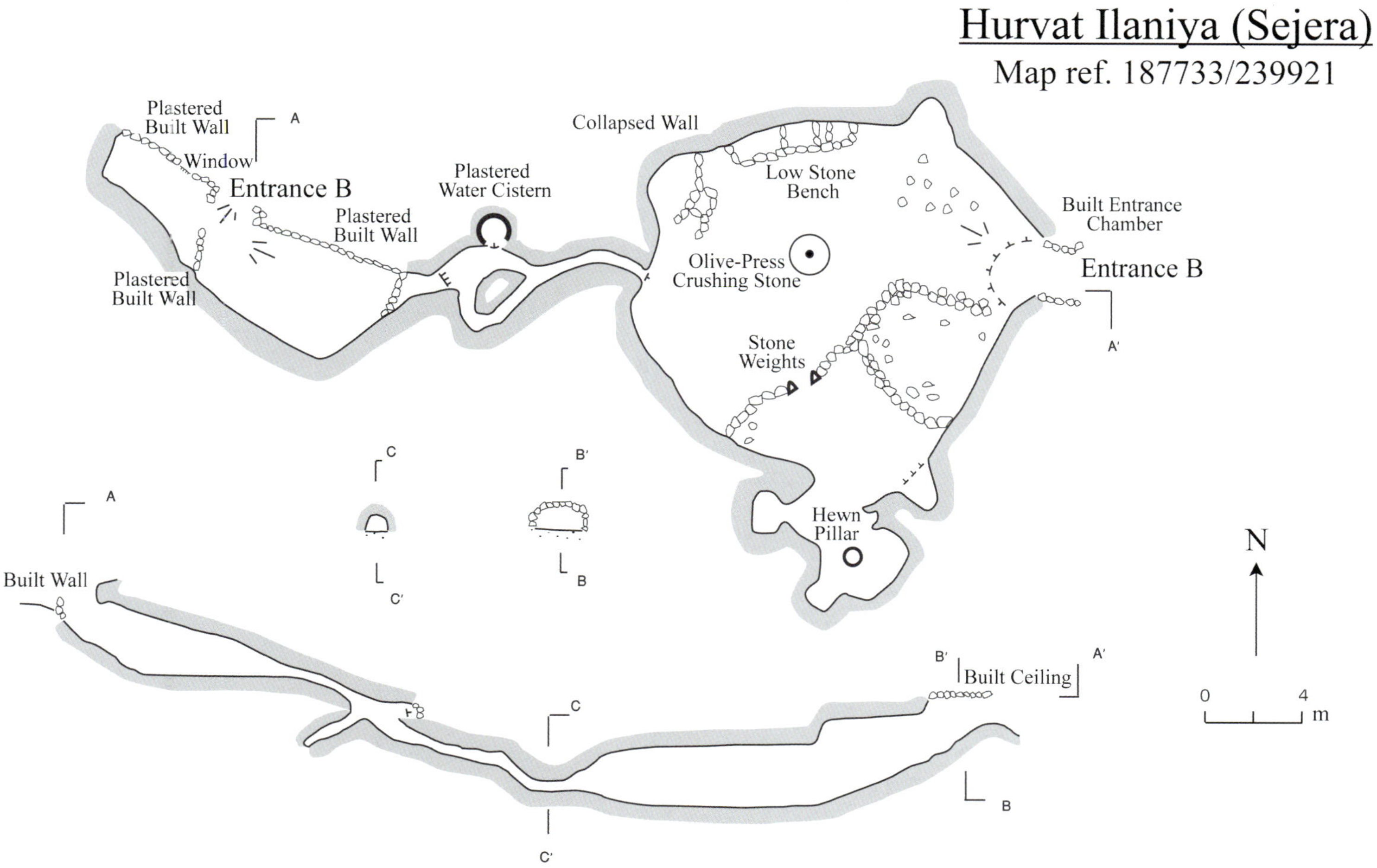

Map 73: Ilaniya, Khirbet Sejera

Fig. 105: Ilaniya, Khirbet Sejera

50. Evtsam, Horvat Evtsam (Kh. Basum), Yavniel Valley (Map ref. 195495/237586)

The ruins lie on top of a ridge on the southwest fringes of Yavniʿel valley and next to an ancient road, about 7 km southwest of Tiberias and 3 km northwest of Moshava Yavniʿel, near Moshav Hazorʿim. I am not aware of any proposal to identify the site with a toponym mentioned in historical records. The site contains remains of walls and dwelling houses and the tomb of an Arab sheikh, Sheikh el-Basum, on its south side. Ancient architectural elements are incorporated in the walls of the structure above the tomb. Three large lintels were found at the site as well as ashlars and other architectural elements that Ilan believes are characteristic of elements found at ancient Galilean synagogues.[103] In the 1920s, Aapeli Saarisalo discovered three large lintels, ashlars, and other architectural elements similar to those found at synagogues in Galilee at the site.[104] Guérin described it as a small, abandoned village. A hiding complex was discovered c. 50 m north of the sheikh's tomb, on the south side and hewn from inside a cave (depth 6 m, width 14 m) in the local rock with basalt inclusions (a previously unknown feature in hiding com-

103 See Ilan 1987:57.
104 See Ilan 1991a:123.

Fig. 106: Horvat Evtsam

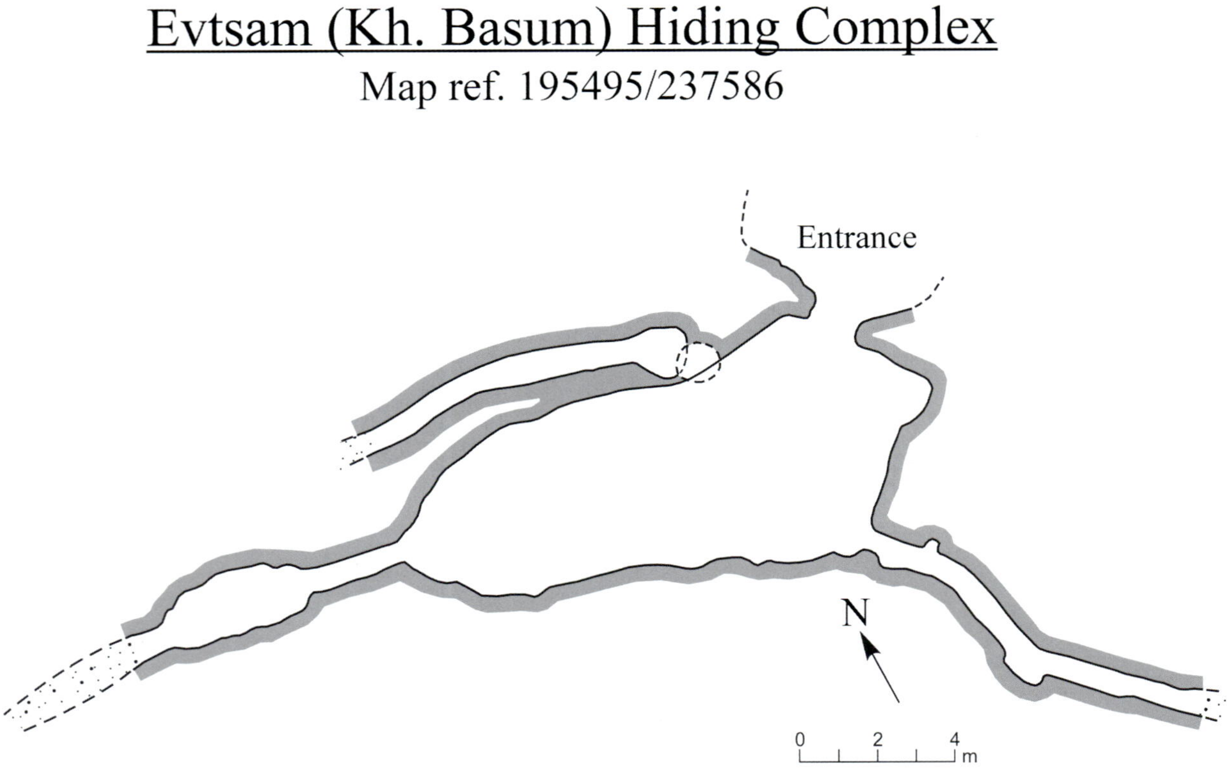

Map 74: Horvat Evtsam

plexes. Three passages are hewn at roof height in the cave. A passage in its south wall can be crawled along for about 10 m until it becomes blocked with earth fill. Niches for oil lamps cut along the passage bear chisel marks showing that it was hewn from the south. A step inside the passage leads to a small chamber. A second passage was hewn in the northwest wall of the main chamber and leads 8 m further down. After about 3 m, the passage widens into a rectangular chamber and then resumes its former width. It is also now blocked with earth. A third passage is cut near the north wall of the cave entrance. It begins in a cist grave, whose floor it damaged, continuing for c. 7 m until it becomes blocked. About 20 m southwest of the complex surveyed by Tepper and Shachar (map ref. 195468/237589) is an irregularly shaped entrance measuring c.1 × 2 m.[105] An entrance to a passage hewn in the south wall of the cavity measures 0.45 × 0.45 m in section. The chisel marks inside the passage are aligned to the south, toward the hiding complex found by Tepper and Shachar, and it appears to have connected the two complexes.

105 See Tepper and Shachar 1987b:316–317; Marcus and Elazari 2000:61.

51. Jebel Qat, north of Zippori (Map ref. 176632/241721)

Jebel Qat rises at the northern end of a ridge formed of a series of hills, c. 3.5 km from the ancient city of Zippori. Scanty traces of an unidentified ancient settlement are visible on the mound. In their survey of the site, Tepper and Shachar found various architectural elements on its summit.[106] They dated the pottery recovered to the 1st and 2nd c. CE and discovered a hiding complex hewn from inside a water cistern. Two passages hewn in the south wall of the cistern lead to a natural cave adapted as a dwelling. Pottery gathered from the cave included bowls and jars dated by Tepper and Shachar to between the second century CE and the Byzantine period. The surveyors believe that it is a hiding complex that lacks all the characteristics of hiding complexes in Judea and Galilee. According to their plan, however, it is difficult to accept their proposal that this is a hiding complex.

106 See Tepper and Shachar 1987b:304.

Fig. 107: Jebel Qat, estimated entrance to the Hiding Complex

52–53. Shikhin, west of Jebel Qat (Shikhin, 1: Map ref. 176111/241636; Shikhin, 2: Map ref. 175670/240906)

Shikhin is mentioned in rabbinical literature and described several times by Josephus as a large settlement near Sepphoris; it is now identified as Asochis (Ἀσωχις) (*War* 1:86).[107] Various scholars attempted to locate the settlement until it was identified by David Adan-Bayewitz, who found a large storage-jar workshop there that supplied jars to the entire north of the country.[108] Shikhin is now identified with the dome-shaped hill on the Sepphoris ridge, c. 2.5 km to the north of the ancient city. From the top of Shikhin hill (188 m asl), St. Anne's Church and the southern part of the Bet Natofa Valley are visible.

107 See Klein 1945:32, 54, 69 and especially 212–213; Strange 2015a; Strange, Groh and Longstaff 1994 and 1995.

108 See Adan-Bayewitz 1993:32.

Our survey discovered two hiding complexes.[109] **Shikhin 1** is located north of Shikhin hill, in the folds of a moderate west slope of a hill south of Jebel Qat. Next to a rock ledge is a very narrow entrance (0.3 × 0.4 m in section) which is a tight crawl and leads to a large plastered hewn chamber (8 × 12 m, height 2.5 m) that was probably a water cistern that became defunct when a round opening (diameter 0.5 m) was cut in its east wall. The opening leads to a 3 m long plastered passage (0.3 × 0.4 m in section) and this leads in turn to another chamber (1.5 × 2.0 m, height 1.2 m) that was also used as a water cistern in an earlier period. In the east wall of the cistern, a wall built of dressed stones and coated with plaster divides it in two. Another pas-

109 Vladimir Boslov, Shmuel Avidan and Boaz Langford participated in the site's exploration. A third hiding complex was discovered at map ref. 175949/241439 during a subsequent survey, but almost all of it is blocked with earth and it is therefore not included in the complexes described here.

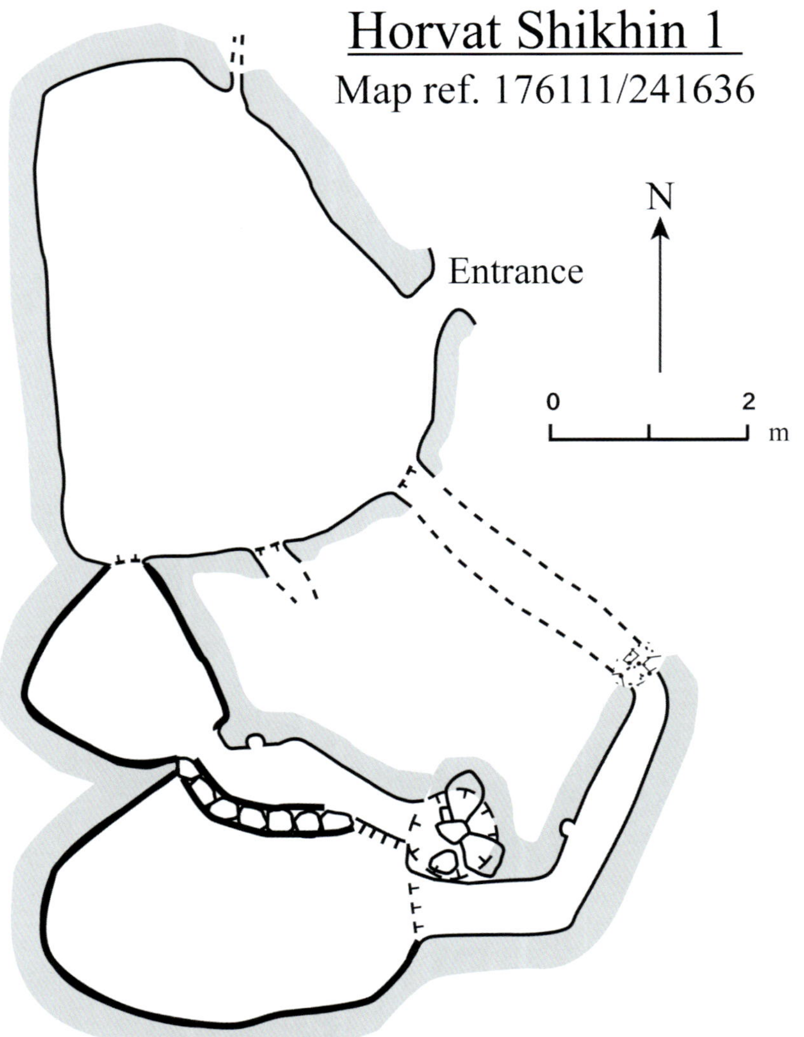

Map 75: Horvat Shikhin, Hiding Complex 1

Fig. 108: Horvat Shikhin, Hiding Complex 1

sage (1.0 × 1.6 m in section) is cut in the south wall of the cistern. On entering the 5 m long passage, it bends eastward and an entrance blocked with dressed stones is visible in its southern wall, through which a little daylight can be glimpsed. About fifteen Roman-period potsherds whose production and distribution are attributed to Shikhin were recovered from the passage, together with a fragment of a Shikhin-ware jar.[110] Halfway along the passage, an opening hewn in the roof probably provided ventilation and a stone wall was built along the west side of the passage, dividing it from a third water cistern that was also rendered obsolete and can be reached via a passage. The cistern measures 2.0 × 4.2 m and has a vaulted plastered roof. A passage cut into its south wall has the same dimensions as those described above and slopes down for 5 m until it is blocked by earth.

Fig. 109: Horvat Shikhin, Hiding Complex 2

Shikhin 2: Situated to the south of Shikhin hill, c. 800 m south of the first hiding complex, this complex is hewn into a terraced hill; a small valley runs between it and the hill where Complex 51 (Shikhin 1) was discovered. Its entrance (1 × 2 m) is hewn into the hill's northern slope, and leads to a rock-hewn chamber (6 × 10 m, height 2 m). A passage cut in the east wall of the chamber is 10 m long and 0.5 × 0.6 m in section. The passage was built in a straight line and preserves the same width along its entire length, but not the same height. Eighteen niches for oil lamps are hewn along it. On reaching the last 3 m, the passage widens to form a 1 × 1 m cavity. The remainder of the passage to the south is blocked with silt.

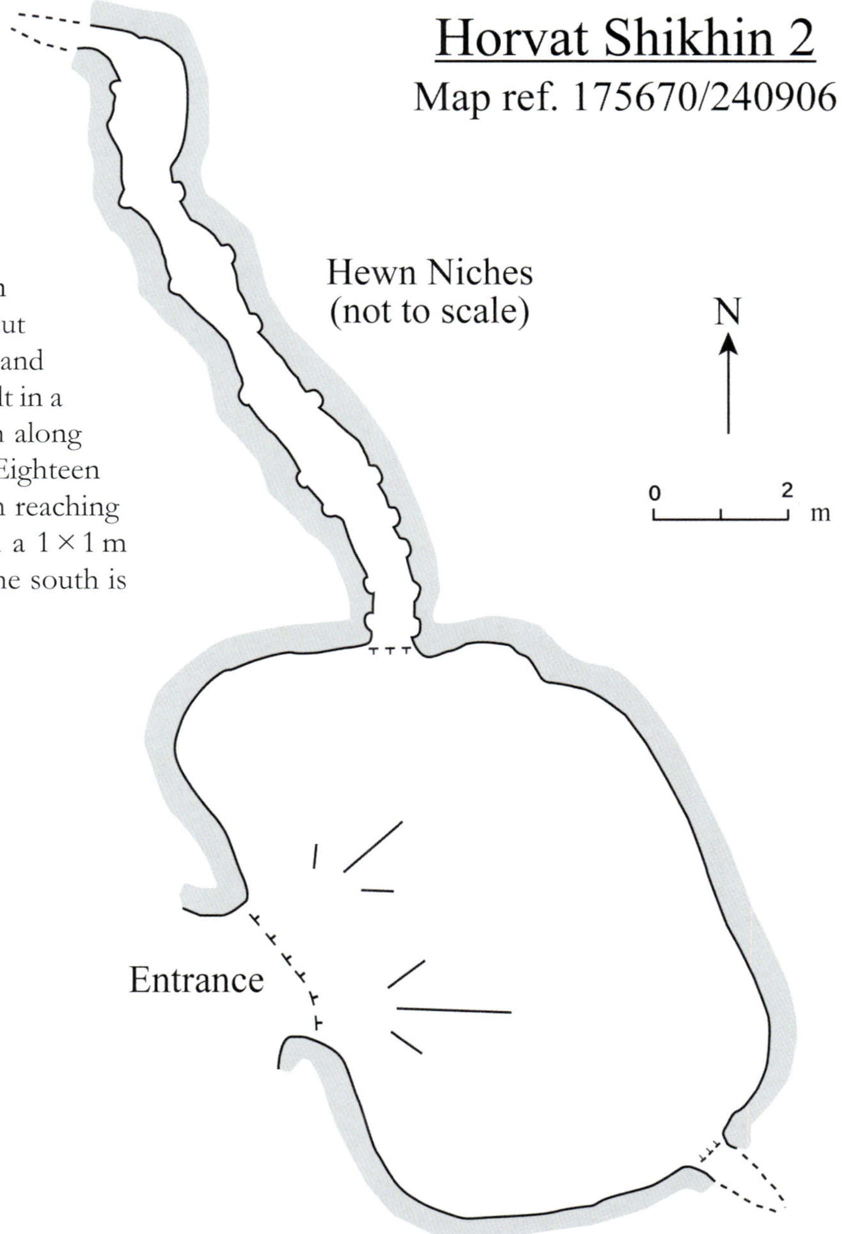

Map 76: Horvat Shikhin, Hiding Complex 2

110 Adan-Bayewitz and Perlman 1990:162–170 fig. 3:1 and 167–169 fig. 3:3.

54. Sepphoris, on Zippori Hill (Saffuriya al Qal'a) (Map ref. 195415/254523)

The Sepphoris hiding complex was discovered and excavated in the upper part of the city as part of excavations directed by James Strange in 1985, who exposed a vertical shaft leading to 20 m long horizontal passages linking three cisterns together, two of which are plastered.[111] The cisterns date to the Early Roman period. Another underground chamber hewn between the cisterns rendered them useless for storing water. Stone doors were found in this chamber. The complex yielded intact jars from the Early Roman period, a bone hairpin, a pottery oil lamp, and potsherds from the 1st–3rd c. CE. Since the archaeologists were unaware that this could be a hiding complex, they identified it as a group of rock-hewn storage rooms. Tepper and Shachar believe that the finds date the complex to the Bar Kokhba Revolt since Sepphoris collaborated with the Romans during the Great Revolt and was not in danger of being attacked.[112] I do not believe that this helps date the hiding complex, since the local population would probably also have prepared refuges in anticipation of a possible war with the Romans on the eve of the Great Revolt as well as during and after the Revolt.

111 See Strange and Longstaff 1985:298.

112 See Tepper and Shachar 1987b:302.

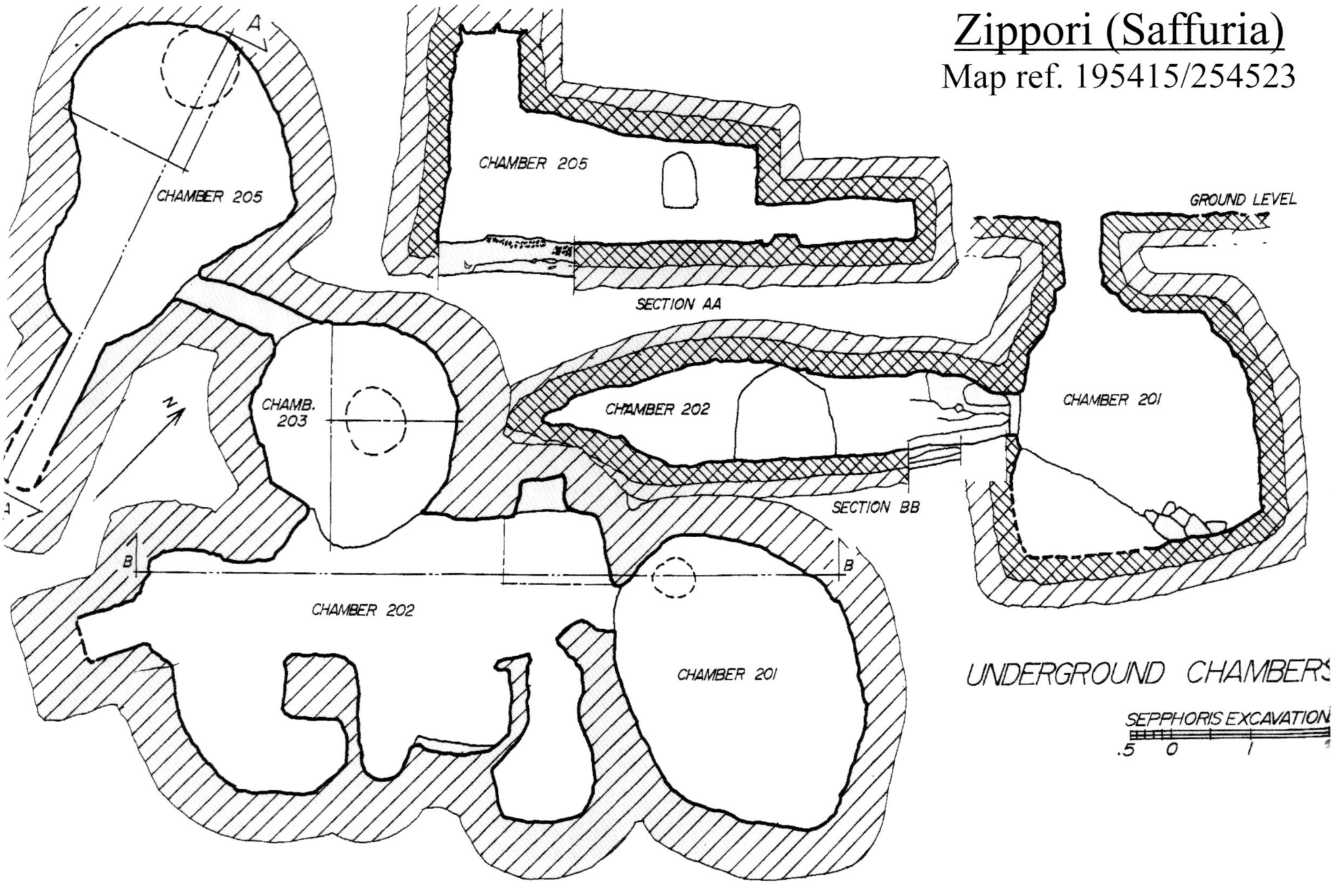

Map 77: Zippori (Saffuria)

Fig. 110: Zippori, the ancient Jewish Quarter

55. Zippori, c. 80 m west of Zippori Citadel
(Map ref. 176411/239903)

This underground cavity was discovered while attempting to identify the complex excavated by Strange. It lies beneath a residential area excavated to the west of the citadel and c. 80 m from the citadel's southwest corner. The complex consists of ten chambers, seven of which were reservoirs and ritual baths that became defunct. Strange interpreted it as underground storerooms.[113]

The underground cavity is reached from a ritual bath in the middle of the residential sector. An irregularly shaped opening (0.88 × 2.55 m) cut in the bath's east wall descends to a large plastered reservoir (4.5 × 10.0 m) whose roof is now 3.34 m above the silted-up floor. The original, oval entrance to the reservoir (1.8 × 2.5 m) is hewn in its west wall. A hole (0.4 × 0.8 m) is hewn high in the wall between the entrance cut from the ritual bath to the reservoir and the original opening, near the roof of the cistern. By climbing up a ladder, one can pass through this hole to a plastered cistern (3 × 5 m). Daylight is visible through a round opening (diameter 0.8 m) in the cistern's north wall. A large oval gap (1.3 × 2.9 m) hewn in the north wall of the large reservoir provides access to an unplastered rectangular chamber (5.18 × 5.32 m). In the west wall of the chamber is the entrance to a passage whose southern wall consists of the plaster in the large reservoir. The entrance is 0.85 × 0.90 m in section and the passage is c. 2 m long. The passage climbs up to another plastered chamber (2.3 × 2.9 m, height 2.4 m). A meticulously hewn arched entrance (0.5 × 0.8 m in section) leads out of the west wall of the chamber, where it is blocked by a rectangular dressed stone. A large entrance (1.0 × 2.2 m) is hewn into the south wall of the chamber and a round opening (diameter 0.5 m) is cut in its roof. In the southeast wall of the large reservoir, about 1 m above the silted-up floor, is an arched entrance (0.65 × 1.45 m). Two triangular windows (0.6 × 0.8 m) flank the upper part of the entrance, which is faced with dressed stones and leads to a hewn chamber with an arched entrance in its west wall surmounted by triangular windows

113 See Strange and Longstaff 1987:278–280.

Fig. 111: Zippori, south of Citadel

resembling those in the north part of the reservoir. An irregularly formed, curved breach in the east wall of the chamber measures 1.0 × 1.7 m. From here, there is a descent to a plastered water cistern (5.2 × 5.7 m). An oval entrance in the roof of the north wall of the cistern measures 1.0 × 2.3 m and is blocked to half its height by dressed stones. In the south wall of the cistern is another arched opening (0.6 × 1.5 m in section). Below this opening, c. 0.5 m above the cistern floor, is another irregularly shaped opening (0.25 × 0.35 m). With a flashlight, it is possible to make out another large cavity through this opening that is inaccessible at present (Fig. 206). Another entrance (0.45 × 0.6 m), hewn into the southwest cistern wall, leads to a further plastered water cistern (3.1 × 5.3 m, height 2.8 m). An opening in the east wall of the cistern is blocked with dressed stones and an irregularly cut gap in its west wall measures 0.4 × 0.6 m. An opening (1.8 × 5.0 m) is cut in the south wall of the cistern abutting its roof. An arched opening (visible dimensions 0.1 × 0.3 m) is hewn beneath the gap leading to this cistern and is now blocked with earth. Another opening cut in the cistern's north wall leads to a water cistern through which the surface can be reached by climbing up a ladder. Yet another opening (0.45 × 0.6 m) in the same wall is blocked. Near the main entrance to the cistern is an arched opening (0.45 × 0.55 m) leading to a plastered water cistern (2.4 × 3.6 m) that is almost completely filled with earth, but it is possible to crawl around its sides beneath the roof. Three fragments of cooking pots and four jar fragments dated to the mid-Roman period were recovered here. From similar examples described in this volume, it can be concluded that here too, the population of Sepphoris constructed an underground hiding complex by cutting into vital previously existing installations (water reservoirs and ritual baths).

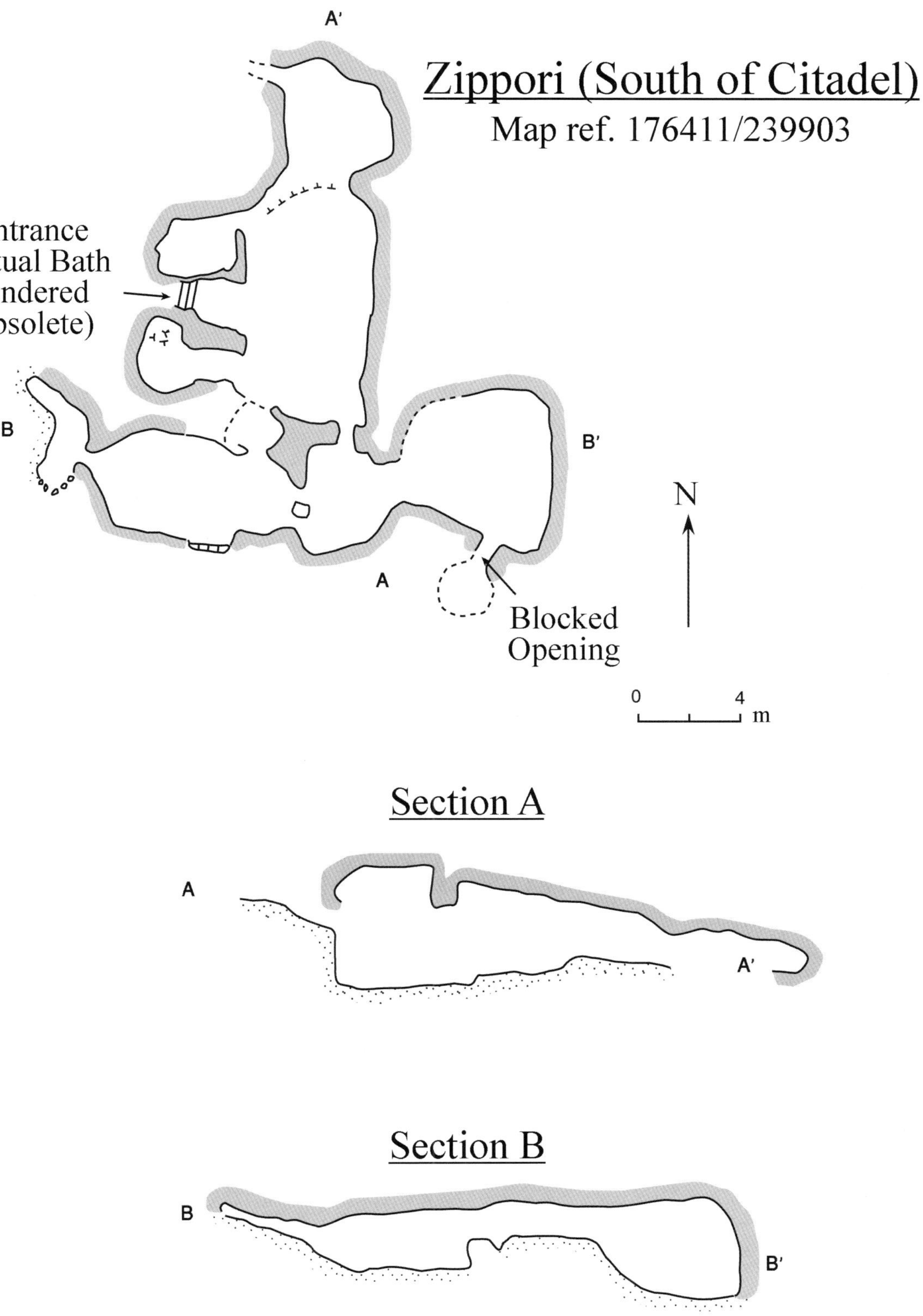

Map 78: 80 m west of Zippori Citadel (entrance into a ritual bath whose wall has been breached)

56. Horvat Bina (Kh. Beiyin), north of 'En Mahel (Map ref. 184383/238060)

The small site lies on a mound southeast of Kafr Kanna and north of 'En Mahel. Surface finds recovered here include pottery from the Early Roman, Late Roman and Byzantine periods. Digging by antiquities robbers exposed the entrance to a hiding passage leading to a chamber containing entrances to three more passages. The passages yielded a few potsherds and a handle of an Early Roman stone vessel.[114] On surveying the site, I discovered that the remains had been completely plowed up and olive trees had been planted there, now making it impossible to locate the hiding complex.

114 See Aviam 2004:129.

57. Horvat Tiriya (Kh. et Tira), on a hill southeast of Nazareth (Map ref. 181136/233775)

Horvat Tiriya is situated on a mound southeast of Nazareth Illit. The hill (514 m asl) is isolated on all sides, the only easy approach being from the north. Its summit has is a south-southeasterly view toward Mount Kesulot, the town of Iksal, Afula, and large parts of Kesulot Valley. Between Horvat Tiriya and Mount Kesulot is the Nahal Barak stream, a tributary of Nahal Tabor. The hill's ancient remains include water cisterns and agricultural installations. Tiriya was a Jewish settlement referred to in rabbinical literature as Tira, Tria, Tiria, and Turia, where it is always linked with the sage Hoshaiah Rabbah of Tiriya. Some scholars place the settlement near Peki'in, whereas others suggest placing it at this site.[115]

Archaeological excavations at the site found no trace of the hiding complex, which was only discov-

115 See Vilnay 1976:2655.

Fig. 112: Horvat Tiriya

ered by the present survey. The complex has three entrances; two are via water cisterns and are only accessible by rope. It was hewn into previously existing ancient water cisterns and natural karstic cavities. Its features are characteristic of the simple type of hiding complex, with narrow, low passages, sudden sharp turns, and multiple exit and access routes. The hiding complex is reached by abseiling 2 m down into a water cistern with a 4.5 m diameter opening whose floor is full of rubble. An entrance to a passage that is now blocked with dressed stones is cut in the east wall of the cistern. Another opening (0.3 × 1.0 m) is hewn in the cistern's west wall and leads to an oval chamber measuring c. 5 × 13 m with a blocked hole in its roof. An opening (0.9 × 0.9 m) cut in the south wall of the chamber leads to a 2.5 m long passage terminating in a chamber with two blocked holes in its roof. The passage continues into the north wall of the chamber, but is now blocked with stones. The chamber measures 4 × 8 m and is aligned north–south. A narrow passage cut in the south wall of this chamber leads to a long, narrow room (1.5 × 5.5 m). The passage continues to the southwest, widening to 2 m in places. After about 12 m, the passage narrows and can only be crawled through with difficulty. The narrow section is c. 2 m long and eventually widens into a chamber 4.0 × 8.5 m in size. This hewn chamber contains two niches (c. 0.50 × 0.55 m) on its north side. Its west side contains a kind of hewn shelf (0.5 × 0.9 m) and another opening is cut in its south wall. Although this opening is almost completely blocked, it clearly leads to another chamber with an exit to a water cistern above it through which daylight is visible. The cistern opening measures c. 0.9 × 1.2 m. The complex is c. 35 m long from one end to the other and covers an area of around 50 square meters. The hiding complex contains five roughly hewn chambers, some with collapsed roofs. The two northeast chambers were water cisterns with openings in the roof that were probably blocked up when they were incorporated into the hiding complex. While mapping the complex, we recovered numerous Early Roman and Byzantine potsherds.

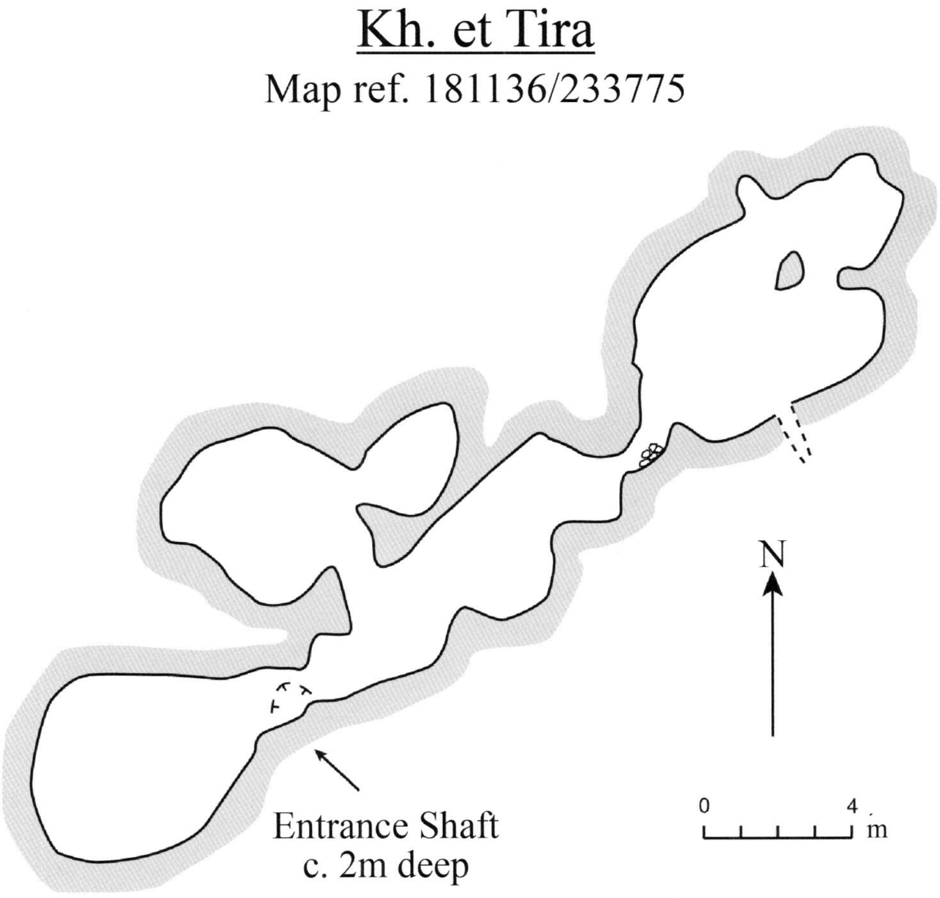

Map 79: Horvat Tiriya

58. Nazareth, St. Joseph's Church (Map ref. 173418/228191)

Nazareth lies in the center of the Lower Galilee, c. 10 km north of Afula. The town is built on a hill and its southern neighborhoods lie on the north side of a ridge sloping down to the Jezreel Valley. To the east, the town is surrounded by the Nazareth hill ridge. Both the New Testament Gospels (e. g. Luke 1:26; John 1:46) and later Christian writings refer to Nazareth as a Jewish town.[116] In 1955, a ritual bath was uncovered during construction work on the new Basilica of the Annunciation. Also found were the remains of a building consisting of building stones, column bases, capitals, and doorjambs. The finds are in the same style as architectural elements found in Galilean synagogues.[117] Hanan Eshel has published a fragment of a Hebrew inscription carved in limestone, originally from Nazareth, in which names of the 24 priestly orders are partially preserved.[118] The hiding complex was discovered in the Church of St. Joseph, beneath the floor of the ancient Byzantine and Crusader churches. It was excavated and cleaned by a Franciscan expedition in 1969 that reported finding pottery dating from Iron Age B to the Roman period.[119] It begins in a spacious cave today known as 'Saint Joseph's Carpentry' that is reached by a stairway leading down from the crypt of the modern church. Inside the crypt, Tepper and Shachar discovered a passage cut in the wall of a bell-shaped water cistern beneath the south wall of the new church.[120] The cistern has two openings, one outside the church and one inside. A glass window recently installed in the inner opening provides a view of the passage entrance. This underground chamber was used as a storage silo. As has been observed in hiding complexes in the Shephela, bell-shaped caves were meticulously finished here as well.[121] A stairway descends from the cistern to the entrance to a passage hewn around the water cistern. It would once have continued to the floor of the crypt, but is now blocked. From the stairway, a passage bends round to enter the cave of Saint Joseph. Round, well-dressed openings are visible in the cave floor and roof. The entrance to Saint Joseph's cave measures 0.70 × 1.70 m. A bell-shaped cavity (diameter 1.4 m) is hewn in the north wall of the cave and its entrance is blocked by a stone slab. The cistern is c. 0.8 m deep and the passage continuing at the bottom of it was made before the steps were hewn. In the north wall of the stairway is another passage whose opening measures 0.60 × 0.65 m, which skirts the cistern in an easterly direction before turning sharply west to reach Saint Joseph's cave. Other openings are hewn in the cave floor, all of which could be sealed with stone covers; they are now covered with iron grids. It is possible to crawl c. 6 m in a westerly direction up another passage in the south wall of the cave.[122] Tepper and Shachar believe the complex was built to conceal agricultural produce. They observed differences between the installations and the passages. Whereas the installations were meticulously hewn, the passages were hastily cut with no attempt to render an even finish.

Fig. 113: Nazareth, St. Joseph's Church, entrance to the Hiding Complex

116 See Strange 2015.
117 See Bagatti 1992:1090.
118 See Eshel 1992:160.
119 See Tepper and Shachar 1987b:306–311; Bagatti 1992:1088–1091.
120 See Tepper and Shachar 1987b:306–311.
121 See Kloner and Tzoran 1987:217–225.
122 Tepper and Shachar 1987b:307.

Saint Joseph's Church, Hiding Complex

Map ref. 173418/228191

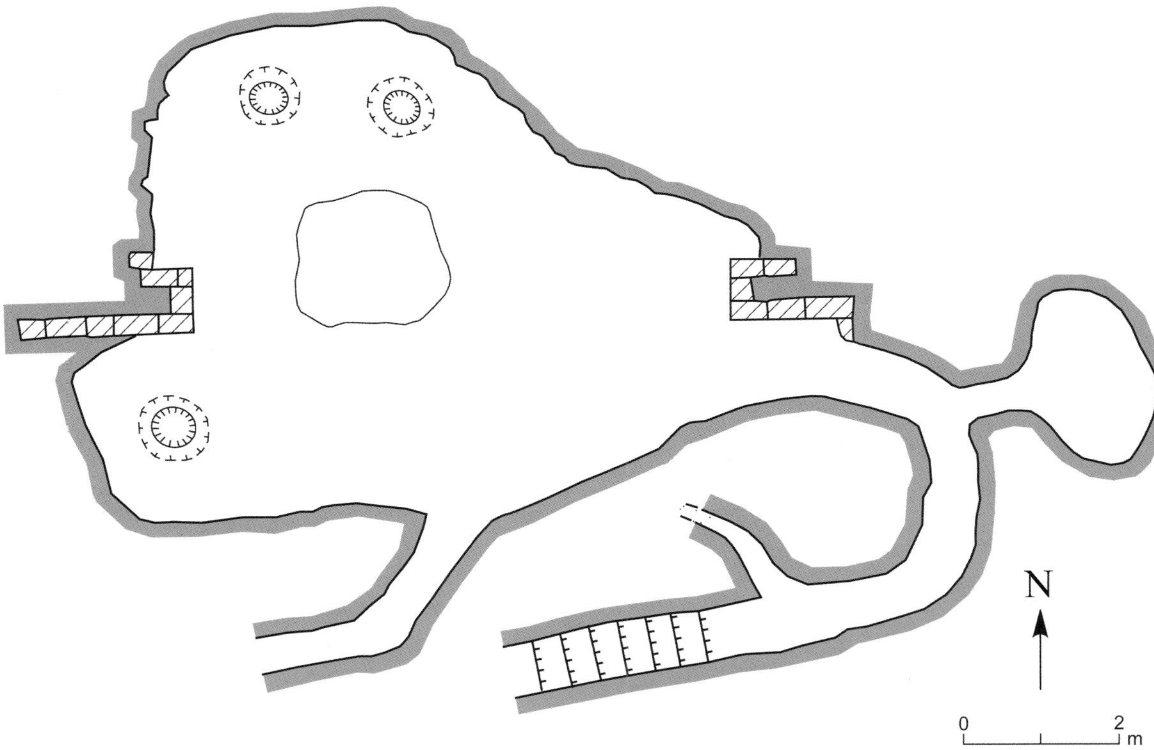

Map 80: Nazareth, St. Joseph's Church. Hiding Complex

59, 60. Horvat Dabbura, Kh. Dabbura,
1 km northeast of Daburiya village
(Map refs. 185950/233653, 185869/233694)

Horvat Dabbura lies about 1 km northeast of the Arab village of Daburiyya, at the foot of Mount Tabor. The site contains numerous Iron Age and Second Temple-period architectural remains. Some scholars have identified it as Dabrita, a Jewish village recorded by Josephus (*Life* 126). Victor Guérin saw the remains here of an ancient building made of ashlars which he identified as a church.[123] Ancient agricultural terraces and rock-hewn water cisterns surround the site. The present survey discovered two underground chambers that appear to be hiding complexes: The first, found in the middle of an olive orchard on the north side of the site, begins in the upper part of the east wall of a water cistern (11 × 17 m) whose original opening is square (0.90 × 0.96 m). A 2 m section is visible of a south–north gutter leading to the opening. The gutter is 0.34 m wide and as it reaches the cistern, it widens further to form a funnel 0.4 m wide. An arched entrance (1.55 × 2.90 m) is hewn in the cistern's north wall, which would have rendered the cistern useless for storing water. The cistern consists of four hewn and plastered cavities and has a cruciform plan: A western section (3.75 × 5.28 m, depth 3.3 m); a southern section (3.33 × 5.26 m, depth 4.56 m); a northern section (4.04 × 5.11 m, depth 2.3 m); and an eastern section (3.14 × 5.94 m, depth 3.11 m). At the south end of the eastern section, c. 3 m above the present floor, is the hewn entrance to a passage (0.56 × 0.64 m) that can be reached with a ladder. The passage is c. 8.5 m long and leads to a rock-hewn chamber (4.35 × 4.90 m). An opening in the north wall of this chamber leads to a small earth-filled chamber and a vertical shaft (0.6 × 1.2 m) hewn in the middle of the chamber reaches a depth of 4.3 m. The shaft is coated with roughly hewn stones and can only be chimneyed down by a skilled speleologist, emerging into a hewn chamber (2.0 × 2.5 m) that is blocked with earth. The complex yielded Early Roman potsherds.

123 See Guérin 1880, vol. 6:95.

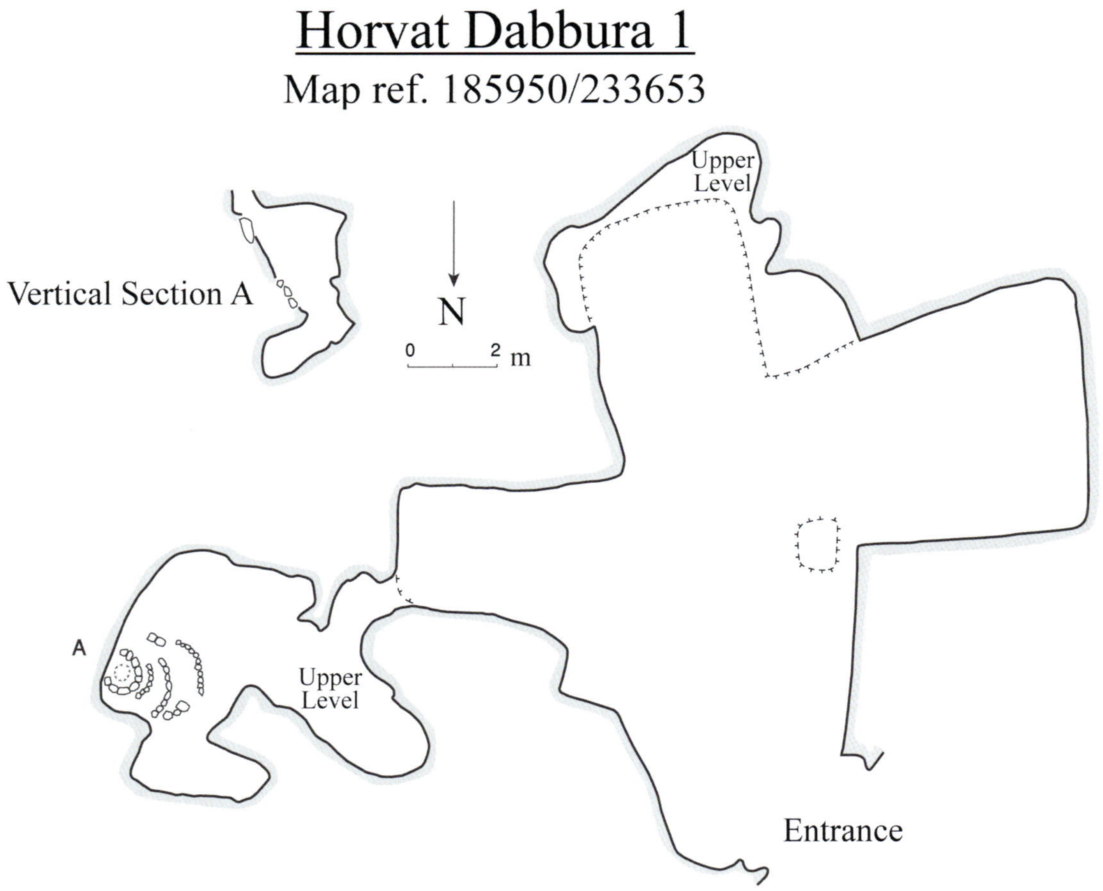

Map 81: Horvat Dabbura, Complex 1

Fig. 114: Horvat Dabbura, Complex 1

The second hiding complex lies c. 150 m east of the first and was hewn in the north part of a protruding ledge of rock that creates a natural fence for the olive grove. Its oval entrance measures 1.0 × 1.3 m. The west side of the entrance is meticulously hewn, whereas the east side is roughly worked. It leads to a large chamber (6 × 8 m, height 2.1 m) whose walls are covered with chisel marks. An entrance cut in the west wall of the chamber leads into a passage that is blocked with earth and broken rock, which may once have linked the two complexes together. The exposed part of the entrance measures 0.3 × 1.0 m. Two niches are hewn in the east wall of the chamber, one round (0.5 diameter) and the other rectangular (0.12 × 0.20 m). Beneath the rectangular niche, an entrance (0.50 × 0.65 m) hewn at floor level leads to a finely dressed passage c. 30 m long containing slight bends and oil-lamp niches. It was built on a moderate 10-degree upward slope and reaches the chamber of a cave (3.0 × 7.5 m, height 1.5 m) whose roof has collapsed, providing access to the surface by clambering over the fallen rocks. Two passage entrances to the east of the rock collapse are blocked with earth.

Fig. 115: Horvat Dabbura, Complex 2

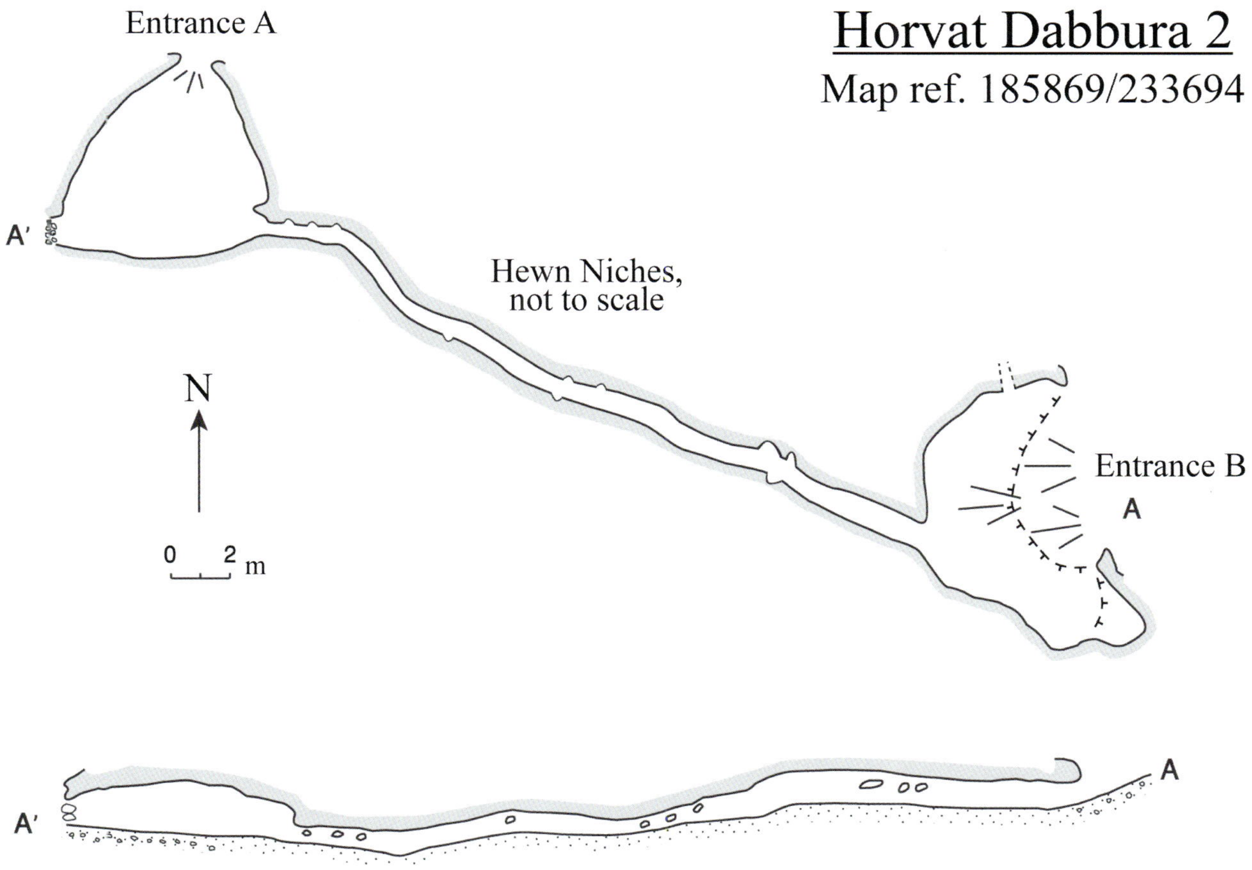

Map 82: Horvat Dabbura, Complex 2

61. Bet She'arim (Sheikh Abreik), in Bet Zayid courtyard, near the synagogue (Estimated map ref. 162546/234244)

Bet She'arim Hill lies in southwest Lower Galilee on the southern slopes of the Alonim-Shefar'am hills and overlooks the western edges of the Jezreel Valley. The summit is within sight of the Jezreel Valley, Kiryat Tiv'on, and the main road between Megiddo Junction and Lower Galilee. Bet She'arim was a Jewish settlement first mentioned by Josephus as Βησαρά, and grain silos belonging to Agrippa II's sister Berenice were located there. Bet She'arim probably belonged to the "King's Lands."[124] Bet She'arim is also mentioned as the place where Josephus drew up his forces while fighting Abutius, governor of the Jezreel Valley (*Life* 119). In Talmudic literature, the town is called "Bet Sherei" or "Bet Sherean."[125] Bet She'arim became famous as the seat of the Sanhedrin at the time of Rabbi Yehuda Hanassi and as the site of his burial, making it a popular burial location. It was probably destroyed in the revolt against Gallus in the fourth century CE.

The first scientific archaeological excavations were conducted at Bet She'arim from the 1930s to the 1950s. The location of the hiding complex can only be roughly surmised, on the southwest side of Sheikh Abreik Hill, between the south wall of the ancient synagogue and the home of the Zayid family (Fig. 222). The hiding complex was discovered in the sixth excavation season, when Nachman Avigad identified it as a tunnel although based on his description it was probably a hiding complex. The excavation exposed remains of rooms and structures built of stone and hewn into the rock. A number of rock-hewn water cisterns were also found beneath the floors of the rooms. In one of the rooms, marked as Room 5 on Avigad's plan, is a rock-hewn water cistern c. 1 m deep whose northwest wall is built of stones. Avigad cleaned out 3 m of a passage cut in the east wall of the water cistern and recovered two 2nd c. CE jar handles, but maintained that the passage should not be dated purely on the strength of these finds.[126] Zvi Safrai was the first to suggest that the tunnel be identified as a hiding complex[127] and Yuval Shachar also includes Bet She'arim in his list of hiding complexes in Galilee.[128] Yigal and Yotam Tepper maintain that the fact that the passage cuts into the water cistern, rendering it useless for water storage, shows that it must have been a hiding complex and they date it to the Bar Kokhba Revolt.[129]

124 See Gil 2009:9.
125 See for example *yKilaim,* 9:32, 2,3.
126 See Avigad 1956:86–87.
127 See Safrai 2001:48–49.
128 See Shachar 2003:232.
129 See Tepper and Shachar 2004:166.

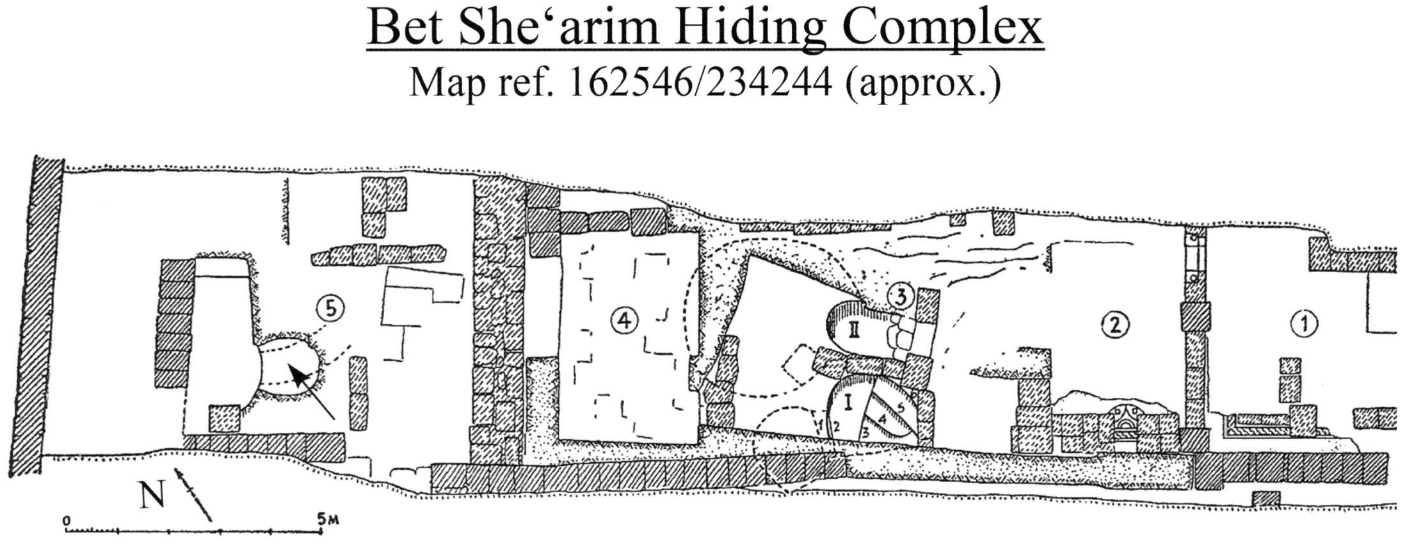

Map 83: Bet She'arim synagogue, estimated site of Hiding Complex

Fig. 116: Bet She'arim synagogue, estimated site of Hiding Complex

62. Migdal Ha-'Emeq (al Mujeidil) *(Map ref. 172134/231257)*

The town of Migdal Ha-'Emeq lies on the slopes of the west spur of the Nazareth hill ridge in central Lower Galilee, c. 6 km southeast of Nazareth and overlooking the northwest part of the Jezreel Valley. The top of the hill has good views of Nahalal to the west and Nazareth to the east. To the north is a broad vista of the settlements and ridges of northern Lower Galilee. Victor Guérin recorded a large village with a Muslim and Greek Orthodox population at the site and surmised that it was built over an ancient town with a name similar to the Hebrew name Magdal, Magdul, or Magdiel.[130]

Salvage excavations conducted in 1993 in the west of the town (map ref. 180836/233549) exposed traces of walls overlying a hewn hiding complex.[131] The 50 m long section of the complex, along both sides of a sewage trench, contained a bell-shaped water cistern whose dimensions were not recorded. Fragments of Gaza Jars and Ottoman-period coins were found in the floor. Cistern B was hewn in a natural cave and exploited its natural walls. The water cistern retained traces of gray plaster and a preserved east corner and original opening, now blocked with dressed stones and large fieldstones. The potsherds date the cistern's use to the Late Roman and Byzantine periods. A coin recovered from the floor of an entrance cut in the west wall of the cave was minted in Tyre in the 1st c. BCE. In another complex (C), c. 10 m from Cave B, five interconnected hewn cavities were discovered. It seems highly likely that passages once joined cisterns A and B to Complex C. An oval chamber with a collapsed roof was exposed at the south end of Complex C. The chamber was blocked with a fill of earth and rocks containing potsherds from the Roman and Byzantine period and part of a "measuring-cup" stone vessel. In the north wall of the chamber, an oval entrance (0.8 m) leads to another chamber. Potsherds dating to the Roman period were found on its floor, together with Early Roman glass fragments

130 See Guérin 1880,6:261.
131 See Shalem 1995:31–36.

Migdal Ha'emeq Hiding Complexes C and D

Map ref. 172134/231257

Plan and sections

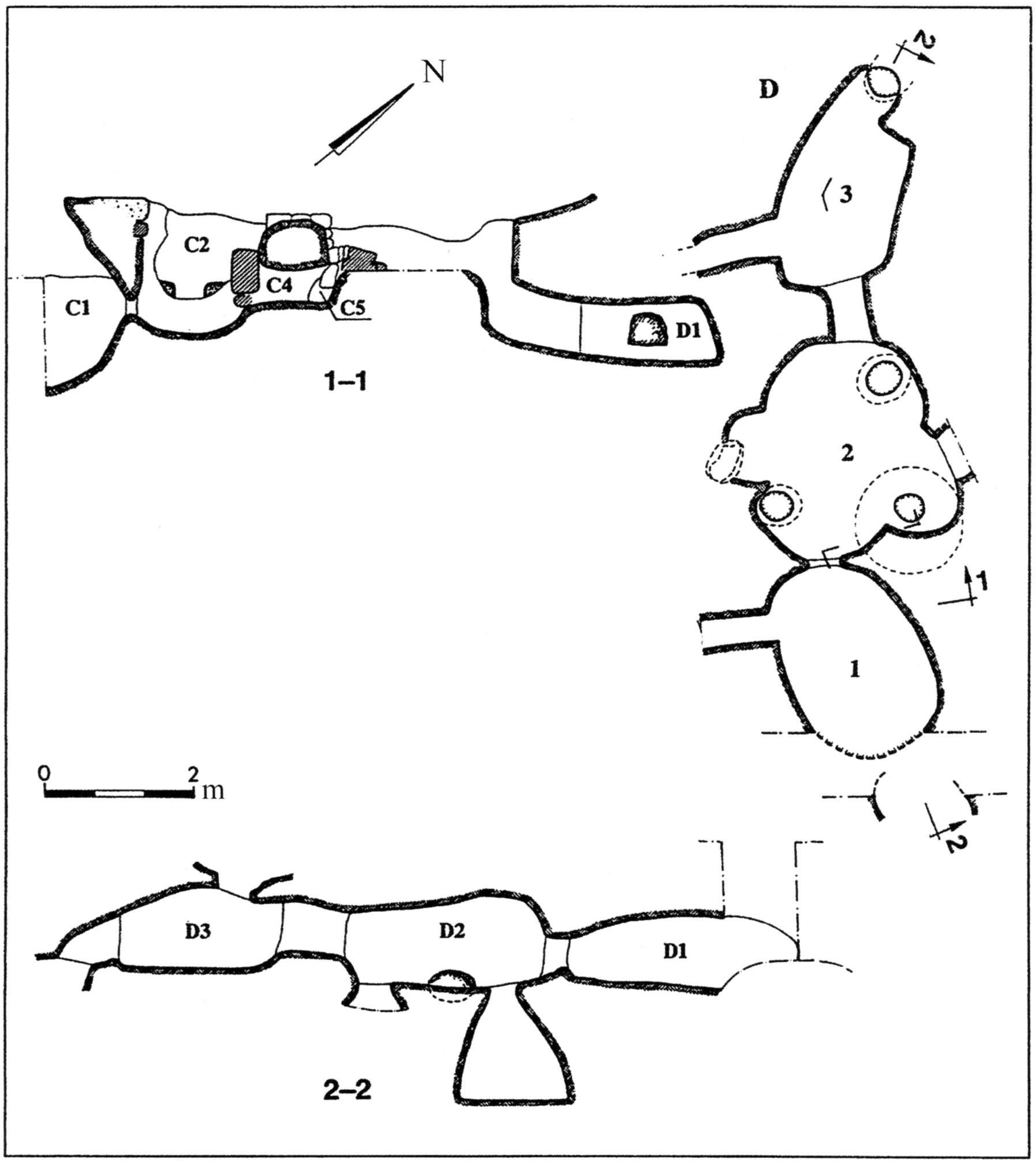

Map 84: Migdal Ha-'Emeq Hiding Complexes, Areas C and D

and a fragment of a "pared-nozzle" (Herodian) pottery oil lamp. The west and north walls of this chamber had collapsed and the rubble contained fragments of sarcophagi, Roman and Byzantine pottery, and part of a stone vessel. To the north of this chamber, another chamber was discovered that was not excavated. Its entrance had been deliberately blocked up with stones, including a threshold stone in secondary use. Roman potsherds and the base of a "measuring-cup" stone vessel were recovered from beneath the fill. An opening in the east wall of the second chamber leads to a third chamber. The threshold and southern doorjamb of the opening are preserved. The third chamber is oval-shaped (diameter 2 m) and its floor is 0.65 m higher than that of the second chamber. A stone wall built along its south wall was probably intended to prevent it from collapsing. Finds recovered here include pottery from the Roman, Byzantine, and Mamluk periods and a coin from the rule of Severus (222–235 CE). The fifth chamber, which was blocked with earth and stone collapse, was only partially explored. In its western part was a fill of dressed stones beneath two built walls; a coin of the procurator Antonius Felix (dated 54 CE) was recovered from between the two walls. The chamber also produced Early Roman potsherds, a stone 'measuring-cup' base, and 17 coins dating to 330–360 CE.

To the south of the modern sewage trench, the remainder of the hiding complex was exposed (Chamber D) and three chambers were excavated that were hewn perpendicular to Complex C on a northwest-southeast alignment. The chamber roofs are preserved, but they are filled with earth and stones. The first chamber measures c. 2.75 × 4.0 m and is 1.5 m high. It is joined by a 1.5 m long passage to a fifth chamber in Complex C. Pottery from the Early Roman, Byzantine, and Mamluk periods was found in the passage as well as human skeletal remains. A round opening (diameter c. 0.6 m) cut in the west wall of the chamber provides access to another chamber to its northwest. The second chamber was damaged when the sewage trench was dug, but appears to have been larger than the first. The upper section of a shaft cut in the south wall of the chamber incorporates dressed stones, beneath which are hewn steps. The north wall of the chamber contains an oil-lamp niche and an opening that was not explored. Three pits were dug in the floor of the chamber, only one of which was excavated; the pit is bell shaped in section (diameter of opening 0.6 m, diameter of floor 2.1 m, depth 2.2 m) and yielded pottery – most from the Early Roman and Byzantine periods and some from the Hellenistic and Mamluk periods. Also recovered from this pit was a pottery oil lamp decorated with a seven-branched menorah from the Late Roman period. Only half of the third chamber (c. 2 × 4 m) was excavated. This chamber was connected to the second chamber by a 1.3 m long passage. A round entrance hewn in its north wall leads to a large bell-shaped water cistern that was not excavated. A narrow passage hewn on the southwest side was also not explored. The chamber has an oval opening (diameter 0.6 m) in its roof. Most of the finds recovered from this chamber date to the Mamluk period and a few to the Hellenistic and Roman periods.

The find of a stone vessel and pottery oil lamp decorated with a seven-branched menorah in a hiding complex resembling those found in Judea and Galilee provides sufficient evidence to identify this as a Jewish settlement whose inhabitants made preparations for one of the revolts against the Romans (the pottery finds suggest that this was probably in the Early Roman period). The archaeologist believes that the passages and rooms were used from the Early Roman to the Late Islamic periods.

63. Horvat Riv (Tirat el Khariba), on the south bank of Nahal Tabor (Map ref. 195256/254516)

Horvat Riv covers an area of c. 5 dunams (c. 1.2 acres) and lies on the south bank of Nahal Tabor, c. 2 km southeast of Kibbutz Gazit. The remains of the ancient ruin are underneath the remains of an Arab village that existed here until Israel's War of

Fig. 117: Horvat Riv

Independence. The site is described in a PEF-survey as a new village, but Tsuri identifies it as a crusader settlement by the name of Castel de Cheris.[132] Architectural elements and cave dwellings have been found at the site as well as pottery and coins from the Roman and Byzantine periods. A seven-branched menorah with a four-footed base was found carved in the lintel of one of the caves.

The present survey identified a dwelling cave in the middle of the site that was originally an ancient water cistern and was probably converted into a hiding complex. The complex is entered via an underground chamber with an arched opening whose visible dimensions are 2 × 4 m. The entrance leads to a hewn chamber (9 × 12 m) whose floor is filled with earth. A round opening in the center of the roof shows that the cavity was used as a water cistern. An entrance (0.4 × 0.8 m) is hewn on the west side of the chamber and was blocked up by a stone wall in front of an earth-filled passage. A passage (0.4 × 0.6 m in section) is cut in the south of the chamber. Although the passage contains an earth fill, it can be crawled along on a gradual incline for 12 m toward another small chamber that is inaccessible. In the middle of the passage, another passage is hewn from the north that is blocked after 1 m.

132 See Tsuri 1977:120; Conder and Kitchener 1882:130.

Horvat Riv

Map ref. 195256/254516

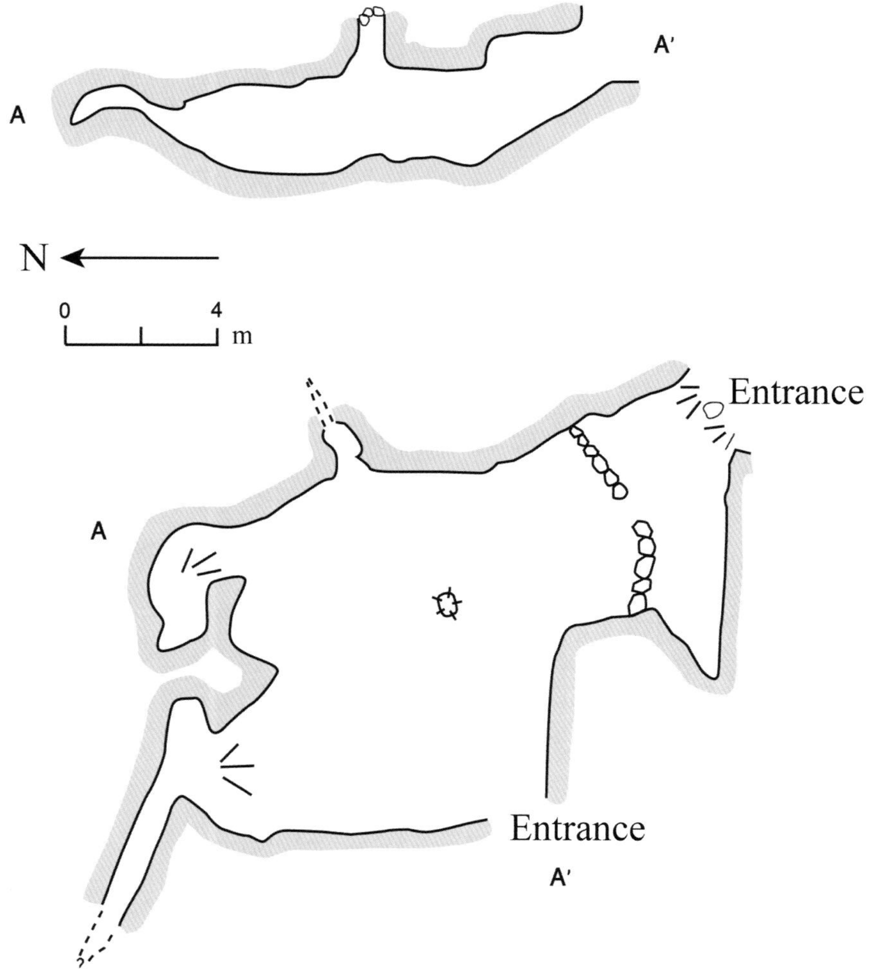

Map 85: Horvat Riv

64. Shunam (Sulam), on the south slope of Givat Hamoreh (Map ref. 181830/224255)

The remains of the village of Shunam, site of the Arab village of Sulam, extend across the sloping southwest spur of Givat Ha-Moreh, at the east end of the Jezreel Valley and c. 4 km east of Afula. The summit has views of the southern and western parts of the Jezreel Valley as far as the eastern Gilboa Ridge. The wide escarpments of Givat Ha-Moreh are clearly visible to the north of the site. The northeast part of the modern village is built over an ancient tell. Victor Guérin described Sulam as a village with a spring flowing into an aqueduct used to irrigate orchards. He noted a possible linguistic link between the name Sulam and the ancient name Shunam.[133]

Tepper and Shachar identified three hiding complexes at Tel Shunam, but only thoroughly surveyed one of them.[134] Called "Sab'a Abu Wab Cave," the site is situated at the end of the southern slope of Givat Ha-Moreh 1 km north of the tell and is an underground cavern divided into three complexes containing hewn chambers with interconnecting passages. The complex is entered via a rock-hewn pool (2.7 × 2.7 m, depth 1.6 m). Steps are hewn in the south wall of the pool and an opening at floor level in the north wall leads into a hewn chamber (3 × 6 m, height 1.8 m). Seven entrances cut in the walls of this chamber lead off to other chambers. A vertical shaft in the west chamber descends to another chamber, most of which is blocked up with earth. A narrow passage cut in the northeast wall of the main chamber leads to a chamber with an opening sealed by a stone in its east wall. An entrance in the south wall of this chamber continues to a small room that connects to the main chamber. From the chamber with the seal stone, a narrow passage (0.45 × 0.45 m) leads to a conically hewn chamber with an arched niche hewn at its east end and an elongated niche cut at its south end. A passage hewn in the east wall of this chamber leads to a third complex. The passage is 0.45 × 0.50 m in section and can only be crawled through with difficulty. A shaft cut at the end of the passage was found to be blocked. At the center of the third complex is a hewn cave (2 × 5 m, height c. 2 m) divided into five parts: Two cavities hewn in the east wall, two in the west wall, and a niche in the north wall. The three complexes yielded coins dating from the first half of the 1st c. CE. Pottery dating to the 1st and early 2nd c. CE was also recovered. Tepper and Shachar believe

133 See Guérin 1880,6:75–76.

134 See Tepper and Shachar 1983:26–29; 1984:228; 1987b:288–290.

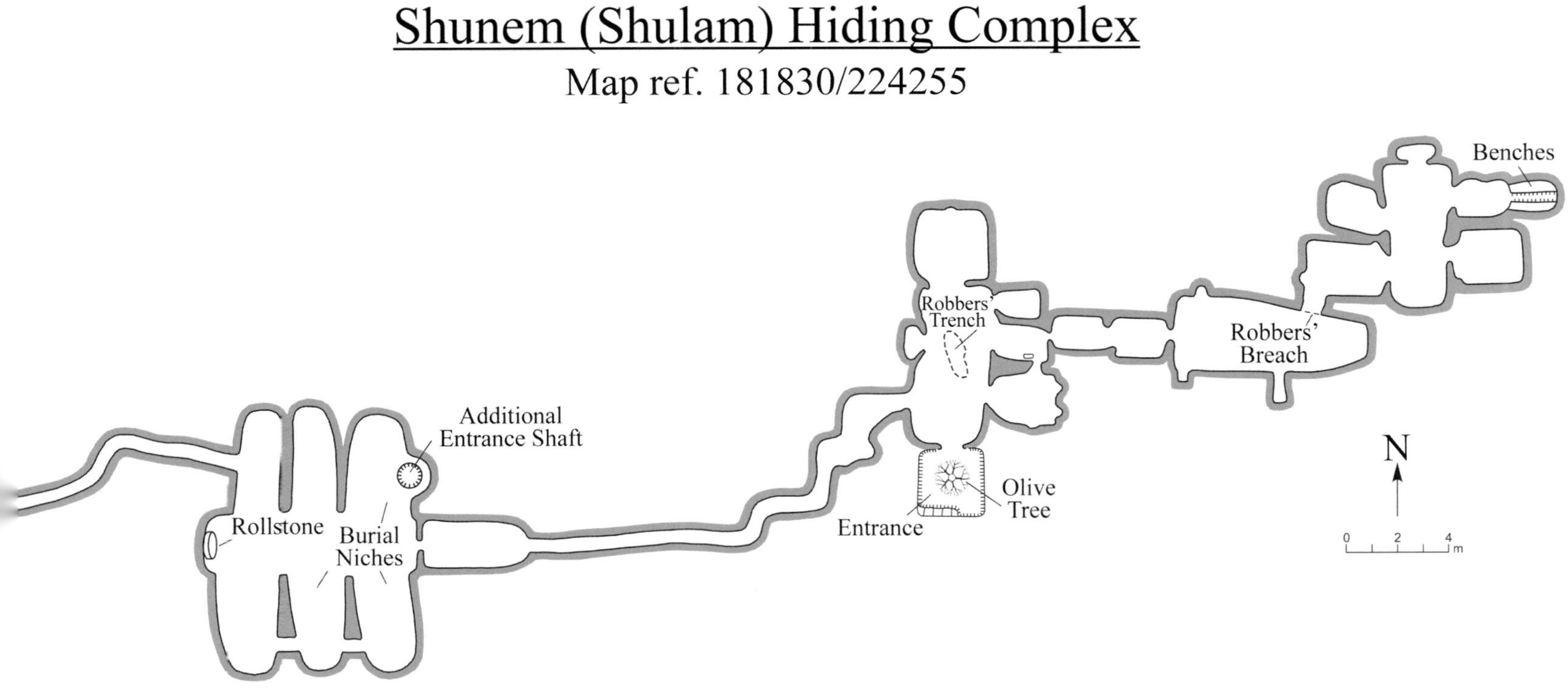

Map 86: Horvat Shunam

Fig. 118: Horvat Shunam

that the hiding complex was installed in two phases and that, even if the dating of the Shunam complex is inconclusive, the settlement at Shunam was probably one of those that rebelled against the Romans in the 1st and 2nd c. CE. The present survey found that the hiding complex was hewn from inside an earlier burial cave in a similar manner to examples identified by myself at other sites.

Further to their detailed survey of the hiding complex, Tepper and Shachar also gained access to one of the blocked complexes consisting of a natural cavity enlarged by hewing out additional sections. In the northeast wall of the cavity is a hewn passage entrance (0.5 × 0.6 m in section). The complex shows signs of arrangements for stone doors that could be used to block the passages and one such door was found *in situ*. The passage terminated in a chamber containing fragments of Early Roman jars and cooking pots.

65. Horvat Buleiq, near Ein Harod (Map ref. 186002/222075)

Horvat Buleiq is located on a low, rocky hill (100 m asl) on the southeast slopes of Givat Hamoreh, c. 10 km southwest of Afula and c. 3. 5 km east of Kibbutz Ein Harod. The Harod Valley, Ramot Issachar and Ramat Kochav, Mount Gilboa, and Mount Gilead are visible from its summit. On 1:500,000-scale maps, the ruins are marked as Buleiq Hill and are close to a site called Horvat Qarah (c. 400 m to the north) containing the remains of numerous buildings. Horvat Buleiq covers c. 30 dunams (7.5 acres). In his survey of the site, Tsuri recorded an abundance of ancient remains with a burial cave, water cisterns, rock-hewn winepresses, and traces of installations.[135] On the north slope of the site, he discovered a burial cave that is accessible via a

135 See Tsuri 1977:57–59.

Fig. 119: Horvat Buleiq

plastered pit (7 × 8 m). Engraved in the plaster at the entrance are four ships similar to examples found at Bet She'arim, flanked by other, unidentifiable objects. Tsuri discovered an engraved Greek inscription next to the ships. Unfortunately, the engravings have been damaged by a crude instrument in the meantime and are no longer extant. To the north of the cave, Tsuri found another burial cave with a red painted inscription in Hebrew or Aramaic above one of its niches, similar to an inscription found in excavations at Bet She'arim. He also uncovered grinding stones from the Roman period, a plain mosaic floor, pottery from the Iron Age, Hellenistic and Byzantine periods, a Hellenistic coin and Roman and Byzantine coins. Tsuri is convinced that the site was a Jewish settlement during the Talmudic period. Zvi Gal recorded two winepresses, an unfinished olive-press crushing stone, and five stone olive-press weights *in situ* on the east side of the hill. The present survey discovered a burial cave containing five sarcophagi. About 200 m west of the burial cave,

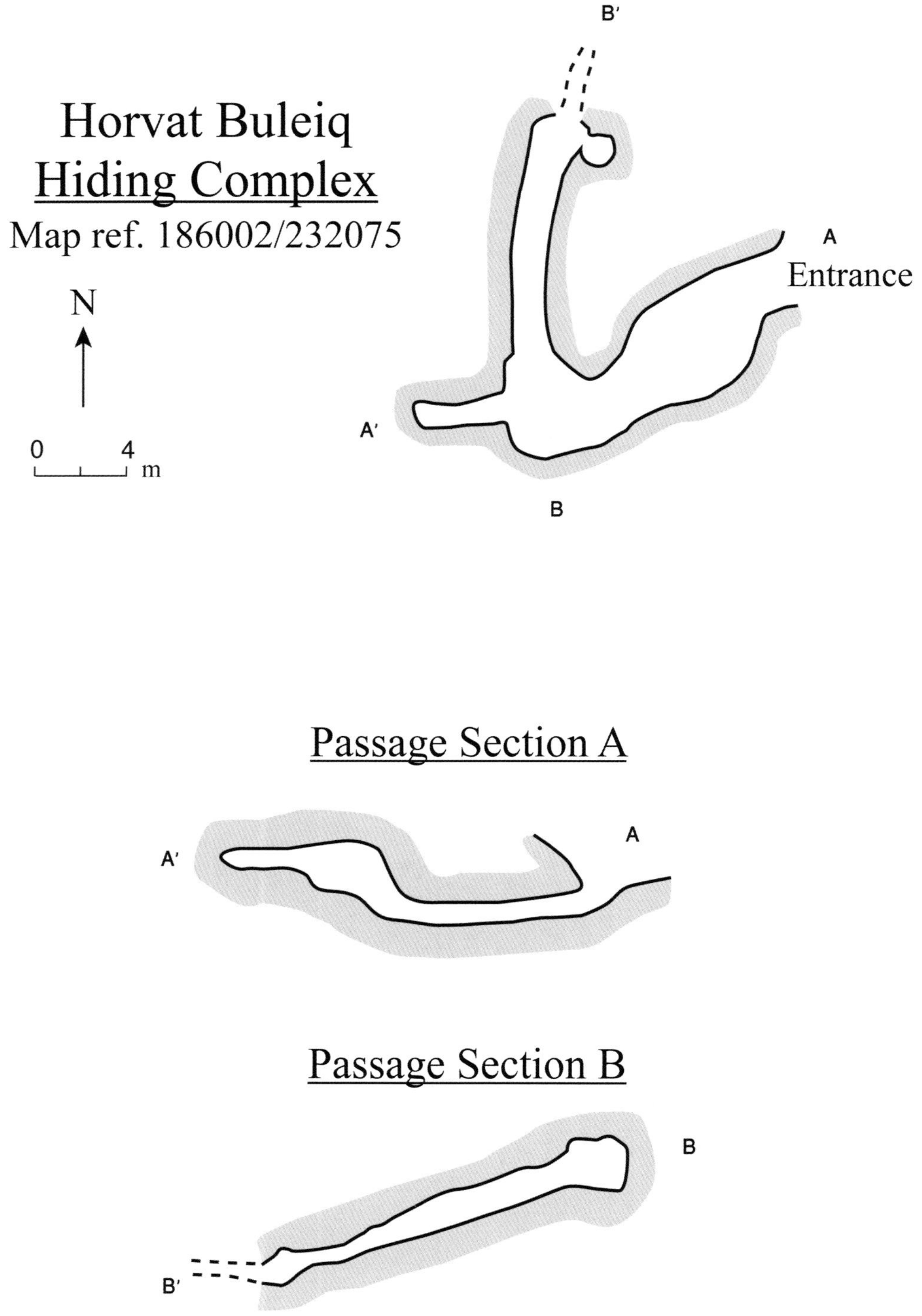

Map 87: Horvat Buleiq

an underground rock-hewn cavern was found bearing all the typical features of a hiding complex. The entrance to the complex is cut into the north slope of the hill, rendering an earlier industrial installation obsolete. The opening (0.6 × 1.0 m) is irregularly shaped and simply hewn. It leads to a 6 m long passage that can only be crawled through with considerable difficulty. The passage turns sharply to the north (making an almost 90-degree turn) and leads to a hewn chamber measuring 2.0 × 2.5 m and 1.3 m high. Branching off in a straight line from this chamber is a hewn passage that is rectangular in section and meticulously dressed. The passage measures 0.7 × 1.0 m across and continues for 7 m, becoming narrower until it reaches a hewn niche that is blocked with earth. The roof of the passage also decreases gradually in height until it can only be crawled through. About 15 m east of the entrance to the hiding complex is another entrance on the east face of the rock, which may be the original entrance to the hiding complex. From this arched entrance (0.9 × 1.0 m) a westerly passage hewn in the direction of the hiding complex is blocked with earth after 5 m. Since Buleiq Hill has few structural remains whereas the nearby site of Horvat Qarah has many, it is highly likely that the inhabitants of Horvat Qarah used Buleiq Hill for quarrying building stones, for industrial purposes, for burial, and as a hiding place.

66. Horvat Nurit (Nuris), on Mount Gilboa (Map ref. 184349/215612)

Horvat Nurit is located on the western slopes of Mount Gilboa at the foot of Mount Mazar. The site lies on a gentle slope and its remains are covered by dense vegetation. Ancient walls built of dressed stones, water cisterns and numerous cave entrances – some used for habitation – are visible at the site. A village Victor Guérin described here had a population of 600 living in dilapidated houses and rock-hewn caves and cellars.[136] Tsuri surveyed the ruins and discovered column drums, capitals, and two pedestals from the Roman and Byzantine periods.[137] Many architectural elements are incorporated in secondary use in the remains of the Arab village. Zvi Ilan surveyed the site and recorded finding items similar to those at ancient synagogues in Galilee.[138] The present survey explored a substantial underground cavern consisting of large chambers with interconnecting hewn passages. The complex has two entrances. The main entrance (2.3 × 6.5 m) has a secondary entrance nearby (1.2 × 1.8 m). A built wall acts as a partition between the two entrances. The main chamber (length 7 m, height 1.5 m) has three round openings in its roof, one of which is blocked. It was probably originally used as a large water reservoir and became obsolete when the hiding complex was hewn. In the middle of the chamber is a stone wall five courses high that splits it into two rooms. Another wall (length 3.5 m, width 1.5 m) was found to the south of the entrance. A passage (0.55 × 1.10 m in section) cut in the north wall of the chamber leads to another chamber; a stone wall was also built along the west wall of this chamber and a nearby passage is now blocked with earth. From this chamber another, 15 m long passage leads to a third chamber with a triangular opening hewn in its north wall that is now blocked with earth.

136 See Guérin 1880,4:215.
137 See Tsuri 1977:4–5.
138 See Ilan 1991a:185.

Fig. 120: Horvat Nurit

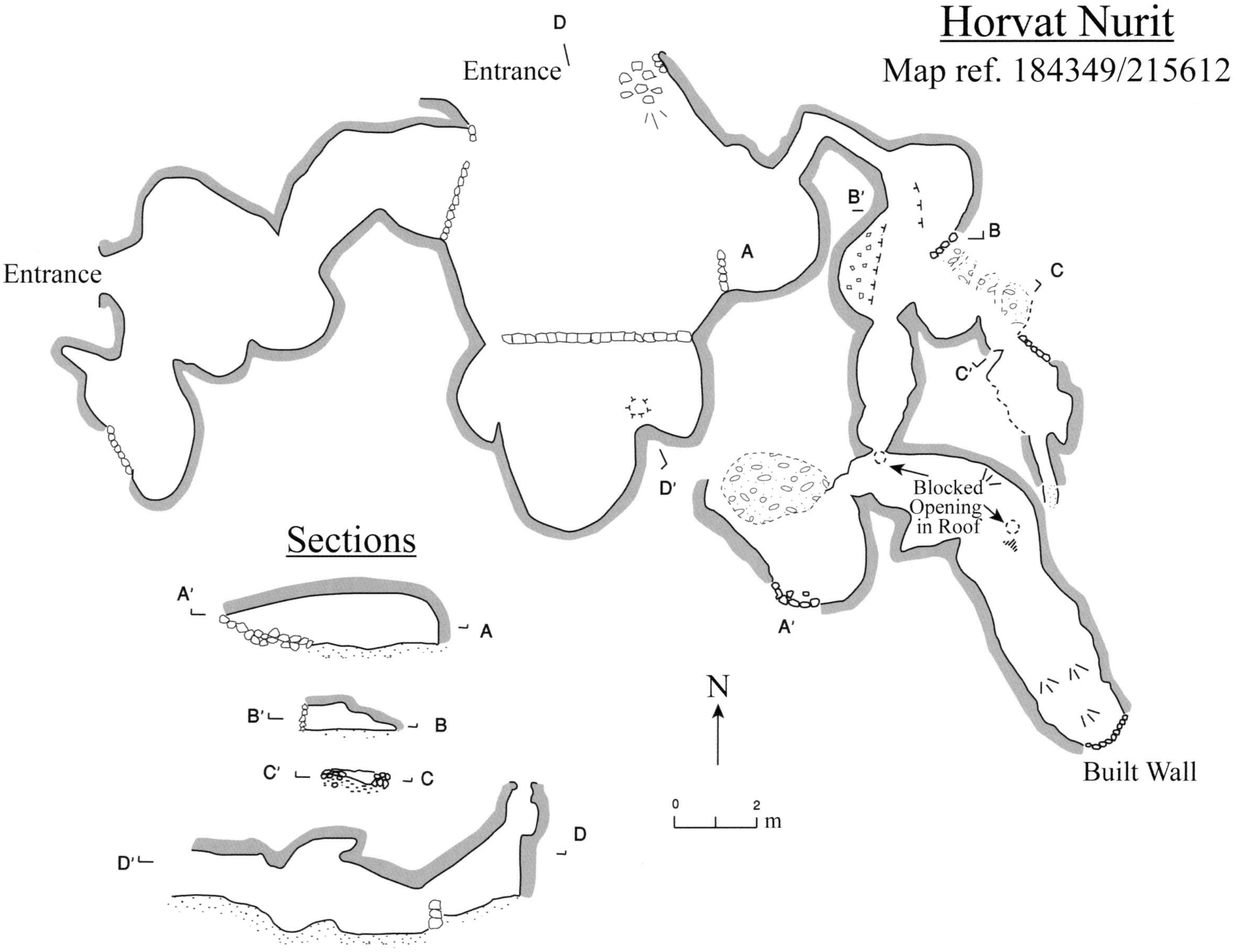

Map 88: Horvat Nurit

67. Tel 'Amal tunnel, Horvat Tel al-Asi, on the south bank of Nahal 'Amal (Map ref. 192594/212313)

Tel 'Amal is on the south bank of Nahal 'Amal, inside Gan Ha-Shlosha National Park. The site covers roughly 3 dunams (c. 0.75 acre) and consists of two mounds separated by a gully. Tsuri excavated the western mound in 1958 and recovered a large quantity of architectural elements and pottery. Salvage excavations on the east mound in 1962–1966 and 1983 exposed five occupation strata dating to Iron Age II and the Persian, Byzantine, and Early Islamic periods.[139]

A tunnel in the southern rock scarp of Nahal 'Amal was doubtless cut to channel water and its opening is still visible today. Tepper and Shachar identified the tunnel as a hiding complex.[140] Its entrance (0.6 × 0.8 m in section) is now filled with earth. Travertine deposits have formed around the entrance to the tunnel, widened to 1.4 × 1.6 m by water erosion (Fig. 240). From this entrance, the tunnel is accessible to a depth of 1.5 m before becoming blocked. Water channeled along the east wall of the tunnel flows into Nahal 'Amal 2.5 m away from the opening. The tunnel is hewn in a slight curve to the south and a plan pub-

139 See Tsuri 1962:184–185; Edelstein and Feig 1992:1583.

140 See Tepper and Shachar 1987b:283.

Fig. 121: Tel ʿAmal tunnel

Fig. 122: Nahal ʿAmal passages

lished by Tepper and Shachar shows that it reaches a length of c. 30 m. The end of the tunnel, or its original opening, is in the western mound where traces of the ancient settlement were found. Tepper and Shachar described a hewn tunnel in three sections. The first section is hewn directly south from the opening facing Nahal ʿAmal and is 17 m in length. The second section continues from the end of the bend for another c. 12 m. The archaeologists believe that a round shaft cut in the tunnel roof in this section leads to the cellar of the ruined building above. The third section was cut in a 9 m bend to the point where it was blocked with mud and plaster. In Tepper and Shachar's opinion, despite the water erosion visible in the tunnel it was not intended as a water channel but as a hiding complex. In light of data gathered while studying the hiding complexes in Judea and Galilee, I do not believe that it should be interpreted as a hiding complex, although it may have been used as an escape tunnel.

68. Nahal ʿAmal passages, in Gan Hashlosha National Park on the north bank of Nahal ʿAmal (Wadi al-Asi) (Map ref. 192446/212351)

Approximately 1 km west of Tel ʿAmal tunnel and further upstream, two rock-hewn openings were discovered in the north bank of Nahal ʿAmal that lead to two passages. Tepper and Shachar identified these passages as hiding complexes and believe they provide evidence that Tel ʿAmal tunnel and the Nahal ʿAmal passages were part of a comprehensive series of hiding complexes hewn at around the time of the Bar Kokhba Revolt.[141] The western passage branches into two more passages that are accessible for c. 20 m before being blocked with earth. Inside the passages, the surveyors found the marks of water that flowed in them in ancient times and hewn oil-lamp niches, some retaining traces of soot. They noted that although Josephus describes this region as having a Jewish population, no evidence has yet been found for the existence of a Jewish settlement at the site in the Early or Late Roman periods. The present survey found that the eastern entrance to the passage is completely blocked; however, it was possible to enter to a depth of c. 3 m from the stream via the western passage opening (0.7 × 0.8 m in section) c. 2 m away from the blocked entrance and up to a point where it is completely blocked with silt and mud. As with the Tel ʿAmal tunnel, the Nahal ʿAmal passages should not be interpreted as hiding complexes although they may have been used as escape tunnels.

69. Horvat ʿAmmudim (Khirbet Umm el-Amad) (Map ref. 188946/246720)

Yitzhak Tur of the Israel Antiquities Authority's Antiquities Robbery Prevention Unit informed me of the hiding complex on the agricultural slopes of Horvat ʿAmmudim. On visiting the site in the 19th c., Victor Guérin cited an ancient synagogue there as proof of an ancient Jewish settlement.[142] Heinrich Kohl and Carl Watzinger excavated it in 1905 and drafted a plan of the synagogue.[143] Israel Levine excavated the synagogue in 1979 and dated its founding to the early fourth century CE. Zvi Maʿoz believes that the building had

141 See Tepper and Shachar 1987b:286.

142 Guérin 1886, vol. 6:242–243.

143 Kohl and Watzinger 1916:71–79.

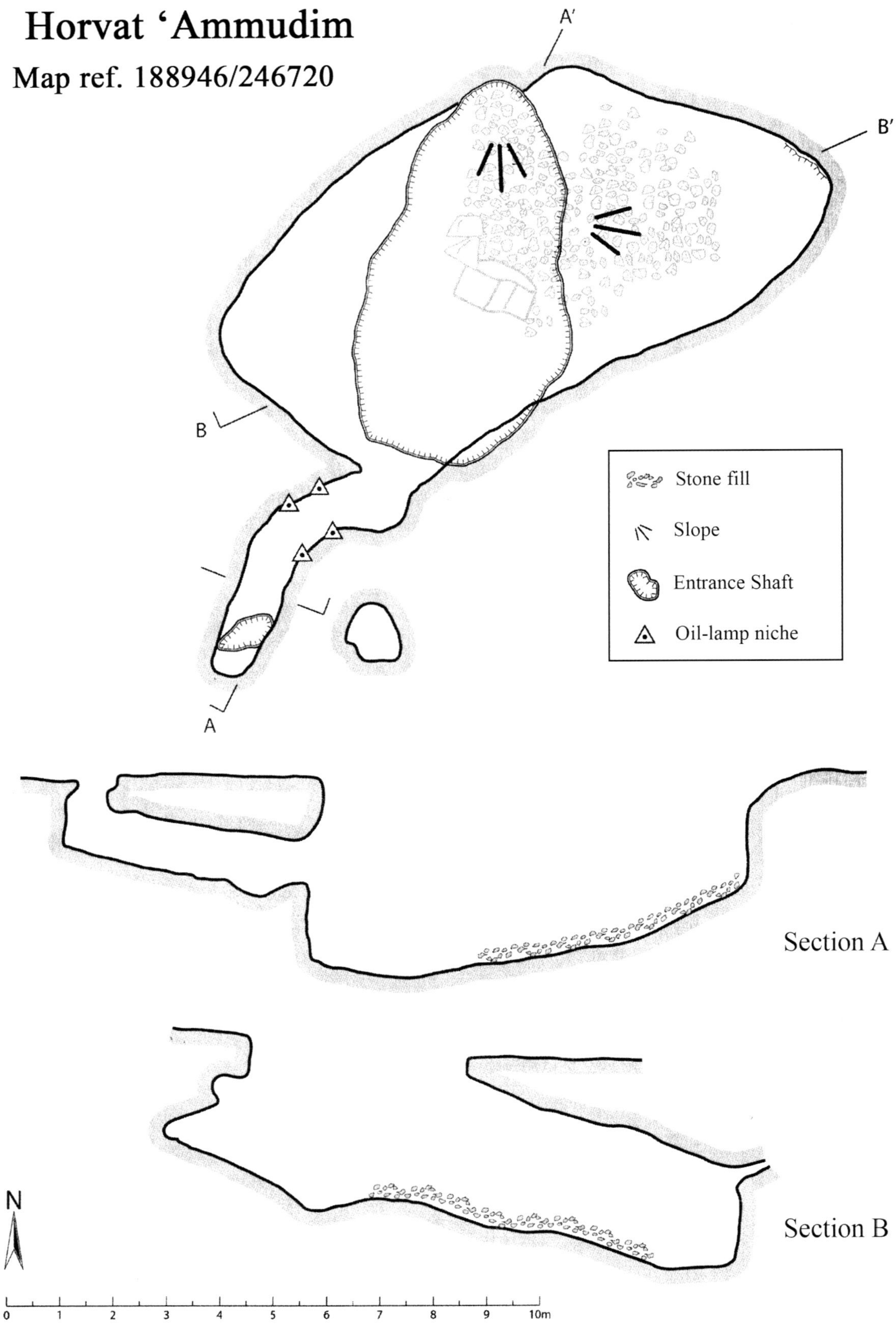

Map 89: Horvat 'Ammudim

an earlier phase in the late 2nd and early 3rd c. CE. Two Aramaic descriptions were discovered here at two different times; one was deciphered by Yosef Naveh and the other by Eleazar Lipa Sukenik.[144] During the years, several surveys and one excavation exposed dozens of agricultural installations various kinds.[145] The hiding complex was discovered inside a water cistern, which was capable of storing water even after the complex was built (as at Horvat Mishtah).[146] The water cistern is located in Horvat ʿAmmudim's agricultural-industrial sector. It is rare to find a hiding complex located outside the boundaries of a settlement.

The complex was hewn in the upper part of the southwest wall of a water cistern with a collapsed roof whose floor is silted up with earth that now provides easy access to the cistern. The cistern lies on the northeast slope, c. 200 m away from the ruins of the synagogue. It contains the only fig tree in a landscape dominated by hawthorn and terebinth trees; fig trees are frequently found in association with cisterns converted into hiding complexes. The cistern is coated with gray plaster covered with a layer of reddish plaster. Traces of the plaster are evident throughout the cistern, which is roughly 12 m long and 6 m wide at its widest point. The entrance to the hiding complex is cut into the upper part of the cistern, 0.6 m higher than the debris inside it and 1.5 m from the present floor of the cistern, now filled with clods of earth and bushy vegetation. The cistern would have been capable of storing water while the hiding complex was still being built or used. The entrance to the complex can be reached by scrambling up the earthen mound and crawling inside to a depth of 3 m, where it becomes a tight squeeze. Two oil-lamp niches were discovered at the entrance to the passage.

A three-day archaeological excavation conducted in the hiding complex by the author and Mechael Osband

144 For a summary of the data and relevant citations see Leibner 2009:243.

145 See Zingboym 2017.

146 See Complex 26.

Fig. 123: Horvat ʿAmmudim

succeeded in exposing the passage for a length of 5 m before encountering a bedrock wall, proving that for some unknown reason the complex was never completed. We discovered four oil-lamp niches along both sides of the passage. The niches were soot free, indicating that not only was the hiding complex not completed, but it was never used since it lacked the soot marks often found in other hiding complexes. The passage was dated by potsherds recovered from two excavation layers inside it; the first layer consisted of the earth accumulated in the cistern, containing a mixture of potsherds from the 1st–5th c. CE and a fragment of a bowl from a stone vessel. The second layer, in which the pottery was separate, was that of the leveled passage floor and contained 1st and 2nd c. CE finds.

70. Horvat Qisi (Map ref. 171811/236353)

Horvat Qisi is a few hundred meters east of the Arab town of Zarzir. The ruins are not marked on PEF surveys or recorded by Guérin, although the latter does mention a route between the village of ʻIllut and Horvat Simonaya that must have passed beside this prominent ruin. Shlomo Grootkerk notes that the site was known as Khirbet Qis in the Ottoman period.[147] This is probably the reason why older local inhabitants call it Khirbet Qisi. The name Kh. Qisi appears for the first time on a British 1:100.000 scale map from 1941–1942 (amended in 1944). The Archaeological Survey of Israel Map of Nazareth records Horvat Qisi as Site No. 31.

On visiting the site with Zeev (Zabbo) Erlich, we saw the remains of a later settlement on top of those of an ancient site, with traces of buildings and natural and man-made underground cavities. On the summit are agricultural installations, water cisterns, hewn basins and other rock-cut features. Caves are scattered throughout the hill. Some are natural and some hewn, and some may recently have been used as dwellings or for storage. A leveled rock surface on the summit contains two openings: The northern one is on its north face and the southern one is reached from the leveled surface, where steps cut in the rock lead to an underground chamber. Slightly to the south of the summit are signs of stone clearance and an assortment of protruding dressed stones.[148]

Avner Raban surveyed the Shefarʻam-Alonim-Zippori hill region, published by the Israel Nature Protection Society in 1990 in a booklet for the general public.[149] The booklet contains limited data on the site and describes ruined buildings and dwellings. Raban located a burial cave and water cisterns on the north slope. At the foot of the hill, near the upper tributary of Nahal Shimron, Raban detected the route of the Roman road from Legio to Sepphoris and a stream flowing from a spring (ʻEn Qisi, which is also not marked on maps although it supplies plentiful water, particularly in rainy years). Raban also maintains that column drums, worked pedestals and other architectural elements that were once visible may well attest to the existence of an ancient synagogue at Horvat Qisi. In his introduction to the survey, Raban provides a thorough description of the entire surrounding region, noting that the Alonim-Shefarʻam hill region had a dense Jewish population. He believes that the Sanhedrin's move to Bet Sheʻarim, together with the seat of Rabbi Yehuda Hanassi, enhanced the Jewish presence in the region. Raban describes a thriving center of Jewish life, consisting of land owning or tenant farmers. In his opinion, Talmudic records of "twenty-four towns of Beit Rabbi" (*ySanhedrin* 1b:2) and the economic prosperity at the time refer to the region that includes Horvat Qisi.

Our survey was the first to recognize the hiding complex on the hilltop. We found hewn steps leading to an underground cavity where we discovered a series of underground chambers connected by passages, providing a clear example of a finely hewn hiding complex of the kind found in the Judean foothills and Galilee and dating from the 2nd–3rd c. CE. The hiding complex was mapped using modern technology, allocating a serial number to each feature.

<u>Chamber A</u>: The complex is hewn from inside a large underground cavity resembling an underground storeroom in three sections incorporated into one by removing the partition walls between them. Chamber A now has two main entrances: One, which is probably the original main entrance, leads to the chamber and is hewn in the east part of the north wall. The entrance consists of two meticulously hewn jambs and most of it is buried in earth. Two boltholes are visible at the top of the jambs. The opening originally led to a square chamber. The other entrance, which was probably a secondary one, is cut in the south side and has a hewn rectangular opening with a double frame. A small round hole for a bolt is hewn on the west side of the

147 Grootkerk 2000:279.

148 We visited the site on 15 March 2016 and completed our exploration soon afterward.

149 Raban 1990:72.

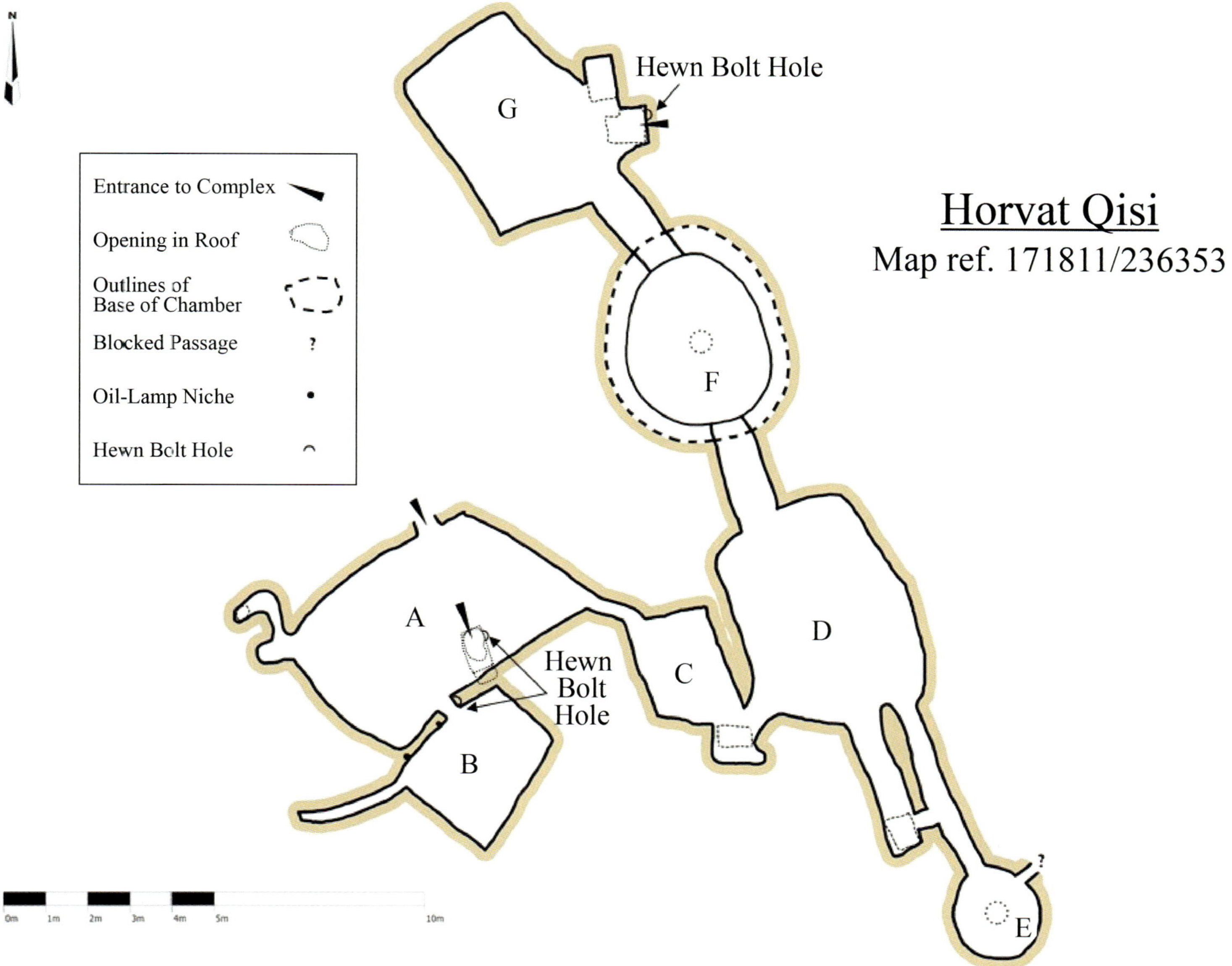

Map 90: Horvat Qisi

rectangular opening (0.55 × 0.95 m). Two steps (length 0.5 m, depth 0.5 m) lead down to a round entrance to the chamber. The opening was probably the upper part of a Giv'on Pit-type storage pit that was converted into an entrance to the complex. Three small rooms were added to the west of these two anterooms at a later stage. Each small room had a separate entrance hewn in the roof, the upper parts of which are preserved. The divisions between the three entrances were removed and the anterooms were combined to form a single space. A short westerly passage is hewn in the west wall of the chamber. The passage bends before emerging at the surface. The exit is now blocked by a stone.

Chamber B: A 0.6 m wide opening hewn 1.3 m up the south wall of Chamber A leads to a meticulously hewn rectangular chamber (1.95 × 3.65 m, height 1.32 m), which is a later addition to Chamber A. A bolthole is cut in the opening and an oil-lamp niche is hewn in the wall near the opening. Both the niche and the finely hewn chamber are free of soot. Horizontal flint veins are visible along the walls of the well-dressed chamber. A passage 2.67 m long and averaging 0.6 m in height leads off the west wall of this chamber. After beginning to hew in a slightly northerly direction, work on the passage ceased after 2.67 m. The clean oil-lamp niche and unfinished passage sug-

Fig. 124: Horvat Qisi

gest that whoever worked on the complex never succeeded in using it.

Chamber C: In the southeast corner of Chamber A, a short easterly passage was hewn to Chamber C, which is roughly worked and measures c. 3 × 3 m and 1.5 m high. An opening hewn in the southeast corner of the south wall of the chamber is a dead end. In the southeast corner of the roof is an opening (0.67 × 0.90 m) blocked by two symmetrically hewn stone slabs that are meticulously worked.

Chamber D: A short easterly passage cut in the east wall of Chamber C leads to Chamber D (c. 5 × 5 m), which is also roughly quarried and chisel marks are visible on its south wall. Its north wall is covered with a glacis of earth debris, hinting that there may be another opening in the roof of the chamber. Two short passages hewn into the east wall of Chamber D lead to very small cavities that continue nowhere.

Chamber E: In the west wall of Chamber D is a short westerly passage leading to Chamber E, which is an ancient water cistern; its plaster coating has evidence of having been used more recently. The cistern (diameter 4.5 m) is now 4 m deep and has an opening that protrudes another 1 m above ground. The floor is strewn with earth debris.

Chamber F: In the middle of the west wall of Chamber E (the water cistern), a short passage cuts through to Chamber F in the west (c. 6 × 6 m). A round opening hewn in the northeast corner of this chamber leads to the surface; this is probably the entrance to a Giv'on Pit-type storeroom. A rectangular alcove is cut 1 m high in the north side of this opening. The alcove is roofed with three symmetrical, well-finished slabs. The capacity of the water cistern was reduced by at least a third by cutting the passage from Chamber E to Chamber F.

Pottery finds from the complex are representative of the late third–early fourth centuries CE. We propose identifying Horvat Qisi as the biblical Qatat, referred to as Qatana in rabbinic literature, whose location is compatible with that of the site.[150]

150 Erlich and Shivti'el 2017:21–22.

Fig. 125: Horvat Maskana 1

71. Horvat Maskana 1 (Map ref. 188751/243262)

Horvat Maskana lies on an elongated spur-like hill c. 1 km north of Golani Junction. Its original name, Maskana, appears in the Jerusalem Talmud as a Jewish settlement on the road from Tiberias to Zippori (*yBerachot* 9:5,14d; *ySanhedrin* 3:1,20a). Uzi Leibner surveyed the ruins and identified agricultural installations, water cisterns, and burial complexes. The pottery recovered shows that the settlement existed from the Early Roman to the Early Islamic period. Most of the ceramic finds date from the Early to the Late Roman Periods.[151]

A hiding complex is hewn in the northeast wall of a large water cistern divided into two sections: A cistern, and a ritual bath. The passage has a regular profile (c. 0.4 × 0.6 m in section). The opening is meticulously hewn and the funnel-like wall above it is rendered completely smooth. The passage is blocked at the entrance. The water cistern itself (8 × 15 m) is plastered and its original opening is blocked by a large stone. In the southern part of the cavity is another opening that now provides access to the water cistern. A ritual bath (?) hewn in the nearby southeast wall probably had a separate entrance and is now flanked by a large barren tree. The ritual bath is coated with thick gray hydraulic plaster. The bath (1 × 2 m) is filled in with earth but a single wide step protruding from the earthen fill is also well plastered. Another passage section, only 0.3 m long and unfinished, was begun in the east wall of the ritual bath. The present opening (opposite the ritual bath) is marked by a massive fig tree. The water cistern in which the hiding complex is hewn has two openings: One, now used to enter the cistern, is on the south side. The other leads directly into the ritual bath where the fig tree is. This entrance is probably the one used by visitors to the ritual bath, which was fed by water from the cistern. Breccia deposits are visible along the walls of the large cistern and on the west wall. In March 2017, antiquities robbers were apprehended inside a new hiding complex that they had been illegally excavating.

151 Leibner 2009: 284.

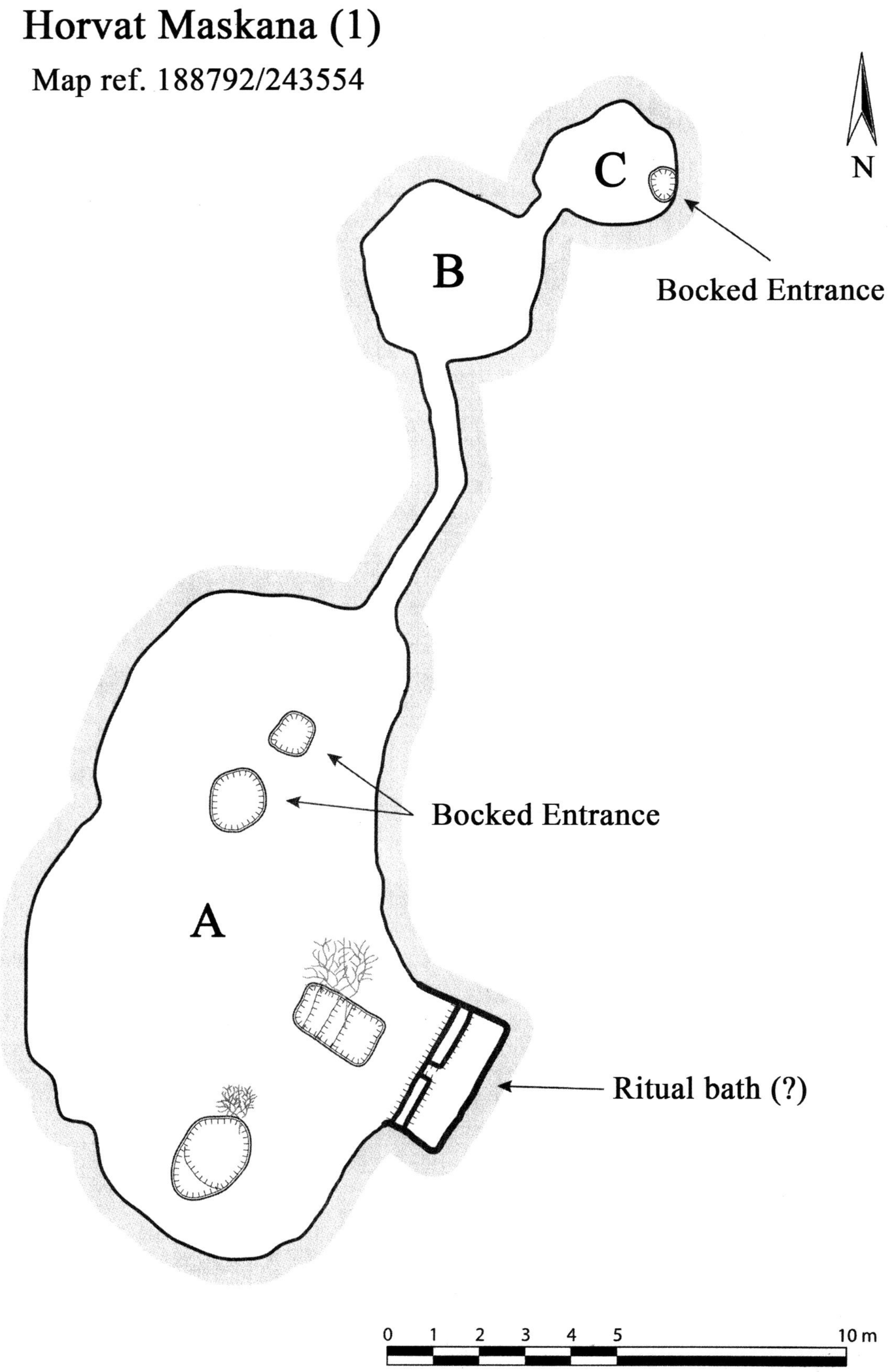

Map 91: Horvat Maskana 1

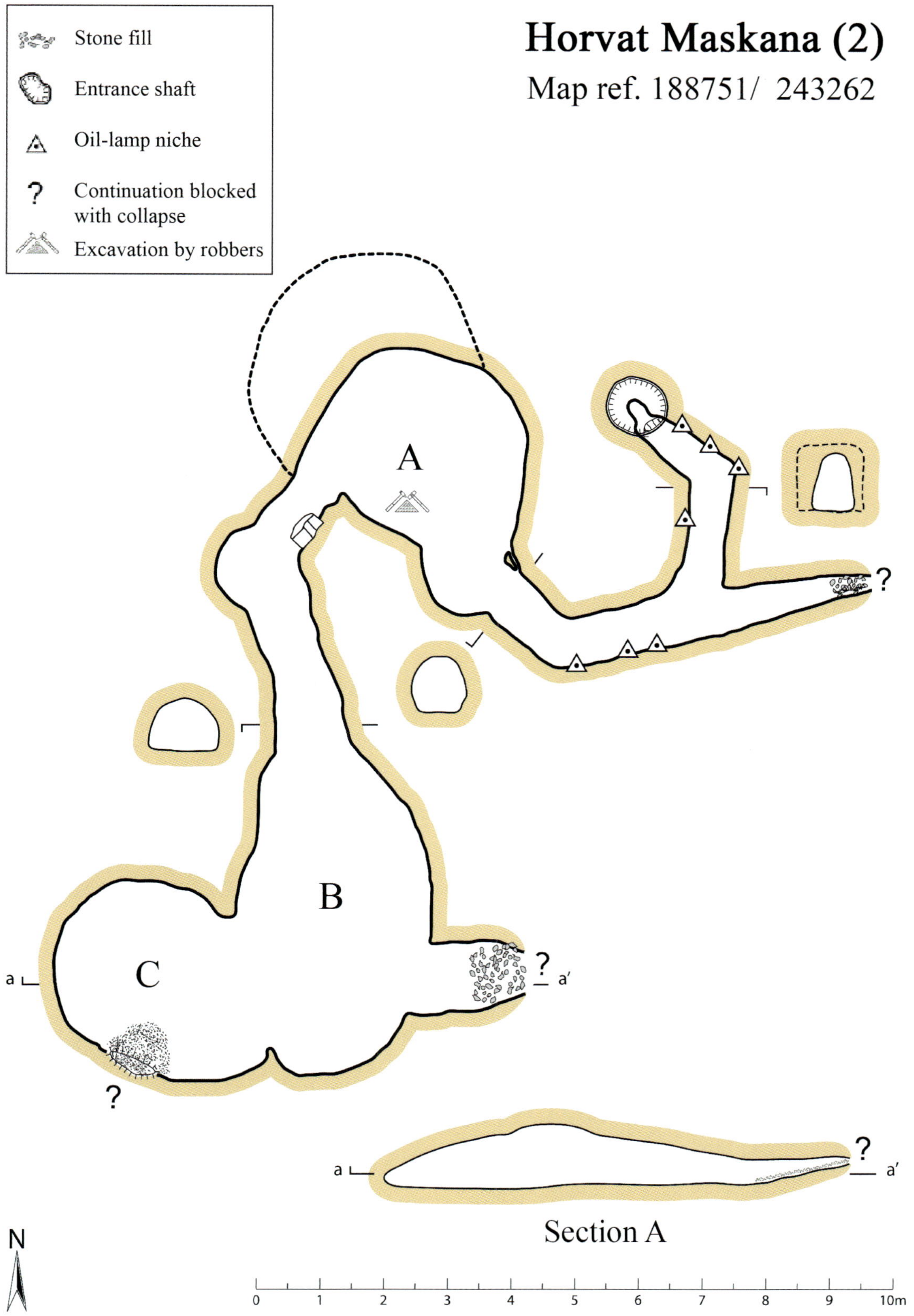

Map 92: Horvat Maskana 2

72. Horvat Maskana 2 (Map ref. 188751/243262)

The second hiding complex at Horbat Maskana was discovered by antiquities robbers who were apprehended inside the complex during the robbery. The hiding complex begins from inside a round, finely hewn shaft that carries on into a roughly, hastily hewn tunnel leading to a large, irregular cavity with massive blocks of earth blocking its southern side. The second part of the hiding complex, including another passage and an additional large cavity (B), was more meticulously hewn.

The cave opening (Cavity A) does not appear to be the original entrance and may have been an emergency exit from the complex. It begins with a circular, symmetrical vertical shaft 0.80 × 1.00 m in diameter. The shaft is smoothly hewn and descends to a depth of one meter. A short incline that may once have had steps on it was quarried down from the bottom of the shaft. At the end of the slope is a finely worked arched opening with a frame similar to that at the entrance to the Huqoq complex (No. 20). The opening leads to a 2 meter-long passage with numerous ellipsoid oil-lamp niches. The passage takes a sharp, right-angled turn to the east and continues for another four meters, leading directly to the second cavity. Toward the middle of the passage is a rock-cut opening that appears to be the beginning of another passage that has either become blocked or was not finished. This section of the passage also contains several ellipsoid oil-lamp niches. The complex has a total of ten such niches.

Cavity B is a large, irregularly-shaped cavity that was partially excavated up to its south wall by the robbers. This created a kind of wide step across the cavity composed entirely of the mud blocks described above. This is probably the reason why the rock on the eastern side of the cavity has a reddish color. A passage was cut in the north wall of Cavity B, on the north side of which is a large rectangular hewn stone measuring 0.50 × 0.50 m and 0.25 m high. It was probably used to seal the passage linking Cavities A and B. The short passage leads to a small, vaulted rock-cut cavity. The passage crosses the small cavity and continues northward for a few meters directly into Cavity C, which is

Fig. 126: Horvat Maskana 2

irregularly shaped. At the south end of the cavity is an arched, rock-cut opening that appears to be the opening to another passage that has either become blocked or was not finished. The entrance to Cavity C leads straight from Cavity B. In the north of Cavity C, near the roof, is a sloping mound of earth fill that may indicate the location of the original entrance, which is now blocked. The east part of the cavity, near the roof of the complex, also contains large blocks of dry mud. Cavity C looks to be roughly hewn and the original opening may belong typologically to the period when the complex was made, prior to the Great Revolt. The meticulous quarrying of the passages with its well-designed escape exit may have been part of the preparations for the Bar Kokhba revolt.

73. Rushmya / Rosh Maya, Citadel (Haifa, Romema) (Map ref. 150229/243889)

The ruins of Rosh Maya fortress (Rushmya; 248 m asl) are on the summit of the Old Romema neighborhood in Haifa, at the end of Palmah St. between Nahal Vardiya and Nahal Giborim and they overlook the entrance to Nahal Rushmya (Nahal Remez), which was the main route to Mount Carmel from the north in antiquity. The site, which covers c. 20 dunams (c. 5 acres), now consists mainly of the remains of a Crusader fortress made of *kurkar* stones with a fine view of the whole of Haifa Bay and the ʻAkko Valley. The hill is now forested, obstructing views in other directions. Although the site is neglected, it has a sign bearing the name "Ha-Banim Grove." Although it retains the name of a Jewish settlement from Mishnaic and Talmudic times (Rosh Maya, Rosh Mayim), the location is not compatible with that of Rosh Maya in the Talmudic list of forbidden towns in the territory of Tyre: "Shetset and Betset and Pi-Metsubah, Upper Hanita and Lower Hanita, Bari and Rosh Maya" (*yDemai* 2:22,4a), which are generally considered to have been near Rosh Hanikra ridge on the border of Western Galilee.[152] Nevertheless, the Arab name "Rushmya" undoubtedly preserves the name of some ancient Jewish settlement. Archaeological excavations conducted in the 1970s by Moshe Prausnitz and Ezriel Seligman have shed some light on its identity. They found that the site was already built as a fortress in the Hasmonean period (2nd–1st c. BCE) and their finds indicate a late 2nd c. BCE date for the fortress. It was occupied until the Byzantine period and a fragment of an oil lamp decorated with a seven-branched candelabra dating from that period is evidence of Jewish occupation there at least until that time.[153]

The excavation exposed the hiding complex in 1972 before the phenomenon of defensive "hiding complexes" received sufficient academic attention; the archaeologists therefore attributed the underground cavities to the Hasmonean fortress. On a recent visit to the site (10 September 2016), I realized that the underground cavities found have all the characteristics of hiding complexes and can be dated to the Hasmonean period.[154] The entrance to the complex is 6 m away from the north wall of the ruined fortress and it is now accessible via a square pit (not plastered; Cavity A; map ref. 150229/243889, with a 6 m deviation) measuring 1.35 × 2.20 m. An entrance (0.5 × 0.6 m) cut in the west wall of the pit and similar to the entrances to most hiding complexes from the first–second centuries CE leads directly into Cavity B. A low 4.5 m long passage hewn from Cavity A can only be crawled through with difficulty, not least because of waste and pine needles accumulated inside it. After 3 m, however, it bends nearly 90 degrees and continues for another 1.5 m to reach a hewn chamber (2.1 × 3.0 m, height 1.1 m; Cavity C). A soot-free oil-lamp niche is hewn in the west wall of the chamber. In its southwest wall, the passage (0.6 × 0.7 m in section) continues in a straight line. After 0.3 m a further passage (0.4 × 1.3 m) cut in its northeast wall is incomplete and has three oil-lamp niches in horizon on the north wall that are also free of soot. This is obviously not a burial niche, since it is only 0.4 m wide. The length of the main passage is 2.3 m on its south side, with an oil-lamp niche, and 1.5 m on its north side with a width of c. 0.6 m. The passage leads to another hewn chamber (1.5 × 1.8 m; Cavity D). From here, an entrance leads to a bell-shaped pit (Cavity E; diameter 1.5 m, height 1.8 m). An opening (0.6 × 1.1 m) cut into the south wall of the pit links it to another pit (Cavity F; diameter 1.2 m, height 2.0 m). Both pits have three niches hewn one above the other in their north wall and in the south wall are two more oil-lamp niches that contain traces of soot. The pits bear no signs of plaster. The complex at Rosh Maya fortress in Haifa is highly significant for research into the distribution of hiding complexes.

152 Klein 1945:159; Ilan 1986a: 503–515.

153 Prausnitz 1974:143.

154 In recent years, hiding complexes from the Hasmonean period have been discovered in extensive archaeological excavations at the Nesher-Ramla quarry; see Melamed 2010:89–243; Shivti'el 2018 (in print).

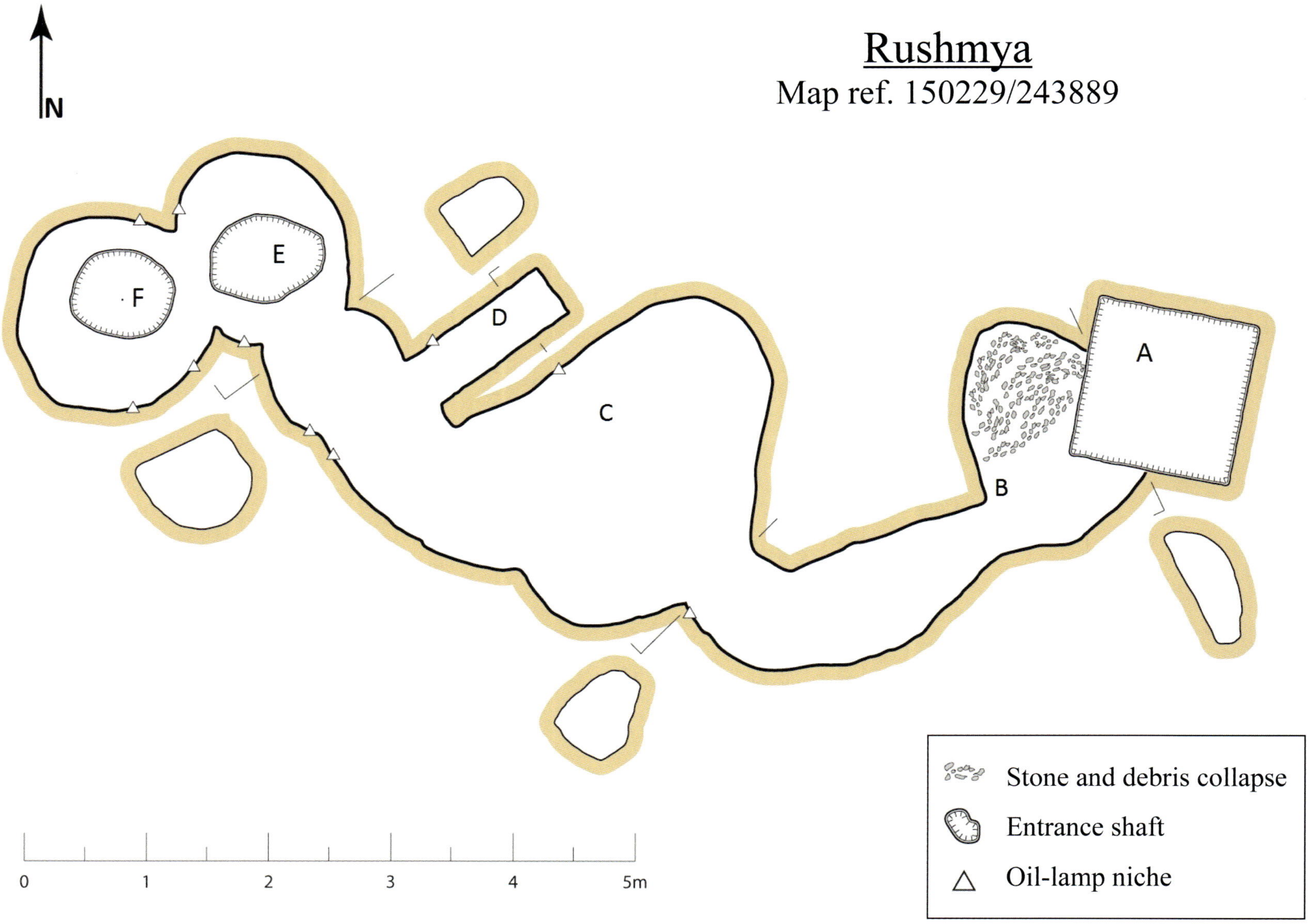

Map 93: Rushmya Hiding Complex

Fig. 127: Rushmya (Rosh Maya) citadel

74. Horvat Usha (Kh. Hoshe) Hiding Complex (Map ref. 163761/244397)

Horvat Usha contains the ruins of an ancient Jewish settlement covering approximately 50 dunams (just over 12 acres; elevation 128 m asl) along the shoulder of a spur to the north of the town of Shefar'am. The site is known to have been an important Jewish settlement in the Early and Middle Roman periods. Most of our information about it is derived from the fact that the leading Sages of Israel gathered there after the Bar Kokhba Revolt to decide on the establishment of a Jewish leadership in the Galilee (*Shir HaShirim Rabbah* 2:5:3). It was at Usha that the laws were compiled on how to conduct the life of the Jewish community in the wake of the severe consequences of the Bar Kokhba Revolt. These laws became known as the 'Ordinances of Usha' (Babylonian Talmud, *Kethuboth,* 88b; 89b, q.v.; Jerusalem Talmud, *Kethuboth,* 4, 8, 28, 4, q.v.). At one stage in its wanderings, the Sanhedrin (rabbinical council) also convened in Usha (Babylonian Talmud, *Rosh Hashanah,* 31b). Sages were ordained between Usha and Shefar'am, although the practice endangered all those present since it was punishable by death (Babylonian Talmud, *Sanhedrin,* 14a). In the early twentieth century, a Greek inscription bearing the phrase 'Shabbat boundary' was discovered at the site.[155]

Archaeological excavations were conducted for the Israel Antiquities Authority in 2008–2009 in five parts of the site, under the direction of Aviram Oshri. During the course of the excavations, a large public building was exposed and potsherds from the Byzantine, Mamluk and Ottoman periods were recovered from a probe pit. Installations and hewn cavities that probably date to the Roman period were also revealed. In one of the excavation areas, on the western fringes of the site, a ritual bath was discovered. From a breach in its floor one can descend to a simple, roughly hewn hiding complex. The complex consists of three cavities interconnected with short passages and it has an escape exit on one side (such hiding complexes are typical of the Great Revolt period). The ritual bath is located on the western slopes of the site and is part of an olive-press complex surrounded by several installations. As at other Jewish sites, the oil produced would probably have conformed to the standards of religious purity. Elongated sockets were carved at the entrance to the ritual bath, apparently to enable the entrance to be sealed with a stone door. The ritual bath has four steps. Since it is 0.30 m high, an imprint is hewn in the second step. The first, third, and fourth steps are 0.20 m high and each step is 0.60 m wide. The hiding complex was probably hewn to shelter the olive-press workers.

The complex consists of three chambers and may contain additional chambers that are now blocked. The entrance to the hiding complex today, and probably also in ancient times, is through the ritual bath. The bath is small, of the type used by a single family, and accessed via steps. The immersion pool measures 1.5 × 1.5 m. The bottom of the bath was hewn into and the descent from there into the first hiding cavity involves a drop of about 2 m, achieved by clinging on with the hands. An opening, probably intended as an escape route, was hewn in the southern side of Chamber A (measuring 6 × 7 m). In the western wall of the chamber is an opening leading to another chamber reached through a crawlway. The second chamber is the same size as the first. An opening blocked with earth fill is visible in the northern wall of the second chamber and this may lead to another chamber. In the western wall of the second chamber is another opening that is also blocked with earth, but using a flashlight it is possible to see that a third chamber exists beyond the blocked section. Approximately 15 m north of the hiding complex (map ref. 244419/163766) is an entrance to a cave with a rectangular hewn opening measuring 1.5 × 2.5 m with an olive tree growing on its west side. The meticulously hewn entrance leads directly into a large chamber measuring 6 × 8 m. There appears to be a continuation on the southwest wall of this chamber and it may be connected to the hiding complex that leads from the ritual bath.

155 Erlich and Shivti'el 2017.

Fig. 128: Horvat Usha (entrance into a ritual bath whose wall has been breached)

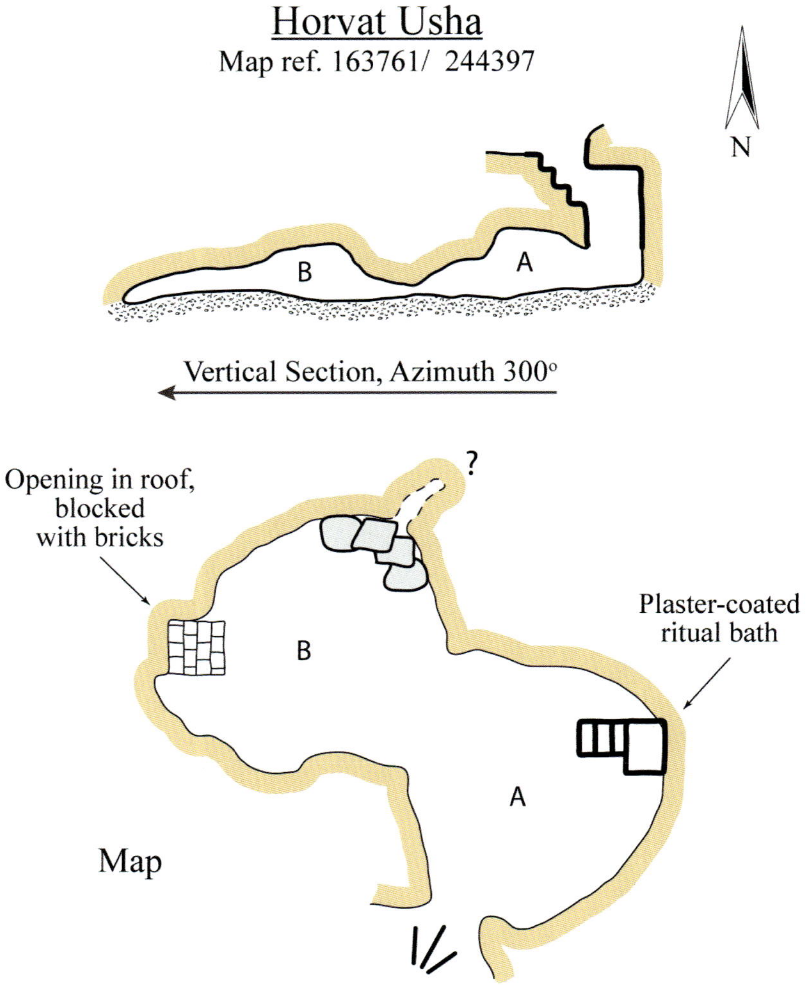

Map 94: Horvat Usha, Hiding Complex

Summary and Conclusions

This book describes my research into two highly significant phenomena discovered at Early Roman Jewish settlements in Galilee, namely cliff shelters and hiding complexes.

Cliff shelters are natural caves that were enlarged and adapted for use as refuges near existing settlements in the vicinity of steep cliffs. Surveys of such shelters show that this is a predominantly Galilean phenomenon, although a single cliff shelter has been found in Judea, at the al-'Aliliat caves in Nahal Michmash, which is comparable with those in Galilee. The uniform style of the cliff shelters, their number, distribution, and the way in which they were used suggest that the phenomenon was probably not a localized initiative, but one that developed as part of an overall strategy adopted by the citizens of Galilee desperate to prepare places of refuge in times of need, from the Hellenistic period onward. The preparation of shelters in cliffs is a distinct phenomenon that is unique to Galilee, leaving tangible evidence that from the end of the Hasmonean period and throughout the entire Roman period, the Jewish population of Galilee lived under a constant state of threat due to Roman persecution and power struggles. The local population resorted to the cliff shelters whenever it felt endangered. Five of the sites where cliff shelters have been discovered are mentioned by Josephus as sites fortified by him prior to the Great Revolt; five other sites have been identified outside the region of Jewish settlement in Galilee. All the cliff shelters share the presence of natural caves located near settlements that were adapted for use as hideouts.

In the cliff shelters at Mount Berenice, thirty natural caves were surveyed that are unusually deep and extend over three levels, although the cliffs they are in are not particularly steep. Some of these caves were used as reservoirs, some as rock-hewn chambers, and some are natural cavities that were linked together by narrow passages with extensions. The longest phreatic cave in Galilee is at Mount Berenice and its winding passages were incorporated in the cliff shelter complex.

The cliff shelters at Mount Arbel and Mount Nittai encompass some 500 caves surveyed over two cliffs. The caves were hewn and prepared in clusters of four to twelve and lie on different levels with interconnecting vertical shafts. Dozens of reservoirs, ritual baths and rock-hewn chambers were found in these shelters, which contained arrowheads, coins, and numerous potsherds from the Hellenistic and Early Roman periods.

Around 200 cliff-shelter caves were surveyed along the steep north bank of central and lower Nahal Amud. The Lower Shovach, Upper Shovach, and 'Shavshevet' cliff shelters aroused great interest among scholars, with their reservoirs, hewn chambers, interconnecting passages, shafts between different levels, and observation windows. All these attest to this having been a site in which a great deal of planning and extremely dangerous manual labor were invested. Numerous arrowheads typical of those used in the Roman army show that, while there may have been attempts to capture this fortified compound, they may have been unsuccessful. Together with Josephus' written testimony, the coins and potsherds recovered at the foot of the site – most dating from the Early Roman period – strengthen the possibility that the events here occurred during the Great Revolt.

At 'Akhbera Rock, about 80 caves were adapted for use as shelters. The caves extend along the entire cliff face over a number of stepped levels. The shelters were hewn as dwelling chambers and interconnected with shafts. Coins dating from the reign of Alexander Jannaeus and minted at Zippori in the early second century CE were recovered from them. The finds raise the question of when the 'Akhbera Rock shelters were used – was it during the Bar Kokhba

Revolt, or in the revolt against Trajan, whose portrait appears on the coins?

The cliff shelters at Mount Evyatar, which are grouped in three main complexes in close proximity to each other along the west and east sides of the cliff, were found to have been hewn differently from the other cliff shelters. The chisel marks indicate that the caves were extensively enlarged to create long, rectangular chambers delving deep into the rock. The pottery finds from the foot of the cliff are diagnostic of the Hellenistic and Early Roman periods. The Mount Evyatar cliff shelters were therefore probably used by the citizens of Meroth, which Josephus mentions as marking the border of Galilee.

Outside the borders of the Jewish Galilee according to Josephus, cliff shelters were also surveyed in Nahal Dishon, Nahal ʿAlmon, and Nahal Aviv. There are dozens of caves in the steep cliffs on both sides of Nahal Dishon, which were recently surveyed for the first time. At present, the shelters of Miglash and Nahal Dishon appear to have been part of a regional defensive system that probably served the population of ʿAlma, Dishon, and possibly also Barʿam. Characteristics of the cliff shelters recorded in Western Galilee were also found at Nahal Aviv, which has caves on a series of levels containing rock-hewn chambers made as dwellings. In some of the caves, niches were cut for oil lamps and two kinds of water reservoirs were detected in them: Some were coated in gray plaster and deliberately hewn beneath active stalactites in places; others were fed by channels hewn along smoothed rock surfaces leading to plastered reservoirs. Loops for attaching ropes were hewn in the entrance jambs. Some of the potsherds found strewn in the shelters were diagnostic of the Early Roman period. The water reservoir found here, which is typical of ritual baths (with steps hewn in the rock that lead down to an immersion basin), further strengthens the conclusion that these shelters served the Jewish settlements of ʿAlma and Dishon.

The cliff shelters explored in Nahal Namer include caves with characteristics identified in Eastern Galilean cliff shelters, including rock-hewn chambers, reservoirs, and passages cut to link different levels together.

In Nahal Bezet, hundreds of caves are scattered along the north bank of the river. They have not yet been explored because the friable rock here makes access to them extremely hazardous. The five caves that have been surveyed exhibit typical cliff-shelter features: They contain clear marks of narrow passages widened by hewing; a few Hellenistic potsherds have been recovered from them and one chamber retains traces of plaster.

In Nahal Keziv, over 100 caves were surveyed of which 80 exhibit features similar to those found in the East Galilee cliff shelters. Furthermore, a few cliff shelters surveyed at Mount Ziv – which rises above Nahal Keziv – have yielded pottery dating from the Early and Late Roman periods. The figure of a Roman soldier chiseled at the entrance to one of the caves provides additional testimony as to the use of the caves in the Hellenistic and Early Roman periods. While these findings suggest that some of the Jewish population of Western Galilee resorted to cliff shelters in times of need, there is not enough data to clarify the enigma surrounding the lack of significant archaeological evidence at present to show the size and distribution of this population.

The second phenomenon described here is that of hiding complexes – those underground cavities hewn in Jewish settlements throughout Galilee that lead to slightly different interpretation. The finds show that a substantial number of these underground cavities were not originally hewn as hiding complexes but for other purposes: For storing and collecting produce, as ritual baths, water cisterns, and burial caves. These cavities were already fashioned prior to the anti-Roman revolts and it is highly probable that such methods were used in as early as the Hasmonean period. Exploration of the hiding complexes indicates that the cavities were transformed into hiding complexes as the result of established organization by the Jewish community in Galilee, mostly in the period preceding the Great Revolt, and that the phenomenon may have become more widespread in preparation for the Bar Kokhba Revolt or even in its wake, when refugees from Judea reached Galilee and made improvements in the security methods used by their fellow citizens. Since the hiding complexes had clearly saved lives in Judea during the Bar Kokhba Revolt, the method was disseminated throughout Galilee, where underground cavities intended for other purposes were transformed into hiding complexes. The recovery of finds dating from the second century CE and often mixed with first-century CE finds at archaeological excavations (some partial) in nineteen hiding complexes indicates that this is quite possible. The distinction between rough, hastily executed work and more refined, elaborate hewing is also reflected in the types of finds recovered: The roughly made hiding complexes yielded mostly first-century CE finds, whereas the more finely finished complexes yielded predominantly second-century CE finds. The impression given at this stage in the research enables us, with all due caution, to date the cruder hiding complexes to the Great Revolt and the more refined ones to the Bar Kokhba Revolt, even if the Galilee did not participate in that revolt – a conclusion that is only supported by the lack of historical sources. For good reason, the Galilean hiding complexes included all the typical features of the Judean hiding complexes. Nevertheless, the Galilean complexes appear to have three unique characteristics: (1) in many cases, and more frequently than in Judea, hiding complexes were hewn from inside an existing installation that was thus rendered obsolete; (2) many of the Galilean complexes were roughly worked without being carefully finished; and (3), most of the hiding complexes in Galilee are neither winding nor particularly long and they contain very few sharp bends.

The two main defensive methods in Galilee – cliff shelters and hiding complexes – show that the Galilean Jewish population was highly motivated to prepare cliff shelters and hiding complexes, even in regions where they were in a minority. I believe that this was a widespread, organized operation involving the adaptation of underground cavities as a means of escape in times of danger. To achieve this, the Jewish community in Galilee would have needed large-scale collective mobilization in order to prepare safe refuges where the population could hide when necessary. During the Jewish revolts against the Romans, the events in Galilee are probably comparable with those in Judea: In Judea, hideouts were prepared, hiding complexes hewn beneath hundreds of Jewish settlements, and provisions brought to those natural cave refuges that were not physically linked to settlements. In Galilee, those living near natural caves prepared cliff shelters for use as secure, clearly temporary refuges; vital installations were hewn in them and basic necessities brought to them. At the same time, hiding complexes were hewn at sites where there were no natural cliffs or caves. In fact, apart from those at Meroth and the escape tunnel at Gush Halav, all the hiding complexes discovered so far are inside the settlements themselves. The difficulty of accessing the cliff shelters in Galilee and the effort required to prepare them attest to the heightened state of urgency that led the Jewish population in Galilee to resort to such hazardous measures. Likewise, the hewing of hiding complexes that eliminated important underground installations – such as ritual baths, water reservoirs, storage and collecting facilities and even burials – show that this work was done out of a concern for personal safety that took precedence over every other consideration.

As for the date when both kinds of underground cavities were prepared in Galilee, we can probably not determine exactly when the cliff shelters were adapted or hiding complexes hewn. The preparation of cliff shelters probably began in the Hellenistic period and it certainly became more widespread just before the Great Revolt. With the hiding complexes, any attempt at dating on the basis of pottery finds is bound to produce inaccurate results, since numerous potsherds from different periods fell into the hiding complexes over the years to form a mixture of debris from various periods. Based on cases where it has been possible to isolate diagnostic potsherds and on other finds described above, together with analysis of the care taken in the hewing, it emerges that a minority of the hideouts were hewn in the Late Hellenistic period (possibly in the Hasmonean period); more than half were made prior to the Great Revolt, some before the Bar Kokhba Revolt (even if Galilee did not actively participate in it), and a minority are of a later date. It is important to note that a similar picture emerges from new research into the hiding complexes in Judea.[1]

The Jewish population in Galilee therefore appears to have used underground cavities as places of refuge and as hideouts over prolonged periods when it felt that its very existence was threatened by the Roman authorities.

1 Melamed 2010.

Coins found in the Cliff Shelters
and Hiding Complexes

List of Figures and Maps

Chapter 1

Chapter 2

Chapter 3

Chapter 4

Bibliography

1. Primary Sources

Albeck H. 1958. *Shisha Sidrei Mishna.* 6 Volumes. Tel-Aviv (Hebrew).

Basola M. 1939. *Travels of Rabbi Moshe Basola in Eretz Israel.* Edited by Y. Ben Zvi. Jerusalem (Hebrew).

Zuckermandel M.S. 1937. *Tosefta, Prospectus zu einer correcten Separat-Ausgabe von Tosefta unter Zugrundlegung der Erfurter und Wiener Handschriften.* Jerusalem (Hebrew).

Tshelebi E. 1980. *Tshelebi's Travels in Palestine (1648–1650).* Jerusalem.

Shimron B. 1991. *Polybius: History* 1. Jerusalem (Hebrew).

Flavius Josephus. *Jewish Antiquities* (1943. LCL 365. Volume V: Books 12–14; ed. and transl. R. Marcus). Cambridge MA/London.

–. *The Jewish Wars* (1927. LCL. Volume II: Books 1–2; ed. and transl. H.St.J. Thackeray). Cambridge MA/London.

–. *The Jewish Wars* (1927. LCL 487. Volume III: Books 3–4; ed. and transl. H.St.J. Thackeray). Cambridge MA/London.

–. *The Life* (1926. LCL 186; ed. and transl. H.St.J. Thackeray). Cambridge MA/London.

2. Secondary Sources

Adan-Bayewitz D. 1990. The Pottery. In: S. Wachsmann (ed.) The Excavation of an Ancient Boat in the Sea of Galilee, *'Atiqot* 19, pp. 89–96.

– 1993. *Common Pottery in Roman Galilee: A Study of Local Trade.* Ramat-Gan.

– /Aviam M. 1997. Iotapata, Josephus and the Siege of 67: Preliminary Report on the 1992–1994 Seasons. *JRA* 10:131–165.

– /Perlman I. 1990. The Local Trade of Sepphoris in the Roman Period. *IEJ* 40:153–172.

Alexandre Y. 2003. West Lubiah. *HA-ESI* 115:27–29 (Hebrew).

– 2008. The Archaeological Evidence of the Great Revolt at Karm er-Ras (Kfar Kanna), in the Lower Galilee. In: O. Guri-Rimon (ed.) *The Great Revolt in the Galilee Catalogue* 28. Haifa. pp. 73–79.

– 2012. Yafi'a, *HA-ESI* 124 (http://www.hadashot-esi.org.il/report_detail_eng.asp?id=25286&mag_id=124).

– 2015. Karm er-Ras near Kafr Kanna. In: D. Fiensy/J.R. Strange (eds.) *Galilee in the Late Second Temple and Mishnaic Periods. The Archaeological Record from Cities, Towns and Villages.* Minneapolis. pp. 146–157.

– 2017. Karm er-Ras (Areas AB, AC), *HA-ESI* 129: http://www.hadashot-esi.org.il/report_detail_eng.aspx?id=25286&mag_id=125

Amit D. 2003. *The Synagogues of Horbat Ma'on and Horbat 'Anim and the Jewish Settlement in the Southern Hebron Hills.* Ph.D. diss. The Hebrew University. Jerusalem (Hebrew; English summary pp. vi–xxxvii).

Appelbaum S./Isaac B./Landau Y. 1981–1982. *Varia Epigraphica.* SCI 6:98–118.
Aviam M. 1982–1983. The Contribution of Secret Tunnels in the Galilee to Research on Secret Tunnels. *Niqrot Zurim* 7:53–59 (Hebrew).
– 1983. The Location and Function of Josephus' Fortifications in Galilee. *Cathedra* 28:33–46 (Hebrew).
– 2004. *Jews, Pagans and Christians in the Galilee.* Rochester.
– 2005. *Yodfat: A Test Case for the Development of Jewish Settlement in the Galilee in the Second Temple Period.* Ph.D. diss. Bar-Ilan University. Ramat-Gan (Hebrew).
– 2008. The Fortified Settlements of Josephus in Galilee Before and During the Revolt, and their Significance in the Context of Finds from Excavations at Yodfat and Gamla. In: O. Guri-Rimon (ed.) *The Great Revolt in the Galilee.* Haifa. pp. 59–71 (Hebrew).
– 2015. Yodefat-Jotapata. A Jewish Galilean Town at the End of the Second Temple Period. In: D. Fiensy/J.R. Strange (eds.). *Galilee in the Late Second Temple and Mishnaic Periods. The Archaeological Record from Cities, Towns and Villages,* Minneapolis. pp. 109–126.
– /Ohel M.Y. 1980. An Archaeology Trip in Nahal Aviv. *Teva VeAretz* 22 (6):245–249 (Hebrew).
– /Richardson P. 2001. Josephus' Galilee in Archaeological Perspective. In S. Mason (ed.) *Life of Josephus: Translation and Commentary* 9. Leiden/Boston/Cologne. pp. 177–209.
– /Syon D. 2002. Jewish Ossilegium in Galilee. In: L.V. Rutgers (ed.) *What Athens Has To Do with Jerusalem. Essays on Classical, Jewish, and Early Christian Art and Archaeology in Honor of Gideon Foerster.* Leuven. pp. 151–187.
Avigad N. 1956. The Sixth Season of Excavations at Beth She'arim, 1954. *EI* 4:83–103 (Hebrew).
– 1968. The Lintel Inscription from the Ancient Synagogue of Kefar Neburaya. *Yediot* 24:136–145 (Hebrew).
– 1968. On the Form of Ancient Synagogues in Galilee. In: H.Z. Hirschberg (ed.) *All the Land of Naphtali.* Jerusalem. pp. 91–100 (Hebrew).
Avi-Yonah M. 1951. The Missing Fortress of Josephus Flavius. *EI* 1:85–103 (Hebrew).
– 1963. *A Historical Geography of Eretz Israel.* Jerusalem (Hebrew).
– 1996. The Madaba Map: Translation and Interpretation. In: G. Barkai/E. Schiller (eds.) *Ariel* 16:15–66 (Hebrew).
Avshalom-Gorni D./Getzov N. 2002. Phoenicians and Jews: A Ceramic Case-Study. In A.M. Berlin/J. Overman (eds.) *The First Jewish Revolt: Archaeology, History and Ideology.* London. pp. 74–83.
– /Najjar, A. 2013. Migdal. Preliminary Report. *HA-ESI* 125: http://www.hadashot-esi.org.il/report_detail_eng.aspx?id=2304&mag_id%20=120
Bagatti B. 1992. Nazareth. In E. Stern (ed.) *The New Encyclopedia of Archaeological Excavations in Eretz-Israel* 3. Jerusalem. pp. 1088–1091 (Hebrew).
– 1974. A Roof Tile of the Legio VI Ferrata and Pottery Vessels from Horvat Hazon. *IEJ* 24:160–169.
– 1983. Mount Hazon—Hideout Complex. *Niqrot Zurim* 7:29–52 (Hebrew).
Balouka M. 2013. Roman Pottery. In E.M. Meyers/C.L. Meyers (eds.). *The Pottery from Ancient Sepphoris.* Winona Lake. pp. 13–129.
Barag D. 1981. Kfar Ata, 'The Missing Fortress' of Josephus Flavius. *EI* 15: 391–395 (Hebrew).
– and Hershkovitz M. 1994. Lamps. In: Aviram J./Foerster G./Netzer (eds.). *Masada IV: The Yigael Yadin Excavations 1963–1965. Final Reports.* Jerusalem: Israel Exploration Society. pp 24–107.
Bar-Kochva B. (a) 1974. Notes on the Fortresses of Josephus in Galilee. *IEJ* 24: 108–116.
– (b) 1974. The Battle of Elasa. *Beit Miqra* 53(3): 419–434 (Hebrew).

– 1976. Gamla in Gaulanitis. *ZDVP* 92: 54–71.
– 2000. The Battle between Ptolemy Lathyros and Alexander Janneus in the Jordan Valley and the Dating of the Scroll of the War of the Sons of Light. *Cathedra* 93:7–56 (Hebrew).
Bar-Yehuda/Pesach N. 1988. The Survey of the Tombs. In: Z. Ilan/E. Damati (eds.) *Meroth: The Ancient Jewish Village.* Tel Aviv. pp. 154–167 (Hebrew).
Be'er S. 1990. Caves Survey in Nahal Kziv. *Niqrot Zurim* 17: 35–44.
Ben-Ephraim Y. 2003. *The Boundary between the Provinces of Palaestina and Phoenicia in the Second and Third Centuries in the Central Golan Heights.* M.A. Thesis. Bar-Ilan University. Ramat-Gan (Hebrew).
– /Dar S. 2007. The Toponym Agrippina on a Boundary Stone in the Golan Heights. In: J. Schwartz et al. (eds.) *Jerusalem and Eretz-Israel* 4–5. *Yehuda Felix Memorial Volume.* Ramat Gan. pp. 157–168 (Hebrew).
Ben-David H. 2006. *The Jewish Settlement in the Golan.* Qazrin (Hebrew).
Berlin A. 2006. *Gamla. Final Reports: The Pottery of the Second Temple Period. IAA Reports.* 29. Vol I. Jerusalem.
Braslavsky Y. 1954. *Studies in Our Country, its Past and Remains.* Tel Aviv (Hebrew).
Britt K./Bustan R. 2017. *The Elephant Mosaic Panel in the Synagogue at Huqoq. Official Publication and Initial Interpretations* (*JRA.Sup* 106). Plymouth RI.
Broshi M. 1983. The Credibility of Josephus Flavius. In: U. Rappaport (ed.) *Josephus Flavius: Historian of Eretz-Israel in the Hellenistic-Roman Period.* Jerusalem. pp. 21–27 (Hebrew).
Cohen A. 1983. Secret Tunnels in Horvat Ruma in the Galilee. *Niqrot Zurim* 7:37–43 (Hebrew).
Conder C.R./Kitchener H.H. 1881. *The Survey of Western Palestine,* I. *Sheets 1–6: Galilee.* London.
Cytryn-Silberman K. 2015. Tiberias, from Its Foundation to the End of the Early Islamic Period. In: D. Fiensy/J.R. Strange (eds.) *Galilee in the Late Second Temple and Mishnaic Periods. The Archaeological Record from Cities, Towns and Villages.* Minneapolis. pp. 188–210.
Damati E. 1986. Kefar Ekho-Huqoq: The Unidentified Fortress of Josephus. *Cathedra* 39: 37–43 (Hebrew).
– 1989. Acbara—1988. *HA-ESI* 6:14.
– /Abu-'Uqsa H. 1992. Gush Halav. *ESI* 10:70–72.
Dan Y. 1983. Josephus and Justus of Tiberias. In: U. Rappaport (ed.) *Josephus Flavius: Historian of Eretz-Israel in the Hellenistic Roman Period.* Jerusalem (Hebrew).
De Luca S./Lena A. 2015. Magdala/Taricheae. In: D. Fiensy/J.R. Strange (eds.) *Galilee in the Late Second Temple and Mishnaic Periods. The Archaeological Record from Cities, Towns and Villages,* Minneapolis. pp. 280–342.
Díez Fernández F. 1983. *Cerámica común romana de la Galilea: Aproximaciones y diferencias con la cerámica del resto de Palestina y regiones circundantes.* Madrid.
Douglas E.R. 2002. Khirbet Qana: From Jewish Village to Christian Pilgrim Site. In: J.H. Humphrey (ed), *The Roman and Byzantine Near East 3 (JRA.Sup)* Plymouth RI. pp. 101–128.
Edelstein G./Feig N. 1993. Tel 'Amal. In: E. Stern/A. Lewinson-Gilboa/J. Aviram (eds.) *The New Encyclopedia of Archaeological Excavations in the Holy Land* 4. Jerusalem. pp. 1583–1586 (Hebrew).
Elizur V. 1990. Dabura and Daburiyeh at the Foot of Mt. Tabor: The Meaning and Origins of the Two Names. *Cathedra* 54:3–16 (Hebrew).
Erlich Z./Shivti'el Y. 2017. The 'Shabbat' Inscription and the Hiding Places of Hurvat Qisi – Towards Identifying an Unnamed Settlement in the Lower Galilee. *'Al 'Atar* 19:5–23 (Hebrew).
Eshel H. 1983. Hiding Complexes at Horbat Bet Natufa. *Niqrot Zurim* 7:51 (Hebrew).
– 1992. A Fragmentary Hebrew Inscription of the Priestly Courses from Nazareth? *Tarbiz* 61:159–162 (Hebrew).
– Amit D. 1999. *The Bar-Kokhba Refuge Caves.* Tel Aviv and Jerusalem (Hebrew).
Fiensy D./Strange J.R. (eds.) 2015. *Galilee in the Late Second Temple and Mishnaic Periods. The Archaeological Record from Cities, Towns and Villages.* Minneapolis.
Foerster G. 1972. *Galilean Synagogues and their Relation to Hellenistic and Roman Architecture.* Ph.D. diss. Hebrew University. Jerusalem.

– 1983a. The Great Revolt against the Romans (66–73) and the Archaeological Evidence. In: U. Rappaport (ed.) *Judea and Rome: The Jewish Revolts.* Jerusalem. pp. 138–152 (Hebrew).
– 1983b. The Synagogues of the Galilee. In: A. Shmueli/A. Sofer/N. Kliot (eds.) *The Lands of the Galilee* 1. Haifa. pp. 231–256 (Hebrew).
Frankel R. 1986. A Relief of a Human Figure in Nahal Keziv. *Qad* 19:51–52 (Hebrew).
– /Getzov N. 1997. *Map of Akhziv (1), Map of Hanita (2) (Archaeological Survey of Israel).* Jerusalem (Hebrew).
– et al. 2001. *Settlement Dynamics and Regional Diversity in Ancient Upper Galilee* (IAA Reports 14). Jerusalem.
Frumkin A. 1984. Caves in the Lower Galilee. *Niqrot Zurim* 10:94–96 (Hebrew).
– 1990. Berenike Cave: The Longest Phreatic Cave in Galilee. *Niqrot Zurim* 17:77–83 (Hebrew).
Furrer K. 1889. Taricheae und Gamala. *ZDPV* 12:148–151.
Gal Z. 1990. *The Lower Galilee, Historical Geography in the Biblical Period.* Tel Aviv (Hebrew).
– 1998. *Map of Har Tavor (41), Map of 'En Dor (45) (Archaeological Survey of Israel).* Jerusalem (Hebrew).
Getzov Z. 1961. Bamat Eilon. In: M. Yedaya/A. Gil (eds.) *The Western Galilee, Sulam Tzur-Ga'aton.* pp. 52–56 (Hebrew).
Gil M. 2009. *And the Romans were in the Land. Eleven Chapters in the History of the Land of Israel.* Tel Aviv (Hebrew).
Grey M.S./Spigel C.S. 2015. Huqoq in the Late Hellenistic and Early Roman Periods. In: D. Fiensy/J.R. Strange (eds.) *Galilee in the Late Second Temple and Mishnaic Periods. The Archaeological Record from Cities, Towns and Villages.* Minneapolis. pp. 362–378.
Grootkerk S. 2000. *Ancient Sites in Galilee: A Toponymic Gazetteer.* Leiden/Boston/Cologne.
Guérin V. 1880. *Description géographique, historique et archéologique de la Palestine: Galilée VI, VII.* (vol 6, 7) Paris.
Har-El M. 1968. The Zealots' Fortresses in Galilee. In: H.Z. Hirschberg ed. *All the Land of Naphtali.* Jerusalem. pp. 203–213 (Hebrew).
Hartal M. 2006. *Land of the Itureans: Archaeology and History of Northern Golan in the Hellenistic, Roman and Byzantine Periods* (Golan Studies 2). Qazrin (Hebrew; English summary).
Hirschfeld Y. 1990. Has the Site Where the Talmud was Composed Been Discovered? *Teva Va'aretz* 32:18–22 (Hebrew).
– /Meir E. 2006. Tiberias 2004. *HA-ESI* 118: http://www.hadashot-esi.org.il/report_detail_eng.aspx?id=337&mag_id=111
Ilan Z. 1969. *The Land of the Golan.* Tel Aviv (Hebrew).
– 1984. The Location of Meroth. *Qad* 16:83–85 (Hebrew).
– 1986a. Excavations in the Western Church in Khirbet 'Erav ('Erabbin). In: M. Yedaya (ed.) *The Western Galilee Antiquities.* Mateh Asher. pp. 503–515 (Hebrew).
– 1986b. Horvat Gelil: Its Identification and Finds. In: M. Yedaya (ed.) *The Western Galilee Antiquities.* Mateh Asher. pp. 516–524 (Hebrew).
– 1987. Synagogues in the Galilee and the Golan. *Ariel* 52. Jerusalem (Hebrew).
– 1989. The Identification of Two Ancient International Roads in Galilee. In: Y. Ben-Artzi/A. Segal/B. Kipnis (eds.) *The 4 th Conference of Galilee Studies.* Haifa. pp. 18–20 (Hebrew).
– 1991a. *Ancient Synagogues in Israel.* Tel Aviv (Hebrew).
– 1991b. New Finds from the Cave Village at Arbel. *Niqrot Zurim* 17:11–21 (Hebrew).
– 1992. *Arbel: Two Thousand Years of History in the Eastern Galilee.* Ofra (Hebrew).
– /Damati E. 1988. *Meroth: The Ancient Jewish Village.* Tel Aviv (Hebrew).
– /Izdarechet A. 1988. *Arbel: An Ancient Jewish Settlement in the Eastern Lower Galilee.* Tel Aviv (Hebrew).
Isaac B./Oppenheimer A. 1985. The Revolt of Bar Kokhba: Ideology and Modern Scholarship. *JJS* 36:33–60.
Ishtori Haparchi (1852). *Caftor wa-Phrach,* Jerusalem. H. Edelmann (ed.). Berlin.
Kahane P.P. 1961. Rock-Cut Tombs at Huqoq. *'Atiqot (ES)* 3:121–127.

Kindler A. 1961. Registration of coins found in the Western Galilee. In: M. Yedaya/A. Gil (eds.) *The Western Galilee*. Haifa. pp. 15–17 (Hebrew).
Klein S. 1939. *Sefer ha-Yishuv*. Jerusalem (Hebrew).
–. 1945. *The Land of Galilee*. Jerusalem (Hebrew).
Kloner A. 1983. The Hiding Complexes in the Judean Shephelah. *Cathedra* 26:4–23 (Hebrew).
– 1987a. An Un-Named Ruin. In: A. Kloner/Y. Tepper (eds.) *The Hiding Complexes in the Judean Shephela*. Tel Aviv. pp. 113–114 (Hebrew).
– 1987b. Horbat Midras. In: A. Kloner/Y. Tepper (eds.) *The Hiding Complexes in the Judean Shephela*. Tel Aviv. pp. 137–145 (Hebrew).
– /Zissu B. 2005. Hiding Complexes in Judea. Update on the Extent of the Bar Kokhba Revolt. In: M. Mor et al. (eds.) *For Uriel. Studies in the History of Israel in Antiquity Presented to Professor Uriel Rappaport*. Jerusalem. pp. 125–147.
– /Tepper Y. 1987. *The Hiding Complexes in the Judean Shephelah*. Tel Aviv (Hebrew).
– /Zissu B. 2006. The Hiding Complexes in Judea: An Archaeological and Geographical Update on the Area of the Bar Kokhba Revolt. In: M. Mor et al. (eds.) *For Uriel, Studies in the History of Israel in Antiquity Presented to Uriel Rappaport*. Jerusalem. pp. 125–147 (Hebrew).
– et al. 1983. The Hiding Complexes in the Judean Shephelah from the Bar-Kokhba Period. *Cathedra* 26:4–45 (Hebrew).
Kohl H./Watzinger C. 1916. Antike Synagogen in Galiläa. Leipzig (Wissenschaftliche Veröffentlichungen der Deutschen Orientgesellschaft. Band 29).
Kotansky, R. 1991. An Inscribed Copper Amulet from 'Evron. *Atiqot* 20. pp. 81–87.
Kokkinos N. 1998. *The Herodian Dynasty: Origins, Role in Society and Eclipse* (*JSP.Sup* 30). Sheffield.
Leibner U. 2004. *History of The Settlement of the Eastern Galilee in the Hellenistic, Roman and Byzantine Periods in Light of Finds from an Archaeological Survey*. Ph.D. diss. Bar-Ilan University. Ramat-Gan (Hebrew).
– 2009. Settlement and History in Hellenistic, Roman, and Byzantine Galilee. An Archaeological Survey of the Eastern Galilee (*TSAJ* 127). Tübingen.
– 2010. Khirbet Wadi Hamam: A Roman Period Village and Synagogue in the Galilee. *Qad* 139:30–45 (Hebrew).
– /Bijovsky G. 2014. Two Hoards from Khirbet Wadi Hamam and the Scope of the Bar Kokhba Revolt, *Israel Numismatic Research* 8. pp.109–134.
– 2015. Khirbet Wadi Hamam in the Early and Middle Roman Periods. In: D. Fiensy/J.R. Strange (eds.) *Galilee in the Late Second Temple and Mishnaic Periods. The Archaeological Record from Cities, Towns and Villages*, Minneapolis. pp. 343–361.
– Shivti'el Y./Distelfeld N. 2015. An Early Roman Hiding Complex at 'Enot Sho'im, Central Lower Galilee. *Tel Aviv* 42:127–143.
Levine L.I. 1978. R. Simeon b. Yohai and the Purification of Tiberias: History and Tradition, *HUCA* 49:143–185.
Louis B. 1956. Eretz Israel Fifty Years after Ottoman Rule According to the Ottoman Land Registry. In: H.Z. Hirschberg/B. Mazar (eds.) *Eretz-Israel*. Jerusalem. pp. 170–187 (Hebrew).
Luca F.M. 2015. Kafr Kanna (The Franciscan Church). In: D. Fiensy/J.R. Strange (eds.) *Galilee in the Late Second Temple and Mishnaic Periods. The Archaeological Record from Cities, Towns and Villages*. Minneapolis. pp. 158–166.
Magen Y. 2002. *The Stone Vessel Industry in the Second Temple Period. Excavations at Hizma and the Jerusalem Temple Mount*. Jerusalem.
Malamut E. 1951. Mount Tabor as a Battle Scene in the Biblical Period. *Kovets Le-Yediat Ha-Aretz Ve-Qadmoniotaya* ('Exploration of the Land and its Ancient Past, Collected Papers'). Tel Aviv. pp. 64–73 (Hebrew).
Marcus M./Elazari Y. 2000. *Mapa Encyclopedia* 1–8. Tel Aviv (Hebrew).
Margaliot M. 1958. *Encyclopedia of the Sages of the Talmud and Geonim*. Jerusalem (Hebrew).

McCollough C.T. 2015. Khirbet Qana. In: D. Fiensy/J.R. Strange (eds.) *Galilee in the Late Second Temple and Mishnaic Periods. The Archaeological Record from Cities, Towns and Villages.* Minneapolis. pp. 127–145.

Melamed E.Z. 1966. The Onomasticon of Eusebius. *Tarbiz* 19–21:1–93 (Hebrew).

Melamed, A. 2010. Hiding Complexes. In: S. Kol-Ya'akov (ed.) *Salvage Excavations at Nesher Ramla Quarry* 1. Haifa, pp. 89–97.

Merril S. 1881. *East of the Jordan.* London.

Meshorer Y. 1978. The Coins of Sepphoris as a Historical Source. *Zion* 43:185–200 (Hebrew).

Meyers E.M. 2015. Nabratein: Synagogue and Environs. In: D. Fiensy/J.R.Strange (eds.) *Galilee in the Late Second Temple and Mishnaic Periods. The Archaeological Record from Cities, Towns and Villages,* Minneapolis. pp. 404–413.

– /Meyers C.L. 2015. Meiron in Upper Galilee. In: D. Fiensy/J.R. Strange (eds.) *Galilee in the Late Second Temple and Mishnaic Periods. The Archaeological Record from Cities, Towns and Villages.* Minneapolis. pp. 379–388.

–. Strange J.F./Groh D.E. 1978. The Meiron Excavation Project. Archaeological Survey in Galilee and Golan, 1976. *BASOR* 230:1–24.

– /Strange J.F./Meyers C.L. 1981. Second Preliminary Report on the 1981 Excavations at en-Nabratein, Israel. *BASOR* 246:35–54.

Meyers E./Carol L./Strange F. 1990. Excavations at the Ancient Synagogue of Gush Halav. University Park PA (Meiron Excavation Project Reports 5).

Mokary A. 1999. 'Ibillin. *HA-ESI* 109:24–26 (Hebrew).

Neumann F. et al. 2013. Galilee Blooming: First Palynological and Archaeological Data from an Early Byzantine Cistern at Horvat Kur. *Environmental Archaeology: The Journal of Human Palaeoecology* 19:39–54.

Oppenheimer A. 1988. Leadership Establishments and Tiberias. In: Y. Hirschfeld (ed.) *Tiberias: From its Foundation to the Muslim Conquest.* Jerusalem. pp. 24–33 (Hebrew).

– 1991. *Galilee in the Mishnaic Period.* Jerusalem (Hebrew).

Ovadiah A./Shivti'el Y. 2016. The Caves in the Cliff Shelters of Keziv Stream (Nahal Keziv) and the Relief of "The Man in the Wall". *Liber Annuus* 66:351–375.

Patrich J. 1985. Caves of Refuge and Jewish Inscriptions on the Cliffs of Nahal Michmas. *EI* 18:153–166 (Hebrew).

Porat R./Eshel H. 2008. The Judean Desert Caves in the First Revolt (the Great Revolt). In: S. Bar (ed.) *In the Hill-Country and in the Arabah (Joshua 12, 8): Studies and Researches Presented to Adam Zertal on the Thirtieth Anniversary of the Manasseh Hill-Country Survey.* Jerusalem. pp. 223–235 (Hebrew).

– /Eshel H./Frumkin A. 2006. Refuge Caves from the Bar-Kokhba Periods in Nahal 'Arugot. In: Y. Eshel (ed.) *Judea and Samaria Research Studies* 15. Ariel. pp. 107–132 (Hebrew).

Prausnitz M.W. 1986. Remains of Synagogues Re-Discovered in Western Galilee at Kfar Yassif, Hanita, and Mi'ilia. In: M. Yedaya (ed.) *The Western Galilee Antiquities.* Tel Aviv. pp. 461–465 (Hebrew).

– 1974. Romema, Haifa. *IEJ* 24:132–144.

Press I. (ed.) 1952. *A Topographical-Historical Encyclopedia of Palestine* 3. Jerusalem (Hebrew).

Raban A. 1990. Ancient Jewish Towns and Synagogues from the Mishnaic and Talmudic Periods. In: Y. Shorer/U. Shefer (eds). *The Hill of Oaks: Landscape and People.* Kiryat Tivon. pp. 67–73 (Hebrew).

Rahmani L.Y. 1994. *A Catalogue of Jewish Ossuaries in the Collection of the State of Israel.* Jerusalem.

Rappaport U. 1983. The Course of the Great Revolt. In: U. Rappaport (ed.) *Judea and Rome: The Jewish Revolts.* Jerusalem. pp. 22–65 (Hebrew).

Rapuano Y. 2013. The Pottery of Judea Between the First and Second Jewish Revolt. *BAIAS* 31:57–102.

Ravani B. 1961. Rock-Cut Tombs at Huqoq: The Excavations. *'Atiqot (ES)* 3:128–143.

Ravak S. 1976. We Looked for Eagles' Eggs and Found a Jar. *Sal'it* 4 (6):10–21 (Hebrew).

Robinson E. 1970. *Biblical Researches in Palestine and Adjacent Regions, 1838 and 1852* II, III. Jerusalem.
Rochman A. 1986. Excavations in the Hiding Complex at Khirbet Rumah. *Niqrot Zurim* 11–21:32–36 (Hebrew).
Romanoff P. 1937. *Onomasticon of Palestine.* New York.
Rosenthal-Heginbottom R./Sivan R. 1978. *Ancient Lamps in the Schloessinger Collection.* Jerusalem (Hebrew).
Safrai Z. 1981. *The Galilee in the time of the Mishnah and Talmud.* Ma'alot (Hebrew).
– 1982. A Historical Geography of Mount Tabor from the Early Hellenistic to the Late Byzantine Periods. *Qardom* 4:21–25 (Hebrew).
– 2001. Beit She'arim: An Important Jewish Settlement in Galilee. *'Al'Atar* 8–9:45–82 (Hebrew).
Savage C.E. 2015. Hamath Tiberias. In: D. Fiensy/J.R. Strange (eds.) *Galilee in the Late Second Temple and Mishnaic Periods. The Archaeological Record from Cities, Towns and Villages.* Minneapolis. pp. 211–216.
Schultz E.G. 1849. Mitteilungen über eine Reise durch Samarien und Galilea. *ZDMG* 3:46–52.
Schumacher G. 1888. *The Jaulan.* London.
Schürer E./Millar F./Vermes, G. 2000. *The History of the Jewish People in the Age of Jesus.* Vol. I. Edinburgh.
Schwager G./Miron Y. 1991. Survey of the Mount Berenice Caves. *Niqrot Zurim* 17:61–76 (Hebrew).
Schwartz S. 1994. Josephus in Galilee: Rural Patronage and Social Breakdown. In: F. Parente/J. Sievers (eds.) *Josephus and the History of the Greco-Roman Period* (Studia Post-Biblica 41). Leiden/New York/Cologne. pp. 290–306.
Schwartz D. 2008. *Flavius Josephus (Yosef Ben-Matatyahu): The Life of Josephus.* Jerusalem (Hebrew).
Seybold K. 2000. Dalmanutha (Mk 8,10). *ZDPV* 116:42–48.
Shachar Y. 1987. *The Great Jewish Revolt in Galilee.* M.A. Thesis. Tel Aviv University. Tel Aviv (Hebrew).
– 2001. The Hiding Complexes in Galilee: Finds, Geographical Distribution and Historical Significance. In: H. Eshel/B. Zissu (eds.) *New Studies on the Bar Kokhba Revolt, Proceedings of the 21 th Annual Conference of the Martin (Szusz) Department of Land of Israel Studies.* Ramat-Gan. pp. 91–93 (Hebrew).
– 2003. The Underground Hideouts in Galilee and Their Historical Meaning. In: P. Schäfer (ed.) *The Bar Kokhba War Reconsidered. New Perspectives on the Second Jewish Revolt Against Rome.* Tübingen (TSAJ 100). pp. 217–240.
Shaked I./Avshalom-Gorni D. 2004. Jewish Settlement in the Southeastern Hula Valley in the First Century C.E. In: D.R. Edwards (ed.) *Religion and Society in Roman Palestine.* New York. pp. 28–36.
Shalem D. 1995. Migdal Ha'Emek. *HA-ESI* 103:31–36 (Hebrew).
Schechter S.Z. 1928. *Schechter's Genizah: Midrash and Haggadah Fragments* 1. Jerusalem (Hebrew).
Shenhav A. 1984. Lavi Forest Survey. *HA-ESI* 84:18 (Hebrew).
Shivti'el Y. 2004. The Third Line of Defense. *Eretz* 93:71–75.
– 2008. Cliff Settlements, Shelters and Refuge Caves in the Galilee. In: S. Bar (ed.) *In the Hill-Country and in the Arabah (Joshua 12, 8). Studies and Researches Presented to Adam Zertal on the Thirtieth Anniversary of the Manasseh Hill-Country Survey.* Jerusalem. pp. 223–235.
– 2010. *Rock Shelters and Hiding Complexes in the Galilee: The History of the Jewish Settlement in the Galilee during the Early Roman Period, Based on a Study of Rock-Cut Caves.* Ph.D. diss. Bar-Ilan University. Ramat Gan (Hebrew).
– 2011a. Hiding Complexes in Galilee: Update and Renewed Discussion. *Cathedra* 142:7–26 (Hebrew).
– 2011b. Cliff Shelters in the Galilee and the Land of Benjamin: Equivalent Typology, Historical Affinity. *The Highland's Depth 1: Ephraim Range and Binyamin Research Studies.* Beit El. pp. 45–58 (Hebrew).

– 2012a. Versteckt in Höhlen und Schluchten, Rebellen und Zeloten am See Gennesaret. In: J. Zangenberg/J. Schröter (eds.) *Bauern, Fischer und Propheten – Galilaa zur Zeit Jesu.* Mainz. pp. 65–82.

– 2012b. Ritual Purification in Troubled Times: The Phenomenon of Ritual Baths in Cliff Shelters in Galilee and Similar Instances in the Land of Benjamin. *The Highland's Depth 2: Ephraim Range and Binyamin Research Studies.* Beit El. pp. 101–118 (Hebrew).

– 2013a. Safe Caves: The Distinctive Features of Hideout Complexes in the Galilee in the Early Roman Period and Parallels in the Judean Lowlands (Shephelah). In: M. Filippi/ P. Bosak (eds.) *16 th International Congress of Speleology,* 2. Brno. pp. 247–253.

– /Stepansky Y. 2013b. Iyei Ma'arot: A Cave and Hiding Complexes Settlement in Upper Galilee. *Jerusalem and Eretz-Israel* 8–9:241–266 (Hebrew).

– /Zissu B. 2007–2008. Coins from 'Akbara and Nahal 'Amud Cliffs. *INJ* 16:112–117.

– /Frumkin A. 2014, The Use of Caves as Security Measures in the Early Roman Period in the Galilee: Cliff Settlements and Shelter Caves. *Caderno de Geografia* 24/41: 77–85.

– 2016. "Because of Midian the people of Israel made for themselves the dens which are in the mountains, and the caves." Historical Sources for the Use of Rock-Cut Caves in Times of Distress. *The Highland's Depth* 6. Bet El. pp. 175–200 (Hebrew).

– /Zissu B./Eshel H. 2009–2010. The Distribution of Coins of the Jewish War against Rome in Galilee and Phoenicia. *INJ* 17:77–87.

– 2018. The Hiding Complex at Horbat Rosh Maya, Haifa: A Landmark in the Appearance of Hiding Complexes during the Hasmonean Period. In: T. Grossmark et al. (eds.) *Tel Hai Galilee Studies 3.* Tel Hai (in print).

Sickenberger J. 1934. Dalmanutha (Mk 8,10). *ZDPV* 57:281–285.

Sklar-Parnes D. A. 2004. Excavations in Northeast Jerusalem: A Jewish Site in Between the Revolts. In: A. Faust/E. Baruch (eds.) New Studies on Jerusalem, 10. Jerusalem. pp. 35–41.

Smithline H. 2006. 'Iyei Me'arot. *HA-ESI* 118: http://www.hadashot-esi.org.il/report_detail_eng.aspx?id=309&mag_id=111

Stiebel G.D. 2007. *Armis et Litteris: The Military Equipment of Early Roman Palestine in Light of the Archaeological and Historical Sources.* Ph.D. diss. University of London. London.

Stepansky Y. 2000a. The Inscription 'Yosef Ben Elazar Ben Shila of Horsha' from Tiberias. In: Y. Eshel (ed.) *Judea and Samaria Research Studies* 9. Kedumim and Ariel. pp. 135–146 (Hebrew; English summary pp. XVII–XVIII).

– 2003. Zefat and its Sites in Antiquity. *Ariel* 157–158:51–58 (Hebrew).

Strange J.F. 2015a. Sepphoris: The Jewel of the Galilee. In: D. Fiensy/J.R. Strange (eds.) *Galilee in the Late Second Temple and Mishnaic Periods. The Archaeological Record from Cities, Towns and Villages.* Minneapolis. pp. 22–38.

– 2015b. Gush Halav. In: D. Fiensy/J.R. Strange (eds.) *Galilee in theLate Second Temple and Mishnaic Periods. The Archaeological Record from Cities, Towns and Villages.* Minneapolis. pp. 389–403.

– /Groh D.E./Longstaff T.R.W. 1994. The Location and Identification of Shikhin, Part I. *IEJ* 44:216–227.

– /Groh D.E./Longstaff T.R.W./Adan-Bayewitz D. 1995. Excavations at Sepphoris: The Location and Identification of Shikhin, Part II. *IEJ* 45:171–187.

– /Longstaff T.R.W. 1985. Sepphoris (Sippori) 1985 (II). *IEJ* 35:297–299.

– /Longstaff T.R.W. 1987. Sepphoris (Sippori). *IEJ* 37:278–281.

– 2015. Kefar Shikhin. In: D. Fiensy/J.R. Strange (eds.) *Galilee in theLate Second Temple and Mishnaic Periods. The Archaeological Recordfrom Cities, Towns and Villages.* Minneapolis. pp. 88–108.

Sukenik E.L. 1951. The Ancient Synagogue at Yafa near Nazareth: Preliminary Report. *Bulletin of the Louis Rabinowitz Fund* 2. pp. 6–24.

Syon D. 1996. *The Identification of Gamla: Through the Sources and by the Results of the Excavations. Cathedra* 78:3–24 (Hebrew).

– 2016. *Gamla III. The Shmarya Gutmann Excavations 1976–1989. Finds and Studies Part 2* (IAA Reports 59). Jerusalem.

Tal O./Tepper Y./Fantalkin A. 2000. Josephus' Fortifications at Beersheba (Galilee). In: J. Schwartz/Z. Amar/I. Ziffer (eds.) *Jerusalem and Eretz Israel, Arie Kindler Volume.* Tel Aviv. pp. 155–163 (Hebrew, English abstract).

Talgam R./Weiss Z. 1989. *The Mosaics of the House of Dionysos at Sepphoris: Excavated by E.M. Meyers, E. Netzer and C.L. Meyers* (Qedem 44). Jerusalem.

Tepper Y. 1987. Exploration of the Hiding Complexes. In: A. Kloner/Y. Tepper (eds.) *The Hiding Complexes in the Judean Shephelah.* Tel Aviv. pp. 37–71 (Hebrew).

– Der'in G./Tepper Y. 2000. *Nahal 'Amud Region: Chapters on the Settlement Outpost.* Tel Aviv (Hebrew).

– /Shachar Y. 1983. Underground Secret Tunnels near Shunem. *Niqrot Zurim* 7:25–30 (Hebrew).

– /Shachar Y. 1984. *Jewish Settlements in Galilee during the Revolts against the Romans and the Underground Hiding-Places.* Tel Aviv (Hebrew).

– /Shachar Y. 1985. *Jewish Settlements in Galilee and their Underground Hiding-Places.* Tel Aviv (Hebrew).

– /Shachar Y. 1987a. The Hideout at Ga'ada. In: A. Kloner/Y. Tepper (eds.) *The Hiding Complexes in the Judean Shephelah.* Tel Aviv. pp. 104–106 (Hebrew).

– /Shachar Y. 1987b. The Underground Hiding-Places. In: A. Kloner/Y. Tepper (eds.) *The Hiding Complexes in the Judean Shephelah.* Tel Aviv. pp. 279–326 (Hebrew).

– /Shachar Y. 1992. Galilean Arbel. *Cathedra* 61:25–53 (Hebrew).

Thackeray H. St. J. 1967. *Josephus: The Man and the Historian.* New York.

Tsafrir Y. 1996. Eretz Israel on the Madaba Map. *Ariel* 116:9–11 (Hebrew).

Tsuk T. 1995. Zippori and its Surroundings. *Ariel* 109:64–79 (Hebrew).

Tsuri N. 1962. An Archaeological Survey in the Beth She'an Valley. In: Y. Aviram (ed.) *The Beth She'an Valley.* Jerusalem. pp. 135–198 (Hebrew).

– 1977. *The Land of Issachar: Archaeological Survey of the Gilboa and its Slopes, the Jezreel Valley, and Eastern Upper Galilee.* Jerusalem (Hebrew).

Urman D. 1995. Public Structures and Jewish Communities in the Golan Heights. In: D. Urman/P.V.M. Flesher (eds.) *Ancient Synagogues: Historical Analysis and Archaeological Discovery.* Leiden. pp. 373–617.

Van Kasteren J.P. 1890. Bemerkungen über einige alte Ortschaften im Ostjordanland. *ZDVP* 13:213–219.

Vilnay Z. 1976. Tiria (Tiraya, Tiria, Turiya). *Ariel: An Encyclopedia of Israel.* Tel Aviv. pp. 26–55 (Hebrew).

– 1981. *Ariel: An Encyclopedia of Israel.* Tel Aviv (Hebrew).

Vincent L.H. 1921. Vestiges d'une synagogue antique à Yafa de Galilée. *RB* 30: 434–438.

Wachsmann S. 1990. The Excavations of an Ancient Boat in the Sea of Galilee (Lake of Kinneret). *'Atiqot (ES)* 19:89–96.

Wehr H. 1974. *A Dictionary of Modern Written Arabic.* Beirut/London.

Weiss Z. 1992a. Sepphoris. In: E. Stern (ed.) *The New Encyclopedia of Archaeological Excavations in the Holy Land* 4. Jerusalem. pp. 1324–1328.

– 1992b. The Synagogue of Hammat Tiberias (Stratum II). A Suggestion for Reconstruction. *EI* 23:320–326 (Hebrew).

– /Netzer E. 1992. Two Excavation Seasons at Sepphoris. *Qad* 24:113–121 (Hebrew).

Ya'ari A. 1946. *Jewish Travels to the Land of Israel.* Tel Aviv (Hebrew).

Yadin Y. 1971. *Bar Kokhba: The Discoveries in Judean Desert Caves and the Letters of the Leader of the Revolt against the Romans.* Jerusalem (Hebrew).

Yitach M. 2000. 'Ibillin. *HA-ESI* 110:112–113 (Hebrew).

Zangenberg J.K. et al. 2013. The Kinneret Regional Project Excavations of a Byzantine Synagogue at Horvat Kur, Galilee, 2010–2013: A Preliminary Report. *Hebrew Bible and Ancient Israel* 2:557–576.

– 2016. Performing the Sacred in a Community Space. Observations from the 2010–2015 Kinneret Regional Project Excavations in the Byzantine Synagogue of Horvat Kur (Galilee). In:

J. Day et al. (eds.) *Spaces in Late Antiquity: Cultural, Theological and Archaeological Perspectives.* London/New York. pp. 166–189.

– 2017. The Menorah on the Mosaic Floor from the Late Roman/Early Byzantine Synagogue at Ḥorvat Kur. *IEJ* 67:110–126.

Zidan O./Alexandre Y. 2012. Kabul. *HA-ESI* 124: http://www.hadashot-esi.org.il/report_detail_eng.aspx?id=2177&mag_id=119

Zilberstien A./Ben Efraim N.N. 2013. The Stone Vessels and Furniture of the Early Roman Period, Jerusalem: Excavations in the Tyropoeon Valley (Giv'ati Parking Lot) Vol. I, IAA, 52, fig. 9.6.4, pp. 213–228.

Zingboym A. 2017. Accepting the Dark in the Area. A Discussion of a Talmudic Passage on the Basis of Archeological Findings in Hurvat 'Amudim in the Galilee. *'Al 'Atar* 19:25–36.

Zissu B. 2002. *Rural Settlement in the Judean Hills and Foothills from the Late Second Temple Period to the Bar Kokhba Revolt.* Ph.D. diss. The Hebrew University. Jerusalem (Hebrew).

Zussman Y. 1981. A Halachic Inscription from Bet She'an. In: J. Naveh (ed.) *Likkutei Tabitz A Jewish Epigraphy Reader,* Jerusalem. pp. 117–195 (Hebrew).

Abbreviations

AASOR	Annual of the American Schools of Oriental Research
ʿAtiqot (ES)	ʿAtiqot (English series)
BASOR	Bulletin of the American Schools of Oriental Research
SCI	Scripta Classica Israelica
EI	Eretz Israel
HA-ESI	Hadashot Arkheologiyot-Excavations and Surveys in Israel
HUCA	Hebrew Union College Annual
IAA Reports	Israel Antiquities Authority Reports
IEJ	Israel Exploration Journal
INJ	Israel Numismatic Journal
IES	Israel Exploration Society
JAOS	Journal of the American Oriental Society
JJS	Journal of Jewish Studies
JPOS	Journal of the Palestine Oriental Society
JRA	Journal of Roman Archaeology
JSP.Sup	Journal for the Study of the Pseudepigrapha, Supplement Series
LA	Liber Annuus – Studium Biblicum Franciscanum
PJB	Palästina-Jahrbuch
TSAJ	Texts and Studies in Ancient Judaism
ZDPV	Zeitschrift des Deutschen Palästina-Vereins

List of Sources for Illustrations

I am grateful to the following persons and institutions:

Map 1a, Aviam, M. 1982. On the Function and Identification of Josephus' Fortifications in Galilee, *Cathedra* 28:35 (Hebrew).
Map 1b, Damati E. 1986. Caphareccho-Huqoq: The Unknown Fortress of Josephus Flavius, *Cathedra* 39:39 (Hebrew).
Map 2, Frumkin A., Schwager G. and Miron Y. 1990. Survey of the Mount Berenice Caves. *Niqrot Zurim* 17:61–76 (Hebrew).
Map 38, Meyers, E. and Meyers, L. 2009. Excavation at Ancient Nabratein: Synagogue and Environs, Indiana, p. 62.
Map 50, Bahat D. 1983. Mount Hazon-Hideout Complex? *Niqrot Zurim* 7:29–52 (Hebrew).
Map 83, Avigad N. 1956. The Sixth Season of Excavations at Beth She'arim, 1954. *EI* 4:86 (Hebrew).
Map 84, Shalem D. 1995. Migdal Ha'Emek. *HA* 103:32–33 (Hebrew).
Map 60, Fig. 92, Zidan O. and Y. Alexandre 2012. Kabul. *HA (Electronic Journal)* 124.
Map 61, Mokary A. 1999. I'billin. *HA* 109:25 (Hebrew).
Map 65, Cohen A. 1983. Secret Tunnels in Horvat Ruma in the Galilee. *Niqrot Zurim* 7:39 (Hebrew).
Map 67, Yardena Alexandre Y. 2008. The Archaeological Evidence of the Great Revolt at Karm er-Ras (Kfar Kanna), in the Lower Galilee. In: O. Guri-Rimon ed. *The Great Revolt in the Galilee Catalogue* 28. Haifa. p. 77.
Map 68, Kfar Kanna file, ICRC.
Map 70, Frumkin A. 1984. Caves in the Lower Galilee. *Niqrot Zurim* 10:95 (Hebrew).
Map 77, Strange and Longstaff, 1985. Israel Antiquities Authority archives: Zippori file, G35/1985.
Yinon Shivti'el: all photographs except those listed below:

Sources of Photographs

Fig. 10: Louis HuguesVincent (1921).
Fig. 18: Yaakov Schweig, (photograph taken during the third excavation season, 11 December 1938–1 February 1939. With thanks to Dr Nili Greizer for sending me the photograph, which is on file in the Rockefeller Museum's British Mandate Archive).
Fig. 28: Avraham Greicer.
Fig. 31: Vladimir Boslov.
Fig. 84: Yosef Stepansky.
Fig. 88: Yehuda Ziv.

Index of Names and Sites

Index of Names

Index of Places